THE **NEW** PETER NORTON
PROGRAMMER'S GUIDE TO
THE IBM®
PC & PS/2®

THE **NEW** PETER NORTON
PROGRAMMER'S GUIDE TO
THE IBM®
PC & PS/2®

Peter Norton
Richard Wilton

Microsoft PRESS ®

PUBLISHED BY
Microsoft Press
A Division of Microsoft Corporation
16011 NE 36th Way, Box 97017, Redmond, Washington 98073-9717

Library of Congress Cataloging in Publication Data

Norton, Peter, 1943- .
The new Peter Norton programmer's guide to the IBM PC and PS/2 :
the ultimate reference guide to the entire family of IBM Personal
Computers / Peter Norton and Richard Wilton.
        p.   cm.
Includes index.
1. IBM microcomputers--Programming.   2. IBM Personal Computer.
3. IBM Personal System/2 (Computer system)   I. Wilton, Richard, 1953- .
II. Title.   III. Title: Programmer's guide to the IBM Personal Computers.
QA76.8.I1015N67   1988   88-21104
005.265--dc19   CIP
ISBN 1-55615-131-4

Printed and bound in the United States of America.

1 2 3 4 5 6 7 8 9   FGFG   3 2 1 0 9 8

Distributed to the book trade in the United States
by Harper & Row.

Distributed to the book trade in Canada by General
Publishing Company, Ltd.

Distributed to the book trade outside the United States
and Canada by Penguin Books Ltd.

Penguin Books Ltd., Harmondsworth, Middlesex, England
Penguin Books Australia Ltd., Ringwood, Victoria, Australia
Penguin Books N.Z. Ltd., 182-190 Wairau Road, Auckland 10, New Zealand

British Cataloging in Publication Data available

Microsoft®, Flight Simulator®, and GW-BASIC® are registered trademarks of Microsoft
Corporation.

IBM®, PC/AT®, Personal System/2®, and PS/2® are registered trademarks, and Micro Channel™,
PCjr™, and PC/XT™ are trademarks of International Business Machines Corporation.
Norton Utilities™ is a trademark of Peter Norton.

Project Editor: Megan E. Sheppard   **Technical Editors:** Bob Combs and Jim Johnson

CONTENTS

INTRODUCTION

The world of personal computers has come a long way in the few years since the original edition of this book appeared, yet the goal of this book remains a simple but ambitious one: to help you master the principles of programming the IBM personal computer family. From the time that the first IBM Personal Computer (known simply as "the PC") was introduced in the fall of 1981, it was clear that it was going to be a very important computer. Later, as PC sales zoomed beyond the expectations of everyone (IBM included) and as the original model was joined by a sibling or two, the PC became recognized as *the* standard for serious desktop computers. From the original PC, a whole family of computers—a family with many branches—has evolved. And at the same time the importance of the PC family has also grown.

The success and significance of the PC family has made the development of programs for it very important. However, the fact that each member of the family differs in details and characteristics from its relatives has also made the development of programs for the family increasingly complex.

This book is about the knowledge, skills, and *concepts* that are needed to create programs for the PC family—not only for one member of the family (though you might perhaps cater to the peculiarities and quirks of one member) but for the family as a whole—in a way that is universal enough that your programs should work not only on all the present family members, but on future members as well.

This book is for anyone involved in the development of programs for the PC family. It is for programmers, but not *only* for programmers. It is for anyone who is involved in or needs to understand the technical details and working ideas that are the basis for PC program development, including anyone who manages programmers, anyone who plans or designs PC programs, and anyone who uses PC programs and wants to understand the details behind them.

Some Comments on Philosophy

One of the most important elements of this book is the discussion of *programming philosophy*. You will find throughout this book explanations of the ideas underlying IBM's design of the PC family and of the principles of sound PC programming, viewed from experience.

If this book were to provide you with only facts — tabulations of technical information — it would not serve you well. That's why we've interwoven with the technical discussion an explanation of what the PC family is all about, of the principles that tie the various family members together, and of the techniques and methods that can help you produce programs that will endure and prosper along with the PC family.

How to Use This Book

This book is both a reading book and a reference book, and you can approach it in at least two ways. You may want to read it as you would any other book, from front to back, digging in where the discussion is useful to you and quickly glancing through the material you don't yet need. This approach provides a grand overview of the workings (and the ideas behind the workings) of PC programs. You can also use this book as a pure reference, and dip into specific chapters for specific information. We've provided a detailed table of contents at the beginning of each chapter and an extensive index to help you find what you need.

When you use this book as a random-access reference to the details of PC programming, you'll find that much of the material is intricately interrelated. To help you understand the interrelationships, we have repeated some details when it was practical to do so and have referred you to other sections when such repetition was less practical.

What's New in This Edition

As you might guess, this edition of the *Programmer's Guide* has been brought up to date for the new generation of IBM personal computers: the Personal System/2 computers, or PS/2s.

In some ways this book is more complex and more detailed than the original. There's a good reason for this: The newer members of the PC and PS/2 family are more complicated computers, and the later versions of DOS are more complicated and have more features than their predecessors. It was inevitable that this revised version of the *Programmer's Guide* would reflect this greater complexity in the hardware, the ROM BIOS, and DOS.

Still, you'll find that a few members of the extended PC family aren't covered in this book. The PCjr, the XT/286, and the PC Convertible are used relatively infrequently, and the PS/2 Model 70 was released too recently to be included. Nevertheless, each of these machines is similar to one of the PCs or PS/2s whose innards we will examine in detail, so this book should be a useful guide even if you are programming a Model 70 or one of the less widely used PCs.

Here are some of the changes you'll find in this new edition:

New video subsystems. Since the original edition appeared, IBM's Enhanced Graphics Adapter (EGA) became a de facto hardware standard for PC programmers and users. Then the PS/2s introduced two new video subsystems, the Multi-Color Graphics Array (MCGA) and the Video Graphics Array (VGA). These new video subsystems receive extensive coverage in Chapters 4 and 9.

New keyboards. IBM supports a new, extended keyboard with later versions of the PC/AT and with all PS/2s. Chapters 6 and 11 have been expanded to cover the new hardware.

A new focus on C programming. For better or worse, the most recent versions of DOS have been strongly influenced by the C programming language. This influence is even more apparent in such operating environments as Microsoft Windows, UNIX, and OS/2—all of which were designed by C programmers. For this reason you'll find new examples of C programming in several different chapters. Of course, we haven't abandoned Pascal and BASIC—in fact, Chapter 20 examines each of these programming languages.

A new perspective on DOS. DOS has evolved into a mature operating system whose design can now be viewed with the clarity of hindsight. The past several years of working with DOS have helped us view this immensely popular operating system with a practical perspective born of experience. Our discussions of DOS emphasize which of its features are obsolescent and which are pointers to the future.

Despite these changes, the direction and philosophy of this book remain the same. When you write a program for a PC or PS/2, you can actually program for an entire family of computers. Each member of the family—the PC, the PC/XT, the PC/AT, and all PS/2s—has hardware and software components that are identical or similar to those in other members of the family. When you keep this big picture in mind, you'll be able to write programs that take advantage of the capabilities of the different PC and PS/2 models without sacrificing portability.

Other Resources

One book, of course, can't provide you with all the knowledge that you might possibly need. We've made this book as rich and complete as we reasonably can, but there will always be a need for other kinds of information. Here are some of the places you might look for material to supplement what you find here.

For detailed technical information about the PC family, the ultimate source is IBM's series of technical reference manuals. Specific technical reference manuals exist for the original PC, for the XT, for the AT, and for PS/2 models 30, 50, 60, and 80. In addition, the detailed *IBM BIOS Interface Technical Reference Manual* summarizes the capabilities of the Basic Input/Output System in all members of the extended PC family. You should know a few things about using these model-specific manuals:

- Information specific to one model is not differentiated from general information for the whole PC family. To be sure of the differences, you should use common sense, compare the different manuals, and consult *this* book.

- Remember that each new model in the PC family adds new features. If you turn to the manual for a later model, you will find information on a wide variety of features; if you turn to the manual for an earlier model, you'll avoid being distracted by features that do not apply to all models in the family.

There is also an *IBM Options and Adapters Technical Reference Manual* for the various options and adapters used by the PC family, such as different disk drives or display screens. Technical information about this kind of equipment is gathered into this manual, which is updated periodically. (The updates are available by subscription.) Little of the information in this technical reference manual is of use to programmers, but you might find some parts of interest.

IBM also publishes technical reference manuals for special extensions to the PC, such as PC Network.

Perhaps *the* most important of the IBM technical reference manuals is the series for DOS. These manuals contain a wealth of detailed technical information which we have summarized in this book.

A number of other sources can provide information to supplement the IBM manuals:

- For a somewhat broader perspective on the IBM Personal Computer — one that is not focused on programming — see Peter Norton's *Inside the IBM Personal Computer,* published by Robert J. Brady Company.

- For a broader perspective on DOS, see the third edition of Van Wolverton's *Running MS-DOS,* and *The MS-DOS Encyclopedia*, both published by Microsoft Press.

Because this book covers the subject of PC programming in a broad fashion, it can provide you with only a few key details about individual programming languages. For details on particular programming languages and the many specific compilers for those languages, you will need more books than we could begin to list or recommend.

With these introductory remarks completed, it's time to plunge into the task of mastering the principles of programming the PC family!

Chapter 1

Anatomy of the PCs and PS/2s

From the programmer's point of view, all members of the PC family consist of a processor, memory chips, and several smart, or programmable, circuit chips. All the main circuit components that make the computer work are located on the system board; other important parts are located on expansion boards, which can be plugged into the system board.

The *system board* (Figures 1-1 through 1-3) contains the microprocessor, which is tied to at least 64 KB of memory; some built-in ROM programs, such as BASIC and the ROM BIOS; and several very important support chips. Some of these chips control external devices, such as the disk drive or the display screen, and others help the microprocessor perform its tasks.

In this section, we discuss each major chip and give a few important technical specifications. These chips are frequently known by more than one name. For example, some peripheral input/output hardware is supervised by a chip known as the 8255. This chip is also referred to as the 8255A and the 8255A-5. The suffixes A and 5 refer to revision numbers and to parts rated for operation at different speeds. For programming purposes, any Intel chip part number that starts with 8255 is identical to any other chip whose part number starts with 8255, regardless of the suffix. However, when you replace one of these chips on a circuit board, note the suffix. If the suffixes are different, the part may not operate at the proper speed.

The Microprocessor

In all PCs, the *microprocessor* is the chip that runs programs. The microprocessor, or central processing unit (CPU), carries out a variety of computations, numeric comparisons, and data transfers in response to programs stored in memory.

The CPU controls the computer's basic operation by sending and receiving control signals, memory addresses, and data from one part of the computer to another along a group of interconnecting electronic pathways called a *bus*. Located along the bus are input and output (I/O) ports that connect the various memory and support chips to the bus. Data passes through these I/O ports while it travels to and from the CPU and the other parts of the computer.

In the IBM PCs and PS/2s, the CPU always belongs to the Intel 8086 family of microprocessors. (See Figure 1-4.) We'll point out the similarities and differences between the different microprocessors as we describe them.

8088
microprocessor

8259A
interrupt
controller

8087 math
coprocessor
plugs in here

8284A clock
generator

8253
programmable
timer

8255
programmable
peripheral
interface

ROM

8253
programmable
timer

RAM

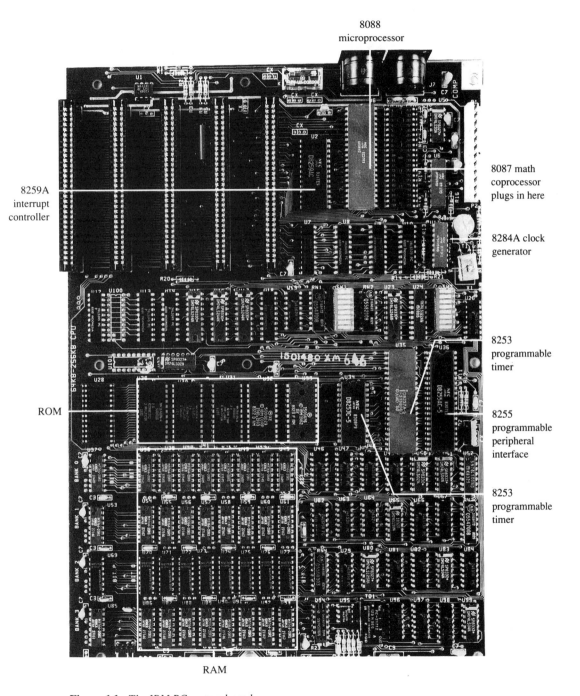

Figure 1-1. *The IBM PC system board.*

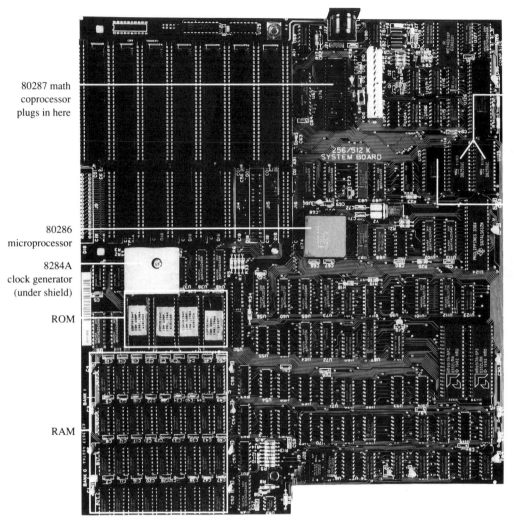

80287 math
coprocessor
plugs in here

80286
microprocessor

8284A
clock generator
(under shield)

ROM

RAM

8259A
interrupt
controllers

8254-2
programmable
timer

Figure 1-2. *The PC/AT system board.*

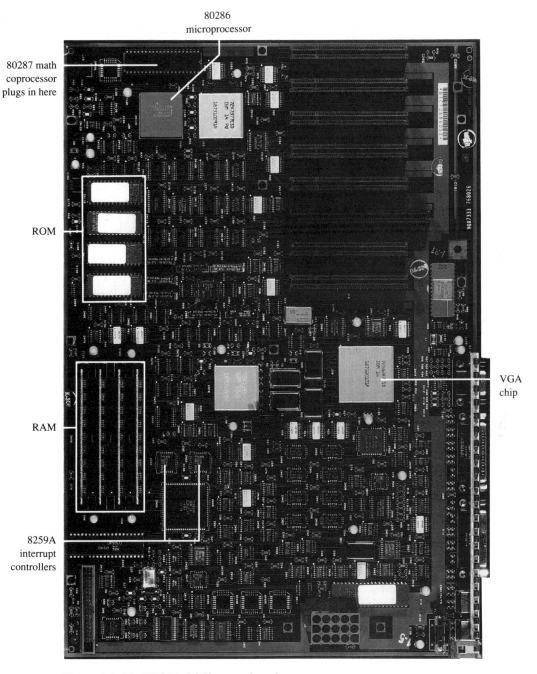

Figure 1-3. *The PS/2 Model 60 system board.*

Model	Microprocessor
PC	8088
PC/XT	8088
PC/AT	80286
PS/2 Models 25, 30	8086
PS/2 Models 50, 60	80286
PS/2 Model 80	80386

Figure 1-4. *Microprocessors used in IBM PCs and PS/2s.*

The 8088 Microprocessor

The 8088 is the 16-bit microprocessor that controls the standard IBM personal computers, including the original PC, the PC/XT, the Portable PC, and the PCjr. Almost every bit of data that enters or leaves the computer passes through the CPU to be processed.

Inside the 8088, 14 registers provide a working area for data transfer and processing. These internal registers, forming an area 28 bytes in size, are able to temporarily store data, memory addresses, instruction pointers, and status and control flags. Through these registers, the 8088 can access 1 MB (megabyte), or more than one million bytes, of memory.

The 8086 Microprocessor

The 8086 is used in the PS/2 models 25 and 30 (and also in many IBM PC clones). The 8086 differs from the 8088 in only one minor respect: It uses a full 16-bit data bus instead of the 8-bit bus that the 8088 uses. (The difference between 8-bit and 16-bit buses is discussed on page 12.) Virtually anything that you read about the 8086 also applies to the 8088; for programming purposes, consider them identical.

The 80286 Microprocessor

The 80286 is used in the PC/AT and in the PS/2 models 50 and 60. Although fully compatible with the 8086, the 80286 supports extra programming features that let it execute programs much more quickly than the 8086. Perhaps the most important enhancement to the 80286 is its support for multitasking.

Multitasking is the ability of a CPU to perform several tasks at a time — such as printing a document and calculating a spreadsheet — by quickly switching its attention among the controlling programs.

The 8088 used in a PC or PC/XT can support multitasking with the help of sophisticated control software. However, an 80286 can do a much better job of multitasking because it executes programs more quickly and addresses much more memory than the 8088. Moreover, the 80286 was designed to prevent tasks from interfering with each other.

The 80286 can run in either of two operating modes: *real mode* or *protected mode*. In real mode, the 80286 is programmed exactly like an 8086. It can access the same 1 MB range of memory addresses as the 8086. In protected mode, however, the 80286 reserves a predetermined amount of memory for an executing program, preventing that memory from being used by any other program. This means that several programs can execute concurrently without the risk of one program accidentally changing the contents of another program's memory area. An operating system using 80286 protected mode can allocate memory among several different tasks much more effectively than can an 8086-based operating system.

The 80386 Microprocessor

The PS/2 Model 80 uses the 80386, a faster, more powerful microprocessor than the 80286. The 80386 supports the same basic functions as the 8086 and offers the same protected-mode memory management as the 80286. However, the 80386 offers two important advantages over its predecessors:

- The 80386 is a 32-bit microprocessor with 32-bit registers. It can perform computations and address memory 32 bits at a time instead of 16 bits at a time.

- The 80386 offers more flexible memory management than the 80286 and 8086.

We'll say more about the 80386 in Chapter 2.

The Math Coprocessor

The 8086, 80286, and 80386 can work only with integers. To perform floating-point computations on an 8086-family microprocessor, you must represent floating-point values in memory and manipulate them using only integer operations. During compilation, the language translator represents each floating-point computation as a long, slow series of integer operations. Thus, "number-crunching" programs can run very slowly—a problem if you have a large number of calculations to perform.

A good solution to this problem is to use a separate math coprocessor that performs floating-point calculations. Each of the 8086-family microprocessors has an accompanying math coprocessor: The 8087 math

7

coprocessor is used with an 8086 or 8088; the 80287 math coprocessor is used with an 80286; and the 80387 math coprocessor is used with an 80386. (See Figure 1-5.) Each PC and PS/2 is built with an empty socket on its motherboard into which you can plug a math coprocessor chip.

From a programmer's point of view, the 8087, 80287, and 80387 math coprocessors are fundamentally the same: They all perform arithmetic with a higher degree of precision and with much greater speed than is usually achieved with integer software emulation. In particular, programs that use math coprocessors to perform trigonometric and logarithmic operations can run up to 10 times faster than their counterparts that use integer emulation.

Programming these math coprocessors in assembly language can be an exacting process. Most programmers rely on high-level language translators or commercial subroutine libraries when they write programs to run with the math coprocessors. The techniques of programming the math coprocessors directly are too specialized to cover in this book.

Data Type	Approximate Range (from)	(to)	Bits	Significant Digits (decimal)
Word integer	−32,768	+32,767	16	4
Short integer	$−2 \times 10E9$	$+2 \times 10E9$	32	9
Long integer	$−9 \times 10E18$	$+9 \times 10E18$	64	18
Packed decimal	−99...99	+99...99	80	18
Short real	$8.43 \times 10E−37$	$3.37 \times 10E38$	32	6–7
Long real	$4.19 \times 10E−307$	$1.67 \times 10E308$	64	15–16
Temporary real	$3.4 \times 10E−4932$	$1.2 \times 10E4932$	80	19

Figure 1-5. *The range of numeric data types supported by the 8087, 80287, and 80387 math coprocessors.*

The Support Chips

The microprocessor cannot control the entire computer without some help — nor should it. By delegating certain control functions to other chips, the CPU is free to attend to its own work. These support chips can be responsible for such processes as controlling the flow of information throughout the internal circuitry (as the interrupt controller and the DMA controller are) and controlling the flow of information to or from a particular device (such as a video display or disk drive) attached to the computer. These so-called *device controllers* are often mounted on a separate board that plugs into one of the PC's expansion slots.

Many support chips in the PCs and PS/2s are *programmable,* which means they can be manipulated to perform specialized tasks. Although direct programming of these chips is generally not a good idea, the following descriptions will point out which chips are safe to program directly and which aren't. Because this book does not cover direct hardware control, you should look in the IBM technical manuals as well as in the chip manufacturers' technical literature for details about programming individual chips.

The Programmable Interrupt Controller

In a PC or PS/2, one of the CPU's essential tasks is to respond to *hardware interrupts.* A hardware interrupt is a signal generated by a component of the computer, indicating that component's need for CPU attention. For example, the system timer, the keyboard, and the disk drive controllers all generate hardware interrupts at various times. The CPU responds to each interrupt by carrying out an appropriate hardware-specific activity, such as incrementing a time-of-day counter or processing a keystroke.

Each PC and PS/2 has a *programmable interrupt controller* (PIC) circuit that monitors interrupts and presents them one at a time to the CPU. The CPU responds to these interrupts by executing a special software routine called an *interrupt handler.* Because each hardware interrupt has its own interrupt handler in the ROM BIOS or in DOS, the CPU can recognize and respond specifically to the hardware that generates each interrupt. In the PC, PC/XT, and PS/2 models 25 and 30, the PIC can handle 8 different hardware interrupts. In the PC/AT and PS/2 models 50, 60, and 80, two PICs are chained together to allow a total of 15 different hardware interrupts to be processed.

Although the programmable interrupt controller is indeed programmable, hardware interrupt management is not a concern in most programs. The ROM BIOS and DOS provide nearly all of the services you'll need for managing hardware interrupts. If you do plan to work directly with the PIC, we suggest you examine the ROM BIOS listings in the IBM technical reference manuals for samples of actual PIC programming.

The DMA Controller

Some parts of the computer are able to transfer data to and from the computer's memory without passing through the CPU. This operation is called *direct memory access,* or DMA, and it is handled by a chip known as the DMA controller. The main purpose of the DMA controller is to allow disk drives to read or write data without involving the microprocessor. Because disk I/O is relatively slow compared to CPU speeds, DMA speeds up the computer's overall performance quite a bit.

The Clock Generator

The *clock generator* supplies the multiphase clock signals that coordinate the microprocessor and the peripherals. The clock generator produces a high-frequency oscillating signal. For example, in the original IBM PC, this frequency was 14.31818 megahertz (MHz, or million cycles per second); in the newer machines, the frequency is higher. Other chips that require a regular timing signal obtain it from the system clock generator by dividing the base frequency by a constant to obtain the frequency they need to accomplish their tasks. For example, the IBM PC's 8088 is driven at 4.77 MHz, one-third of the base frequency. The PC's internal bus and the programmable interval timer (discussed shortly) use a frequency of 1.193 MHz, running at a quarter of the 8088 rate and one-twelfth of the base rate.

The Programmable Interval Timer

The *programmable interval timer* generates timing signals at regular intervals controlled by software. The chip can generate timing signals on three different channels at once (four channels in the PS/2 models 50, 60, and 80).

The timer's signals are used for various system tasks. One essential timer function is to generate a clock-tick signal that keeps track of the current time of day. Another of the timer's output signals can be used to control the frequency of tones produced with the computer's speaker. See Chapter 7 for more information about programming the system timer.

Video Controllers

The many video subsystems available with the PCs and PS/2s present a variety of programmable control interfaces to the video hardware. For example, all PC and PS/2 video subsystems have a cathode ray tube (CRT) controller circuit to coordinate the timing signals that control the video display.

Although the video control circuits can be programmed in application software, all video subsystems have different programming interfaces. Fortunately, all PCs and PS/2s are equipped with basic video control routines in the ROM BIOS. We'll describe these routines in Chapter 9.

Input/Output Controllers

PCs and PS/2s have several input/output subsystems with specialized control circuitry that provides an interface between the CPU and the actual I/O hardware. For example, the keyboard has a dedicated controller chip that transforms the electrical signals generated by keystrokes into 8-bit codes that represent the individual keys. All disk drives have separate controller circuitry that directly controls the drive; the CPU communicates with the controller through a consistent interface. The serial and parallel communications ports also have dedicated input/output controllers.

You rarely need to worry about programming these hardware controllers directly because the ROM BIOS and DOS provide services that take care of these low-level functions. If you need to know the details of the interface between the CPU and a hardware I/O controller, see the IBM technical reference manuals and examine the ROM BIOS listings in the PC and PC/AT manuals.

Linking the Parts: The Bus

As we mentioned, the PC family of computers links all internal control circuitry by means of a circuit design known as a *bus*. A bus is simply a shared path on the main circuit board to which all the controlling parts of the computer are attached. When data is passed from one component to another, it travels along this common path to reach its destination. Every microprocessor, every control chip, and every byte of memory in the computer is connected directly or indirectly to the bus. When a new adapter is plugged into one of the expansion slots, it is actually plugged directly into the bus, making it an equal partner in the operation of the entire unit.

Any information that enters or leaves a computer system is temporarily stored in at least one of several locations along the bus. Data is usually placed in main memory, which in the PC family consists of thousands or millions of 8-bit memory cells (bytes). But some data may end up in a port or register for a short time while it waits for the CPU to send it to its proper location. Generally, ports and registers hold only 1 or 2 bytes of information at a time and are usually used as stopover sites for data being sent from one place to another. (Ports and registers are described in Chapter 2.)

Whenever a memory cell or port is used as a storage site, its location is known by an address that uniquely identifies it. When data is ready to be transferred, its destination address is first transmitted along the address bus; the data follows along behind on the data bus. So the bus carries more than data: It carries power and control information, such as timing signals (from the system clock) and interrupt signals, as well as the addresses of the thousands or millions of memory cells and the many devices attached to the bus. To accommodate these four different functions, the bus is divided into four parts: the *power lines,* the *control bus,* the *address bus,* and the *data bus.* We're going to discuss the subjects of address and data buses in greater detail because they move information in a way that helps to explain some of the unique properties of the PC family.

The Address Bus

The address bus in the PC, PC/XT, and PS/2 models 25 and 30 uses 20 signal lines to transmit the addresses of the memory cells and devices attached to the bus. (Memory addressing is discussed more fully on page 13 and in Chapter 3.) Because two possible values (either 1 or 0) can travel along each of the 20 address lines, these computers can specify 2^{20} addresses — the limit of the addressing capability of the 8088 and 8086 microprocessors. This amounts to more than a million possible addresses.

The 80286 used in the PC/AT can address 2^{24} bytes of memory, so the AT has a 24-line address bus. The bus in the 80286-based PS/2 models 50 and 60 also supports 24-bit memory addressing; in the 80386-based PS/2 Model 80, the bus has 32-bit addressing capability.

The Data Bus

The data bus works with the address bus to carry data throughout the computer. The PC's 8088-based system uses a data bus that has 8 signal lines, each of which carries a single binary digit (bit); data is transmitted across this 8-line bus in 8-bit (1-byte) units. The 80286 microprocessor of the AT uses a 16-bit data bus and therefore passes data in 16-bit (1-word) units.

The 8088, being a 16-bit microprocessor, can work with 16 bits of data at a time, exactly like its relative the 80286. Although the 8088 can work with 16-bit numbers internally, the size of its data bus allows the 8088 to pass data only 8 bits at a time. This has led some people to comment that the 8088 is not a true 16-bit microprocessor. Rest assured that it is, even though it is less powerful than the 80286. The 16-bit data bus of the 80286 does help it move data around more efficiently than the 8088, but the real difference in speed between the 8088 and the AT comes from the AT's faster clock rate and its more powerful internal organization.

There is an important practical reason why so many computers, including the older members of the PC family, use the 8088 with its 8-bit data bus, rather than the 8086 with its 16-bit bus. The reason is simple economics. A variety of 8-bit circuitry elements are available in large quantities at low prices. When the PC was being designed, 16-bit circuitry was more expensive and was less readily available. The use of the 8088, rather than the 8086, was important not only to hold down the cost of the PC, but also to avoid a shortage of parts. The price of 16-bit circuitry elements has decreased significantly since then, however, and it has become economically feasible to use the more efficient 80286 with its 16-bit bus. Furthermore, the 80286 is able to use a mixture of 8-bit parts and 16-bit parts, thereby maintaining compatibility within the PC family.

Micro Channel Architecture

The PS/2 models 50, 60, and 80 introduced a new bus hardware design that IBM calls *Micro Channel architecture*. Both the Micro Channel bus in the PS/2s and the earlier PC and PC/AT bus accomplish the same task of communicating addresses and data to plug-in adapters. The Micro Channel bus hardware is designed to run at higher speeds than its predecessors as well as to allow for more flexible adapter hardware designs. The Micro Channel differs from the PC and PC/AT bus design both in its physical layout and in its signal specifications, so an adapter that can be used with one bus is incompatible with the other.

The differences between the original PC bus, the PC/AT bus, and the Micro Channel bus are important in operating system software but not in applications programs. Although all programs rely implicitly on the proper functioning of the address and data buses, very few programs are actually concerned with programming the bus directly. We'll come back to the Micro Channel architecture only when we describe PS/2 ROM BIOS services that work specifically with it.

Memory

So far, we've discussed the CPU, the support chips, and the bus, but we've only touched on memory. We've saved our discussion of memory for the end of this chapter because memory chips, unlike the other chips we've discussed, don't control or direct the flow of information through a computer system; they merely store information until it is needed.

The number and storage capacity of memory chips that exist inside the computer determine the amount of memory we can use for programs and data. Although this may vary from one computer to another, all PCs and PS/2s come with at least 40 KB of read-only memory (ROM) — with space for more — and between 64 KB and 2 MB of random-access memory (RAM). Both ROM and RAM capacities can be augmented by installing additional memory chips in empty sockets on the motherboard as well as by installing a memory adapter in one of the system expansion slots. But this is only the physical view of memory. A program sees memory not as a set of individual chips, but as a set of thousands or millions of 8-bit (1-byte) storage cells, each with a unique address.

Programmers must also think of memory in this way — not in terms of how much physical memory there is, but in terms of how much *addressable* memory there is. The 8088 and 8086 can address up to 1 MB (1024 KB, or exactly 1,048,576 bytes) of memory. In other words, that's the maximum number of addresses, and therefore the maximum number of individual bytes of information, the processors can refer to. Memory addressing is discussed in more detail in Chapter 2.

CPU Address Space

Each byte is referred to by a 20-bit numeric address. In the 8086 memory scheme, the addresses are 20 bits "wide" because they must travel along the 20-bit address bus. This gives the 8086 an address space with address values that range from 00000H through FFFFFH (0 through 1,048,576 in decimal notation). If you have trouble understanding hex notation, you might want to take a quick look at Appendix B.

Similarly, the 80286's 24-bit addressing scheme lets it use extended address values in the range 000000H through FFFFFFH, or 16 MB. The 80386 can use extended 32-bit addresses, so its maximum address value is FFFFFFFFH; that is, the 80386 can directly address up to 4,294,967,296 bytes, or four gigabytes (GB), of memory. This is enough memory for most practical purposes, even for the most prolific programmer.

Although the 80286 and 80386 can address more than 1 MB of memory, any program compatible with the 8086 and with DOS must limit itself to addresses that lie in the 1 MB range available to the 8086. When the IBM PC first appeared in 1981, 1 MB seemed like a lot of memory, but large business-applications programs, memory-resident utility programs, and system software required for communications and networking can easily fill up the entire 8086 address space.

One way to work around the 1 MB limit is with the LIM (Lotus-Intel-Microsoft) Expanded Memory Specification (EMS). The EMS is based on special hardware and software that map additional RAM into the 8086 address space in 16 KB blocks. The EMS hardware can map a number of different 16 KB blocks into the same 16 KB range of 8086 addresses. Although the blocks must be accessed separately, the EMS lets up to 2048 different 16 KB blocks map to the same range of 8086 addresses. That's up to 32 MB of expanded memory.

❑ NOTE: *Don't confuse EMS "expanded" memory with the "extended" memory located above the first megabyte of 80286 or 80386 memory. Although many memory expansion adapters can be configured to serve as either expanded or extended memory (or both), these two memory configurations are very different from both a hardware and software point of view.*

The System Memory Map

On the original IBM PC, the 1 MB address space of the 8088 was split into several functional areas. (See Figure 1-6.) This memory map has been carried forward for compatibility in all subsequent PC and PS/2 models.

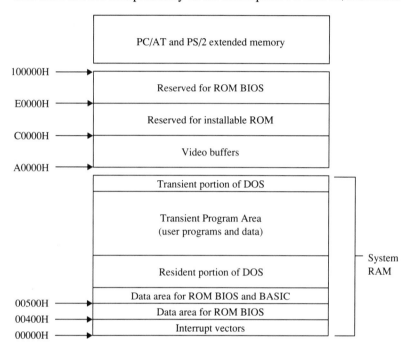

Figure 1-6. *An outline of memory usage in PCs and PS/2s.*

Some of the layout of the PC and PS/2 memory map is a consequence of the design of the 8086 microprocessor. For example, the 8086 always maintains a list of *interrupt vectors* (addresses of interrupt handling routines) in the first 1024 bytes of RAM. Similarly, all 8086-based microcomputers have ROM memory at the high end of the 1 MB address space, because the 8086, when first powered up, executes the program that starts at address FFFF0H.

The rest of the memory map follows this general division between RAM at the bottom of the address space and ROM at the top. A maximum of 640 KB of RAM can exist between addresses 00000H and 9FFFFH. (This is the memory area described by the DOS CHKDSK program.) Subsequent memory blocks are reserved for video RAM (A0000H through BFFFFH), installable ROM modules (C0000H through DFFFFH), and permanent ROM (E0000H through FFFFFH). We'll explore each of these memory areas in greater detail in the chapters that follow.

Design Philosophy

Before leaping into the following chapters, we should discuss the design philosophy behind the PC family. This will help you understand what is (and what isn't) important or useful to you.

Part of the design philosophy of the IBM personal computer family centers around a set of ROM BIOS service routines (see Chapters 8 through 13) that provide essentially all the control functions and operations that IBM considers necessary. The basic philosophy of the PC family is: Let the ROM BIOS do it; don't mess with direct control. In our judgment, this is a sound idea that has several beneficial results. Using the ROM BIOS routines encourages good programming practices, and it avoids some of the kludgy tricks that have been the curse of many other computers. It also increases the chances of your programs working on every member of the PC family. In addition, it gives IBM more flexibility in making improvements and additions to the line of PC computers. However, it would be naive for us to simply say to you, "Don't mess with direct control of the hardware." For good reasons or bad, you may want or may need to have your programs work as directly with the computer hardware as possible, doing what is colorfully called "programming down to the bare metal."

Still, as the PC family has evolved, programmers have had the opportunity to work with increasingly powerful hardware and system software. The newer members of the PC family provide faster hardware and better system software, so direct programming of the hardware does not necessarily result in significantly faster programs. For example, with an IBM PC running DOS, the fastest way to display text on the video display is to use assembly-language routines that bypass DOS and directly program the video hardware. Video screen output is many times slower if you route it through DOS. Contrast this with a PC/AT or PS/2 running OS/2, where the best way to put text on the screen is to use the operating system output functions. The faster hardware and the efficient video output services in OS/2 make direct programming unnecessary.

As you read the programming details we present in this book, keep in mind that you can often obtain a result or accomplish a programming task through several means, including direct hardware programming, calling the ROM BIOS, or using a DOS service. You must always balance portability, convenience, and performance as you weigh the alternatives. The more you know about what the hardware, the ROM BIOS, and the operating system can do, the better your programs can use them.

Chapter 2

The Ins and Outs

Generally speaking, the more you know about how your computer works, the more effective you'll be at writing programs for it. High-level programming languages, such as BASIC and C, are not designed to include every possible function that you might need while programming — though admittedly, some are better than others. At some point, you will want to go deeper into your system and use some of the routines the languages themselves use, or perhaps go even deeper and program at the hardware level.

Although some languages provide limited means to talk directly to memory (as with PEEK and POKE in BASIC) or even to some of the chips (as with BASIC's INP and OUT statements), most programmers eventually resort to assembly language, the basic language from which all other languages and operating systems are built. The 8086 assembly language, like all other assembly languages, is composed of a set of symbolic instructions, as shown in Figure 2-1. An assembler translates these instructions and the data associated with them into a binary form, called *machine language,* that can reside in memory and be processed by the 8086 to accomplish specific tasks.

Mnemonic	Full Name	Mnemonic	Full Name
Instructions recognized by all 8086-family microprocessors:			
AAA	ASCII Adjust After Addition	CWD	Convert Word to Doubleword
AAD	ASCII Adjust After Division	DAA	Decimal Adjust After Addition
AAM	ASCII Adjust After Multiplication	DAS	Decimal Adjust After Subtraction
AAS	ASCII Adjust After Subtraction	DEC	DECrement
ADC	ADd with Carry	DIV	Unsigned DIVide
ADD	ADD	ESC	ESCape
AND	AND	HLT	HaLT
CALL	CALL	IDIV	Integer DIVide
CBW	Convert Byte to Word	IMUL	Integer MULtiply
CLC	CLear Carry flag	IN	INput from I/O port
CLD	CLear Direction flag	INC	INCrement
CLI	CLear Interrupt flag	INT	INTerrupt
CMC	CoMplement Carry flag	INTO	INTerrupt on Overflow
CMP	CoMPare	IRET	Interrupt RETurn
CMPS	CoMPare String	JA	Jump if Above
CMPSB	CoMPare String (Bytes)	JAE	Jump if Above or Equal
CMPSW	CoMPare String (Words)	JB	Jump if Below

Figure 2-1. *The instruction set used with the 8086, 80286, and 80386.* *(continued)*

Figure 2-1. *continued*

Mnemonic	Full Name	Mnemonic	Full Name

Instructions recognized by all 8086-family microprocessors: (continued)

Mnemonic	Full Name	Mnemonic	Full Name
JBE	Jump if Below or Equal	LES	Load pointer using ES
JC	Jump if Carry	LOCK	LOCK bus
JCXZ	Jump if CX Zero	LODS	LOaD String
JE	Jump if Equal	LODSB	LOaD String (Bytes)
JG	Jump if Greater than	LODSW	LOaD String (Words)
JGE	Jump if Greater than or Equal	LOOP	LOOP
JL	Jump if Less than	LOOPE	LOOP while Equal
JLE	Jump if Less than or Equal	LOOPNE	LOOP while Not Equal
JMP	JuMP	LOOPNZ	LOOP while Not Zero
JNA	Jump if Not Above	LOOPZ	LOOP while Zero
JNAE	Jump if Not Above or Equal	MOV	MOVe data
JNB	Jump if Not Below	MOVS	MOVe String
JNBE	Jump if Not Below or Equal	MOVSB	MOVe String (Bytes)
JNC	Jump if No Carry	MOVSW	MOVe String (Words)
JNE	Jump if Not Equal	MUL	MULtiply
JNG	Jump if Not Greater than	NEG	NEGate
JNGE	Jump if Not Greater than or Equal	NOP	No OPeration
JNL	Jump if Not Less than	NOT	NOT
JNLE	Jump if Not Less than or Equal	OR	OR
JNO	Jump if Not Overflow	OUT	OUTput to I/O port
JNP	Jump if Not Parity	POP	POP
JNS	Jump if Not Sign	POPF	POP Flags
JNZ	Jump if Not Zero	PUSH	PUSH
JO	Jump if Overflow	PUSHF	PUSH Flags
JP	Jump if Parity	RCL	Rotate through Carry Left
JPE	Jump if Parity Even	RCR	Rotate through Carry Right
JPO	Jump if Parity Odd	REP	REPeat
JS	Jump if Sign	REPE	REPeat while Equal
JZ	Jump if Zero	REPNE	REPeat while Not Equal
LAHF	Load AH with Flags	REPNZ	REPeat while Not Zero
LDS	Load pointer using DS	REPZ	REPeat while Zero
LEA	Load Effective Address	RET	RETurn

(continued)

Figure 2-1. *continued*

Mnemonic	Full Name	Mnemonic	Full Name

Instructions recognized by all 8086-family microprocessors: (continued)

Mnemonic	Full Name	Mnemonic	Full Name
ROL	ROtate Left	STD	SeT Direction flag
ROR	ROtate Right	STI	SeT Interrupt flag
SAHF	Store AH into Flags	STOS	STOre String
SAL	Shift Arithmetic Left	STOSB	STOre String (Bytes)
SAR	Shift Arithmetic Right	STOSW	STOre String (Words)
SBB	SuBtract with Borrow	SUB	SUBtract
SCAS	SCAn String	TEST	TEST
SCASB	SCAn String (Bytes)	WAIT	WAIT
SCASW	SCAn String (Words)	XCHG	eXCHanGe
SHL	SHift Left	XLAT	transLATe
SHR	SHift Right	XOR	eXclusive OR
STC	SeT Carry flag		

Instructions recognized by the 80286 and 80386 only:

Mnemonic	Full Name	Mnemonic	Full Name
ARPL	Adjust RPL field of selector	LTR	Load Task Register
BOUND	Check array index against BOUNDs	OUTS	OUTput String to I/O port
CLTS	CLear Task-Switched flag	POPA	POP All general registers
ENTER	Establish stack frame	PUSHA	PUSH All general registers
INS	INput String from I/O port	SGDT	Store Global Descriptor Table register
LAR	Load Access Rights	SIDT	Store Interrupt Descriptor Table register
LEAVE	Discard stack frame	SLDT	Store Local Descriptor Table register
LGDT	Load Global Descriptor Table register	SMSW	Store Machine Status Word
LIDT	Load Interrupt Descriptor Table register	STR	Store Task Register
LLDT	Load Local Descriptor Table register	VERR	VERify a segment selector for Reading
LMSW	Load Machine Status Word	VERW	VERify a segment selector for Writing
LSL	Load Segment Limit		

(continued)

Figure 2-1. *continued*

Mnemonic	Full Name	Mnemonic	Full Name
Instructions recognized by the 80386 only:			
BSF	Bit Scan Forward	SETL	SET byte if Less
BSR	Bit Scan Reverse	SETLE	SET byte if Less or Equal
BT	Bit Test	SETNA	SET byte if Not Above
BTC	Bit Test and Complement	SETNAE	SET byte if Not Above or Equal
BTR	Bit Test and Reset	SETNB	SET byte if Not Below
BTS	Bit Test and Set	SETNBE	SET byte if Not Below or Equal
CDQ	Convert Doubleword to Quadword	SETNC	SET byte if No Carry
CMPSD	CoMPare String (Doublewords)	SETNE	SET byte if Not Equal
CWDE	Convert Word to Doubleword in EAX	SETNG	SET byte if Not Greater
LFS	Load pointer using FS	SETNGE	SET byte if Not Greater or Equal
LGS	Load pointer using GS	SETNL	SET byte if Not Less
LSS	Load pointer using SS	SETNLE	SET byte if Not Less or Equal
LODSD	LOaD String (Doublewords)	SETNO	SET byte if Not Overflow
MOVSD	MOVe String (Doublewords)	SETNP	SET byte if Not Parity
MOVSX	MOVe with Sign-eXtend	SETNS	SET byte if Not Sign
MOVZX	MOVe with Zero-eXtend	SETNZ	SET byte if Not Zero
SCASD	SCAn String (Doublewords)	SETO	SET byte if Overflow
SETA	SET byte if Above	SETP	SET byte if Parity
SETAE	SET byte if Above or Equal	SETPE	SET byte if Parity Even
SETB	SET byte if Below	SETPO	SET byte if Parity Odd
SETBE	SET byte if Below or Equal	SETS	SET byte if Sign
SETC	SET byte if Carry	SETZ	SET byte if Zero
SETE	SET byte if Equal	SHLD	SHift Left (Doubleword)
SETG	SET byte if Greater	SHRD	SHift Right (Doubleword)
SETGE	SET byte if Greater or Equal	STOSD	STOre String (Doublewords)

❑ NOTE: *Although this chapter discusses the details of 8086 pro-gramming, remember that we're implicitly talking about the 8088, 80286, and 80386 as well. Information pertaining exclusively to the 80286 or 80386 will be noted.*

The operations that the 8086 instructions can perform break down into only a few categories. They can do simple, four-function integer arithmetic. They can move data around. They can, using only slightly clumsy methods, manipulate individual bits. They can test values and take logical action based on the results. And last but not least, they can interact with the circuitry around them. The size of each instruction varies, but generally the most basic and often-used instructions are the shortest.

Assembly-language programming can be carried out on one of two levels: to create *interface routines* that will tie high-level programs to the lower-level DOS and ROM-BIOS routines; or to create full-fledged assembly-language programs that are faster and smaller than equivalent high-level programs, or that perform exotic tasks at the hardware level, perhaps accomplishing a feat that is accomplished nowhere else. Either way, to understand how to use assembly language, you must understand how 8086-family microprocessors process information and how they work with the rest of the computer. The rest of this chapter describes how the microprocessor and the computer's other parts communicate.

How the 8086 Communicates

The 8086, 80286, and 80386 interact with the circuitry around them in three ways: through direct and indirect memory access, through input/output (I/O) ports, and with signals called *interrupts*.

The microprocessor uses **memory** by reading or writing values at memory locations that are identified with numeric addresses. The memory locations can be accessed in two ways: through the direct memory access (DMA) controller or through the microprocessor's internal registers. The disk drives and the serial communications ports can directly access memory through the DMA controller. All other devices transfer data to and from memory by way of the microprocessor's registers.

Input/Output ports are the microprocessor's general means of communicating with any computer circuitry other than memory. Like memory locations, I/O ports are identified by number, and data can be read from or written to any port. I/O port assignment is unique to the design of any particular computer. Generally, all members of the IBM PC family use the same port specifications, with just a few variations among the different models. (See page 37.)

Interrupts are the means by which the circuitry outside the microprocessor reports that something (such as a keystroke) has happened and requests that some action be taken. Although interrupts are essential to the microprocessor's interaction with the hardware around it, the concept of an interrupt is useful for other purposes as well. For example, a program can use the INT instruction to generate a software interrupt that requests a service from DOS or from the system ROM BIOS. Interrupts are quite important when programming the PC family, so we'll devote a special section to them at the end of this chapter.

The 8086 Data Formats

Numeric data. The 8086 and 80386 are able to work with only four simple numeric data formats, all of which are integer values. The formats are founded on two building blocks: the 8-bit byte and the 16-bit (2-byte) word. Both of these basic units are related to the 16-bit processing capacity of the 8086. The byte is the more fundamental unit; and when the 8086 and 80286 address memory, bytes are the basic unit addressed. In a single byte, these microprocessors can work with unsigned positive numbers ranging in value from 0 through 255 (that is, 2^8 possibilities). If the number is a signed value, one of the 8 bits represents the sign, so only 7 bits represent the value. Thus a signed byte can represent values ranging from -128 through $+127$. (See Figure 2-2.)

The 8086 and 80286 can also operate on 16-bit signed and unsigned values, or words. Words are stored in memory in two adjacent bytes, with the low-order byte preceding the high-order byte. (See the discussion of ''back-words storage'' on page 24.)

Size	Signed?	Range Dec	Hex
8	No	0 through 255	00H through FFH
8	Yes	−128 through 0 through +127	80H through 00H through 7FH
16	No	0 through 65,535	0000H through FFFFH
16	Yes	−32,768 through 0 through +32,767	8000H through 0000H through 7FFFH
32	No	0 through 4,294,967,295	00000000H through FFFFFFFFH
32	Yes	−2,147,483,648 through +2,147,483,647	00000000H through 00000000H through 7FFFFFFFH

Figure 2-2. *The six data formats used in the 8086 family. (Only the 80386 supports 32-bit formats.)*

A word interpreted as an unsigned, positive number can have 2^{16} different values ranging from 0 through 65,535. As a signed number, the value can range from $-32,768$ through $+32,767$.

The 80386 differs from its predecessors in that it can also work with 32-bit integer values, or *doublewords*. A doubleword represents a signed or unsigned 4-byte integer with any of 2^{32} (or 4,294,967,295) different values.

Character data. Character data is stored in the standard ASCII format, with each character occupying 1 byte. The 8086 family knows nothing about ASCII characters and treats them as arbitrary bytes, with one exception: The instruction set accommodates decimal addition and subtraction performed on binary coded decimal (BCD) characters. The actual arithmetic is done in binary, but the combination of the AF flag (see page 33) and a few special instructions makes it practical to work on decimal characters and get decimal results, which can easily be converted to ASCII.

Back-Words Storage

While the PC's memory is addressed in units of individual 8-bit bytes, many operations involve 16-bit words. In memory, a 16-bit word is stored in any two adjacent 8-bit bytes. The least-significant byte of the word is stored in the lower memory location, and the most significant byte is stored in the higher memory location. From some points of view, storing a word this way is the opposite of what you might expect. Due to the backward appearance of this storage scheme, it is sometimes whimsically called ''back-words'' storage.

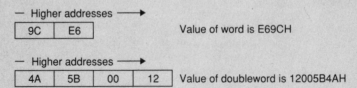

If you are working with bytes and words in memory, you should take care not to be confused by back-words storage. The source of the confusion has mostly to do with how you write data. For example, if you are writing a word value in hex, you write it like this: ABCD. The order of significance is the same as if you are writing a decimal number: The most significant digit is written first. But a word is stored in memory with the lowest address location first. So, in memory, the number ABCD appears as CDAB, with the bytes switched.

See Appendix C for more information on ASCII and the PC family's extended ASCII character set.

How the 8086 Addresses Memory

The 8086 is a 16-bit microprocessor and cannot therefore work directly with numbers larger than 16 bits. Theoretically, this means that the 8086 should be able to access only 64 KB of memory. But, as we noted in the previous chapter, it can in fact access much more than that — 1024 KB to be exact. This is possible because of the 20-bit addressing scheme used with the 8086, which expands the full range of memory locations that the 8086 can work with from 2^{16} (65,536) to 2^{20} (1,048,576). But the 8086 is still limited by its 16-bit processing capacity. To access the 20-bit addresses, it must use an addressing method that fits into the 16-bit format.

Segmented Addresses

The 8086 divides the addressable memory space into *segments,* each of which contains 64 KB of memory. Each segment begins at a *paragraph address* — that is, a byte location that is evenly divisible by 16. To access individual bytes or words, you use an *offset* that points to an exact byte location within a particular segment. Because offsets are always measured relative to the beginning of a segment, they are also called *relative addresses* or *relative offsets.*

Together, a segment and an offset form a *segmented address* that can designate any byte in the 8086's 1 MB address space. The 8086 converts a given 32-bit segmented address into a 20-bit physical address by using the segment value as a paragraph number and adding the offset value to it. In effect, the 8086 shifts the segment value left by 4 bits and then adds the offset value to create a 20-bit address.

Figure 2-3 shows how this is done for a segment value of 1234H and an offset of 4321H. The segmented address is written as 1234:4321, with 4-digit hexadecimal values and with a colon separating the segment and offset.

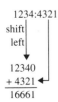

```
   1234:4321
shift |
left  |
      ▼
   12340 |
 + 4321 ◄┘
   ─────
   16661
```

Figure 2-3. *Decoding an 8086 segmented address. The segment value 1234H is shifted left 4 bits (one hex digit) and added to the offset 4321H to give the 20-bit physical address 16661H.*

On the 8086, there's obviously a great deal of overlap in the range of values that can be expressed as segmented addresses. Any given physical address can be represented by up to 2^{12} different segmented addresses. For example, the physical address 16661H could be represented not only as 1234:4321, but also as 1666:0001, 1665:0011, 1664:0021, and so on.

80286 and 80386 Protected-Mode Addresses

The 80286 also uses segmented addresses, but when the 80286 runs in protected mode, the addresses are decoded differently than on an 8086 or in 80286 real mode. The 80286 decodes protected-mode segmented addresses through a table of segment descriptors. The "segment" part of a segmented address is not a paragraph value, but a "selector" that represents an index into a segment descriptor table (Figure 2-4). Each descriptor in the table contains a 24-bit base address that indicates the actual start of a segment in memory. The resulting address is the sum of the 24-bit base address and the 16-bit offset specified in the segmented address. Thus, in protected mode the 80286 can access up to 2^{24} bytes of memory; that is, physical addresses are 24 bits in size.

This table-driven addressing scheme gives the 80286 a great deal of control over memory usage. In addition to a 24-bit base address, each segment descriptor specifies a segment's attributes (executable code, program data, read-only, and so on), as well as a privilege level that lets an operating system restrict access to the segment. This ability to specify segment attributes and access privileges is of great use to a multitasking operating system like OS/2.

The 80386 supports both 8086 and 80286 protected-mode addressing. The 80386 enhances the protected-mode addressing scheme by allowing 32-bit segment base addresses and 32-bit offsets. Thus a single segmented

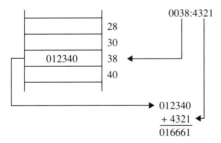

Figure 2-4. *Decoding an 80286 protected-mode segmented address. The segment selector 38H indicates an entry in a segment descriptor table. The segment descriptor contains a 24-bit segment base address which is added to the offset 4321H to give the 24-bit physical address 016661H.*

address, consisting of a 16-bit selector and a 32-bit offset, can specify any of 2^{32} different physical addresses.

The 80386 also provides a "virtual 8086" addressing mode, in which addressing is the same as the usual 8086 16-bit addressing, but with the physical addresses corresponding to the 1 MB 8086 address space mapped anywhere in the 4 gigabyte (GB) 80386 address space. This lets an operating system execute several different 8086 programs, each in its own 1 MB, 8086-compatible address space.

Address Compatibility

The different addressing schemes used by the 80286 and 80386 are generally compatible (except, of course, for 32-bit addressing on the 80386). However, if you are writing an 8086 program that you intend to convert for use in protected mode, be careful to use segments in an orderly fashion. Although it's possible to specify a physical 8086 address with many different segment-offset combinations, you will find it easier to convert 8086 programs to 80286 protected-mode addressing if you keep your segment values as constant as possible.

For example, imagine that your program needs to access an array of 160-byte strings of characters, starting at physical address B8000H. A poor way to access each string would be to exploit the fact that the strings are each 10 paragraphs long by using a different segment value to locate the start of each string:

B800:0000H (physical address B8000H)
B80A:0000H (physical address B80A0H)
B814:0000H (physical address B8140H)
B81E:0000H (physical address B81E0H)

A better way to accomplish the same addressing would be to keep a constant segment value and change the offset value:

B800:0000H (physical address B8000H)
B800:00A0H (physical address B80A0H)
B800:0140H (physical address B8140H)
B800:01E0H (physical address B81E0H)

Although the result is the same on an 8086 and in real mode on an 80286, you'll find that the second method is much better suited to 80286 protected mode, where each different segment selector designates a different segment descriptor.

The 8086 Registers

The 8086 was designed to execute instructions and perform arithmetic and logical operations as well as receive instructions and pass data to and from memory. To do this, it uses a variety of 16-bit registers.

There are fourteen registers in all, each with a special use. Four *scratch-pad registers* are used by programs to temporarily hold the intermediate results and operands of arithmetic and logical operations. Four *segment registers* hold segment values. Five *pointer and index registers* hold the offsets that are used with the values in the segment registers to locate data in memory. Finally, one *flags register* contains nine 1-bit flags that are used to record 8086 status information and control 8086 operations. (See Figure 2-5.)

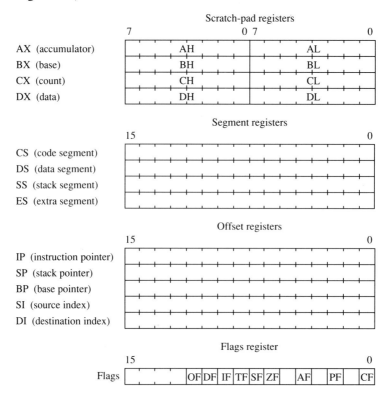

Figure 2-5. *The 8086 registers and flags.*

The Scratch-Pad Registers

When a computer is processing data, a great deal of the microprocessor's time is spent transferring data to and from memory. This access time can be greatly reduced by keeping frequently used operands and results inside the 8086. Four 16-bit registers, usually called the *scratch-pad* or *data registers,* are designed for this purpose.

The scratch-pad registers are known as AX, BX, CX, and DX. Each of them can also be subdivided and separately used as two 8-bit registers. The high-order 8-bit registers are known as AH, BH, CH, and DH, and the low-order 8-bit registers are known as AL, BL, CL, and DL.

The scratch-pad registers are used mostly as convenient temporary working areas, particularly for arithmetic operations. Addition and subtraction can be done in memory without using the registers, but the registers are faster.

Although these registers are available for any kind of scratch-pad work, each also has some special uses:

- The AX (accumulator) register is the main register used to perform arithmetic operations. (Although addition and subtraction can be performed in any of the scratch-pad or offset registers, multiplication and division must be done in AX or AL.)

- The BX (base) register can be used to point to the beginning of a translation table in memory. It can also be used to hold the offset part of a segmented address.

- The CX (count) register is used as a repetition counter for loop control and repeated data moves. For example, the LOOP instruction in assembly language uses CX to count the number of loop iterations.

- The DX register is used to store data for general purposes, although it, too, has certain specialized functions. For example, DX contains the remainder of division operations performed in AX.

The Segment Registers

As we discussed earlier, the complete address of a memory location consists of a 16-bit segment value and a 16-bit offset within the segment. Four registers, called CS, DS, ES, and SS, are used to identify four specific segments of memory. Five offset registers, which we'll discuss shortly, can be used to store the relative offsets of the data within each of the four segments.

Each segment register is used for a specific type of addressing:

- The CS register identifies the code segment, which contains the program that is being executed.

- The DS and ES registers identify data segments where data used in a program is stored.

- The SS register identifies the stack segment. (See page 32 for more information about stacks.)

Programs rarely use four separate segments to address four different 64 KB areas of memory. Instead, the four segments specified in CS, DS, ES, and SS usually refer to overlapping or identical areas in memory. In effect, the different segment registers identify areas of memory used for different purposes.

For example, Figure 2-6 shows how the values in the segment registers correspond to the memory used in a hypothetical DOS program. The values in the segment registers are chosen to correspond to the start of each logically different area of memory, even though the 64 KB areas of memory identified by each segment overlap each other. (See Chapter 20 for more about segments and the memory layout of DOS programs.)

All 8086 instructions that use memory have an implied use of a particular segment register for the operation being performed. For example, the MOV instruction, because it acts on data, uses the DS register. The JMP instruction, which affects the flow of a program, automatically uses the CS register.

This means that you can address any 64 KB segment in memory by placing its paragraph address in the appropriate segment register. For example, to access data in the video buffer used by IBM's Color Graphics Adapter, you place the paragraph address of the start of the buffer in a segment register and then use the MOV instruction to transfer data to or from the buffer.

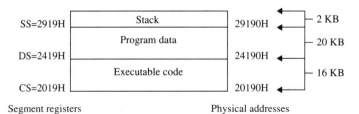

Figure 2-6. *Segment usage in a typical DOS program. Each segment register contains the starting paragraph of a different area of memory.*

```
mov ax,0B800h              ; move the segment value into DS
mov ds,ax
mov al,[0000]              ; copy the byte at B800:0000
                           ; into AL
```

In interpreted BASIC you can use this method with the DEF SEG statement:

```
DEF SEG = &HB800           ' move the segment value into DS
X = PEEK(0000)             ' copy the byte at B800:0000 into X
```

The Offset Registers

Five offset registers are used with the segment registers to contain segmented addresses. One register, called the *instruction pointer* (IP), contains the offset of the current instruction in the code segment; two registers, called the *stack registers,* are intimately tied to the stack; and the remaining two registers, called the *index registers,* are used to address strings of data.

The instruction pointer (IP), also called the program counter (PC), contains the offset within the code segment where the current program is executing. It is used with the CS register to track the location of the next instruction to be executed.

Programs do not have direct access to the IP register, but a number of instructions, such as JMP and CALL, change the IP value implicitly.

The stack registers, called the *stack pointer* (SP) and the *base pointer* (BP), provide offsets into the stack segment. SP gives the location of the current top of the stack. Programs rarely change the value in SP directly. Instead, they rely on PUSH and POP instructions to update SP implicitly. BP is the register generally used to access the stack segment directly. You'll see BP used quite often in the assembly-language examples that appear in Chapters 8 through 20.

The index registers, called the *source index* (SI) and the *destination index* (DI), can be used for general-purpose addressing of data. Also, all string move and comparison instructions use SI and DI to address data strings.

The Flags Register

The fourteenth and last register, called the *flags register,* is really a collection of individual status and control bits called *flags*. The flags are maintained in a register, so they can be either saved and restored as a coordinated set or inspected as ordinary data. Normally, however, the flags are set and tested as independent items — not as a set.

There are nine 1-bit flags in the 8086's 16-bit flags register, leaving 7 bits unused. (The 80286 and 80386 use some of the unused flags to support protected-mode operation.) The flags can be logically divided into two groups: six *status flags,* which record processor status information (usually indicating what happened with a comparison or arithmetic operation), and three *control flags,* which direct some of the 8086 instructions. Be prepared to see a variety of notations for the flags, including distinct names for whether they are set (1) or clear (0). The terms used in Figures 2-7 and 2-8 are the most common.

The Stack

The *stack* is a built-in feature of the 8086. It provides programs with a place to store and keep track of work in progress. The most important use of the stack is to keep a record of where subroutines were invoked from and what parameters were passed to them. The stack can also be used for temporary working storage, although this is less fundamental and less common.

The stack gets its name from an analogy to a spring-loaded stack of plates in a cafeteria: New data is "pushed" onto the top of the stack and old data is "popped" off. A stack always operates in last-in-first-out (LIFO) order. This means that when the stack is used to keep track of where to return to a program, the most recent calling program is returned to first. This way, a stack maintains the orderly workings of programs, subroutines, and interrupt handlers, no matter how complex their operation.

A stack is used from the bottom (highest address) to the top (lowest address) so that when data is pushed onto the top of the stack, it is stored at the memory addresses just below the current top of the stack. The stack grows downward so that as data is added, the location of the top of the stack moves to lower and lower addresses, decreasing the value of SP each time. You need to keep this in mind when you access the stack, which you are likely to do in assembly-language interface routines.

Any part of any program can create a new stack space at any time, but this is not usually done. Normally, when a program is run, a single stack is created for it and used throughout the operation of the program.

Code	Name	Use
CF	Carry flag	Indicates an arithmetic carry
OF	Overflow flag	Indicates signed arithmetic overflow
ZF	Zero flag	Indicates zero result, or equal comparison
SF	Sign flag	Indicates negative result/comparison
PF	Parity flag	Indicates even number of 1 bits
AF	Auxiliary carry flag	Indicates adjustment needed in binary-coded decimal (BCD) arithmetic operations

Figure 2-7. *The six status flags in the 8086's flags register.*

There is no simple way to estimate the size of stack that a program might need, and the 8086's design does not provide any automatic way of detecting when stack space is in short supply or exhausted. This can make programmers nervous about the amount of space that should be set aside for a stack. A conservative estimate of how much stack space to maintain is about 2 KB (2048 bytes), the default amount allocated by many high-level language compilers.

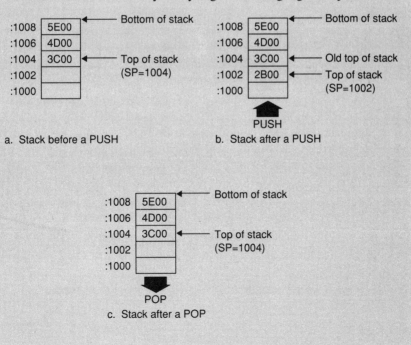

Code	Name	Use
DF	Direction flag	Controls increment direction in string operations (CMPS, LODS, MOVS, SCAS, STOS)
IF	Interrupt flag	Controls whether interrupts are enabled
TF	Trap flag	Controls single-step operation (used by DEBUG) by generating an interrupt at the end of every instruction

Figure 2-8. *The three control flags in the 8086's flags register.*

Addressing Memory Through Registers

We've seen that memory is always addressed by a combination of a segment value and a relative offset. The segment value always comes from one of the four segment registers.

In contrast, the relative offset can be specified in many different ways. (See Figure 2-9.) For each machine instruction that accesses memory, the 8086 computes an effective address by combining one, two, or three of the following:

- The value in BX or BP

- The value in SI or DI

- A relative-offset value, called a *displacement,* that is part of the instruction itself

Name	Effective Address	Example	Comments
Immediate	Value "addressed" is part of the 8086 instruction	mov ax,1234h	Stores 1234H in AX.
Direct	Specified as part of the 8086 instruction	mov ax,[1234h]	Copies the value at 1234H into AX. The default segment register is DS.
Register indirect	Contained in BX, SI, DI, or BP	mov ax,[bx]	Copies the value at the offset contained in BX into AX. The default segment register for [BX], [SI], and [DI] is DS; for [BP] the default is SS.

Figure 2-9. *8086 Addressing Modes. In assembly language, some instructions can be specified in several different ways.* (continued)

Figure 2-9. *continued*

Name	Effective Address	Example	Comments
Based	The sum of a displacement (part of the instruction) and the value in BX or BP	mov ax,[bx+2] *or* mov ax,2[bx]	Copies the value 2 bytes past the offset contained in BX into AX. The default segment register for [BX] is DS; for [BP] the default is SS.
Indexed	The sum of a displacement and the value in SI or DI	mov ax,[si+2] *or* mov ax,2[si]	Copies the value 2 bytes past the offset contained in SI into AX. The default segment register is DS.
Based indexed	The sum of a displacement, the value in SI or DI, and the value in BX or BP	mov ax,[bp+si+2] *or* mov ax,2[bp+si] *or* mov ax,2[bp][si]	The offset is the sum of the values in BP and SI, plus 2. When BX is used, the default segment register is DS; when BP is used, the default is SS.
String addressing	Source string: register indirect using SI Destination string: register indirect using DI	movsb	Copies the string from memory at DS:[SI] to ES:[DI].

Each of the various ways of forming an effective address has its uses. You can use the Immediate and Direct methods when you know the offset of a particular memory location in advance. You must use one of the remaining methods when you can't tell what an address will be until your program executes. In the chapters ahead, you'll see examples of most of the different 8086 addressing modes.

The notation used in specifying 8086 addresses is straightforward. Brackets, [ ], are used to indicate that the enclosed item specifies a relative offset. This is a key element of memory addressing: Without brackets, the actual value stored in the register is used in whatever operation is specified.

Rules for Using Registers

It is important to know that various rules apply to the use of registers, and it is essential to be aware of these rules when writing assembly-language interface routines. Because the rules and conventions of usage vary by circumstance and by programming language, exact guidelines are not always available, but the general rules that follow will apply in most cases. (You will find additional guidance, and working models to copy, in the examples in Chapters 8 through 20.) Keep in mind, though, that the following rules are general, not absolute.

Probably the most useful rule for using the registers is simply to use them for what they are designed for. The idea that each of the 8086 registers has certain special uses may seem somewhat quirky, particularly to a programmer who is accustomed to working with a CPU that has a less specialized set of registers (such as the 68000, for example). On the 8086, using the registers for their natural functions leads to cleaner, more efficient source code and ultimately to more reliable programs.

For example, the segment registers are designed to contain segment values, so don't use them for anything else. (In 80286 protected mode you can't use them for anything else anyway without generating an error condition.) The BP register is intended for stack addressing; if you use it for anything else, you'll have to do some fancy footwork when you need to address values in the stack segment.

Particular rules apply to the four segment registers (CS, DS, ES, and SS). The CS register should be changed only through intersegment jumps and subroutine calls.

Most programmers use the DS register to point to a default data segment that contains the data most frequently used in a program. This means that the value in the DS register is usually initialized at the beginning of a program and then left alone. Should it be necessary to use DS to address a different segment, its original value is saved, the new segment is accessed, and then the original value is restored. In contrast, most people use the ES register as needed to access arbitrary segments in memory.

The stack segment (SS) and stack pointer (SP) registers should usually be updated implicitly, either by PUSH and POP instructions or by CALL and RET instructions that save subroutine return addresses on the stack. When DOS loads a program into memory to be executed, it initializes SS and SP to usable values. In .COM programs, SS:SP points to the end of the program's default segment; in .EXE programs, SS:SP is determined explicitly by the size and location of the program's stack segment. In either case, it's rare that you need to change SS or SP explicitly.

If you need to discard a number of values from the stack or reserve temporary storage space on top of the stack, you can increment or decrement SP directly:

```
add sp,8                        ; discard four words (8 bytes)
                                ; from stack
sub sp,6                        ; add three empty words (6 bytes)
                                ; to top of stack
```

If you need to move the stack to a different location in memory, you must generally update both SS and SP at the same time:

```
cli                              ; disable interrupts
mov ss,NewStackSeg               ; update SS from a memory variable
mov sp,NewStackPtr               ; update SP from a memory variable
sti                              ; re-enable interrupts
```

Be careful when you change SS and SP explicitly. If you modify SS but fail to update SP, SS will be specifying a new stack segment while SP will be pointing somewhere inside another stack segment — and that's asking for trouble the next time you use the stack.

It's hard to be explicit about the use of the other registers. In general, most programmers try to minimize memory accesses by keeping the intermediate results of lengthy computations in registers. This is because it takes longer to perform a computation on a value stored in memory than on a value stored in a register. Of course, the 8086 has only so many registers to work with, so you may find yourself running out of registers before you run out of variables.

How the 8086 Uses I/O Ports

The 8086-family microprocessors communicate with and control many parts of the computer through the use of input and output (I/O) ports. The I/O ports are doorways through which information passes as it travels to or from an I/O device, such as a keyboard or a printer. Most of the support chips we described in Chapter 1 are accessed through I/O ports; in fact, each chip may use several port addresses for different purposes.

Each port is identified by a 16-bit port number, which can range from 00H through FFFFH (65,535). The CPU identifies a particular port by the port's number.

As it does when accessing memory, the CPU uses the data and address buses as conduits for communication with the ports. To access a port, the CPU first sends a signal on the system bus to notify all I/O devices that the address on the bus is that of a port. The CPU then sends the port address. The device with the matching port address responds.

The port number addresses a memory location that is associated with an I/O device but is not part of main memory. In other words, an I/O port number is not the same as a memory address. For example, I/O port 3D8H has nothing to do with memory address 003D8H. To access an I/O port, you don't use data-transfer instructions like MOV and STOS. Instead, you use the instructions IN and OUT, which are reserved for I/O port access.

❑ NOTE: *Many high-level programming languages provide functions that access I/O ports. The BASIC functions* INP *and* OUT, *and the C functions* inp *and* outp, *are typical examples.*

The uses of specific I/O ports are determined by the hardware designers. Programs that make use of I/O ports need to be aware of the port numbers, as well as their use and meaning. Port number assignments differ slightly among the PC family members, but, in general, IBM has reserved the same ranges of I/O port numbers for the same input/output devices in all PCs and PS/2s. (See Figure 2-10.) For details on how each I/O port is used, see the descriptions of the various input/output devices in the IBM technical reference manuals.

Description	I/O Port Numbers	Comment
Programmable Interrupt Controller (master)	20H–3FH	
System timer	40H–5FH	
Keyboard controller	60H–6FH	On PS/2 Model 30, ports 60H–6FH are reserved for system-board control and status
System control port B	61H	PS/2 models 50, 60, and 80 only
Real-time clock, NMI mask	70H–7FH	On PC, PC/XT, and PS/2 Model 30, NMI mask is at port A0H
System control port A	92H	PS/2 models 50, 60, and 80 only
Programmable Interrupt Controller (slave)	A0H–BFH	On PS/2 Model 30, A0H–AFH
Real-time clock	B0H–BFH, E0H–EFH	PS/2 Model 30 only
Clear math coprocessor busy	F0H	
Reset math coprocessor	F1H	
Math coprocessor	F8H–FFH	
Fixed-disk controller	1F0H–1F8H	
Game control adapter	200H–207H	
Parallel printer 3	278H–27BH	
Serial communications 2	2F8H–2FFH	
Fixed-disk controller	320H–32FH	PC/XT and PS/2 Model 30
PC network	360H–363H, 368H–36BH	
Parallel printer 2	378H–37BH	

Figure 2-10. *PC and PS/2 input/output port assignments. This table lists the most frequently used I/O ports. For a complete list, see the IBM Technical Reference manuals.*

(continued)

Figure 2-10. *continued*

Description	I/O Port Numbers	Comment
Monochrome Display Adapter	3B0H–3BBH	Also used by EGA and VGA in monochrome video modes
Parallel printer 1	3BCH–3BFH	
Enhanced Graphics Adapter (EGA), Video Graphics Array (VGA)	3C0H–3CFH	
Color Graphics Adapter (CGA), Multi-Color Graphics Array (MCGA)	3D0H–3DFH	Also used by EGA and VGA in color video modes
Diskette controller	3F0H–3F7H	
Serial communications 1	3F8H–3FFH	

How the 8086 Uses Interrupts

An interrupt is an indication to the microprocessor that its immediate attention is needed. The 8086-family microprocessors can respond to interrupts from either hardware or software. A hardware device can generate an interrupt signal that is processed by the programmable interrupt controller (PIC) and passed to the microprocessor; in software, the INT instruction generates an interrupt. In both cases, the microprocessor stops processing and executes a memory-resident subroutine called an *interrupt handler*. After the interrupt handler has performed its task, the microprocessor resumes processing at the point the interrupt occurred.

The 8086 supports 256 different interrupts, each identified by a number between 00H and FFH (decimal 255). The segmented addresses of the 256 interrupt handlers are stored in an interrupt vector table that starts at 0000:0000H (that is, at the very beginning of available memory). Each interrupt vector is 4 bytes in size, so you can locate the address of any interrupt handler by multiplying the interrupt number by 4. You can also replace an existing interrupt handler with a new one by storing the new handler's segmented address in the appropriate interrupt vector.

Software Interrupts

Probably the most familiar type of interrupts are generated by the INT instruction. Consider what happens when the CPU executes the following instruction:

```
INT 12H
```

The CPU pushes the current contents of the flags register, the CS (code segment) register, and the IP (instruction pointer) register onto the stack. Then it transfers control to the interrupt handler corresponding to interrupt number 12H, using the segmented address stored at 0000:0048H. The CPU then executes the interrupt 12H handler, which responds appropriately to interrupt 12H. The interrupt handler terminates with an IRET instruction that pops CS:IP and the flags back into the registers, thus transferring control back to the interrupted program.

Hardware Interrupts

The microprocessor responds to a hardware interrupt in much the same way it responds to a software interrupt: by transferring control to an interrupt handler. The important difference lies in the way the interrupt is signalled.

Devices such as the system timer, the hard disk, the keyboard, and the serial communications ports can generate interrupt signals on a set of reserved interrupt request (IRQ) lines. These lines are monitored by the PIC circuit, which assigns interrupt numbers to them. When a particular hardware interrupt occurs, the PIC places the corresponding interrupt number on the system data bus where the microprocessor can find it.

The PIC also assigns priorities to the various interrupt requests. For example, the highest-priority PIC interrupt in all PCs and PS/2s is the timer-tick interrupt, which is signalled on interrupt request line 0 (IRQ0) and is assigned interrupt 08H by the PIC. When a system timer generates a timer-tick interrupt, it does so by signalling on IRQ0; the PIC responds by signalling the CPU to execute interrupt 08H. If a lower-priority hardware interrupt request occurs while the timer-tick interrupt is being processed, the PIC delays the lower-priority interrupt until the timer interrupt handler signals that it has finished its processing.

When you coldboot the computer, the system start-up routines assign interrupt numbers and priorities to the hardware interrupts by initializing the PIC. In 8088- and 8086-based machines (PCs, PC/XTs, PS/2 models 25 and 30), interrupt numbers 08H through 0FH are assigned to interrupt request levels 0 through 7 (IRQ0 through IRQ7). In PC/ATs and PS/2 models 50, 60, and 80, an additional eight interrupt lines (IRQ8 through IRQ15) are assigned interrupt numbers 70H through 77H.

One hardware interrupt bypasses the PIC altogether. This is the *non-maskable interrupt* (NMI), which is assigned interrupt number 02H in the 8086 family. The NMI is used by devices that require absolute, ''now-or-never'' priority over all other CPU functions. In particular, when a hardware memory error occurs, the computer's RAM subsystem generates an NMI. This causes the CPU to pass control to an interrupt 02H handler; the default handler in the PC family resides in ROM and issues the "PARITY CHECK" message you see when a memory error occurs.

When you debug a program on any member of the PC family, remember that hardware interrupts are occurring all the time. For example, the system timer-tick interrupt (interrupt 08H) occurs roughly 18.2 times per second. The keyboard and disk-drive controllers also generate interrupts. Each time these hardware interrupts occur, the 8086 uses the current stack to save CS:IP and the flags register. If your stack is too small, or if you are manipulating SS and SP when a hardware interrupt occurs, the 8086 may damage valuable data when it saves CS:IP and the flags.

If you look back at our example of updating SS and SP on page 36, you'll see that we explicitly disable hardware interrupts by executing the CLI instruction prior to updating SS. This prevents a hardware interrupt from occurring between the two MOV instructions while SS:SP is pointing nowhere. (Actually, this is a problem only in very early releases of the 8088; the chip was later redesigned to prevent this problem by disabling interrupts during the instruction that follows a data move into SS.)

We'll talk in more detail about how PCs and PS/2s use interrupts in Chapters 3 and 8.

Chapter 3

The ROM Software

It takes software to make a computer go. And getting a computer going and keeping it going is much easier if some of that software is permanently built into the computer. That's what the ROM programs are all about. ROM stands for *read-only memory* — memory permanently recorded in the circuitry of the computer's ROM chips, that can't be changed, erased, or lost.

PCs and PS/2s come with a substantial amount of ROM that contains the programs and data needed to start and operate the computer and its peripheral devices. The advantage of having a computer's fundamental programs stored in ROM is that they are right there — built into the computer — and there is no need to load them into memory from disk the way that DOS must be loaded. Because they are permanent, the ROM programs are very often the foundation upon which other programs (including DOS) are built.

There are four elements to the ROM in IBM's PC family: the *start-up routines,* which do the work of getting the computer started; the *ROM BIOS* — an acronym for Basic Input/Output System — which is a collection of machine-language routines that provide support services for the continuing operation of the computer; the *ROM BASIC,* which provides the core of the BASIC programming language; and the *ROM extensions,* which are programs that are added to the main ROM when certain optional equipment is added to the computer. We'll be examining each of these four major elements throughout the rest of this chapter.

The ROM programs occupy addresses F000:0000H through F000:FFFFH in the PC/XT/AT family and the PS/2 models 25 and 30, and E000:0000H through F000:FFFFH in the other PS/2s. However, the routines themselves are not located at any specific addresses in ROM as they are in other computers. The address of a particular ROM routine varies among the different members of the PC/XT/AT and PS/2 families.

Although the exact addresses of the ROM routines can vary, IBM provides a consistent interface to the ROM software by using interrupts. Later in this book we'll show you exactly how to use interrupts to execute the ROM routines.

The Start-Up ROM

The first job the ROM programs have is to supervise the start-up of the computer. Unlike other aspects of the ROM, the start-up routines have little to do with programming the PC family — but it is still worthwhile to understand what they do.

The start-up routines perform several tasks:

- They run a quick reliability test of the computer (and the ROM programs) to ensure everything is in working order.

- They initialize the chips and the standard equipment attached to the computer.

- They set up the interrupt-vector table.

- They check to see what optional equipment is attached.

- They load the operating system from disk.

The following paragraphs discuss these tasks in greater detail.

The *reliability test,* part of a process known as the Power On Self Test (POST), is an important first step in making sure the computer is ready. All POST routines are quite brief except for the memory tests, which can be annoyingly lengthy in computers that contain a large amount of memory.

The *initialization process* is slightly more complex. One routine sets the default values for interrupt vectors. These default values either point to the standard interrupt handlers located inside the ROM BIOS, or they point to do-nothing routines in the ROM BIOS that may later be superseded by the operating system or by your own interrupt handlers. Another initialization routine determines what equipment is attached to the computer and then places a record of it at standard locations in low memory. (We'll be discussing this equipment list in more detail later in the chapter.) How this information is acquired varies from model to model — for example, in the PC it is taken mostly from the settings of two banks of switches located on the computer's system board; in the PC/AT and the PS/2s, the ROM BIOS reads configuration information from a special nonvolatile memory area whose contents are initialized by special setup programs supplied by IBM. The POST routines learn about the computer's hardware by a logical inspection and test. In effect, the initialization program shouts to each possible option, ''Are you there?'', and listens for a response.

No matter how it is acquired, the status information is recorded and stored in the same way for every model so that your programs can examine it. The initialization routines also check for new equipment and extensions to ROM. If they find any, they momentarily turn control over to the ROM extensions so that they can initialize themselves. The initialization routines then continue executing the remaining start-up routines (more on this later in the chapter).

The final part of the start-up procedure, after the POST tests, the initialization process, and the incorporation of ROM extensions, is called the *bootstrap loader*. It's a short routine that loads a program from disk. In essence, the ROM bootstrap loader attempts to read a disk boot program from a disk. If the boot program is successfully read into memory, the ROM loader passes control of the computer to it. The disk boot program is responsible for loading another, larger disk program, which is usually a disk operating system such as DOS, but can be a self-contained and self-loading program, such as Microsoft Flight Simulator. If the ROM bootstrap loader cannot read a disk's boot program, it either activates the built-in ROM BASIC or displays an error message if the disk boot program contains an error. As soon as either of these two events occurs, the system start-up procedure is finished and the other programs take over.

The ROM BIOS

The ROM BIOS is the part of ROM that is in active use whenever the computer is at work. The role of the ROM BIOS is to provide the fundamental services that are needed for the operation of the computer. For the most part, the ROM BIOS controls the computer's peripheral devices, such as the display screen, keyboard, and disk drives. When we use the term BIOS in its narrowest sense, we are referring to the device control programs — the programs that translate a simple command, such as read-something-from-the-disk, into all the steps needed to actually perform the command, including error detection and correction. In the broadest sense, the BIOS includes not only routines needed to control the PC's devices, but also routines that contain information or perform tasks that are fundamental to other aspects of the computer's operation, such as keeping track of the time of day.

Conceptually, the ROM BIOS programs lie between programs that are executing in RAM (including DOS) and the hardware. In effect, this means that the BIOS works in two directions in a two-sided process. One side receives requests from programs to perform the standard ROM BIOS input/output services. A program invokes these services with a combination of an interrupt number (which indicates the subject of the service request, such as printer services) and a service number (which indicates the specific service to be performed). The other side of the ROM BIOS communicates with the computer's hardware devices (display screen, disk drives, and so on), using whatever detailed command codes each device requires. This side of the

ROM BIOS also handles any hardware interrupts that a device generates to get attention. For example, whenever you press a key, the keyboard generates an interrupt to let the ROM BIOS know.

Of all the ROM software, the BIOS services are probably the most interesting and useful to programmers — as a matter of fact, we have devoted six chapters to the BIOS services in Chapters 8 through 13. Since we deal with them so thoroughly later on, we'll skip any specific discussion of what the BIOS services do and instead focus on how the BIOS as a whole keeps track of the computer's input and output processes.

Interrupt Vectors

The IBM PC family, like all computers based on the Intel 8086 family of microprocessors, is controlled largely through the use of interrupts, which can be generated by hardware or software. The BIOS service routines are no exception; each is assigned an interrupt number that you must call when you want to use the service.

When an interrupt occurs, control of the computer is turned over to an interrupt-handling subroutine that is often stored in the system's ROM (a BIOS service routine is nothing more than an interrupt handler). The interrupt handler is called by loading its segment and offset addresses into registers that control program flow: the CS (code segment) register and the IP (instruction pointer) register — together known as the CS:IP register pair. Segment addresses that locate interrupt handlers are called *interrupt vectors.*

During the system start-up process, the BIOS sets the interrupt vectors to point to the interrupt handlers in ROM. The interrupt vector table starts at the beginning of RAM, at address 0000:0000H. (See Chapter 2 for more about interrupts and interrupt vectors.) Each entry in the table is stored as a pair of words, with the offset portion first and the segment portion second. The interrupt vectors can be changed to point to a new interrupt handler simply by locating the vector and changing its value.

As a general rule, PC-family interrupts can be divided into six categories: microprocessor, hardware, software, DOS, BASIC, and general use.

Microprocessor interrupts, often called *logical interrupts,* are designed into the microprocessor. Four of them (interrupts 00H, 01H, 03H, and 04H) are generated by the microprocessor itself, and another (interrupt 02H, the nonmaskable interrupt) is activated by a signal generated by certain hardware devices, such as the 8087 math coprocessor.

Hardware interrupts are built into the PC hardware. In PCs, XTs, and PS/2 models 25 and 30, interrupt numbers 08H through 0FH are used for hardware interrupts; in ATs and PS/2 models 50, 60, and 80, interrupt numbers 08H through 0FH and 70H through 77H are reserved for hardware interrupts. (See Chapter 2 for more about hardware interrupts.)

Software interrupts incorporated into the PC design are part of the ROM BIOS programs. ROM BIOS routines invoked by these interrupts cannot

The Part DOS Plays

The ROM bootstrap loader's only function is to read a bootstrap program from a disk and transfer control to it. On a bootable DOS disk, the disk bootstrap program verifies that DOS is stored on the disk by looking for two hidden files named IBMBIO.COM and IBMDOS.COM. If it finds them, it loads them into memory along with the DOS command interpreter, COMMAND.COM. During this loading process, optional parts of DOS, such as installable device drivers, may also be loaded.

The IBMBIO.COM file contains extensions to the ROM BIOS. These extensions can be changes or additions to the basic I/O operations and often include corrections to the existing ROM BIOS, new routines for new equipment, or customized changes to the standard ROM BIOS routines. Because they are part of disk software, the IBMBIO.COM routines provide a convenient way to modify the ROM BIOS. All that is necessary, besides the new routine, is that the interrupt vectors for the previous ROM BIOS routines be changed to point to the location in memory where the new disk BIOS routines are placed. Whenever new devices are added to the computer, their support programs can be included in the IBMBIO.COM file or as installable device drivers, eliminating the need to replace ROM chips. See Appendix A for more on device drivers.

You can think of the ROM BIOS routines as the lowest-level system software available, performing the most fundamental and primitive I/O operations. The IBMBIO.COM routines, being extensions of the ROM BIOS, are essentially on the same low level, also providing basic functions. By comparison, the IBMDOS.COM routines are more sophisticated; think of them as occupying the next level up, with applications programs on top.

The IBMDOS.COM file contains the DOS service routines. The DOS services, like the BIOS services, can be called by programs

be changed, but the vectors that point to them can be changed to point to different routines. Reserved interrupt numbers are 10H through 1FH (decimal 16 through 31) and 40H through 5FH (decimal 64 through 95).

DOS interrupts are always available when DOS is in use. Many programs and programming languages use the services provided by DOS through the DOS interrupts to handle basic operations, especially disk I/O. DOS interrupt numbers are 20H through 3FH (decimal 32 through 63).

through a set of interrupts whose vectors are placed in the interrupt-vector table in low memory. One of the DOS interrupts, interrupt 21H (decimal 33), is particularly important because when invoked, it gives you access to a rather large group of DOS functions. The DOS functions provide more sophisticated and efficient control over the I/O operations than the BIOS routines do, especially with regard to disk file operations. All standard disk processes — formatting diskettes; reading and writing data; opening, closing, and deleting files; performing directory searches — are included in the DOS functions and provide the foundation for many higher-level DOS programs, such as FORMAT, COPY, and DIR. Your programs can use the DOS services when they need more control of I/O operations than programming languages allow, and when you are reluctant to dig all the way down to the BIOS level. The DOS services are a very important part of this book, and we have devoted five chapters to them. (See Chapters 14 through 18.)

The COMMAND.COM file is the third and most important part of DOS, at least from a utilitarian standpoint. This file contains the routines that interpret the commands you type in through the keyboard in the DOS command mode. By comparing your input to a table of command names, the COMMAND.COM program can differentiate between internal commands that are part of the COMMAND.COM file, such as RENAME or ERASE, and external commands, such as the DOS utility programs (like DEBUG) or one of your own programs. The command interpreter acts by executing the required routines for internal commands or by searching for the requested programs on disk and loading them into memory. The whole subject of the COMMAND.COM file and how it works is intriguing and well worth investigating — as are the other DOS programs. We recommend you read the *DOS Technical Reference Manual* or *Inside the IBM PC* for additional information.

BASIC interrupts are assigned by BASIC itself and are always available when BASIC is in use. The reserved interrupt numbers are 80H through F0H (decimal 128 through 240).

General-use interrupts are available for temporary use in your programs. The reserved interrupt numbers are 60H through 66H (decimal 96 through 102).

Most of the interrupt vectors used by the ROM BIOS, DOS, and BASIC contain the addresses of interrupt handlers. A few interrupt vectors, however, point to tables of useful information. For example, interrupt 1EH contains the address of a table of diskette drive initialization parameters; the interrupt 1FH vector points to a table of bit patterns used by the ROM BIOS to display text characters; and interrupts 41H and 46H point to tables of fixed-disk parameters. These interrupt vectors are used for convenience, not for interrupts. If you tried to execute interrupt 1EH, for instance, you'd probably crash the system because the interrupt 1EH vector points to data, not to executable code.

The interrupt vectors are stored at the lowest memory locations; the very first location in memory contains the vector for interrupt number 00H, and so on. Because each vector is two words in length, you can find a particular interrupt's location in memory by multiplying its interrupt number by 4. For example, the vector for interrupt 05H, the print-screen service interrupt, would be at byte offset 20 (5 × 4 = 20); that is, at address 0000:0014H. You can examine the interrupt vectors by using DEBUG. For example, you could examine the interrupt 05H vector with DEBUG in the following way:

```
DEBUG
D 0000:0014 L 4
```

DEBUG will show 4 bytes, in hex, like this:

```
54 FF 00 F0
```

Converted to a segment and offset address and allowing for "backwords" storage, the interrupt vector for the entry point in ROM of the print-screen service routine (interrupt 05H) is F000:FF54H. (Of course, this address may be different in different members of the PC and PS/2 families.) The same DEBUG instruction finds any other interrupt vector just as easily.

Figure 3-1 lists the main interrupts and their vector locations. These are the interrupts that programmers will probably find most useful. Details are available for most of these interrupts in Chapters 8 through 18. Interrupts that are not mentioned in this list are, for the most part, reserved for future development by IBM.

Interrupt		Offset in Segment		Interrupt		Offset in Segment	
Hex	Dec	0000	Use	Hex	Dec	0000	Use
00H	0	0000	Generated by CPU when division by zero is attempted	13H	19	004C	Invokes disk services in ROM BIOS
01H	1	0004	Used to single-step through programs (as with DEBUG)	14H	20	0050	Invokes communications services in ROM BIOS
				15H	21	0054	Invokes system services in ROM BIOS
02H	2	0008	Nonmaskable interrupt (NMI)	16H	22	0058	Invokes standard keyboard services in ROM BIOS
03H	3	000C	Used to set break-points in programs (as with DEBUG)	17H	23	005C	Invokes printer services in ROM BIOS
04H	4	0010	Generated when arithmetic result overflows	18H	24	0060	Activates ROM BASIC language
05H	5	0014	Invokes print-screen service routine in ROM BIOS	19H	25	0064	Invokes bootstrap start-up routine in ROM BIOS
08H	8	0020	Generated by hardware clock tick	1AH	26	0068	Invokes time and date services in ROM BIOS
09H	9	0024	Generated by keyboard action	1BH	27	006C	Interrupt by ROM BIOS for Ctrl-Break
0EH	14	0038	Signals diskette attention (e.g. to signal completion)	1CH	28	0070	Interrupt generated at each clock tick
0FH	15	003C	Used in printer control	1DH	29	0074	Points to table of video control parameters
10H	16	0040	Invokes video display services in ROM BIOS				
11H	17	0044	Invokes equipment-list service in ROM BIOS	1EH	30	0078	Points to diskette drive parameter table
12H	18	0048	Invokes memory-size service in ROM BIOS				

Figure 3-1. *Important interrupts used in the IBM personal computer family.*   *(continued)*

Figure 3-1. *continued*

Interrupt		Offset in Segment 0000		Interrupt		Offset in Segment 0000	
Hex	*Dec*		*Use*	*Hex*	*Dec*		*Use*
1FH	31	007C	Points to CGA video graphics characters	25H	37	0094	Invokes absolute disk-read service in DOS
20H	32	0080	Invokes program-terminate service in DOS	26H	38	0098	Invokes absolute disk-write service in DOS
21H	33	0084	Invokes all function-call services in DOS	27H	39	009C	Ends program, but keeps it in memory under DOS
22H	34	0088	Address of DOS program-terminate routine	2FH	47	00BC	DOS Multiplex interrupt
23H	35	008C	Address of DOS keyboard-break handler	41H	65	0104	Points to fixed-disk drive parameter table
24H	36	0090	Address of DOS critical-error handler	43H	67	010C	Points to video graphics characters (EGA, PS/2s)
				67H	103	019CH	Invokes LIM Expanded Memory Manager

Changing Interrupt Vectors

The main programming interest in interrupt vectors is not to read them but to change them to point to a new interrupt-handling routine. To do this, you must write a routine that performs a different function than the standard ROM BIOS or DOS interrupt handlers perform, store the routine in RAM, and then assign the routine's address to an existing interrupt in the table.

A vector can be changed byte by byte on an assembly-language level, or by using a programming-language instruction like the POKE statement in BASIC. In some cases, there may be a danger of an interrupt occurring in the middle of a change to the vector. If you are not concerned about this, go ahead and use the POKE method. Otherwise, there are two ways to change a vector while minimizing the likelihood of interrupts: by suspending interrupts during the process, or by using a DOS interrupt specially designed to change vectors.

The first method requires that you use assembly language to suspend interrupts while you change the interrupt vector. You can use the clear interrupts instruction (CLI), which suspends all interrupts until a subsequent STI (set interrupts) instruction is executed. By temporarily disabling interrupts with CLI you ensure that no interrupts can occur while you update an interrupt vector.

❑ NOTE: *CLI does not disable the nonmaskable interrupt (NMI). If your application is one of the rare ones that needs to supply its own NMI handler, the program should temporarily disable the NMI while changing the NMI interrupt vector. (See PC or PS/2 technical reference manuals for details.)*

The following example demonstrates how to update an interrupt vector with interrupts temporarily disabled. This example uses two MOV instructions to copy the segment and offset address of an interrupt handler from DS:DX into interrupt vector 60H:

```
xor     ax,ax                       ; zero segment register ES
mov     es,ax
cli                                 ; disable interrupts
mov     word ptr es:[180h],dx       ; update vector offset
mov     word ptr es:[182h],ds       ; update vector segment
sti                                 ; enable interrupts
```

The second method of updating an interrupt vector is to let DOS do it for you using DOS interrupt 21H, service 25H (decimal 37), which was designed for this purpose. There are two very important advantages to letting DOS set interrupts for you. One advantage is that DOS takes on the task of putting the vector into place in the safest possible way. The other advantage is more far-reaching. When you use DOS service 25H to change an interrupt vector, you allow DOS to track changes to any interrupt vectors it may itself be using. This is particularly important for programs that might run in the DOS "compatibility box" in OS/2. Using a DOS service to set an interrupt vector instead of setting it yourself is only one of many ways that you can reduce the risk that a program will be incompatible with new machines or new operating-system environments.

The following example demonstrates how to use interrupt 21H, service 25H to update the vector for interrupt 60H from values stored in a memory variable:

```
mov     dx,seg Int60Handler        ; copy new segment to DS
mov     ds,dx
mov     dx,offset Int60Handler     ; store offset address in DX
mov     al,60h                     ; interrupt number
mov     ah,25h                     ; DOS set-interrupt function number
int     21h                        ; DOS function-call interrupt
```

This example shows, in the simplest possible way, how to use the DOS service. However, it glosses over an important and subtle difficulty: You have to load one of the addresses that you're passing to DOS into the DS (data segment) register—which effectively blocks normal access to data through the DS register. Getting around that problem requires you to preserve the contents of the DS register. Here is one way this can be done. In this example, taken from the Norton Utilities programs, the interrupt 09H vector is updated with the address of a special interrupt handler:

```
push    ds                          ; save current data segment
mov     dx,offset PGROUP:XXX        ; store handler's offset in DX
push    cs                          ; move handler's code segment...
pop     ds                          ; ...into DS
mov     ah,25h                      ; request set-interrupt function
mov     al,9                        ; change interrupt number 9
int     21h                         ; DOS function-call interrupt
pop     ds                          ; restore original data segment
```

Key Low-Memory Addresses

Much of the operation of the PCs and PS/2s is controlled by data stored in low-memory locations, particularly in the two adjacent 256-byte areas beginning at segments 40H and 50H (addresses 0040:0000H and 0050:0000H). The ROM BIOS uses the 256 bytes from 0040:0000H through 0040:00FFH as a data area for its keyboard, video, disk, printer, and communications routines. The 256 bytes between 0050:0000H and 0050:00FFH are used primarily by BASIC, although a few ROM BIOS status variables are located there as well.

Data is loaded into these areas by the BIOS during the start-up process. Although the control data is supposed to be the private reserve of the BIOS, DOS, and BASIC, your programs are allowed to inspect or even change it. Even if you do not intend to use the information in these control areas, it is worth studying because it reveals a great deal about what makes the PC family tick.

The ROM BIOS Data Area

Some memory locations in the BIOS data area are particularly interesting. Most of them contain data vital to the operation of various ROM BIOS and DOS service routines. In many instances, your programs can obtain information stored in these locations by invoking a ROM BIOS interrupt; in all cases, they can access the information directly. You can easily check out the values at these locations on your own computer, using either DEBUG or BASIC.

To use DEBUG, type a command of this form:

```
DEBUG
D XXXX:YYYY L 1
```

XXXX represents the segment part of address you want to examine. (This would be either 0040H or 0050H, depending on the data area that interests you.) *YYYY* represents the offset part of the address. The L 1 tells DEBUG to display one byte. To see two or more bytes, type the number of bytes (in hex) you want to see after the L instruction. For example, the BIOS keeps track of the current video mode number in the byte at 0040:0049H. To inspect this byte with DEBUG, you would type

```
DEBUG
D 0040:0049 L 1
```

To display the data with BASIC, use a program of the following form, making the necessary substitutions for *segment* (&H0040 or &H0050), *number.of.bytes*, and *offset* (the offset part of the address you want to inspect):

```
10 DEF SEG = segment
20 FOR I = 0 TO number.of.bytes - 1
30   VALUE = PEEK(offset + I)
40   IF VALUE < 16 THEN PRINT "0";    ' needed for leading zero
50   PRINT HEX$ (VALUE);" ";
60 NEXT I
```

The following pages describe useful low-memory addresses.

0040:0010H (a 2-byte word). This word holds the equipment-list data that is reported by the equipment-list service, interrupt 11H (decimal 17). The format of this word, shown in Figure 3-2, was established for the PC and XT; certain parts may appear in a different format in later models.

0040:0013H (a 2-byte word). This word contains the usable memory size in KB. BIOS interrupt service 12H (decimal 18) is responsible for reporting the value in this word.

0040:0017H (2 bytes of keyboard status bits). These bytes are actively used to control the interpretation of keyboard actions by the ROM BIOS routines. Changing these bytes actually changes the meaning of keystrokes. You can freely change the first byte, at address 0040:0017H, but it is not a good idea to change the second byte. See pages 137 and 138 for the bit settings of these 2 bytes.

Bit F E D C B A 9 8	7 6 5 4 3 2 1 0	Meaning
X X	. . . .	Number of printers installed
. . X	. . . .	(Reserved)
. . . X	. . . .	1 if game adapter installed
. . . . X X X .	. . . .	Number of RS-232 serial ports
. . . . X	. . . .	(Reserved)
. . . .	X X	+1 = number of diskette drives: 00 = 1 drive; 01 = 2 drives; 10 = 3 drives; 11 = 4 drives (see bit 0)
. . . .	. . X X	Initial video mode: 01 = 40-column color; 10 = 80-column color, 11 = 80-column monochrome; 00 = none of the above
. . . .	. . . . X X . .	For PC with 64 KB motherboard: Amount of system board RAM (11 = 64 KB, 10 = 48 KB, 01 = 32 KB, 00 = 16 KB) For PC/AT: Not used For PS/2s: Bit 3: Not used; Bit 2: 1 = pointing device installed
. . . .	. . . . . . X .	1 if math coprocessor installed
. . . .	 X	1 if any diskette drives present (if so, see bits 7 and 6)

Figure 3-2. *The coding of the equipment-list word at address 0040:0010H.*

0040:001AH (a 2-byte word). This word points to the current head of the BIOS keyboard buffer at 0040:001EH, where keystrokes are stored until they are used.

0040:001CH (a 2-byte word). This word points to the current tail of the BIOS keyboard buffer.

0040:001EH (32 bytes, used as sixteen 2-byte entries). This keyboard buffer holds up to 16 keystrokes until they are read via the BIOS services through interrupt 16H (decimal 22). As this is a circular queue buffer, two pointers indicate the head and tail. It is not wise to manipulate this data.

0040:003EH (1 byte). This byte indicates if a diskette drive needs to be recalibrated before seeking to a track. Bits 0 through 3 correspond to drives 0 through 3. If a bit is clear, recalibration is needed. Generally, you will find that a bit is clear if there was any problem with the most recent use of a drive. For example, the recalibration bit will be clear if you try to request a directory (DIR) on a drive with no diskette, and then type A in response to the following display:

```
Not ready reading drive A
Abort, Retry, Fail?
```

0040:003FH (1 byte). This byte returns the diskette motor status. Bits 0 through 3 correspond to drives 0 through 3. If the bit is set, the diskette motor is running.

0040:0040H (1 byte). This byte is used by the ROM BIOS to ensure that the diskette drive motor is turned off. The value in this byte is decremented with every tick of the system clock (that is, about 18.2 times per second). When the value reaches 0, the BIOS turns off the drive motor.

0040:0041H (1 byte). This byte contains the status code reported by the ROM BIOS after the most recent diskette operation. (See Figure 3-3.)

0040:0042H (7 bytes). These 7 bytes hold diskette controller status information.

Beginning at 0040:0049H is a 30-byte area used for video control. This is the first of two areas in segment 40H that the ROM BIOS uses to track critical video information.

Value	Meaning
00H	No error
01H	Invalid diskette command requested
02H	Address mark on diskette not found
03H	Write-protect error
04H	Sector not found; diskette damaged or not formatted
06H	Diskette change line active
08H	DMA diskette error
09H	Attempt to DMA across 64 KB boundary
0CH	Media type not found
10H	Cyclical redundancy check (CRC) error in data
20H	Diskette controller failed
40H	Seek operation failed
80H	Diskette timed out (drive not ready)

Figure 3-3. *Diskette status codes in the ROM BIOS data area at 0040:0041H.*

Although programs can safely inspect any of this data, you should modify the data only when you bypass the ROM BIOS video services and program the video hardware directly. In such cases, you should update the video control data to reflect the true status of the video hardware.

0040:0049H (1 byte). The value in this byte specifies the current video mode. (See Figure 3-4.) This is the same video-mode number used in the ROM BIOS video services. (See Chapter 9 for more on these services and page 72 for general information concerning video modes.)

We've already shown how to use DEBUG to determine the current video mode by inspecting the byte at 0040:0049H. BASIC programs can use the following instructions to read this byte and determine the video mode:

```
DEF SEG = &H40              ' set BASIC data segment to 40H
VIDEO.MODE = PEEK(&H49)     ' look at location 0040:0049H
```

0040:004AH (a 2-byte word). This word indicates the number of characters that can be displayed in each row of text on the screen.

0040:004CH (a 2-byte word). This word indicates the number of bytes required to represent one screenful of video data.

Number	Description
00H	40 × 25 16-color text (CGA composite color burst disabled)
01H	40 × 25 16-color text
02H	80 × 25 16-color text (CGA composite color burst disabled)
03H	80 × 25 16-color text
04H	320 × 200 4-color graphics
05H	320 × 200 4-color graphics (CGA composite color burst disabled)
06H	640 × 200 2-color graphics
07H	80 × 25 monochrome text
0DH	320 × 200 16-color graphics
0EH	640 × 200 16-color graphics
0FH	640 × 350 monochrome graphics
10H	640 × 350 16-color graphics
11H	640 × 480 2-color graphics
12H	640 × 480 16-color graphics
13H	320 × 200 256-color graphics

Figure 3-4. *BIOS video mode numbers stored at address 0040:0049H.*

0040:004EH (a 2-byte word). This word contains the starting byte offset into video display memory of the current display page. In effect, this address indicates which page is in use by giving the offset to that page.

0040:0050H (eight 2-byte words). These words give the cursor locations for eight separate display pages, beginning with page 0. The first byte of each word gives the character column and the second byte gives the row.

0040:0060H (a 2-byte word). These 2 bytes indicate the size of the cursor, based on the range of cursor scan lines. The first byte gives the ending scan line, the second byte the starting scan line.

0040:0062H (1 byte). This byte holds the current display page number.

0040:0063H (a 2-byte word). This word stores the port address of the hardware CRT controller chip.

0040:0065H (1 byte). This byte contains the current setting of the CRT mode register on the Monochrome Display Adapter and the Color Graphics Adapter.

0040:0066H (1 byte). This byte contains the current setting of the Color Graphics Adapter's CRT color register. This byte ends the first block of ROM BIOS video control data.

0040:0067H (5 bytes). The original IBM PC BIOS used the 5 bytes starting at 0040:0067H for cassette tape control. In PS/2 models 50, 60, and 80, which don't support a cassette interface, the 4 bytes at 0040:0067H can contain the address of a system reset routine that overrides the usual BIOS startup code. (See the BIOS technical reference manual for details.)

0040:006CH (4 bytes stored as one 4-byte number). This area is used as a *master clock count,* which is incremented once for each timer tick. It is treated as if it began counting from 0 at midnight. When the count reaches the equivalent of 24 hours, the ROM BIOS resets the count to 0 and sets the byte at 0040:0070H to 1. DOS or BASIC calculates the current time from this value and sets the time by putting the appropriate count in this field.

0040:0070H (1 byte). This byte indicates that a clock rollover has occurred. When the clock count passes midnight (and is reset to 0), the ROM BIOS sets this byte to 1, which means that the date should be incremented.

❑ NOTE: *This byte is set to 1 at midnight and is not incremented. There is no indication if two midnights pass before the clock is read.*

0040:0071H (1 byte). The ROM BIOS sets bit 7 of this byte to indicate that the Ctrl-Break key combination was pressed.

0040:0072H (a 2-byte word). This word is set to 1234H after the initial power-up memory check. When a warm boot is instigated from the keyboard (via Ctrl-Alt-Del), the memory check will be skipped if this location is already set to 1234H.

0040:0074H (4 bytes). These 4 bytes are used by various members of the PC family for diskette and fixed-disk drive control. See the *IBM BIOS Interface Technical Reference Manual* for details.

0040:0078H (4 bytes). These bytes control time-out values for the parallel printers. (In the PS/2, only the first 3 bytes are used for this purpose.)

0040:007CH (4 bytes). These bytes contain time-out values for up to four RS-232 serial ports.

0040:0080H (a 2-byte word). This word points to the start of the keyboard buffer area.

0040:0082H (a 2-byte word). This word points to the end of the keyboard buffer area.

The next 7 bytes are used by the ROM BIOS in the EGA and PS/2s for video control:

0040:0084H (1 byte). The value of this byte is one less than the number of character rows displayed on the screen. The BIOS can refer to this value to determine how many character rows of data to erase when the screen is cleared or how many rows to print when Shift-PrtSc is pressed.

0040:0085H (2 bytes). This word indicates the height, in scan lines, of characters on the screen.

0040:0087H (4 bytes). These 4 bytes are used by the BIOS video support routines to indicate the amount of video RAM available, the initial settings of the EGA configuration switches, and other miscellaneous video status information.

0040:008BH (11 bytes). The ROM BIOS uses this data area for control and status information regarding the diskette and fixed-disk drives.

0040:0098H (9 bytes). This data area is used by the PC/AT and PS/2 BIOS to control certain functions of the real-time clock.

0040:00A8H (4 bytes). In the EGA and PS/2 BIOS, these bytes contain the segmented address of a table of video parameters and overrides for default ROM BIOS video configuration values. The actual contents of the table vary, depending on which video hardware you are using. The *IBM ROM BIOS Interface Technical Reference Manual* describes this table in detail.

0050:0000H (1 byte). This byte is used by the ROM BIOS to indicate the status of a print-screen operation. Three possible hex values are stored in this location:

00H	Indicates OK status
01H	Indicates a print-screen operation is currently in progress
FFH	Indicates an error occurred during a print-screen operation

0050:0004H (1 byte). This byte is used by DOS when a single-diskette system mimics a two-diskette system. The value indicates whether the one physical drive is acting as drive A or drive B. These values are used:

00H	Acting as drive A
01H	Acting as drive B

0050:0010H (a 2-byte word). This area is used by ROM BASIC to hold its default data segment (DS) value.

BASIC lets you set your own data segment value with the DEF SEG = *value* statement. (The offset into the segment is specified by the PEEK or POKE function.) You can also reset the data segment to its default setting by using the DEF SEG statement without a value. Although BASIC does not give you a simple way to find the default value stored in this location, you can get it by using this little routine:

```
DEF SEG = &H50
DATA.SEGMENT = PEEK(&H11) * 256 + PEEK(&H10)
```

❑ NOTE: *BASIC administers its own internal data based on the default data segment value. Attempting to change this value is likely to sabotage BASIC's operation.*

0050:0012H (4 bytes). In some versions of ROM BASIC, these 4 bytes contain the segment and offset address of BASIC's clock-tick interrupt handler.

❑ NOTE: *In order to perform better, BASIC runs the system clock at four times the standard rate, so BASIC must replace the ROM BIOS clock interrupt routine with its own. The standard BIOS interrupt routine is invoked by BASIC at the normal rate; that is, once for every four fast ticks. There's more about this on page 146.*

0050:0016H (4 bytes). This area contains the address of ROM BASIC's break-key handling routine.

0050:001AH (4 bytes). This area contains the address of ROM BASIC's diskette error-handling routine.

The Intra-Application Communications Area

In the PC/XT/AT family, the 16 bytes starting at 0040:00F0H are reserved as an *intra-application communication area* (ICA). This data area provides an area of RAM at a known address that an application can use for sharing data among separate program modules. In the PS/2 BIOS, however, the ICA is no longer documented.

Few applications actually use the ICA because the amount of RAM is so small and because the data within the ICA can be unexpectedly modified when more than one program uses it. If you do write a program that uses the ICA, we recommend that you include a checksum and also a signature so that you can ensure that the data in the ICA is yours and that it has not been changed by another program.

❏ WARNING: *The ICA is definitely located in the 16 bytes from 0040:00F0H through 0040:00FFH. A typographic error in some editions of the* IBM PC Technical Reference Manual *places it at 0050:0000H through 0050:00FFH. This is incorrect.*

The BIOS Extended Data Area

The PS/2 ROM BIOS start-up routines allocate an additional area of RAM for their own use. The BIOS routines use this *extended data area* for transient data storage. For example, the BIOS routines that support the pointing-device (mouse) controller hardware use part of the extended data area for temporary storage.

You can determine the starting address of the extended data area by using a system service available through ROM BIOS interrupt 15H. (See Chapter 12.) The first byte in the extended data area contains the size of the data area in KB.

The ROM Version and Machine-ID Markers

Because the BIOS programs are fixed in memory, they can't be easily changed when additions or corrections are needed. This means that ROM programs must be tested very carefully before they are frozen onto memory chips. Although there is a good chance for serious errors to exist in a system's ROM programs, IBM has a fine track record; so far, only small and relatively unimportant errors have been found in the PC family's ROM programs, and IBM has done well to correct errors by revising the BIOS.

The different versions of ROM software could present a small challenge to programmers who discover that the differences affect the operating characteristics of their programs. But an even greater challenge for programmers is that the PC, XT, AT, and PS/2s each have a slightly different set of ROM BIOS routines.

To ensure that programs can work with the appropriate ROM programs and the right computer, IBM has supplied two identifying markers that are permanently available at the end of memory in the system ROM. One marker identifies the ROM release date, which can be used to identify the BIOS version, and the other gives the machine model. These markers are always present in IBM's own machines and you'll also find them supplied by the manufacturers of a few PC compatibles. The following paragraphs describe these markers in detail.

The *ROM release date* can be found in an 8-byte storage area from F000:FFF5H to F000:FFFCH (2 bytes before the machine ID byte). It consists of ASCII characters in the common American date format; for example, 06/01/83 stands for June 1, 1983. This release marker is a common feature of the IBM personal computers, but is present in only a few IBM compatibles. For example, the Compaq Portable I does not have it, but the Panasonic Senior Partner does.

You can look at the release date with DEBUG by using the following command:

```
DEBUG
D F000:FFF5 L 8
```

Or you can let your program look at the bytes using this technique:

```
10 DEF SEG = &HF000
20 FOR I = 0 TO 7
30   PRINT CHR$(PEEK(&HFFF5 + I));
40 NEXT
50 END
```

The *model ID* is a byte located at F000:FFFEH. This byte identifies which model of PC or PS/2 you are using. (See Figure 3-5.) In addition, a ROM BIOS service in the PC/AT and PS/2s returns more detailed identification information, including the submodel byte listed in the figure. (See Chapter 12.)

Machine	Date	Model	Submodel	BIOS	Revision Notes
PC	04/24/81	FFH	**	00	
	10/19/81	FFH	**	01	Some BIOS bugs fixed
	10/27/82	FFH	**	02	Upgrade of PC BIOS to XT level
PC/XT	11/08/82	FEH	**	00	
	01/10/86	FBH	00	01	256/640 KB system board
	05/09/86	FBH	00	02	
PC/AT	01/10/84	FCH	**	00	6 MHz 80286
	06/10/85	FCH	00	01	
	11/15/85	FCH	01	00	8 MHz 80286
PS/2 Model 25	06/26/87	FAH	01	00	
PS/2 Model 30	09/02/86	FAH	00	00	
	12/12/86	FAH	00	01	
PS/2 Model 50	02/13/87	FCH	04	00	
PS/2 Model 60	02/13/87	FCH	05	00	
PS/2 Model 80	03/30/87	F8H	00	00	16 MHz 80386
PS/2 Model 80	10/07/87	F8H	01	00	20 MHz 80386
PCjr	06/01/83	FDH	**	00	
PC Convertible	09/13/85	F9H	00	00	
PC/XT Model 286	04/21/86	FCH	02	00	

** not applicable

Figure 3-5. *Machine and ROM BIOS version identification.*

It is possible that IBM-compatible computers can be identified in the same way, but we do not know of any reliable published information. You may need to rely on improvised methods to identify non-IBM compatibles.

You can examine the machine ID byte with DEBUG by using the following command:

```
DEBUG
D F000:FFFE L 1
```

A BASIC program can inspect this byte using techniques such as this:

```
10 DEF SEG = &HF000
20 MODEL = PEEK(&HFFFE)
30 IF MODEL < &HF8 THEN PRINT "I'm not an IBM computer" : STOP
40 ON (MODEL - &HF7) GOTO 100,110,120,130,140,150,160,170
100 PRINT "I'm a PS/2 Model 80" : STOP
110 PRINT "I'm a PC convertible" : STOP
120 PRINT "I'm a PS/2 Model 30" : STOP
130 PRINT "I'm a PC/XT" : STOP
140 PRINT "I'm an 80286-based machine (PC/AT, PS/2 Model 50 or 60)" :
        STOP
150 PRINT "I'm a PCjr" : STOP
160 PRINT "I'm a PC/XT" : STOP
170 PRINT "I'm a PC" : STOP
```

The ROM BASIC

Now we move on to the third element of ROM: the ROM BASIC. The ROM BASIC acts in two ways. First, it provides the core of the BASIC language, which includes most of the commands and the underlying foundation — such as memory management — that BASIC uses. The disk versions of interpreted BASIC, which are found in the program files BASIC.COM and BASICA.COM, are essentially supplements to ROM BASIC, and they rely on ROM BASIC to get much of their work done. The second role of ROM BASIC is to provide what IBM calls "cassette" BASIC — the BASIC that is activated when you start up your computer without a disk.

Whenever you use any of the interpreted, disk-based BASICs, the ROM BASIC programs are also used — although there's nothing to make you aware of it. On the other hand, compiled BASIC programs don't make use of the ROM BASIC.

The ROM Extensions

The fourth element of the ROM has more to do with the PC's design than with the actual contents of its memory. The PC was designed to allow for installable extensions to the built-in software in ROM. The additional ROM is usually located on a plug-in adapter such as the Enhanced Graphics Adapter or a fixed-disk controller card. Computers in the PC/XT/AT family also have empty sockets on their system boards to accommodate additional ROM chips. Because the original ROM BIOS could not include support programs for future hardware, ROM extensions are obviously a necessary and helpful addition.

Several memory areas are reserved for ROM extensions. Addresses C000:0000H through C000:7FFFH are reserved for video adapter ROM. The area between C800:0000H and D000:FFFFH can be used by nonvideo adapters. (For example, the IBM XT fixed-disk adapter occupies addresses starting at C800:0000H.) Finally, ROM extensions on chips placed onto the system board of a PC, XT, or AT occupy the address range E000:0000H through E000:FFFFH. In the PS/2 models 50, 60, and 80, you cannot add ROM chips to the system board. The system ROM in these computers occupies the entire address range between E000:0000H and F000:FFFFH.

Comments

As the PC family has evolved, the amount and complexity of the ROM software has increased to accommodate the greater sophistication of the computer hardware. The source code listings in the PC, XT, and AT technical reference manuals consist of tens of thousands of assembly-language instructions. Despite the size of the ROM BIOS, a browse through the source code can be fun and enlightening.

We have made every effort in this book to point out when and how to use the ROM BIOS routines. We recommend that you read Chapters 8 through 13 before you begin your own exploration of the ROM BIOS.

Chapter 4

Video Basics

To many people, the video display is the computer. Programs are often judged by their display quality and visual design alone. In this chapter, you'll see what kinds of video display output the IBM PC family can produce. More importantly, we'll describe how to manipulate the video displays to get the effects you want.

The Video Subsystems

Every PC and PS/2 has a *video subsystem* responsible for producing the image that appears on the screen. At the heart of the video subsystem is the special-purpose circuitry that must be programmed to generate the electrical signals that control the video display. Most members of the PC/XT/AT family require you to install a *display adapter,* a special video circuit board that plugs into one of the computer's expansion slots. On the other hand, all PS/2s are equipped with built-in video circuitry and, therefore, require no display adapter.

The *video circuitry* consists of a group of interrelated components that control signal timing, colors, and the generation of text characters. All IBM video subsystems have a *video buffer,* a block of dedicated memory that holds the text or graphics information displayed on the screen. The video subsystem performs the unique task of translating the raw data in the video buffer into the signals that drive the video display.

The various video subsystems used in PCs and PS/2s all evolved from the two video adapters originally released by IBM for the PC: the Monochrome Display Adapter (MDA) and the Color Graphics Adapter (CGA). IBM later released its Enhanced Graphics Adapter (EGA), a more powerful successor to the MDA and CGA.

When the PS/2s appeared, IBM introduced two more video subsystems: the Multi-Color Graphics Array (MCGA), built into the PS/2 models 25 and 30, and the Video Graphics Array (VGA), built into the PS/2 models 50, 60, and 80. At the same time the PS/2s appeared, IBM introduced a VGA adapter that can be used in the PC/XT/AT family as well as in the PS/2 Model 30.

We'll be discussing all five of these IBM subsystems — MDA, CGA, EGA, MCGA, and VGA — in this chapter. Although clear differences in hardware design exist between the various video subsystems, their strong family resemblance should encourage you to consider what they have in common before worrying about the differences between them.

Most of the five video subsystems can be programmed into two fundamentally different modes, called *text mode* and *graphics mode* by IBM. (The lone exception is the MDA, which operates only in text mode.) In text mode you can display only text characters, though many of these characters are suitable for producing simple line drawings. (See Appendix C for more on characters.) Graphics mode is mainly used for complex drawings but you can also use it to draw text characters in a variety of shapes and sizes.

The CGA can operate in both text and graphics modes to produce drawings and characters in several formats and colors. By contrast, the MDA can operate only in text mode, using a stored set of ASCII alphanumeric and graphics characters and displaying them in only one color. The MDA works only with the IBM Monochrome Monitor (or its equivalent) while the CGA must be connected to either a direct-drive or a composite color monitor. (See page 74 for more on monitors.) Many business and professional users prefer a monochrome display to a color display because a monochrome screen is easier on the eyes and less expensive than an equivalent color display. But in choosing monochrome, they sacrifice color, a valuable asset for any computer display.

The MDA's most obvious drawback is its inability to display images in graphics mode. For this reason, PC/XT/AT users who prefer a monochrome display, yet need to view graphics, must turn to an EGA or to a non-IBM adapter like the Hercules Graphics Card, which emulates the MDA's text mode but supports a monochrome graphics mode as well.

Roughly two-thirds of all PCs are equipped with the standard MDA and therefore have no graphics or color capability. While there are real advantages to using color and graphics, most PCs get along nicely without either. Although the clear trend is toward higher-performance video subsystems that can display graphics as well as text, keep in mind as you plan computer applications that many PCs display text *only*.

The best way to understand the video capabilities of the PCs and PS/2s is to cover the features that their various video subsystems have in common. As we go along, we'll point out the differences and improvements that distinguish the newer and more complicated subsystems (EGA, MCGA, and VGA) from their predecessors (MDA and CGA).

Memory and the Video Subsystems

The video buffer memory is connected directly to the display circuitry so that the data in the video buffer can be repeatedly read out of the buffer and displayed. However, the video buffer is also logically (to the CPU) a part of the computer's main memory address space. A full 128 KB of the memory address space is set aside for use as video buffers, at addresses A000:0000H through B000:FFFFH, but the two original display adapters use only two small parts of this memory area. The Monochrome Display Adapter (MDA) provides 4 KB of display memory located at segment B000H. The original CGA provides 16 KB of display memory located at segment B800H.

With the other IBM video subsystems, the address at which video memory is located isn't fixed—it depends on how the subsystem is configured. For example, when an EGA is used with a monochrome display, its text-mode video buffer is placed at B000H, just as with an MDA. When an EGA is attached to a color display, its video buffer can be addressed at B800H. And when you use an EGA in non-CGA graphics modes, the starting buffer address is A000H. Like the EGA, the MCGA and the VGA also support this chameleon-like method of buffer addressing.

Creating the Screen Image

You can describe the screen display created by IBM video subsystems as a *memory-mapped display,* because each address in the display memory corresponds to a specific location on the screen. (See Figure 4-1.) The display circuitry repeatedly reads information from memory and places it on the screen. The information can be changed as quickly as the computer can

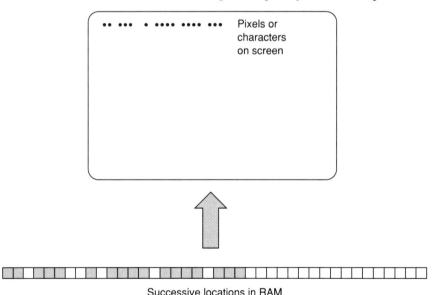

Pixels or characters on screen

Successive locations in RAM

Figure 4-1. *The memory-mapped display.*

write new information from your programs into memory. The display circuitry translates the stream of bits it receives from memory into bursts of light at particular locations on the screen.

These dots of light are called *pixels* and are produced by an electron beam striking the phosphorescent surface of the CRT. The electron beam is produced by an electron gun that scans the screen line by line. As the gun moves across and down the screen in a fixed path called a *raster scan,* the video subsystem generates video control signals that turn the beam on and off, matching the pattern of the bits in memory.

The video circuitry refreshes the screen between 50 and 70 times a second (depending on the video mode), making the changing images appear clear and steady. At the end of each screen-refresh cycle, the electron beam must move from the bottom right corner to the top left corner of the screen to begin a new cycle. This movement is called the *vertical retrace.* During the retrace, the beam is blanked and no pixels are written to the screen.

The vertical retrace period (about 1.25 milliseconds) is important to programmers for one main reason, which requires some explanation. The special dual-ported design of the video memory gives the CPU and the display-refresh circuitry equal access to the display memory. This allows the CPU and the display circuitry to access video memory at the same time.

This causes a problem on the Color Graphics Adapter (CGA). If the CPU happens to read or write to the video buffer at the same time the display circuitry is copying data out of the buffer to display onscreen, a "snow" effect may briefly appear on the screen. However, if you instruct the CPU to access memory only during vertical retrace, when the display circuitry is not accessing the video buffer, then snow can be eliminated. A program running on a CGA can test the value of bit 3 in the adapter's I/O port at 3DAH. This bit is set on at the beginning of vertical retrace and then set off at the end. During this 1.25-millisecond pause, you can have your programs write as much data as possible to the video display memory. At the end of the retrace, the display circuitry can write this data to the screen without snow.

This technique is useful for any application that directly accesses data in the video buffer in text mode on a CGA. Fortunately, the hardware design of all other IBM video subsystems avoids this access conflict and makes this specialized programming technique unnecessary.

The Video Display Modes

Originally, there were eight video modes defined for the IBM personal computers: seven on the CGA and one on the MDA. The more sophisticated EGA, MCGA, and VGA introduced several new modes plus variations on the original eight. As a result, among the five IBM video subsystems are 12 text and graphics modes and, depending how you count them, seven or eight variations—and that's not counting the extra modes available with non-IBM video hardware and with defunct IBM systems like the PCjr. There's plenty of variety when you're working with IBM video subsystems.

Despite the perplexing proliferation of video modes, what is striking about the different modes is not their differences but their similarities (Figure 4-2): All video modes are related in resolution and in video buffer organization to the original MDA and CGA modes.

The MDA's 80-column, 25-row monochrome text mode is supported on the EGA and VGA. Similarly, the CGA's two text modes (40 × 25 and 80 × 25 16-color modes) are also supported on the EGA, MCGA, and VGA. Don't let the redundant mode numbers in Figure 4-2 confuse you: The difference between mode 0 and mode 1, for example, is that the composite color signal on

| BIOS Mode Number | | | | | |
Hex	Dec	Type	Resolution	Colors	Video Subsystem
00H,01H	0, 1	Text	40 × 25	16	CGA, EGA, MCGA, VGA
02H,03H	2, 3	Text	80 × 25	16	CGA, EGA, MCGA, VGA
04H,05H	4, 5	Graphics	320 × 200	4	CGA, EGA, MCGA, VGA
06H	6	Graphics	640 × 200	2	CGA, EGA, MCGA, VGA
07H	7	Text	80 × 25	Mono	MDA, EGA, VGA
08H,09H,0AH	8, 9, 10				(PCjr only)
0BH,0CH	11, 12				(Used internally by EGA BIOS)
0DH	13	Graphics	320 × 200	16	EGA,VGA
0EH	14	Graphics	640 × 200	16	EGA,VGA
0FH	15	Graphics	640 × 350	Mono	EGA,VGA
10H	16	Graphics	640 × 350	16	EGA,VGA
11H	17	Graphics	640 × 480	2	MCGA,VGA
12H	18	Graphics	640 × 480	16	VGA
13H	19	Graphics	320 × 200	256	MCGA,VGA

Figure 4-2. *Video modes available on IBM video subsystems.*

the CGA is modified for composite monochrome monitors in mode 0. (See page 74 for more on monitors.) With all other monitors and in all other video subsystems, modes 0 and 1 are the same, as are modes 2 and 3 and modes 4 and 5.

The evolutionary pattern is the same for graphics modes. The CGA supports two graphics modes, a 320 × 200 pixel, 4-color mode and a 640 × 200, 2-color mode. These same two modes are supported on the EGA, MCGA, and VGA. The EGA introduced three new graphics modes with more colors and better resolution than the original CGA graphics modes: the 320 × 200, 16-color; 640 × 200, 16-color; and 640 × 350, 16-color modes. The EGA also introduced a 640 × 350 monochrome graphics mode that could be used only with an MDA-compatible monochrome display.

When the PS/2s appeared, their video subsystems supported the same modes as did the MDA, CGA, and EGA — but again, a few new graphics modes were introduced. The MCGA in the PS/2 models 25 and 30 followed the CGA tradition: It supported all CGA modes, plus new 640 × 480, 2-color and 320 × 200, 256-color graphics modes. The VGA in the other PS/2 models strongly resembles the EGA. It provides all the EGA's text and graphics modes, the two new MCGA graphics modes, and one more graphics mode not supported by the other subsystems — a 640 × 480, 16-color mode.

How do you know which mode to use in a program? Clearly, if broad compatibility is a concern, the MDA and CGA modes are the least common denominator. If you need more colors or better graphics resolution than the CGA modes provide, you can turn to one of the EGA, MCGA, or VGA graphics modes. Of course, if your program requires an EGA or a VGA to run, users who have only a CGA will be out of luck.

Many commercial software vendors solve this problem by distributing installable video output routines along with their products. Before you can use a package like Microsoft Windows or Lotus 1-2-3, for example, you must run a special installation program that binds output routines for your particular video hardware to the software application. This approach is more work for both the people who write software and the people who use it, but it is a good way to make applications deliver the best possible video performance without stumbling over the diversity of video hardware and video modes.

Video Mode Control

Before we get into the details about resolution and color in video modes, let's consider how you select which video mode to use. The most efficient way to set up a video mode is to use assembly language to call the ROM

BIOS. ROM BIOS interrupt 10H (decimal 16), service 00H, provides a way to select a video mode using the mode numbers listed in Figure 4-2. (See Chapter 9 for more details on this.)

Many programming languages also offer high-level commands that select video modes for you. For example, BASIC gives you control over the

Monitors

The type of video display, or monitor, that might be used has an important effect on program design. Many monitors cannot produce color or graphics, and a few produce such a poor quality image that you can use only the 40-column text display format. The many kinds of monitors that can be used with the PC family of computers can be broken down into five basic types.

Direct-drive monochrome monitors. These monitors are designed to work with the Monochrome Display Adapter (MDA), although you can also use them with an Enhanced Graphics Adapter (EGA). The green IBM Monochrome Display is reminiscent of IBM's 3270 series of mainframe computer terminals; it's no surprise that many business users are comfortable with the combination of an MDA and a green monochrome display.

Composite monochrome monitors. These monitors are still among the most widely used and least expensive monitors available. They connect to the composite video output on the Color Graphics Adapter (CGA) and provide a fairly clear one-color image (usually green or amber). Don't confuse the composite monochrome monitor with the direct-drive monochrome monitor. The composite monochrome monitor can be attached only to the CGA, whereas the direct-drive monochrome monitor must be used with an MDA or EGA.

Composite color monitors and TV sets. Composite color monitors use a single combined signal such as the composite video output of the CGA. The composite color monitor produces color and graphics but has limitations: An 80-column display is often unreadable; only certain color combinations work well; and graphics resolution is low in quality, so graphics must be kept simple by using low-resolution graphics modes.

Although the standard television set (color or black-and-white) is technically a composite monitor, it usually produces an even lower-quality image than the dedicated composite monitor. Text displays

video modes through the SCREEN statement but refers to them in its own way, using different mode numbers than the ROM BIOS routines. You can also control some of the video modes through the DOS MODE command. (See Figure 4-3.)

must be in 40-column mode to ensure that the display is readable. TVs are connected to the composite video output of the CGA, but the composite signal must be converted by an RF adapter before going into the TV.

RGB color monitors. The RGB monitors are considered the best of both worlds. They combine the high-quality text display of the monochrome monitors with high-resolution graphics and color. RGB stands for *red-green-blue,* and RGB monitors are so named because they use separate red, green, and blue color signals, unlike the composite monitors, which use only one composite signal. The image and color quality of an RGB monitor is much better than that available through any screen that connects to the composite video output.

Variable-frequency monitors. One of the problems created by the proliferation of different video subsystems is that some subsystems produce color and timing signals with different frequencies or different encodings than other subsystems. For example, you cannot use a PS/2-compatible monitor with a CGA because the color information in the monitor drive signals is encoded differently by a CGA than it is by a PS/2 video subsystem (MCGA or VGA).

Monitor manufacturers addressed this problem by designing variable-frequency RGB monitors that can be used with a wide range of signal frequencies and with more than one type of color signal encoding. For example, NEC's MultiSync monitors can adjust to the different signal frequencies generated by the CGA, the EGA, and the PS/2 video subsystems. These monitors also have a switch that lets you adapt them either to the digital color signal encoding used by the CGA and EGA or to the analog color signals used by the PS/2 subsystems.

Many people use variable-frequency monitors because they anticipate the need to upgrade their video subsystems at some time in the future, and they don't want to be stuck with an incompatible monitor.

| BIOS Mode Number | | BASIC Statement to | DOS Statement to |
Hex	Dec	Change Mode	Change Mode
00H	0	SCREEN 0,0: WIDTH 40	MODE BW40
01H	1	SCREEN 0,1:WIDTH 40	MODE CO40
02H	2	SCREEN 0,0:WIDTH 80	MODE BW80
03H	3	SCREEN 0,1:WIDTH 80	MODE CO80
04H	4	SCREEN 1,0	n/a
05H	5	SCREEN 1,1	n/a
06H	6	SCREEN 2	n/a
07H	7	n/a	MODE MONO

Figure 4-3. *The BASIC and DOS commands used to change video modes.*

Display Resolution

Video images consist of a large number of closely spaced pixels. The display resolution is defined by the number of pixel rows, or *scan lines*, from top to bottom and the number of pixels from left to right in each scan line. The horizontal and vertical resolution is limited by the capabilities of the video monitor as well as the display circuitry inside the computer. The video modes available on the different subsystems were carefully designed so that the horizontal and vertical resolution in each mode is within the limits imposed by the hardware.

The MDA's single text mode has 720 × 350 pixel resolution; that is, the screen has 350 scan lines, each of which contains 720 pixels. Because 25 rows of 80 characters of text are displayed in this mode, each character is 9 pixels wide (720 ÷ 80) and 14 pixels high (350 ÷ 25). The CGA's text modes are a bit lower resolution, because the CGA's pixel resolution is only 640 × 200. Thus the 25 rows of 80-character text on a CGA consist of characters that are only 8 pixels wide (640 ÷ 80) and 8 pixels high (200 ÷ 25). That's why text looks sharper on an MDA screen than on a CGA.

The trend in the newer IBM video subsystems is to provide better vertical resolution. For example, the EGA's 80 × 25 text mode has 640 × 350 pixel resolution, so text characters are 8 × 14 pixels. On the MCGA, the default 80 × 25 text mode has 640 × 400 resolution (8 × 16 characters), and on the VGA the same text mode has 720 × 400 resolution, so characters are each 9 pixels wide and 16 pixels high. From a program's point of view, the 80 × 25 text mode is the same on the CGA, the MCGA, and the VGA — it's display mode 3 in all cases — but a user sees much higher resolution when using a VGA or MCGA than when using one of the older subsystems.

You see the same trend towards better resolution when you examine the graphics modes available with the newer video subsystems. The VGA's 640 × 480, 16-color mode has more than twice as many pixels on the screen as the original CGA's 640 × 200 graphics mode. It's ironic that this CGA mode was known as a "high-resolution" mode when the CGA was new.

The Use of Color

A variety of colors is available in every video mode except of course on a monochrome display. You may have noticed that among the various modes there are substantial differences in the number of colors available. In this section, we will describe the color options for the video modes.

Colors for the video display screens are produced by combinations of four elements: three color components — red, green, and blue — plus an intensity, or brightness, component. Text and graphics modes use the same colors and intensity options, but they combine them in different ways to produce their colored displays. The text modes, whose basic unit is a character composed of several pixels, use an entire byte to set the color, the intensity, and the blinking characteristics of the character and its background. In graphics modes, each pixel is represented by a group of 1 through 8 bits whose value determines the color and brightness of the displayed pixel.

In 16-color text and graphics modes, the four basic color and brightness components can be combined in 16 ways. Colors are specified by a group of 4 bits. Each bit designates whether a particular color component is on or off. The result is 16 color combinations that correspond to the 16 4-bit binary numbers. (See Figure 4-4.)

In some video modes, the data in the video buffer consists of 4-bit attribute values that correspond exactly to the 16 possible color combinations on the screen. In other video modes, the attribute values do not directly specify colors. For example, on the EGA, each attribute value designates one of 16 palette registers, each of which contains a color value. (See Figure 4-5.) It is the palette color values that determine the color combinations displayed on the screen.

The use of palettes makes it possible to specify one of a broad range of colors using relatively few bits of data in the video buffer. Each of the

Intensity	Red	Green	Blue	Binary	Hex	Description
0	0	0	0	0000B	00H	Black
0	0	0	1	0001B	01H	Blue
0	0	1	0	0010B	02H	Green
0	0	1	1	0011B	03H	Cyan (blue-green)
0	1	0	0	0100B	04H	Red
0	1	0	1	0101B	05H	Magenta
0	1	1	0	0110B	06H	Brown (or dark yellow)
0	1	1	1	0111B	07H	Light gray (or ordinary white)
1	0	0	0	1000B	08H	Dark gray (black on many screens)
1	0	0	1	1001B	09H	Light blue
1	0	1	0	1010B	0AH	Light green
1	0	1	1	1011B	0BH	Light cyan
1	1	0	0	1100B	0CH	Light red
1	1	0	1	1101B	0DH	Light magenta
1	1	1	0	1110B	0EH	Yellow (or light yellow)
1	1	1	1	1111B	0FH	Bright white

Figure 4-4. *Default colors available in 16-color text and graphics modes.*

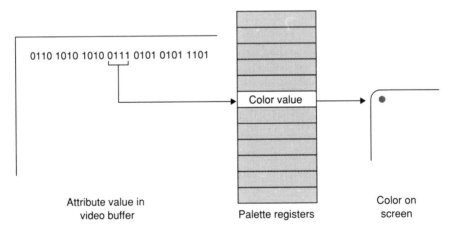

Figure 4-5. *How EGA colors are specified using palette registers. Each attribute value in the video buffer designates a palette register whose contents specify a color.*

EGA's 16 palette registers, for example, can contain one of 64 different 6-bit color values. In this way, any 2 of 64 different colors can be used in a 2-color EGA video mode, any 4 out of 64 can be used in a 4-color mode, and any 16 of 64 can be used in a 16-color mode.

All IBM video subsystems except the MDA can use palettes to display colors. The CGA has three built-in, 4-color palettes for use in 320 × 200, 4-color mode. The EGA, as we have seen, has a 16-color palette in which each color can be selected from a set of 64 colors. The MCGA and the VGA, which can display an even wider range of colors, use a separate palette-like component, the *video digital to analog converter* (video DAC), to send color signals to the screen.

The video DAC contains 256 color registers, each of which contains 6-bit color values for red, green, and blue. Since there are 64 possible values for each of the RGB components, each video DAC color register can contain one of 64 × 64 × 64, or 262,144 different color values. That wide range of colors can help you display very subtle color shades and contours.

With the MCGA, the video DAC color registers serve much the same purpose as the palette registers do with the EGA. Attribute values in the video buffer designate video DAC color registers whose contents specify the colors that appear on the screen. Unfortunately, only one MCGA video mode can take full advantage of the video DAC's capabilities: 320 × 200, 256-color mode. Only this video mode uses 8-bit attribute values that can specify all 256 of the video DAC's color registers. All remaining video modes use attribute values that have no more than 4 bits, so only the first 16 video DAC color registers are used.

The VGA gets around this limitation (and complicates matters somewhat) by using a set of 16 palette registers like the EGA's, as well as a set of 256 video DAC color registers like the MCGA's. An attribute value in the video buffer selects one of the 16 palette registers, whose contents select one of the 256 video DAC color registers — whose contents "in turn" determine the color displayed on the screen. (See Figure 4-6.)

Specifying colors on an EGA, MCGA, or VGA is clearly more complicated than it is on the CGA. To simplify this process, however, the ROM BIOS loads the palette registers (on the EGA and VGA) and the video DAC color registers (on the MCGA and VGA) with color values that exactly match those available on the CGA. If you use CGA-compatible text and graphics modes on the newer subsystems and ignore the palette and video DAC registers, you'll see the same colors you would on a CGA.

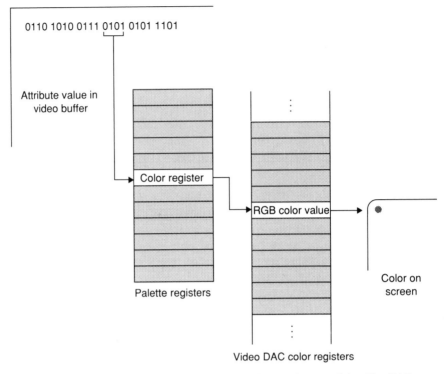

Figure 4-6. *How VGA colors are specified using palette registers and the video DAC.*

For this reason it's usually best to ignore the palette and video DAC registers when you start developing an application. Once your application works properly with the CGA-compatible colors, you can add program code that changes the palette and/or the video DAC colors. The ROM BIOS provides a complete set of services that let you access the palette and video DAC registers. Chapter 9 covers these services in detail.

In considering color, read each of the remaining sections, which discuss important color-related items.

Color-Suppressed Modes

In an effort to make the graphics modes compatible with a wide range of monitors, both color and monochrome, IBM included a few modes on the Color Graphics Adapter that do not produce color: *color-suppressed modes*. There are three color-suppressed modes: modes 0, 2, and 5. In these modes, colors are converted into shades of gray, or whatever color the screen phosphor produces. There are four gray shades in mode 5, and a variety of shades in modes 0 and 2. CGA's color is suppressed in the composite output but *not* in its RGB output. This inconsistency is the result of an unavoidable technical limitation.

> ❏ NOTE: *For each color-suppressed mode, there is a corresponding color mode, so modes 0 and 1 correspond to 40-column text, modes 2 and 3 to 80-column text, and modes 4 and 5 to medium-resolution graphics. The fact that modes 4 and 5 reverse the pattern of modes 0 and 1 and modes 2 and 3, where the color-suppressed mode comes first, has led to a complication in BASIC. The burst parameter of the BASIC SCREEN statement controls color. The meaning of this parameter is reversed for modes 4 and 5 so that the statement SCREEN,1 activates color in the text modes (0, 1, 2, and 3) but suppresses color in the graphics modes (4 and 5). This inconsistency may have been a programming error at first, but it is now part of the official definition of the SCREEN statement.*

Color in Text and Graphics Modes

Text and graphics modes use the same color-decoding circuitry, but differ in the way they store the color attribute data in the video buffer. In text modes, no matter what video subsystem you use, the foreground and background colors of each character are specified by two 4-bit fields in a single attribute byte. (See Figure 4-7.) Together, the foreground and background attributes describe all of a character's pixels: All foreground pixels are displayed with the character's foreground attribute, and all background pixels assume the background attribute.

Bit *7 6 5 4 3 2 1 0*	*Use*
1	Blinking of foreground character or intensity component of background color
. 1	Red component of background color
. . 1	Green component of background color
. . . 1	Blue component of background color
. . . . 1 . . .	Intensity component of foreground color
. . . . . 1 . .	Red component of foreground color
. . . . . . 1 .	Green component of foreground color
. . . . 1	Blue component of foreground color

Figure 4-7. *The coding of the color attribute byte.*

In graphics modes, each pixel's attribute is determined by the contents of a bit field in the video buffer. The size and format of a pixel's bit field depend on the video mode: The smallest bit fields are only 1 bit wide (as in 640 × 200, 2-color mode), and the largest bit fields are 8 bits wide (as in 320 × 200, 256-color mode).

The reason for having both text and graphics modes becomes clear if you think about how much data it takes to describe the pixels on the screen. In graphics modes, you need between 1 and 8 bits of data in the video buffer for every pixel you display. In 640 × 350, 16-color mode, for instance, with 4 bits per pixel, you need 640 × 350 × 4 ÷ 8 (112,000) bytes to represent one screenful of video data. But if you display 25 rows of 80 characters in a text mode with the same resolution, you need only 80 × 25 × 2, or 4000, bytes.

The tradeoff is clear: Text modes consume less memory and require less data manipulation than do graphics modes — but you can manipulate each pixel independently in graphics modes, as opposed to manipulating entire characters in text modes.

Setting color in text modes

Let's take a closer look at how you control colors in text modes. (We'll get back to graphics modes later in this chapter.) In text modes, each character position on the display screen is controlled by a pair of adjacent bytes in the video buffer. The first byte contains the ASCII code for the character that will be displayed. (See Appendix C for a chart of characters.) The second byte is the character's *attribute byte*. It controls how the character will appear, that is, its colors, brightness (intensity), and blinking.

We've already mentioned two attributes that affect a character's appearance: color and intensity (brightness). You can assign several other attributes to text characters, depending on which video subsystem you're using. With all IBM video subsystems, text characters can blink. On monochrome-capable subsystems (the MDA, EGA, and VGA), characters can also be underlined. Also, on some non-IBM subsystems like the Hercules Graphics Card Plus, characters can have attributes such as overstrike and boldface.

In all cases, you assign these alternate attributes by using the same 4-bit attributes that specify color. A case in point is the blinking attribute. Character blinking is controlled by setting a bit in a special register in the video subsystem. (On the CGA, for example, this enable-blink bit is bit 5 of the 8-bit register mapped at input/output port 3D8H.) When this bit is set to 1, the high-order bit of each character's attribute byte is not interpreted as part of the character's background color specification. Instead, this bit indicates whether the character should blink.

If you have a CGA, watch what happens when you run the following BASIC program:

```
10 DEF SEG = &HB800        ' point to start of video buffer
20 POKE 0,ASC("A")         ' store the ASCII code for A in the buffer
30 POKE 1,&H97             ' foreground attribute = 7 (white)
                           ' background attribute = 9 (intense blue)
```

You'll see a blinking white letter A on a blue background. If you add the following statement to the program, you'll clear the enable-blink bit and cause the CGA to interpret the background attribute as intense blue:

```
40 OUT &H3D8,&H09          ' clear the "enable-blink" bit
```

The default attribute used by DOS and BASIC is 07H, normal white (7) on black (0), without blinking, but you can use any combination of 4-bit foreground and background attributes for each character displayed in a text mode. If you exchange a character's foreground and background attributes, the character is displayed in "reverse video." If the foreground and background attributes are the same, the character is "invisible."

Setting attributes in the monochrome mode

The monochrome mode (mode 7) used by the Monochrome Display Adapter has a limited selection of attributes that take the place of color. Like the CGA, the MDA uses 4-bit foreground and background attributes, but their values are interpreted differently by the MDA attribute decoding circuitry.

Only certain combinations of foreground and background attributes are recognized by the MDA. (See Figure 4-8.) Other useful combinations, like "invisible" (white-on-white) or a reverse-video/underlined combination, aren't supported by the hardware.

Like the CGA, the MDA has an enable-blink bit that determines whether the high-order bit of each character's attribute byte controls blinking or the intensity of the background attribute. On the MDA, the enable-blink bit is bit 5 of the register at port 3B8H. As on the CGA, the enable-blink bit is set by the ROM BIOS when it establishes monochrome text mode 7, so you must explicitly clear this bit if you want to disable blinking and display characters with intensified background.

With the EGA, MCGA, and VGA, text-mode attributes work the same as with the MDA and CGA. Although the enable-blink bit is not in the same

Attribute	Description
00H	Nondisplayed
01H	Underlined
07H	Normal (white on black)
09H	High-intensity underlined
0FH	High-intensity
70H	White background, black foreground ("reverse video")
87H*	Blinking white on black (if blinking enabled)
	Dim background, normal foreground (if blinking disabled)
8FH*	Blinking high-intensity (if blinking enabled)
	Dim background, high-intensity foreground (if blinking disabled)
F0H	Blinking "reverse video" (if blinking enabled)
	High-intensity background, black foreground (if blinking disabled)

* Not displayed by all monochrome monitors

Figure 4-8. *Monochrome text-mode attributes. The appearance of some attributes depends on the setting of the enable-blink bit at I/O port 3B8H.*

hardware register in the newer subsystems, the ROM BIOS offers a service through interrupt 10H that toggles the bit on an EGA, MCGA, or VGA. (See Chapter 9, page 178 for more information about this service.)

Setting color in graphics modes

So far, we've seen how to set color (and the monochrome equivalent of color) in text modes. Setting color in graphics modes is quite different. In graphics modes, each pixel is associated with a color. The color is set the same way attributes are set in text mode, but there are important differences. First, since each pixel is a discrete dot of color, there is no foreground and background—each pixel is simply one color or another. Second, pixel attributes are not always 4 bits in size—we've already mentioned that pixel attributes can range from 1 to 8 bits, depending on the video mode being used. These differences give graphics-mode programs a subtly different "feel" than they have in text modes, both to programmers and to users.

The most important difference between text-mode and graphics-mode attributes, however, is this: In graphics modes you can control the color of each pixel. This lets you use colors much more effectively than you can in text modes. This isn't so obvious with the CGA and its limited color capabilities, but with an MCGA or VGA it's quite apparent.

Let's start with the CGA. The CGA's two graphics modes are relatively limited in terms of color: In 320 × 200, 4-color mode, pixel attributes are only 2 bits wide, and you can display only four different colors at a time. In 640 × 200, 2-color mode, you have only 1 bit per pixel, so you can display only two different colors. Also, the range of colors you can display in CGA graphics modes is severely limited.

In 320 × 200, 4-color mode, pixels can have value 0, 1, 2, or 3, corresponding to the 2-bit binary values 00B, 01B, 10B, and 11B. You can assign any one of the CGA's 16 color combinations to zero-value pixels, but colors for nonzero pixels are derived from one of three built-in palettes. (See Figure 4-9.) In 640 × 200, 2-color mode, nonzero pixels can be assigned any one of the 16 color combinations, but zero-value pixels are always black. In both modes, you can assign palette colors using ROM BIOS interrupt 10H services described in Chapter 9.

The EGA, MCGA, and VGA are considerably more flexible in terms of color management, because you can assign any color combination to any palette or video DAC color register. Equally important is the fact that you have larger pixel values and therefore more colors to work with on the

Pixel Bits	Pixel Value	Pixel Color
Mode 4, palette 0:		
0 1	1	Green
1 0	2	Red
1 1	3	Yellow or brown
Mode 4, palette 1:		
0 1	1	Cyan
1 0	2	Magenta
1 1	3	White
Mode 5:		
0 1	1	Cyan
1 0	2	Red
1 1	3	White

Figure 4-9. *Palettes in CGA 320 × 200, 4-color graphics mode.*

screen. The most frequently used graphics modes on the EGA and VGA are the 16-color modes with pixels that require 4 bits to define the colors. In most applications, 16 colors are adequate, because you can select those 16 colors from the entire range of color combinations the hardware can display (64 colors on the EGA and 262,144 colors on the MCGA and VGA). Again, the ROM BIOS provides services that let you assign arbitrary color combinations to the palette and video DAC color registers on the EGA, MCGA, and VGA. See Chapter 9 for details.

Inside the Display Memory

Now we come to the inner workings of the video buffer map. In this section, we'll see how the information in the video memory is related to the display screen.

Although the video buffer memory map varies according to the video mode you use, a clear family resemblance exists among the video modes. In text modes, the video buffer map in all IBM video subsystems is the same. In graphics modes, there are two general layouts, a *linear map* based on the map used with the original CGA graphics modes and a *parallel map* that was first used in EGA graphics modes.

Video Mode	Starting Paragraph Address (hex)	Memory Used (bytes)	Subsystem
00H, 01H	B800H	2000	CGA, EGA, MCGA, VGA
02H, 03H	B800H	4000	CGA, EGA, MCGA, VGA
04H, 05H	B800H	16,000	CGA, EGA, MCGA, VGA
06H	B800H	16,000	CGA, EGA, MCGA, VGA
07H	B000H	4000	MDA, EGA, VGA
0DH	A000H	32,000	EGA, VGA
0EH	A000H	64,000	EGA, VGA
0FH	A000H	56,000	EGA, VGA
10H	A000H	112,000	EGA, VGA
11H	A000H	38,400	MCGA, VGA
12H	A000H	153,600	VGA
13H	A000H	64,000	MCGA, VGA

Figure 4-10. *Video buffer addresses in IBM video modes.*

Before we examine the actual map of the video buffer, let's look at the addresses where the video buffer is located. (See Figure 4-10.) The breakdown is straightforward: Color text modes start at paragraph address B800H, and monochrome text mode starts at B000H. CGA-compatible graphics modes start at B800H. All other graphics modes start at A000H. The amount of RAM required to hold a screenful of data varies according to the number of characters or pixels displayed, and, in the case of graphics modes, with the number of bits that represent a pixel.

Display Pages in Text Modes

The amount of RAM physically installed in the various video subsystems is frequently more than enough to contain more than one screen's worth of video data. In video modes where this is true, all IBM video subsystems support multiple display pages. When you use display pages, the video buffer is mapped into two or more areas, and the video hardware is set up to selectively display any one of these areas in the map.

Because only one page is displayed at any given time, you can write information into nondisplayed pages as well as directly to the displayed page. Using this technique you can build a screen on an invisible page while another page is being displayed and then switch to the new page when the appropriate time comes. Switching screen images this way makes screen updates seem instantaneous.

The display pages are numbered 0 through 7, with page 0 starting at the beginning of the video buffer. Of course, the amount of available RAM may be insufficient to support eight full display pages; the actual number of pages you can use (see Figure 4-11) depends on how much video RAM is available and on how much memory is required for one screenful of data. Each page begins on an even kilobyte memory boundary. The display page offset addresses are shown in Figure 4-12.

To select a display page, use ROM BIOS interrupt 10H, service 05H. To determine which page is actively displayed, use interrupt 10H, service 0FH. (See Chapter 9 for information about these ROM BIOS services.)

In any of these modes, if the pages are not actively used (actually displayed on the screen), then the unused part of the display memory can conceivably be used for data besides text or pixels, although this usage is neither normal nor advisable. Making any other use of this potentially free memory is asking for trouble in the future.

Video Mode	Subsystem	Number of Pages	Notes
00H, 01H	CGA, EGA, MCGA, VGA	8	
02H, 03H	CGA	4	
	EGA, MCGA, VGA	8	
04H, 05H	CGA, MCGA	1	
	EGA, VGA	2	Not fully supported by ROM BIOS
06H	CGA, EGA, MCGA, VGA	1	
07H	MDA	1	
	EGA, VGA	8	
0DH	EGA, VGA	8	
0EH	EGA, VGA	4	
0FH	EGA, VGA	2	
10H	EGA, VGA	2	
11H	MCGA, VGA	1	
12H	VGA	1	
13H	MCGA, VGA	1	

Figure 4-11. *Display pages available in IBM video subsystems.*

Page	40 × 25, 16-color	80 × 25, 16-color	80 × 25 Mono
0	B800:0000H	B800:0000H	B000:0000H
1	B800:0800H	B800:1000H	B000:1000H*
2	B800:1000H	B800:2000H	B000:2000H*
3	B800:1800H	B800:3000H	B000:3000H*
4	B800:2000H	B800:4000H*	B000:4000H*
5	B800:2800H	B800:5000H*	B000:5000H*
6	B800:3000H	B800:6000H*	B000:6000H*
7	B800:3800H	B800:7000H*	B000:7000H*

* EGA and VGA only

Figure 4-12. *Start addresses for text-mode display pages in IBM video subsystems.*

Display Pages in Graphics Modes

For the EGA, the MCGA, and the VGA, the page concept is as readily available in graphics modes as in text modes. Obviously there is no reason not to have graphics pages if the memory is there to support them.

The main benefit of using multiple pages for either graphics or text is to be able to switch instantly from one display screen to another without taking the time to build the display information from scratch. In theory, multiple pages could be used in graphics mode to produce smooth and fine-grained animation effects, but there aren't enough display pages to take the animation very far.

Displaying Characters in Text and Graphics Modes

As you have learned, in text modes no character images are stored in video memory. Instead, each character is represented in the video buffer by a pair of bytes containing the character's ASCII value and display attributes. The pixels that make up the character are drawn on the screen by a character generator that is part of the display circuitry. The Color Graphics Adapter has a character generator that produces characters in an 8 × 8 pixel block format, while the Monochrome Display Adapter's character generator uses a 9 × 14 pixel block format. The larger format is one of the factors that makes the MDA's display output easier to read.

The standard ASCII characters (01H through 7FH [decimal 1 through 127]) represent only half of the ASCII characters available in the text modes. An additional 128 graphics characters (80H through FFH [decimal 128 through 255]) are available through the same character generator. More than half of them can be used to make simple line drawings. A complete list of both the standard ASCII characters and the graphics characters provided by IBM is given in Appendix C.

The graphics modes can also display characters, but they are produced quite differently. Graphics-mode characters are drawn, pixel by pixel, by a ROM BIOS software character generator, instead of by a hardware character generator. (ROM BIOS interrupt 10H provides this service; see Chapter 9.) The software character generator refers to a table of bit patterns to determine which pixels to draw for each character. The ROM of every PC and PS/2 contains a default table of character bit patterns, but you can also place a custom bit pattern table in RAM and instruct the BIOS to use it to display your own character set.

In CGA-compatible graphics modes (640 × 200, 2-color and 320 × 200, 4-color), the bit patterns for the second 128 ASCII characters are always found at the address stored in the interrupt 1FH vector at 0000:007CH. If you store a table of bit patterns in a buffer and then store the buffer's segment and offset at 0000:007CH, the ROM BIOS will use the bit patterns in the buffer for ASCII characters 80H through FFH (decimal 128 through 255). In other graphics modes on the EGA, MCGA, and VGA, the ROM BIOS provides a service through interrupt 10H that lets you pass the address of a RAM-based table of character bit patterns for all 256 characters.

Mapping characters in text modes

In text modes, the memory map begins with the top left corner of the screen, using 2 bytes per screen position. The memory bytes for succeeding characters immediately follow in the order you would read them — from left to right and from top to bottom.

Modes 0 and 1 are text modes with a screen format of 40 columns by 25 rows. Each row occupies $40 \times 2 = 80$ bytes. A screen occupies only 2 KB in modes 0 and 1, which means the CGA's 16 KB memory can accommodate eight display pages. If the rows are numbered 0 through 24 and the columns numbered 0 through 39, then the offset to any screen character in the first display page is given by the following BASIC formula:

```
CHARACTER.OFFSET = (ROW.NUMBER * 80) + (COLUMN.NUMBER * 2)
```

Since the attribute byte for any character is in the memory location next to the ASCII character value, you can locate it by simply adding 1 to the character offset.

Modes 2, 3, and 7 are also text modes, but with 80 columns in each row instead of 40. The byte layout is the same, but each row requires twice as many bytes, or $80 \times 2 = 160$ bytes. Consequently, the 80×25 screen format uses 4 KB, and the 16 KB memory can accommodate four display pages. The offset to any screen location in the first display page is given by the following BASIC formula:

```
CHARACTER.OFFSET = (ROW.NUMBER * 160) + (COLUMN.NUMBER * 2)
```

The beginning of each text display page traditionally starts at an even kilobyte boundary. Because each screen page in the text modes actually uses only 2000 or 4000 bytes, some unused bytes follow each page: either 48 or 96 bytes, depending on the size of the page. So, to locate any screen position on any page in text mode, use the general formula shown on the next page.

```
LOCATION = (SEGMENT.PARAGRAPH * 16)
        + (PAGE.NUMBER * PAGE.SIZE) + (ROW.NUMBER * ROW.WIDTH * 2)
        + (COLUMN.NUMBER * 2) + WHICH
```

LOCATION is the 20-bit address of the screen information.
SEGMENT.PARAGRAPH is the location of the video display memory
(for example, B000H or B800H).
PAGE.NUMBER is in the range 0 through 3 or 0 through 7.
PAGE.SIZE is 2000 or 4000.
ROW.NUMBER is from 0 through 24.
ROW.WIDTH is 40 or 80.
COLUMN.NUMBER is from 0 through 39 or 0 through 79.
WHICH is 0 for the display character or 1 for the display attribute.

Mapping pixels in graphics modes

When you use a graphics mode, pixels are stored as a series of bit fields,
with a one-to-one correlation between the bit fields in memory and the
pixels on the screen. The actual mapping of bit fields in the video buffer
depends on the video mode.

In CGA-compatible graphics modes, the display is organized into 200
lines, numbered 0 through 199. Each line of pixels is represented in the
video buffer in 80 bytes of data. In 640 × 200, 2-color mode, each bit
represents one pixel on the screen, while in 320 × 200, 4-color mode, each
pixel is represented by a pair of bits in the buffer. (See Figure 4-13.) Thus
there are eight pixels to each byte in 640 × 200, 2-color mode, and 80 × 8, or
640, pixels per row. Similarly, there are four pixels to each byte in 320 × 200,
4-color mode, and 80 × 4, or 320, pixels per row.

The storage for the pixel rows is interleaved:

- Pixels in even-numbered rows are stored in the first half of the
  video buffer, starting at B800:0000H.

- Pixels in odd-numbered rows are stored starting at B800:2000H.

For example, in 640 × 200, 2-color mode, the first pixel in the first row
(in the upper-left corner of the screen) is represented by the leftmost bit (bit
7) in the byte at B800:0000H. The second pixel in the row is represented by
bit 6 of the same byte. Because of the interleaved buffer map, however, the
pixel immediately below the first pixel is represented in bit 7 of the byte at
B800:2000H.

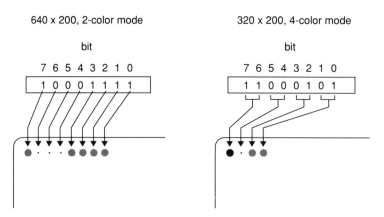

Figure 4-13. *Pixel mapping in CGA-compatible graphics modes.*

In all other graphics modes, the buffer map is linear, as it is in text modes. Pixels are stored from left to right in each byte, and one row of pixels immediately follows another in the video buffer. On the MCGA and VGA, for example, the 1-bit pixels in 640 × 480, 2-color mode and the 8-bit pixels in 320 × 200, 256-color mode are stored starting at A000:0000H and proceeding linearly through the buffer.

The catch is that pixel bit fields are not always mapped linearly in all video modes. On the EGA and VGA, the video buffer in 16-color graphics modes is arranged as a set of four parallel memory maps. In effect, the video memory is configured to have four 64 KB memory maps spanning the same range of addresses starting at A000:0000H. The EGA and VGA have special circuitry that accesses all four memory maps in parallel. Thus in 16-color EGA and VGA graphics modes, each 4-bit pixel is stored with 1 bit in each memory map. (See Figure 4-14.) Another way to visualize this is that a 4-bit pixel value is formed by concatenating corresponding bits from the same address in each memory map.

There is a good reason why the EGA and VGA were designed to use parallel memory maps in graphics modes. Consider the situation in 640 × 350, 16-color mode: With 4 bits per pixel, you need 640 × 350 × 4 (896,000) bits to store one screenful of pixels. That comes out to 112,000 bytes, which is bigger than the 64 KB maximum size of one 8086 segment. If you organize the pixel data in parallel, however, you only need 112,000 ÷ 4 (28,000) bytes in each memory map.

With this variety of memory maps and pixel sizes, it's fortunate that the ROM BIOS provides services that let you read and write individual pixels

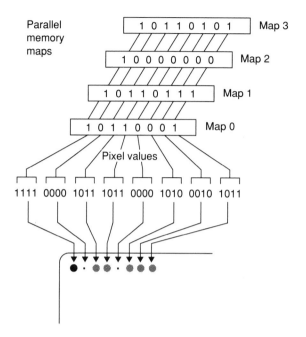

Figure 4-14. *Pixel mapping in 16-color EGA and VGA graphics modes.*

regardless of the video mode. (Chapter 9 describes these services.) Unfortunately, these ROM BIOS pixel-manipulation services are pretty slow. If you're working in graphics modes, you'll probably find that the graphics drawing functions provided in your programming language (such as the PSET, LINE, and CIRCLE functions in BASIC) are the best tools for creating graphics-mode screens.

Controlling the Video Display

In general, control of the display screen, like most other computer operations, can be done in four ways:

- By using the programming-language services (for example, BASIC's SCREEN statement)

- By using the DOS services (see Chapters 16 and 17)

- By using the ROM BIOS video services (see Chapter 9)

- By direct manipulation of the hardware via memory or I/O ports

The video services available through programming languages, DOS, and the ROM BIOS automatically place screen output data in the video buffer, with each type of service offering varying levels of control. The ROM BIOS services are particularly powerful, providing nearly all the functions needed to generate display-screen output, control the cursor, and manipulate screen information. (All video services are fully described in Chapter 9.) For maximum control over the video display, you also have the

About the Cursor

A blinking cursor is a feature of the text modes that is used to indicate the active location on the display screen. The cursor is actually a group of scan lines that fill the entire width of the character box. The size of the character-box varies with the video hardware and video mode: The Monochrome Display Adapter uses a 9-pixels-wide-by-14-scan-lines-high format; the Color Graphics Adapter uses an 8-pixels-by-8-scan-lines format; the EGA's default text-mode character box is 8 pixels wide by 14 scan lines high; and the VGA's is 9 by 16. The higher-resolution video subsystems use character boxes with more scan lines, so their text-mode characters appear sharper and more detailed, as you'll see in Appendix C.

The default cursor format uses two scan lines near the bottom of the character box but may be changed to display any number of scan lines within the character box. Since the blinking cursor used in text modes is a hardware-created feature, software has only limited control over it.

You can change the size of the cursor as well as its location on the screen using the services provided by the ROM BIOS. Interrupt 10H, service 01H lets you set the size of the cursor, whereas service 02H lets you move the cursor to any character position on the screen. The ROM BIOS also provides a service (interrupt 10H, service 03H) that reports the current size and location of the cursor.

So far, we've been talking about the text-mode cursor. In graphics modes there is no hardware-generated cursor, but the ROM BIOS routines keep track of a logical cursor location that tells you the active screen location. As in text modes, you can use ROM BIOS services 02H and 03H to keep track of the graphics-mode cursor location.

To create a cursor in graphics modes, many programs, including BASIC, simulate the block cursor by using a distinctive background color at the cursor location or by using the ASCII block characters.

option of bypassing the software services and placing data directly in the video buffer — when you feel you have good reason to.

Before opting for direct video output, you should know that it does interfere with windowing systems and more advanced multitasking operating environments. All the same, many important programs for the PC family generate direct video output — so many, in fact, that this has become a standard and accepted way of creating output. So, even though in the long run it's probably not wise to place output directly in the video buffer, everyone seems to be doing it.

Basically, you can't mix programs that write directly into the display memory and windowing systems because two programs would be fighting over the control of the same memory and messing up each other's data. But because so many programs now generate direct video output, multitasking operating systems like OS/2 go to great lengths to accommodate programs that write directly to the display memory. A system like OS/2 can make this accommodation simply by keeping a separate copy of the program's display memory; when the program is running, the copy is moved into the display buffer, and when the program is stopped, a fresh copy of the display buffer is made. This technique allows OS/2 to run programs that work directly with the display memory, but at a cost: First, computing and memory overhead go up; second, the program can't run in the background simultaneously with other programs; and third, the display information can't be ''windowed''; that is, it can't be moved or adjusted in size.

Programmers are faced with a conflict here: Direct output to the screen has the benefit of speed and power, but using ROM BIOS or higher-level services for screen output has the benefit of more flexibility for adapting to windowing systems, new video hardware, and so on. The best solution is to use both techniques, trading off portability whenever maximum performance is an absolute priority.

Direct Hardware Control

Much of the information we've provided in this chapter, particularly information on internal mapping of display memory, is meant to help you write video information directly into the display memory. But remember that direct programming has inherent risks, and you'll find it both safer and easier to use the highest available means to control the video display. Lower-level means, particularly direct manipulation, can be very disruptive.

More important, it's not always easy to write ''well-behaved'' programs that access video hardware directly. There are several reasons for this. One is simply that there is a lot of different video hardware to worry about. Apart from the five IBM video subsystems we've discussed here, many non-IBM video adapters and built-in video subsystems exist in non-IBM computers. If you write a program that programs a particular IBM video subsystem directly, the program probably won't be portable to a different IBM subsystem or to non-IBM hardware.

We've already mentioned another reason to avoid direct video hardware programming: Multitasking or windowing operating systems must work overtime to accommodate programs that directly access video hardware. Of course, the designers of newer PC and PS/2 operating environments are well aware of the need for good video performance, so modern operating systems generally offer faster and more flexible video output services than do older systems, such as DOS. Direct hardware programming offers little advantage if the operating system's video I/O services are fast enough.

Also, direct video hardware control can get you into trouble with the ROM BIOS if you aren't careful. The ROM BIOS keeps track of the video hardware status in a set of variables in the data area in segment 40H. (See Chapter 3 for a list of ROM BIOS video status variables.) If you program the video hardware directly, you must be careful to update the ROM BIOS status variables accordingly.

For example, the simple routine we presented earlier for resetting the CGA enable-blink bit bypasses a ROM BIOS status variable. To update the enable-blink bit without causing the ROM BIOS to lose track of the video hardware state, you would update the ROM BIOS status variable at 0040:0065H:

```
10 DEF SEG = &HB800              ' (same as before)
20 POKE 0,ASC("A")
30 POKE 1,&H97
40 DEF SEG = &H0040              ' address the BIOS data area
50 POKE &H0065,(PEEK(&H0065) AND NOT &H20) ' update BIOS status variable
60 OUT &H3D8,PEEK(&H0065)        ' update hardware register
```

If you program carefully, controlling the video hardware directly can be very rewarding. You can maximize the speed of your video output as well as take full advantage of hardware capabilities such as smooth, pixel-by-pixel panning or hardware-generated interrupts. But when you write such a program, keep the pitfalls in mind.

Compatibility Considerations

If you want your program to run on a wide variety of PCs and PS/2s, you must design compatibility into the program. As the various IBM video subsystems have evolved, programmers have developed several approaches to compatibility. These include

- Installable programs

- Self-installing programs

- Hardware-independent programming environments

We've already mentioned how many software vendors provide video compatibility by distributing software that has its video output routines in separate, installable modules: Before the software can be used, the video routines must be linked to the rest of the application. This lets you write programs that take full advantage of each video subsystem's capabilities without sacrificing compatibility.

However, the installation process can be cumbersome, both for a programmer who must write the installation program and for an end-user who must install video routines properly. You can eliminate the installation process if you make your application self-installing. The key to doing this is to incorporate a routine in your program that identifies which video subsystem the program is running on. The program can then tailor its own video output to the capabilities and limitations of the video hardware.

You can use several different programming techniques to identify the video subsystem. In PS/2s, ROM BIOS offers a service that reports the video hardware configuration (see Chapter 9), but in the PC/XT/AT family you must rely on improvised hardware identification techniques documented in the hardware technical manuals.

Once a program has determined the video hardware configuration, it can produce appropriate output. For example, a program running on a Monochrome Display Adapter can use only one video mode with monochrome attributes. If the same program were running on a color subsystem, it could run with color attributes in text modes. If the program needed to produce graphics output, it could select a graphics mode with the highest possible resolution based on its identification of the video subsystem.

In the simplest case, your program can use whatever video mode is in use when the program starts up. ROM BIOS interrupt 10H, service 0FH reports the current video mode number. If you're not using an assembly-language interface to the ROM BIOS, however, you may find it easier simply to use the program on the following page to inspect the ROM BIOS status variable at 0040:0049H that contains the video mode number.

```
10 DEF SEG = &H0040
20 VIDEO.MODE = PEEK(&H0049)
```

You can avoid video hardware dependence in your programs if you use an operating environment like Digital Research's GEM or Microsoft Windows. These environments shield your program from the idiosyncrasies of video hardware by providing a set of consistent, hardware-independent subroutines to perform video I/O. The problem, of course, is that the end-user must also have a copy of the operating environment to be able to run your program.

Whatever approach you take to video compatibility, be sure to consider several compatibility criteria. These criteria are not completely consistent with each other, reflecting the internal inconsistency in the design of the IBM personal computer and the variety of display formats that can be used. Still, there are overall guidelines for compatibility, which we'll outline here.

First, text-only display output increases compatibility. Many PCs are still equipped with Monochrome Display Adapters, which cannot show graphic output. If you are weighing a text-versus-graphics decision in the design of a program, there are two factors to consider. On one hand, as many programs have dramatically demonstrated, you can create very effective drawings using only standard IBM text characters. On the other hand, it is more and more common for computers to include graphics capability. So, in the future, text-only output will probably lose its importance, and you'll be able to use graphics in your programs without worrying about compatibility.

Second, the less your programs depend on color, the wider the range of computers with which they will be compatible. This does not mean that you need to avoid color for compatibility; it simply means that for maximum compatibility, programs should use color as an enhancement rather than as an essential ingredient. If programs can get along without color, they will be compatible with computers that use monochrome displays, including PCs with Monochrome Display Adapters, as well as Compaq Portable computers with built-in monochrome displays.

In general, you must weigh the advantage of broad compatibility against the convenience and simplicity of writing programs for a narrower range of displays. Our own experience and judgment tell us that far too often programmers err by opting for a narrower range of displays, thereby greatly reducing the variety of computers their programs can be used on. Be forewarned.

Chapter 5

Disk Basics

Most computer systems have some way to store information permanently, whether it is on punched paper tape, bar-coded print media, magnetic disks or tape, or laser disks. By far the most widely used media in the PC and PS/2 family are *diskettes* (floppy disks) and *fixed disks* (hard disks). Diskettes and fixed disks come in various sizes and capacities but they all work in basically the same way: Information is magnetically encoded on their surfaces in patterns determined by the disk drive and by the software that controls the drive.

When the PC family was introduced in 1981, it used one main type of storage device: the 5¼-inch diskette, which was double density, single sided, and soft sectored, and stored only 160 kilobytes (KB). Since then, higher-capacity 5¼-inch and 3½-inch diskettes have become standard equipment on PCs and PS/2s, as have fixed disks with capacities from 10 megabytes (MB) on the PC/XT to 314 MB on the PS/2 Model 80.

Although the type of storage device is important, it is the way stored information is laid out and managed that concerns programmers most. In this chapter, we'll focus on how information is organized and stored on both diskettes and fixed disks. Much of the information provided in this chapter applies to RAM disks — that is, the simulation of disk storage in memory — as much as it does to conventional diskettes, fixed disks, and disk cartridges.

Disk Data Mapping

To understand how data is organized on a disk, consider the physical structure of the disk itself and the drive mechanism that reads from and writes to it. We'll start with diskettes, but both diskettes and fixed disks have the same basic geometry.

Inside a diskette's square plastic case is a circular platter made of tough plastic coated with a magnetic medium. A diskette drive stores data on the diskette by writing and reading magnetically encoded patterns that represent digital data. Because both sides of the diskette are coated, both sides can be used to store data.

A diskette drive contains a motor that rotates the diskette at a constant speed. The drive has two read/write heads, one for each side of the diskette. The heads are mounted on an arm that moves them in unison to any position toward or away from the center of the disk. (The original IBM PC came with a diskette drive that had only one read/write head and could access only one side of a diskette. Most PC users perceived this as wasteful, so single-sided diskette drives gradually went the way of the dinosaur.)

Like the tape heads in a common tape recorder, a diskette drive's read/write heads can magnetize the diskette medium to store data on the diskette; they can also retrieve data from the diskette by decoding the magnetically encoded patterns in the diskette medium.

The geometry of a fixed disk is similar to that of a diskette. Fixed disks rotate much faster than diskettes, so the platters are made of magnetically coated metal or glass, not flexible plastic. Also, fixed disks usually consist of a stack of several platters that rotate together, so fixed-disk drives have multiple read/write heads — one for each disk surface.

Data Storage

The way data is mapped on diskettes and fixed disks is a natural result of the geometry of the hardware. When a particular read/write head is held motionless, a ring of magnetic medium moves past it as the disk rotates. For each position of the read/write head, relative to the center of the disk, there is a corresponding ring of disk medium on which data can be stored. These rings are called *tracks*. (See Figure 5-1.)

Because each disk track can store 4 KB or more of data, each track of data is divided into a number of smaller units called *sectors*. All sectors hold the same amount of data — typically, 512 bytes for diskettes and most fixed disks. The sectors and tracks are numbered sequentially, so you can locate any particular byte of data on a disk surface by specifying its track number and its sector number.

Because two-sided diskettes and fixed disks have more than one disk surface, however, you need to think three-dimensionally to locate a byte of data. So the position of the read/write heads for these disks is described by a *cylinder* number. Like tracks, cylinders are numbered sequentially. If you think of a cylinder as a stack of tracks at a given position of the read/write heads, you can see that the location of a particular track is determined by specifying a cylinder number plus a read/write head.

With this in mind, it's easy to make sense of the various diskette formats used in PC and PS/2 disk drives. (See Figure 5-2.) With the original single-sided IBM PC diskette drives you could use diskettes formatted with 40 tracks, each of which contained eight sectors of data, so the capacity of the diskette was 40 × 8 × 512, or 160 KB. Now, with more accurate diskette drives and with high-density diskette media that can store more data per track, you can use diskettes with higher-capacity formats. Fixed-disk drives are mechanically more accurate than diskette drives, and their magnetic media are of comparatively higher density, so the number of tracks and the number of sectors per track are higher than for diskettes.

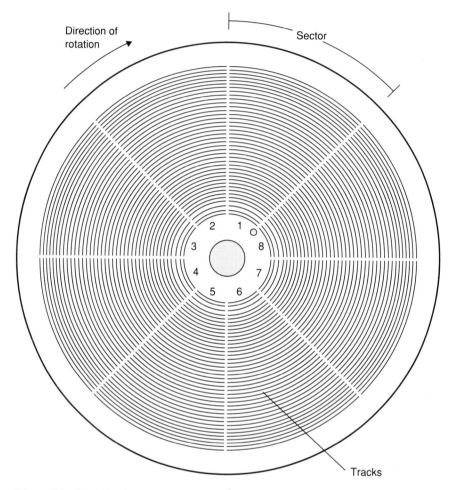

Figure 5-1. *One side of a diskette formatted with 40 concentric tracks and eight sectors per track.*

Manufacturers' terminology and advertising regarding these variations of disk format and disk-storage capacity is somewhat fuzzy. "Quad-density" refers to a diskette or drive that can use an 80-track diskette format. "High-density" and "high-capacity" generally refer to the PC/AT 1.2 MB or PS/2 1.44 MB diskette formats. "Double-density" diskettes can be formatted with eight or nine sectors per track, but they can't be used reliably with higher-capacity formats.

Disk	Capacity	Cylinders	Sectors per Track	Heads
5¼-inch diskette	160 KB	40	8	1
	180 KB	40	9	1
	320 KB	40	8	2
	360 KB	40	9	2
	1.2 MB	80	15	2
3½-inch diskette	720 KB	80	9	2
	1.44 MB	80	18	2

Figure 5-2. *PC and PS/2 diskette formats.*

Bootable Disks

Regardless of their data formats, all diskettes and disks are potentially bootable; that is, they can contain the information necessary to get an operating system running at the time you start your computer. There is nothing special about the format of a bootable disk; it's just one that contains information that lets the ROM BIOS boot the operating system. Here's how it works.

On all PC and PS/2 diskettes and fixed disks, the first sector on the disk — cylinder 0, head 0, sector 1 — is reserved for a short bootstrap program. (The program has to be short because the size of a sector is only 512 bytes.) The function of this bootstrap program is to read the bulk of the operating system into memory from elsewhere on the disk and then to transfer control to the operating system.

When you start or restart your computer, the last tasks performed by the start-up ROM BIOS routines are reading the contents of the disk boot sector into memory and checking those contents for a bootstrap program. The BIOS does this checking by examining the last 2 bytes of the boot sector for a signature (55H and AAH) that indicates that the data in the boot sector represents a bootstrap program. If the signature value isn't correct, the BIOS assumes there's no bootstrap program in the boot sector and, therefore, that the disk isn't bootable.

The bootstrap program's job is to copy the start-up program for an operating system from the disk into memory. There's no restriction on the size and location of the operating system's start-up program, so this stepwise transfer of control — from ROM BIOS to boot sector to operating system — can be used to start DOS, XENIX, OS/2, or even a stand-alone application.

DOS Disk Formats

The diskette formats listed in Figure 5-2 aren't the only ones you can use for diskettes, but because diskettes are intended to be portable, the number of diskette formats that DOS recognizes is limited to those in the list. In the earliest releases of DOS, only the 160 KB and 320 KB formats could be used. Later DOS versions recognize higher-capacity diskette formats and fixed disks in addition to the original diskette formats (Figure 5-3).

Disk	Capacity	DOS Version	Media Descriptor
5¼-inch diskette	160 KB	1.0	FEH
	320 KB	1.1	FFH
	180 KB	2.0	FCH
	360 KB	2.0	FDH
	1.2 MB	3.0	F9H
3½-inch diskette	720 KB	3.2	F9H
	1.44 MB	3.3	F0H
Fixed disk		2.0	F8H

Figure 5-3. *Standard DOS disk formats. The media descriptor value is used by DOS to identify different disk formats.*

Diskette Formats

Beginning with version 2.0, DOS had the potential to recognize virtually any physical disk format. This became possible because DOS versions 2.0 and later provide the necessary tools to write an installable device driver—a machine-language routine that can configure a disk drive to read or write different formats or allow you to hook up a non-IBM disk drive to your system. (See Appendix A for more on installable device drivers.)

Fortunately, installable diskette device drivers have not led to a proliferation of nonstandard, incompatible diskette formats. Instead, software vendors and programmers have relied on the standard DOS formats listed in Figure 5-3. On 5¼-inch diskettes, the 360 KB nine-sector format is used most frequently, while on 3½-inch diskettes, the 720 KB format is most common. These are not the highest capacity formats, but they can be used on machines that aren't equipped with higher-capacity diskette drives as well as on those that are.

If you're interested in creating your own diskette formats, or in understanding DOS diskette formats in more detail, be sure to read about ROM BIOS disk services in Chapter 10.

Fixed-Disk Formats

High-capacity fixed-disk systems present some special problems and opportunities. Fixed-disk formats vary much more than diskette formats do (Figure 5-4). Still, data is organized on fixed disks by cylinder, head, and sector numbers, just as it is on diskettes.

Disk	Capacity	Cylinders	Sectors per Track	Heads
Typical PC/XT fixed disk	10 MB	306	17	4
PC/AT fixed disk type 20	30 MB	733	17	5
PS/2 Model 30 fixed disk, type 26	20 MB	612	17	4
PS/2 Model 60 fixed disk, type 31	44 MB	732	17	7

Figure 5-4. *Some typical fixed-disk formats. All use 512 bytes per sector.*

Because the storage capacity of a fixed disk is relatively large, some PC users prefer to use only part of the disk space for DOS and to use other portions of the disk for other operating systems. To facilitate this, the available space on a fixed disk can be split into as many as four logical partitions, each of which is accessed separately. Each partition's data can be kept completely separate from the data in the other partitions. Each partition can contain its own boot sector and operating system.

The first sector on a fixed disk contains a 64-byte partition table (Figure 5-5) and a disk bootstrap program. The partition table indicates where each partition is located on the disk. The table also designates one bootable partition. The first sector in the bootable partition is a partition boot sector that the ROM BIOS can use to load an operating system.

The disk bootstrap program examines the partition table to determine which one of the partitions is bootable. It then reads the partition's boot sector from the disk into memory. The partition boot sector contains a bootstrap program that reads the operating system from the disk into memory and transfers control to it.

Because bootable partitions are indicated in a table, you can select among fixed-disk partitions simply by updating the table and restarting the computer. All operating systems capable of supporting fixed disks provide a utility program that lets you update the partition table. (The DOS utility FDISK is such a program.)

Offset from Start of Entry	Size (bytes)	Meaning
00H	1	Boot indicator (80H = bootable, 0 = not bootable)
01H	1	Starting head number
02H	2	Starting cylinder number (10 bits) and sector number (6 bits)
04H	1	System indicator: 1 = primary DOS, 12-bit FAT 2 = XENIX 4 = primary DOS, 16-bit FAT 5 = extended DOS 8 = other non-DOS
05H	1	Ending head number
06H	2	Ending cylinder and sector numbers
08H	4	Starting sector (relative to beginning of disk)
0CH	4	Number of sectors in partition

Figure 5-5. *The format of an entry in a fixed-disk partition table. The table consists of four such 16-byte entries, starting at offset 1BEH in the disk boot sector.*

❏ NOTE: *Be very careful if you access a fixed disk's boot sector. The information contained there is intended only for use by the ROM BIOS bootstrap loader. Should the data in a disk's boot sector be erased or corrupted, the entire contents of the disk may become inaccessible.*

The Disk's Logical Structure

Regardless of the type of disk you use, all DOS disks are logically formatted in the same way: The disk's sides, tracks, and sectors are identified numerically with the same notation, and certain sectors are always reserved for special programs and indexes that DOS uses to manage disk operations. Before we describe how DOS organizes space on a disk, we need to briefly cover the conventional notation used by DOS and the ROM BIOS to locate information.

Diskette cylinder numbers start from 0 at the outside edge of the disk surface and increase toward the center of the disk. Read/write heads are also numbered from 0, but sector numbers start with 1. Any location on the disk can thus be described by a unique combination of cylinder, head, and sector numbers. This in fact is how the ROM BIOS services access disk data.

DOS, however, does not recognize cylinders, heads, and sectors. Instead, DOS sees a disk as a linear sequence of *logical sectors*. The sequence of logical sectors begins with the first sector on a disk: Sector 1, cylinder 0, head 0 (the boot sector) is DOS logical sector 0.

Logical sectors are numbered from track to track in the same cylinder, and then are numbered from cylinder to cylinder. Thus the last sector in cylinder 0, head 0, is followed by the first sector in cylinder 0, head 1; the last sector in a cylinder is followed by the first sector in the next cylinder. See page 300 for information on converting DOS notation to ROM BIOS notation and vice versa.

The use of logical sector numbers lets DOS avoid having to deal with cylinder, head, and sector numbers that vary among different types of disk-drive hardware. However, this same feature means that DOS is limited in the amount of disk space it can access on a particular disk drive. Because DOS maintains logical sector numbers as 16-bit integers, it can recognize, at most, 65,536 logical sectors on a disk. Because the default size of a disk sector is 512 bytes, the largest disk DOS can manage is 65,536 × 512, or 32 MB. This certainly is no problem on diskettes, but it's an unwelcome limitation for the many PC/AT and PS/2 users who have fixed disks larger than 32 MB.

To get around this restriction, DOS version 3.3 introduced the notion of the *extended* DOS partition. With DOS 3.3, you can use the DOS utility program FDISK to allocate a fixed-disk partition as an extended DOS partition. You can format the extended partition as one or more separate logical drives. Thus, for example, you could use both a primary and an extended DOS partition on a fixed disk, with the primary partition as drive C and the extended partition as drives D and E.

How DOS Organizes the Disk

When DOS formats a diskette, it erases and verifies every sector. In a fixed-disk partition, DOS verifies the integrity of each sector without erasing pre-existing data. (That is why a program like the Norton Utilities' Format Recover can retrieve data from a fixed disk after you have accidentally reformatted it.) On both diskettes and fixed disks, the format program reserves a certain amount of disk space to store control information and indexes that DOS uses to organize the data you store on the disk.

Every DOS diskette or fixed-disk DOS partition is mapped into four separate areas. These areas, in the order they are stored, are the *reserved area,* the *file allocation table* (FAT), the *root directory,* and the *files area.* (See Figure 5-6.) The size of each area varies among formats, but the structure and the order of the areas don't vary.

Logical sector 0

| Reserved area |
| File allocation table (FAT) |
| Root directory |
| Files area (files and subdirectories) |

Figure 5-6. *DOS disk map.*

The reserved area can be one or more sectors long; the first sector is always the *disk boot sector* (logical sector 0). A table within the boot sector specifies the size of the reserved area, the size (and number of copies) of the file allocation table, as well as the number of entries in the root directory. All diskettes have a reserved area of at least one sector, even if they aren't bootable.

The file allocation table, or FAT, immediately follows the reserved area. The FAT maps the usage of all the disk space in the files area of the disk, including space used for files, space that hasn't been used, and space that is unusable due to defects in the disk medium. Because the FAT maps the entire usable data storage area of a disk, two identical copies of it are stored in case one is damaged. The size of a FAT depends on the size of the disk (or of the partition of a fixed disk): Larger disks usually require larger FATs. Figure 5-7 shows FAT sizes for several different disk sizes.

Disk	Capacity	Reserved Area	FAT	Root Directory
5¼-inch diskette	360 KB	1 sector	4 sectors	7 sectors
	1.2 MB	1	14	14
3½-inch diskette	720 KB	1	6	7
	1.44 MB	1	18	14

Figure 5-7. *Reserved area, FAT, and root-directory overhead for some common DOS diskette formats.*

The root directory is the next item on a DOS disk. It is used as a table of contents, identifying each file on the disk with a directory entry that contains several pieces of information, including the file's name, size, and location on the disk. The size of the root directory varies with the disk format. (See Figure 5-7.)

The files area, which occupies the bulk of the available disk space, is used to store files; in DOS versions 2.0 and later, the files area may contain subdirectories as well as files. For both files and subdirectories, space in the files area is allocated as needed in chunks of contiguous sectors called *clusters*. As with the sizes of the FAT and the root directory, a DOS disk's cluster size varies with the format. (See Figure 5-8.) The number of sectors in a cluster is always a power of 2; generally, the cluster size is one sector for single-sided diskettes, two sectors for double-sided diskettes, and four or more for fixed disks.

Disk	*Capacity*	*Cluster Size*
5¼-inch diskette	360 KB	2 sectors
	1.2 MB	1
3½-inch diskette	720 KB	2
	1.44 MB	1
Typical PC/XT fixed disk	10 MB	8
PC/AT fixed disk, type 20	30 MB	4
PS/2 Model 30, fixed disk, type 26	20 MB	4
PS/2 Model 60, type 31	44 MB	4

Figure 5-8. *Cluster size for some common DOS disk formats.*

The Logical Structure in Detail

Now it's time to delve a little more deeply into each of the four sections of a disk: the boot sector, the root directory, the files area, and the FAT.

The Boot Sector

The boot sector on a DOS diskette or in a DOS partition on a fixed disk consists primarily of a short machine-language program that starts the process of loading DOS into memory. As we mentioned, to perform this task the ROM BIOS checks to see whether the disk is bootable and then proceeds accordingly.

❏ NOTE: *A bootable disk contains the start-up programs for an operating system or for a stand-alone application that runs without operating-system support. In the case of DOS, a bootable disk contains two hidden files that represent the DOS start-up routines and essential low-level DOS functions. See Chapter 3, page 45 for details about these files.*

You can inspect the boot program by using the DOS DEBUG utility, which combines the ability to read data from any sector on a disk with the ability to disassemble — or unassemble — machine language into assembly-language code. If you want to learn more about the boot program and you aren't intimidated by DEBUG's terse command format, place a bootable diskette in drive A and enter the following commands to display the diskette's boot program:

```
DEBUG
L 0 0 0 1          ; load first logical sector
U 0 L 3            ; unassemble and list first and second bytes
```

At this point, DEBUG will display the first instruction in the boot program, a JMP to the address that contains the rest of the program. Use DEBUG's U command with the address specified in the JMP to inspect the rest of the boot program. For example, if the first instruction is JMP 0036, enter

```
U 0036             ; unassemble and list next portion of boot program
```

For all disk formats (except diskettes formatted with eight sectors per track) you will find some key parameters in the boot sector, beginning with the 11th byte. (See Figure 5-9.) These parameters are part of the BIOS parameter block used by DOS to control any disk-type device. If you're using DEBUG to inspect the boot sector of a diskette in drive A, you can see a hexadecimal dump of the BIOS parameter block by entering the following command:

```
D 0B L 1B
```

Offset	Length	Description
03H	8 bytes	System ID
0BH	1 word	Number of bytes per sector
0DH	1 byte	Number of sectors per cluster
0EH	1 word	Number of sectors in reserved area
10H	1 byte	Number of copies of FAT
11H	1 word	Number of root directory entries
13H	1 word	Total number of sectors
15H	1 byte	DOS media descriptor
16H	1 word	Number of sectors per FAT
18H	1 word	Number of sectors per track
1AH	1 word	Number of heads (sides)
1CH	1 word	Number of hidden sectors

Figure 5-9. *The BIOS parameter block in the boot sector.*

The Root Directory

The root directory on a diskette or in a fixed-disk partition is created by the DOS FORMAT program. The root directory's size is determined by FORMAT, so the number of root directory entries is limited. (See Figure 5-10.)

Disk	Capacity	Size	Number of Entries
5¹/₄-inch diskette	180 KB	4 sectors	64
	360 KB	7	112
	1.2 MB	14	224
3¹/₂-inch diskette	720 KB	7	112
	1.44 MB	14	224
Typical PC/XT fixed disk	10 MB	32	512
PC/AT fixed disk, type 20	30 MB	32	512
PS/2 Model 30, fixed disk, type 26	20 MB	32	512
PS/2 Model 60, fixed disk, type 31	44 MB	32	512

Figure 5-10. *Root directory sizes for some common DOS disk formats.*

In DOS versions 1.0 and later, which did not support subdirectories, the size of the root directory limited the number of files that could be stored on a diskette. This restriction disappeared in DOS versions 2.0 and later, where file names could be placed in subdirectories as well as in the root directory.

The root directory contains a series of 32-byte directory entries. Each directory entry contains the name of a file, a subdirectory, or a disk volume label. The directory entry for a file contains such basic information as the file's size, its location on the disk, and the time and date it was most recently modified. This information is contained in the eight fields listed in Figure 5-11.

Offset	Description	Size (bytes)	Format
00H	Filename	8	ASCII characters
08H	Filename extension	3	ASCII characters
0BH	Attribute	1	Bit coded
0CH	Reserved	10	Unused; zeros
16H	Time	2	Word, coded
18H	Date	2	Word, coded
1AH	Starting cluster number	2	Word
1CH	File size	4	Integer

Figure 5-11. *The eight parts of a directory entry.*

Offset 00H: The filename

The first 8 bytes in a directory entry contain the filename, stored in ASCII format. If the filename is less than eight characters, it is filled out to the right with blanks (CHR$(32)). Letters should be uppercase, because lowercase letters will not be properly recognized. Normally, blanks should not be embedded in the filename, as in *AA BB*. Most DOS command programs, such as DEL and COPY, will not recognize filenames with embedded blanks. BASIC works successfully with these filenames, however, and DOS services usually can too. (See Chapters 16 and 17.) This capability suggests some useful tricks, such as creating files that cannot easily be erased.

Two codes, used to indicate special situations, may appear in the first byte of the filename field. When a file is deleted, DOS sets the first byte of the filename field in its directory entry to E5H to indicate that the directory entry can be reused for another filename. In DOS versions 2.0 and later, the first byte of a directory entry can also be set to 00H to indicate the end of the list of directory entries.

When a file is erased, only two things on the disk are affected: The first byte of the directory entry is set to E5H, and the file's space-allocation chain in the FAT is wiped out (we'll cover this in the section on the FAT). All other directory information about the file is retained, including the rest of its name, its size, and even its starting cluster number. The lost information can be recovered, with suitably sophisticated methods, provided that the directory entry has not been reused for another file. Be forewarned, though, that whenever a new directory entry is needed, DOS uses the first available entry, quickly recycling an erased file's entries and making recovery more problematic.

Offset 08H: The filename extension

Directly following the filename is the standard filename extension, stored in ASCII format. It is 3 bytes long and, like the filename, is padded with blanks if it is less than the full three-character length. While a filename must have at least one ordinary character in it, the extension can be all blanks. Generally, the rules that apply to the filename also apply to the filename extension.

❏ NOTE: *When the directory contains a volume ID label entry, the filename and extension fields are treated as one combined field of 11 bytes. In this case, embedded blanks are permitted.*

Offset 0BH: The file attribute

The third field of the directory entry is 1 byte long. The bits of the attribute byte are individually coded as bits 0 through 7, as shown in Figure 5-12, and each bit is used to categorize the directory entry.

Bit 7 6 5 4 3 2 1 0	*Meaning*
. . . . 1	Read-only
. . . . . . 1 .	Hidden
. . . . . 1 . .	System
. . . . 1 . . .	Volume label
. . . 1	Subdirectory
. . 1	Archive
. 1	Unused
1	Unused

Figure 5-12. *The 8 file-attribute bits.*

Bit 0, the low-order bit, is set to mark a file as read-only. In this state, the file is protected from being changed or deleted by any DOS operation. We should point out that many DOS services ignore this attribute, so even though bit 0 can provide worthwhile protection for data, it is not foolproof.

Bit 1 marks a file as hidden and bit 2 marks a file as a system file. Files marked as hidden, system, or both, cannot be seen by ordinary DOS operations, such as the DIR command. Programs can gain access to such files only by using DOS services to search explicitly for hidden or system files. There is no particular significance to the system attribute; it exists to perpetuate a feature of CP/M and has absolutely nothing to do with DOS.

Bit 3 marks a directory entry as a volume label. A volume label entry is properly recognized only in the root directory, and uses only a few of the eight fields available in the directory entry: The label itself is stored in the

Subdirectories

There are two types of directories: *root directories* and *subdirectories*. The contents and use of each type are essentially the same (both store the names and locations of files on the disk) but their characteristics are different. The root directory has a fixed size and is stored in a fixed location on the disk. A subdirectory has no fixed size and can be stored anywhere on the disk. Any version of DOS numbered 2.0 or later can use subdirectories.

A subdirectory is stored in a disk's files area, just like any other file. The format of directory entries in a subdirectory is identical to the format of entries in a root directory, but a subdirectory is not

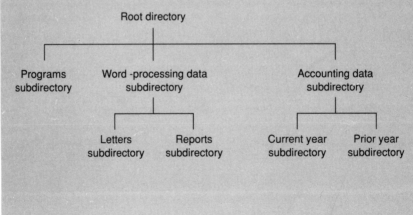

filename and extension fields, which are treated as one unified field for this purpose; the size and starting cluster fields are not used, but the date and time fields are.

Bit 4, the subdirectory attribute, identifies a directory entry as a subdirectory. Because subdirectories are stored like ordinary data files, they need a supporting directory entry. All the directory fields are used for these entries, except the file-size field, which is zero. The actual size of a subdirectory can be found simply by following its space allocation chain in the FAT.

Bit 5, the archive attribute, was created to assist in making backup copies of the many files that can be stored on a fixed disk. This bit is 0 on all files that haven't changed since they were last backed up; DOS sets this bit to 1 whenever a file is created or modified.

limited in size. Like an ordinary file, a subdirectory can grow without bounds as long as disk space is available to hold it.

A subdirectory is always attached to a parent directory, which can be either the root directory or another subdirectory. When you nest subdirectories, one within another, they are related in the form of a tree structure.

A parent directory has one entry for each of its subdirectories. A subdirectory entry is just like a filename entry, except that the attribute byte marks the entry as a subdirectory and the file-size field is set to 0. The actual size of the subdirectory can be found by tracing its allocation chain through the FAT.

When DOS creates a subdirectory, it places two special entries in it, with . and . . as filenames. These act like entries for further subdirectories, but . actually refers to the present subdirectory and . . refers to its parent directory. The starting cluster number in each of these directory entries gives the location of the subdirectory itself or of its parent. When the starting cluster number is 0, the parent of the subdirectory is the root directory.

If the size of a "normal" file is reduced, you can generally count on DOS to release any unused space. In the case of subdirectories, however, clusters of space that are no longer used (because the directory entries that occupied that space are erased) are not released until the entire subdirectory is deleted.

Offset 0CH: Reserved

This 10-byte area is set aside for possible future uses. All 10 bytes are normally set to 0.

Offset 16H: The time

This field contains a 2-byte value that marks the time that the file was created or last changed. It is used in conjunction with the date field, and the two together can be treated as a single 4-byte unsigned integer. This 4-byte integer can be compared with those in other directory entries for greater-than, less-than, or equal values. The time, by itself, is treated as an unsigned word integer. It is based on a 24-hour clock and is built out of the hour, minutes, and seconds with this formula:

$$Time=(Hour \times 2048)+(Minutes \times 32)+(Seconds \div 2)$$

The 2-byte word used to store the time is one bit too short to store all the seconds, so seconds are stored in units of 2 seconds from 0 through 29; a value of 5, for example, would represent 10 seconds. The time 11:32:10 would be stored as the value 5C05H (decimal 23557).

Offset 18H: The date

This field contains a 2-byte value that marks the date the file was created or last changed. It is used in conjunction with the time field, and the two together can be treated as a single 4-byte unsigned integer that can be compared with those in other directory entries for greater-than, less-than, or equal values. The date, by itself, is treated as an unsigned word integer that is built out of the year, month, and day with this formula:

$$Date=((Year-1980) \times 512)+(Month \times 32)+Day$$

This formula compresses the year by subtracting 1980 from it. Thus, the year 1988 is calculated as a value of 8. Using this formula, a date such as December 12, 1988 is stored by the formula as 118CH (decimal 4492):

$$(1988-1980) \times 512+12 \times 32+12=4492$$

Although this scheme allows for years up through 2107, the highest year supported by DOS is 2099.

Offset 1AH: The starting cluster number

The seventh field of a directory entry is a 2-byte value that gives the starting cluster number for the file's data space. This cluster number acts as the entry point into the file's space allocation chain in the FAT. For files with no space allocated and for volume-label entries, the starting cluster number is 0.

Offset 1CH: The file size

The last field of a directory entry gives the size of the file in bytes. It is coded as a 4-byte unsigned integer, which allows file sizes to grow very large — 4,294,967,295 bytes, to be exact — large enough for all practical purposes.

DOS uses the file size in a file's directory entry to determine the *exact* size of the file. Because a file's disk space is allocated in clusters of 512 bytes or more, the actual disk space occupied by a file is usually greater than the value in the directory entry. On disk, the space between the end of the file and the end of the last cluster in the file is wasted.

The Files Area

All data files and subdirectories are stored in the files area, which occupies the last and largest part of each disk.

DOS allocates space to files, one cluster at a time, on an as-needed basis. (Remember, a cluster is one or more consecutive sectors; the number of sectors per cluster is a fixed characteristic of each disk format.) As a file is being created, or as an existing file is extended, the file's allocated space grows. When more space is needed, DOS allocates another cluster to the file. In DOS versions 1 and 2, the first available cluster is always allocated to the file. Later versions of DOS select clusters by more complicated rules that we won't go into here.

Under ideal conditions, a file is stored in one contiguous block of space. However, a file might be broken into several noncontiguous blocks, especially if information is added to an existing file or a new file is stored in the space left by an erased file. So it's not unusual for one file's data to be scattered throughout the disk.

This file fragmentation slows access to the file's data to some degree. Also, it is much harder to ''unerase'' a file you have unintentionally erased if it is fragmented, simply because you have to do a lot more searching for the individual clusters that make up the file's data space. But fragmentation has no other effect, and programs generally do not need to be concerned about where on a disk their data is stored. To determine if a file is fragmented, use CHKDSK or a program such as the Norton Utilities.

If you are concerned about diskette file fragmentation, the DOS COPY command lets you transfer fragmented files to a newly formatted disk. DOS allocates contiguous space for the copied files. This simple technique also works for fixed-disk files, but it is much less convenient unless you have an extra, newly formatted fixed disk to use. If you think that fixed-disk file fragmentation is slowing down a particular application, you can purchase any of several fixed-disk utility programs to rearrange fragmented fixed-disk files and make them contiguous. Most of the time, however, file fragmentation has little impact on the speed of your programs.

Whether you ever look at your fragmented files or not, you should know how DOS uses the file allocation table (FAT) to allocate disk space and how the FAT forms a space allocation chain to connect all of the clusters that make up a file.

The File Allocation Table

The file allocation table (FAT) is DOS's map of how space is utilized in the files area of a disk. We've already discussed how space for the FAT itself is reserved on a diskette or in a fixed-disk partition. Now we'll describe how the FAT is formatted and used.

For most disk formats, DOS maintains two copies of the FAT, just in case one of them is damaged or becomes unreadable. Curiously, the CHKDSK program, which tests for most errors that can occur in the FAT and in directories, does not even notice if the two FATs are different.

The organization of the FAT is simple: There is one entry in the FAT for each cluster in the files area. A FAT entry can contain any of the values listed in Figure 5-13. If the value in a FAT entry doesn't mark an unused, reserved, or defective cluster, then the cluster that corresponds to the FAT entry is part of a file, and the value in the FAT entry itself indicates the next cluster in the file.

This means that the space that belongs to a given file is mapped by a chain of FAT entries, each of which points to the next entry in the chain. (See Figure 5-14.) The first cluster number in the chain is the starting cluster number in the file's directory entry. When a file is created or extended, DOS allocates clusters to the file by searching the FAT for unused

12-bit Value	16-bit Value	Meaning
0	0	Unused cluster
FF0-FF6H	FFF0-FFF6H	Reserved cluster
FF7H	FFF7H	Bad cluster
FF8-FFFH	FFF8-FFFFH	Last cluster in a file
(other values)		Next cluster in a file

Figure 5-13. *FAT values.*

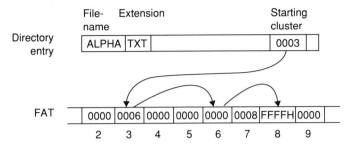

Figure 5-14. *Disk-space allocation using the FAT.*

clusters (that is, clusters whose FAT entries are 0) and adding them to the chain. Conversely, when a file is truncated or deleted, DOS frees the clusters that had been allocated to the file by clearing the corresponding FAT entries.

The FAT can be formatted with either 12-bit or 16-bit entries. The 12-bit format is used for diskettes and fixed-disk partitions with no more than 4078 clusters. (A fixed-disk's partition table indicates whether a DOS partition's FAT uses 12-bit or 16-bit entries.) The entries in a 12-bit FAT are harder to access because they don't fit neatly into the 16-bit word size of the 8086 family of microprocessors, but a 12-bit FAT takes up less room on a diskette, where disk space is scarcer.

The first two entries in the FAT are reserved for use by DOS. The first byte of the FAT contains the same media descriptor value that appears in the BIOS parameter block in the disk boot sector. The remaining bytes of the first two entries are filled with the value 0FFH. Because the first two cluster numbers (0 and 1) are reserved, cluster number 2 corresponds to the first cluster of available disk space in the files area.

Reading the values in the FAT is simple enough for a 16-bit FAT: Multiply a given cluster number by 2 to find the byte offset of the corresponding FAT entry. In the 16-bit FAT in Figure 5-15a, for example, the byte offset of the FAT entry for cluster 2 is 04H, and the value in that entry is 0003; the byte offset of the FAT entry for cluster 3 is 06H, and the value in that entry is 0004; and so on.

For a 12-bit FAT, the computation is a bit trickier, because each pair of FAT entries occupies 3 bytes (0 and 1 occupy the first 3 bytes, 2 and 3 occupy the next 3 bytes, and so forth). Given any cluster number, you can find the FAT entry by multiplying the cluster number by 3, dividing by 2, and then using the whole number of the result as a displacement into the FAT. By grabbing a word at that address, you have the three hex digits of the FAT entry, plus one extraneous hex digit, which can be removed by any one of several quick machine-language instructions. If the cluster number is even, you discard the high-order digit; if it is odd, you discard the low-order digit. Try this on the 12-bit FAT in Figure 5-15b. You'll find that the entries are the same as in the 16-bit FAT in Figure 5-15a.

(a) 16-bit FAT

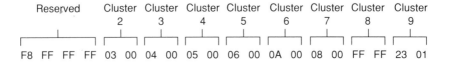

(b) 12-bit FAT

Figure 5-15. *The first few entries in a 16-bit FAT (a) and in a 12-bit FAT (b).*

As we have said, the first two FAT entries, in both 12-bit and 16-bit formats, are not used to indicate the status of clusters; instead, they are set aside so that the very first byte of the FAT can be used as a media descriptor byte that indicates the format of the disk. (See Figure 5-16.) However, you should not assume that these IDs uniquely identify formats: they don't necessarily. If you considered every disk format in use, you'd find quite a few duplications. Beware.

Disk	Capacity	Heads	Sectors per Track	Media Descriptor
5¼-inch diskette	160 KB	1	8	FEH
	320 KB	2	8	FFH
	180 KB	1	9	FCH
	360 KB	2	9	FDH
	1.2 MB	2	15	F9H
3½-inch diskette	720 KB	2	9	F9H
	1.44 MB	2	18	F0H
Fixed disk				F8H

Figure 5-16. *DOS media descriptor values.*

Your programs can learn the format of a disk by reading and inspecting the FAT media descriptor byte. The easy way to do this is to use DOS function 1BH (decimal 27). For more information about this function, see page 335.

Special notes on the FAT

Normally, programs do not look at or change a disk's FAT; they leave the FAT completely under the supervision of DOS. The only exceptions are programs that perform space-allocation functions not supported by DOS — for example, programs that recover erased files, such as the UnErase program in the Norton Utilities program set.

Be aware that a FAT can be logically damaged; for example, an allocation chain can be circular, referring back to a previous link in the chain; or two chains can converge on one cluster; or a cluster can be orphaned, meaning that it is marked as in use even though it is not part of any valid allocation chain. Also, an end-of-file marker (FFFH or FFFFH) may be missing. The DOS programs CHKDSK and RECOVER are designed to detect and repair most of these problems as well as can reasonably be done.

For special notes on the interaction of the space allocation chain in the FAT and DOS's record of a file's size, see page 116.

Comments

Although this chapter has included detailed information for direct use of the logical structure of the disk itself, including the boot sector, FAT, and directories, it is not a good idea to use these elements directly unless you have a compelling reason. In fact, except where such use is completely unavoidable, as in a copy-protection program, it's unwise to incorporate any knowledge of the disk format in your programs. On the whole, your best approach is to consider the standard hierarchy of operations and use the highest level of services that can satisfy your needs:

- First choice: Language services (the facilities provided by your programming language; for example, BASIC's OPEN and CLOSE statements)

- Second choice: DOS services (described in Chapters 16 and 17)

- Third choice: ROM BIOS disk services (described in Chapter 10)

- Last choice: Direct control (for example, direct programming of the disk-drive controller through commands issued via I/O ports)

Most disk operations for the PC family can be handled quite easily with the services that your programming language provides. There are, however, two obvious circumstances that can call for more exotic methods. One, which we've already mentioned, occurs when your programming involves control of a disk on the same level exercised by DOS. This level of control would be called for if you were writing a program similar to DOS's CHKDSK or the Norton Utilities. The other circumstance involves copy protection. In one way or another, all diskette copy-protection schemes involve some type of unconventional diskette I/O. This type of control usually leads to the use of the ROM BIOS services, but may also lead to the extreme measure of directly programming the disk-drive controller itself.

Copy Protection

A variety of copy-protection schemes are commercially available. Some are simple, others are more complex. If you're interested in devising your own scheme, however, here are some things to consider.

For diskettes, there are dozens of ways to approach copy protection. Perhaps the most common methods involve reformatting the sectors in certain tracks on the diskette by using the ROM BIOS format routines. Because DOS cannot read sectors that don't conform to its specific formats, the DOS COPY program can't copy a disk that has an occasional odd sector size interspersed with normal sectors. This DOS limitation inspired a number of companies to produce copy programs that can read and copy sectors of any size, so it is not a particularly effective means of copy protection.

On a more advanced level, there are two special aspects of diskette copy protection that are worth noting. First, some of the most exotic and unbreakable protection schemes have been based on the discovery of undocumented abilities hidden in the diskette-drive controller. Second, some protection schemes are intentionally or unintentionally dependent upon the particular characteristics of different diskette drives. This means that a copy-protected program may function on one model of computer but fail to function on another model, even though the copy protection has not been tampered with. If you use a copy-protection scheme, keep this in mind.

Many of the copy-protection techniques used on diskettes are not appropriate for fixed disks, mainly because most fixed-disk users need to be able to make backup copies of programs on their fixed disks. This means you should avoid copy-protection schemes that prevent fixed-disk backups by making it impossible for DOS or the ROM BIOS to read part of the disk. Most of the fixed-disk copy-protection schemes in use today rely on data-encryption techniques, which discourage software piracy without preventing legitimate copying.

In an encrypted program, the program's executable code and data are stored on the disk in an encrypted, hard-to-unravel format. When you execute the program, a special start-up program decrypts the encrypted code and data so that it can be used. The start-up program might also rely on data saved in hidden files or subdirectories to decrypt the main program.

There is no particular additional guidance that we can give you here, except to remind you that variety and ingenuity are the keys to successful copy protection.

Chapter 6

Keyboard Basics

This chapter is about the IBM PC and PS/2 keyboards. The first part of this chapter explains how the keyboard interacts with the computer on a hardware and software level. In the second part, we'll describe how the ROM BIOS treats keyboard information and makes it available to programs.

❑ NOTE: *If you plan to play around with keyboard control, we urge you to read the comments on page 140 first and then apply the information in this chapter to your programs only if you have a reason to do so (for example, if you are creating a keyboard-enhancer program to modify the operation of the keyboard; see the sidebar on page 133 for more information on such programs). If you have any such application in mind, take a look at the ROM BIOS keyboard services in Chapter 11.*

The keyboard has undergone several modifications since the IBM PC was released. The original IBM PC keyboard had 83 keys. The PC/AT was introduced with an 84-key keyboard that changed the locations of several keys on the 83-key keyboard and added one new key, the Sys Req key.

IBM later upgraded the AT with a 101/102-key keyboard that provided extra function keys and a new keyboard layout. The 101/102-key keyboard became standard equipment in the PS/2 series. The 101/102-key layout includes two extra function keys (F11 and F12), a number of duplicate shift and control keys, and modifications to several keys and keyboard combinations found in the 83- and 84-key layouts (Pause, Alt-Sys Req, and Print Screen).

A trend in IBM's keyboard design has been to increase the similarity between the PC and PS/2 keyboards and the keyboards on their mainframe display terminals. For example, the 101/102-key keyboard's 12 function keys (F1 through F12) are reminiscent of the Program Function (PF) keys on IBM mainframe display terminals. Similarly, the Sys Req key is like the Sys Req key in IBM mainframe terminals: A mainframe terminal-emulator program running on a PC or PS/2 could use the Sys Req key for the same purpose a mainframe terminal would — to switch among terminal sessions or to initiate a keyboard reset function.

Another trend in IBM's keyboard design has been to accommodate non-English alphabets in the keyboard layout. The English-language version of the 101/102-key keyboard released in the United States and United Kingdom has 101 keys, but for other languages the same keyboard has an extra key next to the left Shift key, a different arrangement of keys around the Enter key, and a different map of ASCII characters to key locations. From a programmer's point of view, however, these two keyboards are so similar that IBM describes them together in its technical documentation—and we'll do the same in this chapter.

Keyboard Operation

The keyboard unit contains a dedicated microprocessor that performs a variety of jobs, all of which help cut down on system overhead. The main duty of the keyboard microprocessor is to watch the keys and report to the main computer whenever a key is pressed or released. If any key is pressed continuously, the keyboard microprocessor sends out a repeat action at specific intervals. The keyboard microprocessor controller also has limited diagnostic and error-checking capabilities and has a buffer that can store key actions in the rare instance that the main computer is temporarily unable to accept them.

The PC/AT and PS/2s have sophisticated keyboard control circuitry that can perform several functions the original IBM PC and PC/XT keyboard cannot. These features include programmable typematic control, programmable scan-code sets, and improved hardware for error detection.

On the 83-key keyboard, the typematic delay and repeat rate are built into the hardware: A key must be pressed for 0.5 seconds before auto-repeat begins, and the repeat rate is about 10 characters per second. With the PC/AT and PS/2 keyboards, you can modify the typematic delay and rate by programming the keyboard controller. The most convenient way to do this is through the ROM BIOS keyboard services described in Chapter 11.

The keyboard controller in the PC/AT and PS/2s can also assign any of three different sets of scan-code values to the keys on the 84- and 101/102-key layouts. By default, however, the ROM BIOS establishes a scan-code set that is compatible with that used on the 83-key keyboard. You will probably find use for the alternative scan-code sets only if your program bypasses the ROM BIOS and processes scan codes directly. (See the PC/AT and PS/2 technical reference manuals for details.)

The improved error-detection ability of the AT and PS/2 keyboard controllers is largely invisible to your programs; the keyboard hardware and the ROM BIOS service routines are very reliable. The most common errors you may encounter are a full ROM BIOS keyboard buffer or a key combination that the PS/2 ROM BIOS cannot process. In both situations, the ROM BIOS generates a warning beep to inform you that something unusual has occurred. (For example, try holding down both pairs of Ctrl and Alt keys on a PS/2 keyboard.)

Keystrokes and Scan Codes

Each time you press or release one of the keys on the keyboard, the keyboard circuits transmit a sequence of one or more 8-bit numbers through the connector cable to the computer. This sequence, called a *scan code,* uniquely identifies the key you pressed. The keyboard produces different scan codes, depending on whether the key was pressed or released. Whenever you press a key, the scan-code byte contains a number ranging from 01H through 58H. When you release the key, the keyboard generates a scan code 80H higher than the keystroke scan code by setting bit 7 of the scan-code byte to 1. For example, when you press the letter Z, the keyboard generates a scan code of 2CH; when you release it, the keyboard generates a scan code of ACH (2CH + 80H). The keyboard diagrams in Figures 6-1, 6-2, and 6-3 show the standard keyboard keys and their associated scan codes.

Figure 6-1. *Scan codes for the 83-key keyboard (PC, PC/XT). Scan-code values are in hex.*

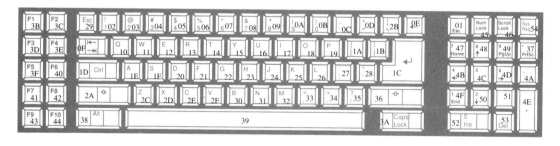

Figure 6-2. *Scan codes for the 84-key keyboard (PC/AT). Scan-code values are in hex.*

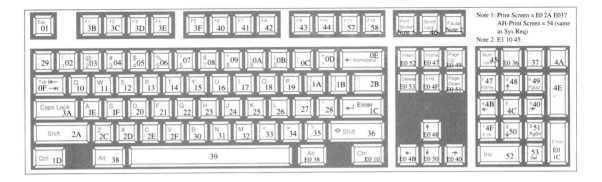

Figure 6-3. *Scan codes for the 101/102-key keyboard (PC/AT and PS/2). Scan-code values are in hex.*

If you compare the scan codes for the 83-, 84-, and 101/102-key keyboards, you'll see that a key generates the same scan code regardless of its location on the keyboard. For example, the Esc key has a scan code of 01H, whether it's next to the 1 key, next to the Num Lock key, or by itself in the upper-left corner. (The 101/102-key keyboard can actually generate different scan codes, but the start-up ROM BIOS suppresses this by configuring the keyboard to be compatible with the 83-key keyboard.)

The 101/102-key layout contains duplicate shift and control keys that don't exist on the other keyboards. The 101/102-key keyboard distinguishes between duplicate keys by transmitting multiple-byte scan codes. For example, the two Alt shift keys have different scan codes: The left Alt key has a scan code of 38H, and the right Alt key has a 2-byte scan code, E0H 38H.

❑ NOTE: *The multiple-byte scan codes for shift and control keys can vary depending on whether one of the shift keys (Ctrl, Alt, Shift), Num Lock, or Caps Lock is pressed at the same time. See IBM's PS/2 technical reference manuals for details.*

The 101/102-key keyboard also assigns special scan codes to certain keystroke combinations. The Alt-Sys Req combination is intended to be the same as the Sys Req key on the 84-key layout, so the 101/102-key keyboard transmits the same scan code, 54H. Because the Print Screen key has the same function as the Shift-PrtSc combination in the other keyboard layouts, the 101/102-key keyboard transmits a Shift key scan code (E0H 2AH) followed by the PrtSc scan code (E0H 37H). The Pause key's scan code, E1H 1DH 45H, resembles the scan-code sequence for the Ctrl-Num Lock combination, but when you press Ctrl-Pause (that is, Ctrl-Break), the keyboard transmits E0H 46H E0H C6H, which is derived from the scan code for the Scroll Lock (Break) key on the 83- and 84-key keyboards. Figure 6-4 lists these keystroke combinations and their associated codes.

101/102-key Keyboard Keystroke Combination	84-key Keyboard Equivalent	Scan Code Transmitted
Alt-Sys Req	Sys Req	54H
Print Screen	Shift-Print Screen	E0H 2AH E0H 37H
Ctrl-Break	Ctrl-Break	E0H 46H E0H C6H

Figure 6-4. *Scan codes for special keystroke combinations on the 101/102-key keyboard.*

❏ NOTE: *The "compact" keyboard available for the PS/2 Model 25 is really a 101/102-key keyboard in disguise. The numeric keypad is mapped to a group of 14 keys on the main keyboard, and the Num Lock key is the shift state of the Scroll Lock key. However, keyboard scan codes and ROM BIOS processing are the same for the compact version as for the full-size 101/102-key keyboard.*

Any program that processes keyboard scan codes must be aware of which machine it's running on and which keyboard is in use. Fortunately, few programs need to respond directly to keyboard scan codes — the ROM BIOS keyboard service routines translate scan codes into meaningful information that a program can use. The following sections describe this translation process more fully.

Communicating with the ROM BIOS

The keyboard-controller circuitry on the computer's system board monitors the keyboard for input. The keyboard controller generates interrupt 09H each time it receives a byte of data from the keyboard. The ROM BIOS contains an interrupt 09H handler that reads the byte from the keyboard controller and processes it. (I/O port 60H contains the keyboard data byte.) The interrupt 09H handler translates scan codes into 2-byte values that are generally more useful to a program than the original scan codes.

The low-order byte of each 2-byte keyboard value contains the ASCII value corresponding to each key pressed. The high-order byte usually contains the corresponding keyboard scan code.

Special keys, such as the function keys and the numeric-keypad keys, have a 0 in the low-order byte, with the keyboard scan code in the high-order byte. (More about this later, on page 134.)

The ROM BIOS routines place the translated byte-pairs in a queue, which is kept in low memory in location 0040:001EH. The byte-pairs are stored there until they are requested by a program, such as DOS or interpreted BASIC, that expects to read keyboard input.

Translating the Scan Codes

The scan-code translation job is moderately complicated because the IBM keyboard recognizes two types of keys that change the meaning of a keystroke: *shift keys* and *toggle keys*.

The shift keys

Three keys—Ctrl, Shift, and Alt—are known as *shift keys*: They change the shift state, and thereby the meaning, of whatever key they are used with. For example, when you press Shift-C, you get a capital *C*; when you press Ctrl-C, you generate the "break" character. The ROM BIOS recognizes that all subsequent key actions will be influenced by that shift state as long as a shift key is pressed.

The toggle keys

In addition to the shift keys, two toggle keys also affect the keyboard's shift state: the Caps Lock key and the Num Lock key. When activated, Caps Lock reverses the shift state of the alphabet keys; it doesn't affect the other keys. When activated, the Num Lock key disables cursor-control functions on the numeric keypad. Toggle keys are activated with a single keystroke and remain active until released by a second keystroke.

The shift-key and toggle-key status information is kept by the ROM BIOS in a low-memory location (0040:0017H), where you can use or change it. When you press a shift key or a toggle key, the ROM BIOS sets a specific bit in one of these two bytes. When the ROM BIOS receives the release scan code of a shift key, it switches the status bit back to its original shift state.

Whenever the ROM BIOS receives a scan code for an ordinary keystroke, such as the letter *z* or a right arrow key, it first checks the shift state and then translates the key into the appropriate 2-byte code. (We'll discuss the status bytes in more detail on page 137.)

The combination keys

While the ROM BIOS routine is translating scan codes, it checks for Sys Req keystrokes and for certain shift-key combinations; specifically, it checks for the Ctrl-Alt-Del, Shift-PrtSc, Ctrl-Num Lock, and Ctrl-Break combinations. These five command-like key actions cause the ROM BIOS to perform a specific task immediately.

Ctrl-Alt-Del causes the computer to reboot. Ctrl-Alt-Del is probably used more often than any other special key combination. It works dependably as long as the keyboard interrupt service is working. If the interrupt service is not working, turn the power off, wait a few seconds, then turn it on again; the power-on program resets all interrupt vectors and services.

Shift-PrtSc (Print Screen on the 101/102-key keyboard) causes the ROM BIOS interrupt 09H handler to execute software interrupt 05H. The default interrupt 05H handler is also part of the ROM BIOS; it prints a ''snapshot'' of the current contents of the screen.

Ctrl-Num Lock (Pause on the 101/102-key keyboard) suspends operation of a program until another keystroke occurs.

Ctrl-Break causes the ROM BIOS to generate software interrupt 1BH and to set bit 7 of the byte at 0040:0071H to 1. The default DOS handler for interrupt 1BH simply sets a flag internal to DOS that causes DOS to interpret Ctrl-Break as Ctrl-C. You can override the default DOS action for Ctrl-Break by pointing the interrupt 1BH vector (located at 0000:006CH) to your own interrupt handler.

Sys Req (on the 84-key keyboard) and **Alt-Sys Req** (on the 101/102-key keyboard) cause the ROM BIOS to issue interrupt 15H with AH = 85H. Your program can provide its own interrupt 15H handler that intercepts and processes Sys Req keystrokes. (See Chapter 12 for details.)

These are the only key combinations that are especially meaningful to the ROM BIOS. When an invalid combination is reported from the keyboard, the ROM BIOS simply ignores it and moves on to the next valid key action.

Two more features of the PC keyboard should be presented before we discuss the details of keyboard coding: *repeat key action* and *duplicate keys*.

Repeat key action

The PC keyboard features automatic repeat key action, a process called *typematic* by IBM. The circuitry inside the keyboard monitors how long each key is pressed, and if a key is held down longer than a defined interval, the circuitry generates repeat key actions. This typematic action is reported as successive keystroke scan codes, without the intervening key-release codes. This makes it possible for an interrupt 09H handler to distinguish between actual keystrokes and typematic action. However, the ROM BIOS does not always distinguish between the two. The ROM BIOS keyboard-handling routine treats each automatic repeat key action as though the key were actually pressed and interprets the key accordingly.

For example, if you press and hold the *A* key long enough for the keyboard to begin generating successive keystroke signals, then the ROM BIOS will create a series of *A*s to be passed on to whatever program is reading keyboard data. On the other hand, when you press and hold a shift key, the ROM BIOS sets bits in its status bytes in segment 40H. While you hold the shift key down, the ROM BIOS continues to set the same bits to 1.

Keyboard-enhancer programs

Thanks to the flexible software design of the PC, it's possible to create programs that customize the keyboard. Such programs are called *keyboard-enhancer programs.*

Keyboard-enhancer programs monitor the scan codes that come in from the keyboard and respond to them in ways that aren't supported by the ROM BIOS or by DOS. Typically, these programs are fed instructions, called *keyboard macros,* that tell them what keystrokes to look for and what changes to make. The change might involve suppressing a keystroke (acting as if it never happened), replacing one keystroke with another, or replacing one keystroke with a long series of keystrokes. The most common use of keyboard macros is to abbreviate frequently used phrases; for example, you might instruct a keyboard enhancer to convert a key combination, such as Alt-S, into a salutation you use in your correspondence, such as *Sincerely yours.* You can also use keyboard macros to condense multiple-keystroke program commands to a single keystroke.

Keyboard enhancers work by combining the powers of two special facilities — one that's part of DOS and one that's part of the PC's ROM BIOS. The DOS facility allows the enhancer program to remain resident in the computer's memory, quietly monitoring the operation of the computer while the ordinary control of the computer is turned over to a conventional program, such as a word processor. The ROM BIOS facility lets programs divert the stream of keyboard information so that it can be inspected and changed before it is passed on to a program. These programs use the DOS Terminate and Stay Resident facility to stay active in memory while other programs are run; then they use the ROM BIOS keyboard-monitoring facility to preview keyboard data and change it as needed.

When you release the key, the ROM BIOS resets the status bits. All this boils down to the simple fact that the ROM BIOS treats repeat key actions in a sensible way, acting on them or ignoring them as needed.

Duplicate keys

We've already described how the keyboard differentiates duplicate keys by assigning different scan codes to each. The ROM BIOS translates duplicate keys into the same ASCII character codes. For example, if you press either of the two asterisk keys, the ROM BIOS returns ASCII 2AH (the ASCII code for an asterisk); if you press either of the two Ctrl keys on a 101/102-key keyboard, the ROM BIOS sets the appropriate bit in its shift-state byte.

The ROM BIOS also lets programs tell the difference between duplicate keys, in some cases. Remember that the ROM BIOS translates each keystroke into a scan code as well as an ASCII code. A program that requests a keystroke from the ROM BIOS can inspect the scan code to determine which key was pressed. In the case of shift keys, a program can inspect the BIOS shift-state bytes at 0040:0017H and 0040:0018H to determine exactly which shift keys are pressed. (See the discussion of the shift-state bytes on pages 137 and 138.)

Entering ASCII Codes Directly

We should mention that the PC keyboard, in conjunction with the ROM BIOS, provides an alternate way to enter nearly any ASCII character code. This is done by holding down the Alt key and then entering the decimal ASCII character code from the numeric keypad on the right side of the keyboard. This method lets you enter any ASCII code from 01H through FFH (decimal 1 through 255).

Keyboard Data Format

Once a keyboard action is translated, it is stored as a pair of bytes in the ROM BIOS buffer. We call the low-order byte the *main byte* and the high-order byte the *auxiliary byte*. The contents of these bytes will vary, depending on whether an ASCII key or a special key was pressed.

The ASCII Keys

When the main byte is an ASCII character value from 01H to FFH, one of two events has occurred: One of the standard keyboard characters was pressed, or an ASCII character was entered directly using the Alt-number method mentioned above. (See Appendix C for the complete ASCII character set.) For these ASCII characters, the auxiliary byte contains the scan code of the pressed key. (The scan code is 0 for characters entered with Alt-number.) Usually you can ignore this scan code. DOS does not report keyboard scan codes, nor do high-level programming language functions like *getch()* in C or INKEY$ in BASIC. However, a program can examine the auxiliary byte (scan code) to differentiate among duplicate keyboard characters.

The Special Keys

When the main byte is null (00H), it means that a special, non-ASCII key was pressed. The special keys include function keys, shifted function keys, cursor-control keys such as Home and End, and some of the Ctrl- and Alt-key combinations. When any of these keys are pressed by themselves or in combination with other keys, the auxiliary byte contains a single value that indicates which key was pressed. Figure 6-5 lists these values in a rough mixture of logical and numeric order. (For a complete breakdown of ROM BIOS key codes, see the *IBM BIOS Interface Technical Reference Manual*.)

❑ NOTE: *With the 101/102-key keyboard, the main byte value for the gray cursor-control keys is E0H. This value distinguishes these keys from their counterparts on the numeric keypad, which have a main byte value of 00H.*

Value (hex)	(dec)	Keys Pressed	Value (hex)	(dec)	Keys Pressed	Value (hex)	(dec)	Keys Pressed
3BH	59	F1	54H	84	Shift-F1	5EH	94	Ctrl-F1
3CH	60	F2	55H	85	Shift-F2	5FH	95	Ctrl-F2
3DH	61	F3	56H	86	Shift-F3	60H	96	Ctrl-F3
3EH	62	F4	57H	87	Shift-F4	61H	97	Ctrl-F4
3FH	63	F5	58H	88	Shift-F5	62H	98	Ctrl-F5
40H	64	F6	59H	89	Shift-F6	63H	99	Ctrl-F6
41H	65	F7	5AH	90	Shift-F7	64H	100	Ctrl-F7
42H	66	F8	5BH	91	Shift-F8	65H	101	Ctrl-F8
43H	67	F9	5CH	92	Shift-F9	66H	102	Ctrl-F9
44H	68	F10	5DH	93	Shift-F10	67H	103	Ctrl-F10
85H	133	F11	87H	135	Shift-F11	89H	137	Ctrl-F11
86H	134	F12	88H	136	Shift-F12	8AH	138	Ctrl-F12

Figure 6-5. *ROM BIOS auxiliary byte values for the special keys.*   *(continued)*

Figure 6-5. *continued*

Value (hex)	(dec)	Keys Pressed	Value (hex)	(dec)	Keys Pressed	Value (hex)	(dec)	Keys Pressed
68H	104	Alt-F1	10H	16	Alt-Q	0FH	15	Shift-Tab
69H	105	Alt-F2	11H	17	Alt-W			
6AH	106	Alt-F3	12H	18	Alt-E	47H	71	Home
6BH	107	Alt-F4	13H	19	Alt-R	48H	72	Up arrow
6CH	108	Alt-F5	14H	20	Alt-T	49H	73	PgUp
6DH	109	Alt-F6	15H	21	Alt-Y			
6EH	110	Alt-F7	16H	22	Alt-U	4BH	75	Left arrow
6FH	111	Alt-F8	17H	23	Alt-I			
70H	112	Alt-F9	18H	24	Alt-O	4DH	77	Right arrow
71H	113	Alt-F10	19H	25	Alt-P			
8BH	139	Alt-F11				4FH	79	End
8CH	140	Alt-F12	1EH	30	Alt-A			
			1FH	31	Alt-S	50H	80	Down arrow
78H	120	Alt-1	20H	32	Alt-D	51H	81	PgDn
79H	121	Alt-2	21H	33	Alt-F	52H	82	Insert
7AH	122	Alt-3	22H	34	Alt-G	53H	83	Del
7BH	123	Alt-4	23H	35	Alt-H			
7CH	124	Alt-5	24H	36	Alt-J	72H	114	Ctrl-PrtSc
7DH	125	Alt-6	25H	37	Alt-K	73H	115	Ctrl-Left arrow
7EH	126	Alt-7	26H	38	Alt-L	74H	116	Ctrl-Right arrow
7FH	127	Alt-8				75H	117	Ctrl-End
80H	128	Alt-9	2CH	44	Alt-Z	76H	118	Ctrl-PgDn
81H	129	Alt-0	2DH	45	Alt-X	77H	119	Ctrl-Home
82H	130	Alt-Hyphen	2EH	46	Alt-C			
83H	131	Alt-=	2FH	47	Alt-V	84H	132	Ctrl-PgUp
			30H	48	Alt-B			
			31H	49	Alt-N			
			32H	50	Alt-M			

Codes generated by the ROM BIOS for the complete set of characters and special keys are handled differently in different programming languages. BASIC, for example, takes a mixed approach to the special keys. When you use ordinary input statements, BASIC returns the ASCII characters and filters out any special keys. Some of these keys can be acted on with the ON KEY statement, but you can use the BASIC INKEY$ function to get directly to the ROM BIOS coding for keyboard characters and find out immediately what special key was pressed. If the INKEY$ function returns a 1-byte string, it is reporting an ordinary or extended ASCII keyboard character. If INKEY$ returns a 2-byte string, the first byte in the string is the ROM BIOS's main byte and will always be 00H; the second byte is the auxiliary byte and will indicate which special key was pressed.

ROM BIOS Keyboard Control

The ROM BIOS stores keyboard status information in several portions of the ROM BIOS data area in segment 40H in low memory. Your programs can use some of the ROM BIOS status variables to check the keyboard status or to modify ROM BIOS keyboard processing.

The two keyboard status bytes at locations 0040:0017H (shown in Figure 6-6) and 0040:0018H (shown in Figure 6-7) are coded with individually meaningful bits that indicate which shift keys and toggle keys are active. All the standard models of the PC family have these two bytes, although the bits representing the Sys Req, left Alt, and left Ctrl keys are updated only for the keyboards that support these keys.

The status byte at 0040:0017H is particularly useful because it establishes the state of ROM BIOS keystroke processing. Changes to this status byte affect the next keystroke that the ROM BIOS processes.

Bit 7 6 5 4 3 2 1 0	Meaning
X	Insert state: 1 = active; 0 = inactive
. X	Caps Lock: 1 = active; 0 = inactive
. . X	Num Lock: 1 = active; 0 = inactive
. . . X	Scroll Lock: 1 = active; 0 = inactive
. . . . X . . .	1 = Alt pressed
. . . . . X . .	1 = Ctrl pressed
. . . . . . X .	1 = Left Shift pressed
. . . . X	1 = Right Shift pressed

Figure 6-6. *The coding of the keyboard status byte at location 0040:0017H. Bits 4–7 are toggles; their values change each time the key is pressed. Bits 0–3 are set only while the corresponding key is pressed.*

Bit 7 6 5 4 3 2 1 0	Meaning
X	1 = Ins pressed
. X	1 = Caps Lock pressed
. . X	1 = Num Lock pressed
. . . X	1 = Scroll Lock pressed
. . . . X . . .	1 = Hold state active (Ctrl-Num Lock or Pause)
. . . . . X . .	1 = Sys Req key pressed
. . . . . . X .	1 = Left Alt key pressed
. . . . X	1 = Left Ctrl key pressed

Figure 6-7. *The coding of the keyboard status byte at location 0040:0018H. These bits are set only while the corresponding key is pressed.*

The Insert State

The ROM BIOS keeps track of the insert state in bit 7 of byte 0040:0017H. However, every program we know of ignores this bit and keeps its own record of the insert state. This means that you should not rely on this status bit to tell you anything about the current state of Insert key processing.

The Caps Lock State

Some programmers force the Caps Lock state to be active by setting bit 6 of byte 0040:0017H. This can confuse or irritate some program users, so we don't recommend it. However, this trick works reliably and precedent exists for using it. If you do you'll see that the ROM BIOS updates the LED indicator on the 84- and 101/102-key keyboards accordingly. This also occurs when you update the Num Lock or Scroll Lock states.

The Num Lock State

Because the Num Lock key's location on the keyboard makes it susceptible to inadvertent keystrokes, some programmers force the Num Lock toggle (bit 5 of byte 0040:0017H) to a predetermined state at the beginning of a program. For example, clearing the Num Lock status bit before requesting user input from the keypad forces keypad keystrokes to be processed as direction keys instead of numbers, even if the Num Lock key was pressed accidentally. This can be particularly helpful with the 83-key keyboard for the IBM PC and PC/XT because this keyboard has no status LEDs and provides no visual indication of the Num Lock state.

The Keyboard-Hold State

The ROM BIOS establishes the keyboard-hold (pause) state when it detects a Ctrl-Num Lock or Pause keystroke. During keyboard hold, the ROM BIOS executes a do-nothing loop until a printable key is pressed; it doesn't return control of the computer to whatever program is running until this happens. This feature is used to suspend the operation of the computer.

During keyboard hold, all hardware interrupts are handled normally. For example, if a disk drive generates an interrupt (signaling the completion of a disk operation), the disk interrupt handler receives the interrupt and processes it normally. But when the interrupt handler finishes working, it passes control back to whatever was happening when the interrupt took place — which is that endless do-nothing loop inside the ROM BIOS. So, during the keyboard hold, the computer can respond to external interrupts but programs are normally completely suspended. The keyboard BIOS continues to handle interrupts that signal key actions, and when it detects a normal keystroke (for example, the Spacebar or a function key, but not just a shift key), it ends the keyboard hold, finally returning control to whatever program was running.

The keyboard-hold state is of no practical use in programming, except that it provides a standard way for users of our programs to suspend a program's operation.

Be aware that the keyboard-hold state is not "bullet-proof." A program can continue working through the keyboard hold by acting on an external interrupt, such as the clock-tick interrupt. If a program really wanted to avoid being put on hold, it could set up an interrupt handler that would work through the hold state, or it could simply turn the hold state off whenever the hold state was turned on.

The Toggle-Key States

Notice that bits 4 through 7 in the bytes at 0040:0017H and 0040:0018H refer to the same keys. In the first byte, the bits show the current state of the toggle keys; in the second byte, they show whether or not the corresponding toggle key is pressed.

You can read the status of any of these bits to your heart's content, but few, if any, are likely to be useful in your programs. With the partial exception of controlling the Caps Lock state, we don't think it's wise to change any of the shift-state bits (bits 4 through 6 of byte 0040:0017H). And it is potentially very disruptive to change any of the key-is-pressed bits (bits 0 through 3 of byte 0040:0017H or any bits in byte 0040:0018H).

Comments

If you want to gain a deeper understanding of the PC's keyboard operation, study the ROM BIOS program listing in the IBM technical reference manuals for the PC, PC/XT, or PC/AT. If you do this, be careful to avoid making a simple mistake that is common when anyone first studies the ROM BIOS, particularly the interrupts used by the ROM BIOS. The ROM BIOS provides two different interrupts for the keyboard: one that responds to keyboard hardware interrupts (interrupt 09H) and collects keyboard data into the low-memory buffer, and one that responds to a software interrupt requesting keyboard services (interrupt 16H, decimal 22) and passes data from the low-memory buffer to DOS and your programs. It is easy to confuse the operation of these two interrupts, and it is just as easy to further confuse them with the break-key interrupts, 1BH and 23H (decimal 27 and 35). The table in Figure 6-8 lists the keyboard interrupts.

| *Interrupt* | | *Origin of Interrupt* | *Use* |
Hex	*Dec*		
09H	9	Keyboard	Signals keyboard action.
16H	22	User program	Invokes standard BIOS keyboard services. (See Chapter 11.)
1BH	27	ROM BIOS	Occurs when Ctrl-Break is pressed under BIOS control; a routine is invoked if you create it.
23H	35	DOS	If you create it, an interrupt routine is invoked when a break-key combination is pressed under DOS control.

Figure 6-8. *The interrupts related to keyboard action.*

A general theme running throughout this book advises you not to play fast and loose, but to play by the rules. This means, again, to write programs that are general to the IBM PC family rather than tied to the quirks of any one model, and to write programs that use portable means (such as DOS or ROM BIOS services) to manipulate data, instead of direct hardware programming. These rules apply to keyboard programming as much as they do to any other type of programming.

Chapter 7

Clocks, Timers, and Sound Generation

Clocks and timers are the heartbeat of a computer. The computer's essential functions of computation and data transfer take place in step with the pulses generated by electronic clocks. PCs and PS/2s play host to several clocks and timers that you should know about:

- The *system timer* generates "clock-ticks" and other timing pulses at precisely controlled intervals.

- The *sound generator* produces tones through a speaker with a wide range of frequencies and durations.

- The *real-time clock/calendar* keeps track of the date and time and can also serve as an "alarm clock." (This is supported only in the PC/AT and PS/2s.)

To understand how to use the system timer, the sound generator, and the real-time clock, you need to know about the basic clock and timing mechanisms in PCs and PS/2s. That is what we'll outline in this chapter.

Clocks and Timers

PCs and PS/2s have several clocks and timers that run at different rates and perform different functions. Some of them are intrinsic to the circuit design of these computers; their operation is independent of software control. Others are designed to support timing functions in software; the operation of these timers can be controlled by software through ROM BIOS services or by direct hardware programming.

The CPU Clock

Probably the most basic of the timed events in a PC or PS/2 is the step-by-step operation of the computer's CPU, whose speed is determined by the frequency of a special oscillator circuit that generates high-frequency pulses at regular intervals. This frequency is the CPU's *clock speed,* and it determines how quickly the CPU can carry out its functions.

The CPU oscillator keeps time for the CPU in much the same way a metronome keeps time for a musician. At each tick of the CPU clock (that is, at each pulse in the CPU oscillator's signal), the CPU carries out part of one machine instruction. All instructions require two or more clock cycles to complete. For example, the register INC instruction requires two clock cycles to execute; more complicated instructions like CALL and MUL take a longer amount of time.

In IBM PCs and PC/XTs, the CPU's clock speed is 4,772,727 cycles per second, or about 4.77 megahertz. (A *megahertz,* or MHz, is one million cycles per second.) One CPU clock cycle thus lasts about 1/4,772,727 of a second, or about 210 *nanoseconds* (billionths of a second). With this clock frequency, a 2-cycle INC instruction executes in roughly 420 nanoseconds (0.42 *microseconds* or millionths of a second).

The odd clock speed of 4.77 MHz was actually a convenient frequency for the designers of the original PC to use. In fact, the CPU clock frequency is derived from a basic oscillator frequency of 14.31818 MHz, which is commonly used in television circuitry. Dividing the basic frequency by 3 gives the CPU clock frequency. Dividing by 4 gives a clock rate of 3.57955 MHz, which is the frequency of the color burst signal used in color televisions and in the PC's Color Graphics Adapter. Dividing the basic frequency by 12 gives 1.19318 MHz, which is the clock frequency used by the PC's system timers.

In later, faster members of the PC and PS/2 family, the CPU clock speed is higher, so the overall computational speed of these computers is greater. The 80286 and 80386 processors also execute many machine instructions in fewer clock cycles than the 8088 used in the PC and PC/XT. For example, the register PUSH instruction in the 8088 executes in 15 clock cycles; in the 80286 the same instruction takes 3 cycles; and in the 80386 only 2 cycles. The combination of a higher CPU clock rate and faster machine instructions means that the 80286- and 80386-based members of the PC family execute programs significantly faster than do the 8088- and 8086-based machines. (See Figure 7-1.)

Model	CPU	CPU Clock Frequency	Approximate Speed Relative to 4.77 MHz IBM PC
PC	8088	4.77 MHz	1.0
PC/XT	8088	4.77 MHz	1.0
PC/AT	80286	6 MHz	3.4
		8 MHz	4.8
PS/2 models 25 and 30	8086	8 MHz	2.5
PS/2 models 50 and 60	80286	10 MHz	6.1
PS/2 Model 80	80386	16 MHz	12.5
		20 MHz	15.5

Figure 7-1. *CPU clock frequencies and relative computation speeds for PCs and PS/2s.*

System Timers

Apart from the operation of the CPU, other basic hardware and software functions occur at regular intervals based on a preset clock frequency. For example, the dynamic RAM chips that constitute the computer's main memory must be accessed at regular intervals to refresh the information represented in them. Also, ROM BIOS and operating system functions such as keeping track of the time of day require the computer to generate a "clock-tick" signal at a predetermined rate. All PCs and PS/2s have circuitry that generates the necessary timing signals.

In the PC and PC/XT, an Intel 8253-5 programmable timer/counter chip produces the RAM refresh and timer-tick signals. In the PC/AT, an Intel 8254-2 is used in the same way. The PS/2 models 25 and 30 use an 8253-5 for the timer tick, but RAM refresh timing is a function of a custom integrated circuit. In the PS/2 models 50, 60, and 80, all timing functions are implemented in custom silicon. Despite these hardware variations, the timer programming interface is the same in all PCs and PS/2s.

In the PC/XT/AT family, the timer chip has three output channels, each with a particular dedicated function:

- *Channel 0* is the system clock-tick timer. When the computer is cold booted, the ROM BIOS programs the timer to oscillate with a frequency of about 18.2 ticks per second. This signal is tied to the computer's interrupt controller in such a way that interrupt 08H is generated each time the clock ticks.

- *Channel 1* is always dedicated to producing the RAM refresh timing signal; it's not intended for use in software applications.

- *Channel 2* is used to control the computer's speaker: The frequency of the timer's channel 2 signal determines the frequency of the sound emitted by the loudspeaker. (We'll come back to this later.)

PS/2 models 50, 60, and 80 also have a timer channel 3. The signal produced on channel 3 is tied to the computer's nonmaskable interrupt (interrupt 02H), and can be used by an operating system as a "watchdog" to ensure that some other critical function, such as servicing a clock-tick interrupt, does not crash the computer by taking too long to execute.

Using the System Timer Tick

In all PCs and PS/2s, the input oscillator to the system timer circuit has a frequency of 1.19318 MHz. On each cycle, the timer chip decrements the values in a set of internal 16-bit counters, one for each of the timer's output channels. When the value in a counter reaches 0, the chip generates a single output pulse on the corresponding channel, resets the count, and starts counting down again.

When the ROM BIOS initializes the system timer, it stores a countdown value of 0 in the count register for channel 0. This means that the timer chip decrements the counter 2^{16} times between output pulses on channel 0, so output pulses occur 1,193,180/65,536, or about 18.2 times per second. The output from timer channel 0 is used as the signal on interrupt request level 0 (IRQ0), so interrupt 08H occurs whenever channel 0 of the system timer counts down to 0 — that is, 18.2 times per second.

The ROM BIOS contains an interrupt handler for interrupt 08H that increments a running count of clock ticks at 0040:006CH in the BIOS data area. This same interrupt handler also decrements the byte at 0040:0040H; if the value in the byte reaches 0, the interrupt handler issues a command to the diskette drive controller to turn off the diskette drive motor if it's on.

The ROM BIOS interrupt 08H handler also issues software interrupt 1CH, which is intended for use in programs that want to be notified when a system timer tick occurs. A program can detect when each timer tick occurs simply by pointing the interrupt 1CH vector at 0000:0070H to its own interrupt handler. If you use an interrupt 1CH handler in a program, however, be aware that the ROM BIOS interrupt 08H handler does not allow subsequent clock-tick interrupts on IRQ0 to occur until your interrupt 1CH handler returns. If you install an interrupt 1CH handler, be certain that it doesn't keep IRQ0 disabled for too long or the system may crash.

The system timer tick and its interrupt are useful in programs that must perform a simple task at a regular interval regardless of what else is going on in the computer. The timer-tick interrupt has the highest priority of any of the hardware interrupts (except the nonmaskable interrupt), so the code in the corresponding interrupt 08H and 1CH handlers takes precedence over all other system software.

For this reason, the timer tick is used primarily in operating system software and in memory-resident "pop-up" programs like SideKick or the Norton Guides. Such programs have their own timer-tick interrupt handlers that check whether it is time to pop up on the screen. These programs generally rely on the system timer tick to occur at the default frequency of 18.2 ticks per second.

.

Because timer-tick function is so essential to the proper operation of the computer, you should change the output frequency of system timer channel 0 only if you are careful to preserve the functionality of the ROM BIOS interrupt 08H handler. For example, BASIC uses the timer tick to measure the duration of tones created with the PLAY or SOUND command. However, because the standard rate of 18.2 ticks per second is not fast enough to provide the precision that some kinds of music demand, BASIC reprograms the timer to tick four times faster, which causes interrupt 08H to occur 72.8 times per second instead of 18.2 times per second. When BASIC counts against the quadruple rate, it is able to more accurately reproduce the proper tempo of a piece of music.

BASIC can do this because it has a special interrupt 08H handler that calls the default interrupt 08H handler on every fourth timer tick. This ensures that the usual interrupt 08H functions still occur 18.2 times per second. If you reprogram system timer channel 0 to a nonstandard rate, your program should use the same technique of preserving interrupt 08H functionality.

Programming system timer channel 2, the sound frequency generator, is not as demanding, because no ROM BIOS or operating system functions rely on it. Before we cover the programming details, however, we'll describe some of the basic mechanics of creating sounds with a computer.

The Physics of Sound

Sounds are simply regular pulses or vibrations in air pressure. Sound is produced when air particles are set into motion by a vibrating source. When the vibrating source pushes out, it compresses the air particles around it. As it pulls in, the pressure release pulls the particles apart. A vibration composed of both the pressing and the pulling actions causes air particles to bump into each other. This motion begins a chain reaction that carries the vibration through the air away from the original source. Such a motion is called a *sound wave*.

The speaker in the IBM PCs and PS/2s is made to vibrate by the electrical impulses sent to it by the computer. Because computers normally deal with binary numbers, the voltages they produce are either high or low. Every transition from one voltage state to another either pushes the speaker cone out or relaxes it. A sound is produced when the voltage to the speaker goes from low to high to low again, causing the speaker to move out and then in. This single vibration, consisting of a pulse out and a pulse in, is called a *cycle*. Through the speaker, a single cycle of sound is heard as a click. A continuous sound is produced when a continuous stream of pulses is sent to the speaker. As the pulse rate increases, so does the pitch of the tone. For example, if you pulse the speaker in and out 261.63 times a second (that is, at a rate of 261.63 *hertz*, or cycles per second), you hear the musical note known as middle C. Figure 7-2 lists the frequencies required to generate other musical notes.

Note	Frequency	Note	Frequency	Note	Frequency	Note	Frequency
C_0	16.35	C_2	65.41	C_4	261.63	C_6	1046.50
$C_{\#0}$	17.32	$C_{\#2}$	69.30	$C_{\#4}$	277.18	$C_{\#6}$	1108.73
D_0	18.35	D_2	73.42	D_4	293.66	D_6	1174.66
$D_{\#0}$	19.45	$D_{\#2}$	77.78	$D_{\#4}$	311.13	$D_{\#6}$	1244.51
E_0	20.60	E_2	82.41	E_4	329.63	E_6	1328.51
F_0	21.83	F_2	87.31	F_4	349.23	F_6	1396.91
$F_{\#0}$	23.12	$F_{\#2}$	92.50	$F_{\#4}$	369.99	$F_{\#6}$	1479.98
G_0	24.50	G_2	98.00	G_4	392.00	G_6	1567.98
$G_{\#0}$	25.96	$G_{\#2}$	103.83	$G_{\#4}$	415.30	$G_{\#6}$	1661.22
A_0	27.50	A_2	110.00	A_4	440.00	A_6	1760.00
$A_{\#0}$	29.14	$A_{\#2}$	116.54	$A_{\#4}$	466.16	$A_{\#6}$	1864.66
B_0	30.87	B_2	123.47	B_4	493.88	B_6	1975.53
C_1	32.70	C_3	130.81	C_5	523.25	C_7	2093.00
$C_{\#1}$	34.65	$C_{\#3}$	138.59	$C_{\#5}$	554.37	$C_{\#7}$	2217.46
D_1	36.71	D_3	146.83	D_5	587.33	D_7	2349.32
$D_{\#1}$	38.89	$D_{\#3}$	155.56	$D_{\#5}$	622.25	$D_{\#7}$	2489.02
E_1	41.20	E_3	164.81	E_5	659.26	E_7	2637.02
F_1	43.65	F_3	174.61	F_5	698.46	F_7	2793.83
$F_{\#1}$	46.25	$F_{\#3}$	185.00	$F_{\#5}$	739.99	$F_{\#7}$	2959.96
G_1	49.00	G_3	196.00	G_5	783.99	G_7	3135.96
$G_{\#1}$	51.91	$G_{\#3}$	207.65	$G_{\#5}$	830.61	$G_{\#7}$	3322.44
A_1	55.00	A_3	220.00	A_5	880.00	A_7	3520.00
$A_{\#1}$	58.27	$A_{\#3}$	233.08	$A_{\#5}$	932.33	$A_{\#7}$	3729.31
B_1	61.74	B_3	246.94	B_5	987.77	B_7	3951.07
						C_8	4186.01

Note: Equal Tempered Chromatic Scale; $A_4 = 440$
   American Standard pitch — adopted by the American Standards Association in 1936

Figure 7-2. *Eight octaves of musical note frequencies.*

The average person can hear sounds ranging from roughly 20 to 20,000 hertz. The IBM PC can generate sounds through its speaker at frequencies that could theoretically range from about 18 to more than a million hertz, far beyond the range of human hearing. To give this frequency range some perspective, compare it to an average human voice, which has a range of only 125 to 1000 hertz.

The speaker that comes with the standard IBM personal computers has no volume control and is not really intended for accurate sound reproduction. As a result, different frequencies will produce different effects; some may sound louder than others and some may have a more accurate pitch. This variation is a by-product of the speaker design and is not something you can control.

How the Computer Produces Sound

You can generate sounds through the speaker in two ways, using one or both of two different sound sources. One method is to write a program that turns the speaker on and off by manipulating two speaker bits in the I/O port that provides access to the speaker-control circuitry. When you use this method, your program controls the timing of the pulse and the resulting sound frequency. The other method is to use channel 2 of the system timer chip to pulse the speaker at a precise frequency. Using the timer chip is a more popular method for two reasons: Because speaker pulses are controlled by the timer chip instead of a program, the CPU can devote its time to the other demands of the computer system; and the timer chip is not dependent on the working speed of the CPU, which varies according to which PC or PS/2 model you use. The program method and timer method can be used together or separately to create many simple and complex sounds.

Timer-Chip Sound Control

The programmable timer chip is the heart of the standard PC models' sound-making abilities. As we have seen, channel 2 of the timer chip is dedicated to sound generation. To create sounds, you must program channel 2 properly and then use the pulses from channel 2 to drive the speaker.

The timer can be programmed to produce pulses at whatever frequency you want, but because it does not keep track of how long the sound continues, the sound will continue forever unless it is turned off. Therefore, your programs must choose when to end a sound through some sort of timing instruction.

Programming the timer chip

To program timer channel 2, load the timer chip with an appropriate countdown value for the channel 2 counter. (The timer chip holds this value in an internal register so that it can reset the counter each time it reaches zero.) The countdown value takes effect immediately after you load it into the timer chip. The timer chip decrements the counter with each cycle of its 1.19318 MHz clock until the counter reaches zero, and then it sends an output pulse on channel 2 to the sound generator circuitry and starts counting down again.

In effect, the timer "divides" the countdown value into the clock frequency to produce an output frequency. The result is that the timer sends out a series of pulses that produce a sound of a certain frequency when you turn on the speaker.

The controlling count and the resulting frequency have a reciprocal relationship, as shown by these formulas:

Count = 1,193,180 ÷ Frequency
Frequency = 1,193,180 ÷ Count

You can see that a low-frequency (low-pitched) sound is produced by a high count and that a high-frequency (high-pitched) sound is produced by a low count. A count of 100 would produce a high pitch of roughly 11,931 cycles per second, and a count of 10,000 would produce a low pitch of about 119 cycles per second.

You can produce just about any frequency, within the limitations of 16-bit arithmetic. The lowest frequency is 18.2 hertz with a divisor of 65,535 (FFFFH), and the highest is 1.193 megahertz with a divisor of 1. BASIC holds this to a practical range of 37 through 32,767 hertz. The following program demonstrates that the actual frequency range of the internal speaker is even less than BASIC provides.

Once you calculate the count that you need for the frequency you want, you send it to the timer channel 2 registers. This is done with three port outputs. The first port output notifies the timer that the count is coming by sending the value B6H (decimal 182) to port 43H (decimal 67). The next two outputs send the low- and high-order bytes of the count, a 16-bit unsigned word, to port 42H (decimal 66) — the low-order byte followed by the high-order byte. The BASIC program on the following page illustrates the process.

```
10 COUNT = 1193280! / 3000      ' 3000 is the desired frequency
20 LO.COUNT = COUNT MOD 256     ' calculate low-order byte value
30 HI.COUNT = COUNT / 256       ' calculate high-order byte value
40 OUT &H43, &HB6               ' get timer ready
50 OUT &H42, LO.COUNT           ' load low-order byte
60 OUT &H42, HI.COUNT           ' load high-order byte
```

Activating the speaker

After you have programmed the timer, you still need to activate the speaker circuitry in order to use the signal that the timer is generating. As with most other parts of the PC and PS/2, the speaker is manipulated by sending certain values to a specific port, a process illustrated in Figure 7-3. The speaker is controlled by changing the values of bits 0 and 1 at I/O port 61H (decimal 97). Only 2 of the port's 8 bits are used by the speaker: the low-order bits numbered 0 and 1. The other 6 bits are used for other purposes, so it is important that you don't disturb them while working with the speaker.

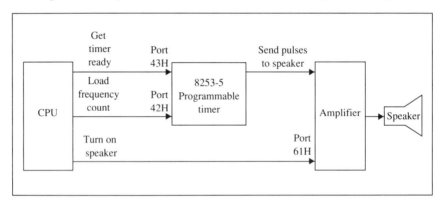

Figure 7-3. *How sound frequencies are generated through the system timer and speaker.*

The lowest bit, bit 0, controls transmission of the timer chip's output signal to the speaker. The second bit, bit 1, controls the pulsing of the speaker. Both bits must be set to make the speaker respond to the timer chip's signal. You can turn them on without disturbing the nonspeaker bits with an operation like this:

```
70 OLD.PORT = INP (&H61)             ' read the value at port 61H
80 NEW.PORT = (OLD.PORT OR &H03)     ' set bits 0 and 1
90 OUT &H61, NEW.PORT                ' turn speaker on
```

Direct Speaker Control

The timer controls the speaker by sending periodic signals that pulse the speaker in and out. You can do the same thing with a program that sends in or out signals directly to the speaker. Do this by setting bit 0 of port 61H (decimal 97) to 0 to turn the speaker off and then alternately setting bit 1 on and off to pulse the speaker. When you use this method, the speed of the program determines the frequency of the sound; the faster the program executes, the higher the pitch. The following BASIC program is an example of this method:

```
10 X = INP (&H61) AND &HFC    ' read port value, turn off bits 1 and 0
20 OUT &H61, X                ' pull speaker in
30 OUT &H61, X OR 2           ' push speaker out
40 GOTO 20
```

The actions in lines 20 and 30 pulse the speaker in and out. Each one is a half-cycle, and the two together produce one complete sound cycle.

This example runs as fast as BASIC can process it, producing as high a note as possible. If you needed more range in your application, you could use a faster language and insert deliberate delays equal to half the frequency cycle time between each complete cycle (half the cycle time, because each ON or OFF operation is a half-cycle). No matter what language you use, you must include a duration count to end the sound. To produce different sounds at a particular frequency, such as clicking or buzzing sounds, just vary the delays between pulses.

Despite all these wonderful possibilities, generating sounds through the speaker by direct program action is not a good way to make sounds. It has three big disadvantages compared to the use of the timer:

- A program requires the constant attention of the CPU, so the computer has a hard time getting any other work done.

- The frequency is at the mercy of the speed of the computer; that is, the same program would make a lower or higher sound on a slower or faster model.

- The clock-tick interrupts interfere with the smoothness of the sound, making a warble. The only way to avoid this is to suspend the clock tick by disabling the interrupts — and that disrupts the computer's sense of time.

As far as we know, there is only one advantage to making sounds using the direct method: With the proper control over the program delays, the direct method lets you make a low-fidelity polyphonic sound. Be forewarned, though, that this requires some very clever and tedious programming and, all in all, may not be worth the trouble.

Speaker Volume and Sound Quality

The computer's internal speaker has no volume control of any kind and, like all speakers, varies in how well it responds to different frequencies; some frequencies may sound louder than others. In the case of a crude speaker like that found in most PCs and PS/2s, the loudness of the sound varies widely with the frequency. You can use the following program to test this — it may help you choose the best sound pitch for your purpose:

```
10 PLAY "MF"                          ' plays each sound separately
20 FREQUENCY = 37
30 WHILE FREQUENCY < 32000            ' use all frequencies to
                                        32000 Hz
40   PRINT USING "##,###"; FREQUENCY  ' display frequency
50   SOUND FREQUENCY, 5               ' produce sound with
                                        duration of 5
60   FREQUENCY = FREQUENCY * 1.1      ' increment frequency by 1/10
70 WEND
```

Be aware that the speakers in the various PC and PS/2 models may not sound alike, partly because the materials of each system housing resonate differently as speaker enclosures. Try the following samples on two different models and be prepared for these variations in sound:

```
100 'sound samples
110 '
120 'warble (two rapidly alternating tones)
130 FOR N% = 0 TO 5
140   SOUND 440, .7
150   SOUND 466.16, .5
160 NEXT
170 WHILE(INKEY$="") : WEND      ' wait for a keystroke
180 '
190 'two tones played quickly
200 SOUND 900, .1
210 SOUND 760, 1
220 WHILE(INKEY$="") : WEND
```

```
230 '
240 'random noise
250 X = INP(&H61) AND &HFC
260 I=20                        ' changing I changes the noise
270 FOR N% = 0 TO 500
280 IF (RND * 100 < I) THEN OUT &H61,X OR 2 : OUT &H61,X
290 NEXT
```

The Real-Time Clock

The PC/AT and the PS/2s all have a real-time clock that keeps track of the current date and time. In the PC/AT, the real-time clock is part of the Motorola MC146818 chip that supports the PC/AT's nonvolatile CMOS RAM. In the PS/2s, the real-time clock is in custom silicon. In all these machines, the real-time clock runs off a battery so that the time and date are maintained even while the computer is turned off.

Using the Date and Time

When you boot a PC/AT or PS/2, the ROM BIOS start-up routines read the time of day from the real-time clock and convert it into the corresponding number of timer ticks. This value is used to initialize the 4-byte count stored at 0040:006CH in the ROM BIOS data area. All versions of DOS use this count value to determine the current time of day. Starting in version 3.0, DOS also obtains the current date from the real-time clock and initializes its own internal record of the date at boot-up time.

To work with the current date and time in a program, we recommend that you use the DOS date and time services (Chapter 16) to get and set the current values. You could also use ROM BIOS services to access the real-time clock (Chapter 10). However, if you call the ROM BIOS to change the date or time, DOS may not be aware of the change and may assume an incorrect time or date.

Setting the Alarm

The real-time clock's alarm feature generates an interrupt at a specific time. To take advantage of this feature, you must create an interrupt handler that performs an action when the alarm interrupt occurs. You can even make this action independent of other programs by leaving the interrupt handler resident in memory with a DOS Terminate-and-Stay-Resident service. (See Chapters 16 and 17.)

The ROM BIOS provides a set of services through interrupt 1AH that give you access to the real-time clock's alarm feature. See Chapter 12 for more details.

Chapter 8

ROM BIOS Basics

One secret of successful programming for the PC family lies in the effective use of the software that is built right into the machine: the ROM BIOS services. Conceptually, the ROM BIOS services are sandwiched between the hardware and the high-level languages (including the operating system). They work directly with the computer's hardware and peripheral devices, performing some of the system's most fundamental tasks, such as reading and writing individual bytes of data to the display screen or disk. DOS services and programming-language services are often built from these basic functions and enhanced to make a particular process more efficient. You can enhance your programs in the same way by plugging them directly into the ROM BIOS, thereby gaining access to an extremely powerful set of tools and using your computers in the way that IBM intended them to be used.

That last point is worth emphasizing. IBM has gone to considerable lengths to create a clean and well-defined method for directing the operation of the computer through the ROM BIOS services. As each new PC model is designed, IBM (and any other computer maker who is faithfully extending the PC family) makes sure its ROM BIOS services are thoroughly compatible with those of the other members of the family. As long as you control your computers through the ROM BIOS, whether directly or indirectly, you are safe from any compatibility problems. If you bypass the ROM BIOS and program directly to the hardware, you are not only asking for trouble, but you are also severely limiting the range and viability of your programs.

That's not to say that you should always use ROM BIOS services when they're available. The input/output functions provided in DOS and in high-level programming languages often provide the same services as the ROM BIOS, but in a form that is easier to use within your programs. However, when a program needs more direct access to the computer's input/output devices than DOS or your programming language can provide, the ROM BIOS services are usually the answer.

The next five chapters discuss the ROM BIOS service routines. Fortunately, the routines fall naturally into groups derived from the hardware devices they support, so the video services, disk services, and keyboard services can all be reviewed separately. But before you take a closer look at the individual services, you need to find out how to incorporate them into your programs. This chapter sets the stage by explaining what goes into writing an *interface routine,* the bridge between programming languages and the ROM BIOS services. First, a word on how the ROM BIOS operates.

The ROM BIOS Philosophy

All ROM BIOS services are invoked by interrupts. Each interrupt instruction selects a particular entry in the interrupt vector table in low memory. The addresses of all ROM BIOS service routines are stored in this table. This design makes it possible for any program to request a service without knowing the specific memory location of the ROM BIOS service routine. It also allows the services to be moved around, expanded, or adapted without affecting the programs that use the services. Although IBM has tried to maintain the absolute memory location of some parts of the ROM BIOS, it would be foolish to use these addresses because they may change in the future. The standard, preferred, and most reliable way to invoke a ROM BIOS service is to use its interrupt rather than its absolute address.

The ROM BIOS services could be supervised by one master interrupt, but instead they are divided into subject categories, each with its own controlling interrupt. This design lets each interrupt handler be easily replaced. For example, if a hardware manufacturer created a radically different video display that operated under a completely new ROM BIOS program, the manufacturer could provide the new ROM BIOS program along with the hardware. The new ROM BIOS program might be stored in RAM, and it would replace the one part of IBM's ROM BIOS that was used with the old hardware. By making the ROM BIOS modular, IBM has made it easier to improve and extend the capabilities of its computers.

The ROM BIOS Service Interrupts

The twelve ROM BIOS interrupts fall into five groups (Figure 8-1):

- Six interrupts serve specific peripheral devices.

- Two interrupts report on the computer's equipment.

- One interrupt works with the time/date clock.

- One interrupt performs the print-screen operation.

- Two interrupts place the computer into another state altogether, activating ROM BASIC and the system start-up routine.

As you'll see, most of the interrupts are tied to a group of subservices that actually do the work. For example, the video service interrupt 10H (decimal 16) has 25 subservices that do everything from setting the video mode to changing the size of the cursor. You call a subservice by invoking its governing interrupt and specifying the subservice number in register AH. This process is explained in the example at the end of this chapter.

Interrupt		
Hex	*Dec*	*Use*

Peripheral Devices Services

10H	16	Video-display services (see Chapter 9)
13H	19	Diskette services (see Chapter 10)
14H	20	Communications services (see Chapter 12)
15H	21	System services (see Chapter 12)
16H	22	Standard keyboard services (see Chapter 11)
17H	23	Printer services (see Chapter 12)

Equipment Status Services

11H	17	Equipment-list service (see Chapter 12)
12H	18	Memory-size service (see Chapter 12)

Time/Date Service

1AH	26	Time and date services (see Chapter 12)

Print-Screen Service

5H	5	Print-screen service (see Chapter 12)

Special Services

18H	24	Activate ROM BASIC (see Chapter 12)
19H	25	Activate bootstrap start-up routine (see Chapter 12)

Figure 8-1. *The 12 ROM BIOS services.*

ROM BIOS Service Operating Characteristics

The ROM BIOS services use some common calling conventions that provide consistency in the use of registers, flags, the stack, and memory. We'll outline the characteristics of these operating conventions, beginning with the segment registers.

The *code segment register* (CS) is automatically reserved, loaded, and restored as part of the interrupt process. Consequently, you don't have to worry about your program's CS. The DS and ES registers are preserved by the ROM BIOS service routines, except in the few cases where they are explicitly used. The *stack segment register* (SS) is left unchanged, and the ROM BIOS services depend on you to provide a working stack. (Everything depends on a working stack!)

The stack requirements of the ROM BIOS services are not spelled out and can vary considerably, particularly because some services invoke other services. Generally, however, most programs ought to be working with a much larger stack than the ROM BIOS services need.

The ROM BIOS varies in its usage of the other 8086 registers. The *instruction pointer* (IP) is preserved by the same mechanism that preserves the code segment. In effect, the *stack pointer* (SP) is preserved because all the ROM BIOS services leave the stack clean, popping off anything that was pushed on during the service-routine execution.

As usual, the general-purpose registers, AX through DX, are considered fair game. The standard rule is not to expect any contents of these registers to be maintained when you pass control to another routine, and that applies to the ROM BIOS services as well. If you closely inspect the coding of the services in the IBM technical reference manuals, you will find that one or more registers are left undisturbed in one service or another, but you would be foolish to try to take advantage of this. As a general rule, when a simple result is returned from a subroutine, it is left in the AX register; this applies to both the ROM BIOS and to all programming languages. We'll see how often this really happens when we cover the ROM BIOS services in detail.

The *index registers* (SI and DI) can be changed, exactly like the AX through DX registers. The *stack frame register* (BP) can also be changed by a few ROM BIOS service routines.

The various flags in the flag register are routinely changed as a by-product of the instruction steps in the ROM BIOS routines. You should not expect any of them to be preserved. In a few instances, the *carry flag* (CF) or the *zero flag* (ZF) is used to signal the overall success or failure of a requested operation.

These details are important but rather tedious, and there is little reason for you to pay much attention to them. If your programs follow the general interface rules given in the next section, and if they follow the specific requirements of your programming language (covered in Chapters 19 and 20), you may not need to be concerned with them at all.

❏ NOTE: *If you set out to use the ROM BIOS services in your programs, you'll naturally be concerned about the possible conflicts between the services and the operating conventions that your language follows. Put your mind at ease. You will find that you do not have to take any extraordinary precautions to protect your programming language from the ROM BIOS, or vice versa.*

Creating an Assembly-Language Interface

In order to make direct use of the ROM BIOS services from your programs, you generally need to create an assembly-language interface routine to link the programming language to the ROM BIOS. When we say "interface routine," we are referring to the conventional program-development subroutines — subroutines that are assembled into object modules (.OBJ files) and then linked into working programs (.EXE or .COM files in DOS). For more on this subject, see Chapter 19.

Working with assembly language can seem a fearsome task if you are not already comfortable with it. While there are plenty of good reasons to be intimidated by assembly language — after all, it is the most difficult and demanding kind of programming — it's really not that difficult to create an assembly-language interface routine.

ROM BIOS Interrupt Conflicts

In the hardware specification for the 8086 family of microprocessors, Intel reserved interrupt numbers 00H through 1FH for use by the microprocessor itself. (See Figure 8-2.) Unfortunately, IBM had appropriated several of these reserved interrupt numbers for its own use in the design of the IBM PC. This wasn't a problem with the PC and PC/XT, which used the Intel 8088, because the 8088 predefined only interrupts 00H through 04H.

When the PC/AT appeared, however, IBM's use of Intel's reserved interrupt numbers led to a conflict. The reason: The AT's 80286 chip predefines some of the same interrupt numbers that IBM's ROM BIOS uses. The conflict appears when you use the 80286 BOUND instruction to validate an array index, because the 80286 signals an out-of-bounds array index by executing interrupt 05H — which IBM had previously assigned to the ROM BIOS print-screen function. If you aren't careful, a program that executes the BOUND instruction can unexpectedly print the screen.

To resolve the conflict, you must install an interrupt 05H handler that inspects the code that caused the interrupt: This handler can determine whether the interrupt was executed in software or by the CPU. You can also avoid this problem by using a protected-mode operating system like OS/2, which bypasses the ROM BIOS. If you use DOS, however, be aware that a programming error can occasionally lead to unexpected execution of a ROM BIOS routine.

To create your own interfaces, you will need to have an assembler that is compatible with the DOS standards for object files. All the examples we give here are for the Microsoft Macro Assembler.

❑ NOTE: *Interpreted BASIC can work with machine-language subroutines put directly into memory. Preparing the sort of assembler subroutine that will work with BASIC can be done as easily with DEBUG's A (assemble) command as it can with an ordinary assembler. See Chapter 20 for more on this subject.*

The Basic Form of an Interface Routine

An interface routine's form varies with its intended use. An assembly-language interface is a handshaker between your programming language

Interrupt	CPU	Function
00H	8088,8086,80286,80386	Divide error
01H	8088,8086,80286,80386	Single-step
02H	8088,8086,80286,80386	NMI (nonmaskable interrupt)
03H	8088,8086,80286,80386	Breakpoint (INT 3)
04H	8088,8086,80286,80386	Overflow (INTO)
05H	80286,80386	BOUND out of range
06H	80286,80386	Invalid opcode
07H	80286,80386	Coprocessor not available
08H	80286,80386	Double exception (double fault)
09H	80286,80386	Coprocessor segment overrun
0AH	80386	Invalid task-state segment
0BH	80386	Segment not present
0CH	80386	Stack fault
0DH	80286,80386	General protection exception
0EH	80386	Page fault
10H	80286,80386	Coprocessor error

Figure 8-2. *Predefined hardware interrupts in Intel microprocessors.*

and a ROM BIOS service, so it has to be tailored to meet the needs of both ends. *It matters* which programming language is being used; *it matters* which ROM BIOS service is being invoked; and *it matters* whether any data is being passed in one direction or the other. However, the general outline of an assembly-language interface is basically the same, no matter what you are doing.

One of the best ways to understand how an assembly-language interface is coded is to view it as five nested parts, which are outlined here:

Level 1: General assembler overhead
  Level 2: Subroutine assembler overhead
    Level 3: Entry code
      Level 4: Get parameter data from caller
        Level 5: Invoke ROM BIOS service
      Level 4: Pass back results to caller
    Level 3: Exit code
  Level 2: Finish subroutine assembler overhead
Level 1: Finish general assembler overhead

In this outline, Levels 1 and 2 tell the assembler what's going on, but don't produce any working instructions. Levels 3 through 5 produce the actual machine-language instructions.

We'll examine each of these levels to show you the rules and explain what's going on. Don't forget that the specific requirements of an interface routine change for different circumstances. We'll point out the few design elements that are universal to all routines.

Here is a simple ROM BIOS interface routine. It's designed to be called from a C program, but the elements of the interface design are the same whether you use this routine as is or adapt it to another programming language.

```
_TEXT           SEGMENT     byte public 'CODE'
                ASSUME      cs:_TEXT

                PUBLIC      _GetMemSize
_GetMemSize     PROC        near

                push        bp
                mov         bp,sp

                int         12H
```

(continued)

162

```
                    pop         bp
                    ret

_GetMemSize         ENDP

_TEXT               ENDS

                    END
```

In the next few pages we'll examine the construction of this routine.

Level 1: General assembler overhead

Here is an outline of a typical Level-1 section of an interface routine, with the lines numbered for reference:

```
1-1  _TEXT          SEGMENT     byte public 'CODE'
1-2                 ASSUME      cs:_TEXT
```

(Levels 2 through 5 appear here)

```
1-3  _TEXT          ENDS
1-4                 END
```

Line 1-1 is a SEGMENT directive that declares the name of a logical grouping of executable machine instructions and informs the assembler (and any person who reads the source code) that what follows consists of executable code. Line 1-2, the ASSUME directive, tells the assembler to associate the CS register with any address labels in the _TEXT segment. This makes sense because the CS register is used by the 8086 to address executable code.

Line 1-3 ends the segment started in line 1-1, and line 1-4 marks the end of the source code for this routine.

The names _TEXT and CODE conform to the conventions used by virtually all C language compilers for PCs and PS/2s, as do the BYTE and PUBLIC attributes. Alternative names and attributes are available to advanced programmers, but for now we'll stick with the simplest.

Level 2: Subroutine assembler overhead

Next, let's look at an outline of a typical Level 2, the assembler overhead for a subroutine (called a *procedure* in assembler parlance). The sample on the following page shows some typical Level-2 coding.

```
2-1                    PUBLIC    _GetMemSize
2-2 _GetMemSize        PROC      near
```

(Levels 3 through 5 appear here)

```
2-3 _GetMemSize        ENDP
```

Line 2-1 instructs the assembler to make the name of the procedure, _GetMemSize, public information, which means that the link program can then connect it to other routines that refer to it by name.

Lines 2-2 and 2-3 bracket the procedure, named _GetMemSize. PROC and ENDP are mandatory and surround any procedure, with PROC defining the beginning of the procedure and ENDP signaling the end of it. Again, the near attribute on the PROC statement follows the conventions established for linking assembly-language routines to C programs. In more advanced C programs and in routines linked with programs written in languages like FORTRAN and BASIC, you must sometimes use a different attribute, far. (More about this in Chapter 20.)

Level 3: Entry and exit code

Levels 3, 4, and 5 contain actual executable instructions. In Level 3, the assembly-language routine handles the housekeeping overhead required if a subroutine is to work cooperatively with the calling program. The key to this cooperation is the stack.

When the calling program transfers control to the subroutine, it does so by means of a CALL instruction. (In this example, the instruction would be CALL _GetMemSize.) When this instruction executes, the 8086 pushes a return address—the address of the instruction following the CALL—onto the stack. Later, the assembly-language routine can return control to the calling program by executing a RET instruction, which pops the return address off the stack and transfers control to the instruction at that address.

If any parameters are to be passed to the assembly-language routine, the calling program pushes them onto the stack before it executes the CALL instruction. Thus, when the routine gets control, the value on top of the stack is the return address, and any parameters are found on the stack below the return address. If you keep in mind that the stack grows from higher to lower addresses and that each value on the stack is 2 bytes in size, you end up with the situation depicted in Figure 8-3.

To access the parameters on the stack, most compilers and assembly-language programmers copy the value in SP into register BP. In this way the values on the stack can be accessed even within a routine that changes SP by pushing parameters or calling a subroutine. The conventional way of doing this is shown by the code on the next page.

```
3-1       push      bp        ; preserve the current contents of BP
3-2       mov       bp,sp     ; copy SP to BP
```

(Levels 4 and 5 appear here)

```
3-3       pop       bp
3-4       ret
```

After lines 3-1 and 3-2 have executed, the stack is addressable as in Figure 8-4. (In a moment, we'll show how useful this is.) When it's time to return control to the calling program, the routine restores the caller's BP register value (line 3-3) and then executes a RET instruction (line 3-4).

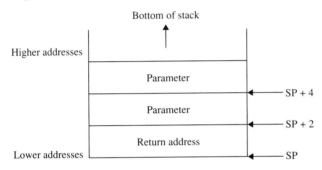

Figure 8-3. *The stack at the time a subroutine is called.*

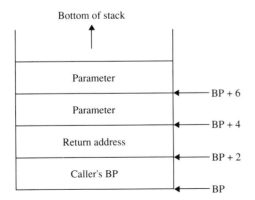

Figure 8-4. *The stack after register BP is initialized.*

If you think about it, you'll realize that things could be more complicated. For example, a calling program might use either a near or a far CALL instruction to transfer control to a subroutine. If your program uses far subroutine calls by convention (instead of the near calls used by default in C), the PROC directive (Line 2-2) would require the far attribute instead of near. This would instruct the assembler to generate a far RET instruction instead of a near RET.

Furthermore, with a far calling convention, the return address on the stack would be 4 bytes in size instead of 2 bytes, so the first parameter would be at address [BP + 6] instead of [BP + 4] as shown in Figure 8-4. In this book, however, we'll stick to the most straightforward case: near PROCs and 2-byte return addresses.

Level 4: Get parameter data from caller

Level 4 deals with the parameters by passing them from the caller to the ROM BIOS, and with the results by passing them from the ROM BIOS to the caller. (Note, however, that the sample program contains no parameters from the caller.) The caller's parameters are on the stack, either in the form of data or addresses. (See Chapter 20 for help with this.) The registers, mostly AX through DX, are used for ROM BIOS input and output. The trick here — and it can be tricky — is to use the correct stack offsets to find the parameters. We'll sneak up on this problem in stages.

First, you get to the parameters on the stack by addressing relative to the address stored in BP in lines 3-1 and 3-2. (Refer to Figure 8-2 to determine how items on the stack relate to the value in BP.) When more than one parameter is present on the stack, you must decide which parameter is which. Most languages push their parameters onto the stack in the order they are written. This means that the *last* parameter is the one closest to the top of the stack, at [BP + 4]. However, C uses the reverse order, so that the parameter at [BP + 4] is the *first* one written in the calling program.

Parameters normally take up 2 or 4 bytes on the stack, although 2 bytes is more common. If any of these parameters were 4 bytes in size, you would need to adjust the subsequent references accordingly.

If *data* were placed on the stack, then you could get it immediately by addressing it like this: [BP + 4]. If an *address* were placed on the stack, two steps would be needed: First, you would get the address, and second, you would use the address to get the data. A Level-4 example showing both data ([BP + 4]) and address ([BP + 6]) retrieval follows on the next page.

```
4-1        mov    ax,[bp+4]      ; value of parameter1
4-2        mov    bx,[bp+6]      ; address of parameter2
4-3        mov    dx,[bx]        ; value of parameter2
```

(Level 5 appears here)

```
4-4        mov    bx,[bp+6]      ; address of parameter2 (again)
4-5        mov    [bx],dx        ; store new value at parameter2 address
```

All of these MOV instructions move data from the second operand to the first operand. Line 4-1 grabs data right off the stack and slaps it into the AX register. Lines 4-2 and 4-3 get data by means of an address on the stack: Line 4-2 gets the address (parking it in BX), and then line 4-3 uses that address to get to the actual data, which is moved into DX. Lines 4-4 and 4-5 reverse this process: Line 4-4 gets the address again, and then line 4-5 moves the contents of DX into that memory location.

❏ NOTE: *A crucial bit of assembler notation is demonstrated here: BX refers to what's in BX, and [BX] refers to a memory location whose address is in BX. A reference like [BP + 6] indicates a memory location 6 bytes past the address stored in register BP.*

While sorting out these references may not be a snap, if you think it through carefully, it works out right.

Level 5: Invoke ROM BIOS service

Level 5 is our final step: It simply invokes the ROM BIOS service.

Once all registers contain appropriate values (usually passed from the calling program and copied into registers by means of the stack), the routine can transfer control to the ROM BIOS using an interrupt:

```
5-1        int    12h
```

In this example, this single INT instruction does all the work for you. The ROM BIOS returns the computer's memory size in register AX, where C expects the routine to leave it when the routine returns control to the calling program. In other cases, you might need to leave a result elsewhere, as in Lines 4-4 and 4-5, above.

Most ROM BIOS interrupts, however, provide access to several different services. In such cases, you must specify a service number in register AH before you execute the interrupt. For example, to access the first video service, you would execute the commands on the following page.

```
mov     ah,0        ; AH=service number 0
int     10h         ; ROM BIOS video services interrupt
```

This five-step process outlines the basic principles of nearly all aspects of an assembly-language interface. In the following chapters, you'll see how this design is used in specific examples.

Advanced BIOS Interface

To conclude this chapter we'd like to mention the alternative BIOS interface that IBM introduced in the PS/2 models 50, 60, and 80. This *Advanced BIOS* (ABIOS) *interface* addresses some of the major design shortcomings of the interrupt-based interface described in this chapter.

The traditional, interrupt-based ROM BIOS interface is limited in two important ways:

- It cannot be used in protected mode in a PS/2 Model 50, 60, or 80.

- It provides poor support for multitasking, so an operating system that offers multitasking cannot rely on the traditional ROM BIOS interface.

IBM's solution to these problems is the Advanced BIOS interface in the PS/2 models 50, 60, and 80. Through the Advanced BIOS interface, BIOS services are accessed through a set of address tables and common data areas designed for use in protected mode as well as with a multitasking operating system. However, the complexity of the Advanced BIOS interface makes it better suited to supporting an operating system than to supporting applications programs. Unless you're writing a protected-mode, multitasking operating system, we recommend that you keep using the traditional ROM BIOS interface that is common to all computers in the PC family.

Chapter 9

ROM BIOS
Video Services

Comments and Example

In this chapter, we will discuss each of the video, or *screen-control,* services provided by the ROM BIOS. We have devoted most of the chapter to detailed descriptions of each video service. Beginning on page 194, we have included some programming hints and an assembly-language routine that makes use of some of the video services. For a more general discussion of video hardware in the PC family, see Chapter 4. For information on low-memory locations used by the ROM BIOS for video status information, turn to page 54.

Accessing the ROM BIOS Video Services

The ROM BIOS video services are all requested by generating interrupt 10H (decimal 16). There are 25 principal services available under this interrupt. (See Figure 9-1.) Like all other ROM BIOS services, the video services are numbered from 00H and are selected by placing the service number in the AH register. The services usually require you to specify additional parameters in register AL, BX, CX, or DX. We'll cover the purpose and placement of the parameters under each service description.

Service		
Hex	*Dec*	*Description*
00H	0	Set Video Mode.
01H	1	Set Cursor Size.
02H	2	Set Cursor Position.
03H	3	Read Cursor Position.
04H	4	Read Light-Pen Position.
05H	5	Set Active Display Page.
06H	6	Scroll Window Up.
07H	7	Scroll Window Down.
08H	8	Read Character and Attribute.
09H	9	Write Character and Attribute.
0AH	10	Write Character.
0BH	11	Set 4-Color Palette.
0CH	12	Write Pixel.
0DH	13	Read Pixel.
0EH	14	Write Character in Teletype Mode.
0FH	15	Get Current Video Mode.
10H	16	Color Palette Interface.

Figure 9-1. *The 25 video services.*   *(continued)*

Figure 9-1. *continued*

Service Hex	Dec	Description
11H	17	Character Generator Interface.
12H	18	"Alternate Select."
13H	19	Write Character String.
14H	20	(PC convertible only)
15H	21	(PC convertible only)
1AH	26	Read/Write Display Combination Code.
1BH	27	Return Functionality/State Information.
1CH	28	Save/Restore Video State.

Service 00H (decimal 0): Set Video Mode

Service 00H (decimal 0) is used to configure your video subsystem into one of the 20 video modes listed in Figure 9-2. For details of the video modes, see page 72.

You may recall from our discussion in Chapter 4 that modes 00H through 06H apply to the standard Color Graphics Adapter; mode 07H applies to the Monochrome Display Adapter; modes 0DH through 10H were added for the Enhanced Graphics Adapter; and modes 11H through 13H

Mode	Type	Resolution	Colors	Video Subsystem
00H, 01H	Text	40 × 25	16	CGA, EGA, MCGA, VGA
02H, 03H	Text	80 × 25	16	CGA, EGA, MCGA, VGA
04H, 05H	Graphics	320 × 200	4	CGA, EGA, MCGA, VGA
06H	Graphics	640 × 200	2	CGA, EGA, MCGA, VGA
07H	Text	80 × 25	Mono	MDA, EGA, VGA
08H, 09H, 0AH				(PCjr only)
0BH, 0CH				(used internally by EGA BIOS)
0DH	Graphics	320 × 200	16	EGA, VGA
0EH	Graphics	640 × 200	16	EGA, VGA
0FH	Graphics	640 × 350	Mono	EGA, VGA
10H	Graphics	640 × 350	16	EGA, VGA
11H	Graphics	640 × 480	2	MCGA, VGA
12H	Graphics	640 × 480	16	VGA
13H	Graphics	320 × 200	256	MCGA, VGA

Figure 9-2. *Video modes available through ROM BIOS video service 00H.*

were introduced with the Multi-Color Graphics Array (PS/2 models 25 and 30) and Video Graphics Array (PS/2 models 50, 60, and 80).

Normally, the ROM BIOS clears the screen memory buffer when the mode is set, even if it is set to the same mode again and again. In fact, resetting the same video mode can be an easy way to clear the screen. In some versions of DOS, in fact, the DOS command CLS clears the screen this way. Setting the video mode also sets the color palette to default color values, however, so don't rely on service 00H to clear the screen if you're working with colors; use video service 06H instead.

On the EGA, MCGA, and VGA, you can also tell the ROM BIOS not to clear the screen when it sets up the video mode. Do this by adding 80H (decimal 128) to the video mode number you specify in AL. For example, to change to 640 × 200, 2-color mode without clearing the screen, call service 00H with AL = 86H. Use this feature with caution, though. Displayable video data is formatted differently in different modes, so a screenful of useful data in one video mode may become unintelligible when you switch to another mode without clearing the screen.

See Chapter 4, page 72 for more on video modes. See page 58, memory location 0040:0049H, for more on how a record of the mode is stored in memory. See service 0FH (decimal 15) to find out how to determine the current video mode.

Service 01H (decimal 1): Set Cursor Size

Service 01H (decimal 1) controls the form and size of the blinking cursor that appears in text modes. The default cursor appears as one or two blinking scan lines at the bottom of a character display position. You can change the default cursor size by redefining the number of lines that are displayed.

The Color Graphics Adapter (CGA) can display a cursor that has 8 scan lines, numbered from 0 at the top to 7 at the bottom. The Monochrome Display Adapter (MDA) and the EGA can display a cursor that has 14 scan lines, also numbered from the top, from 0 through 13. Both the MCGA and the VGA have default text characters that are 16 scan lines high, so the maximum size of the text cursor in default PS/2 text modes is 16 scan lines. You set the cursor size by specifying the starting and ending scan lines. (These are the same as the start and stop parameters of BASIC's LOCATE statement.) The start line number is loaded into the CH register and the stop line number into the CL register. Default cursor settings are CH = 6, CL = 7 for the CGA, CH = 11, CL = 12 for the MDA and EGA, and CH = 13, CH = 14 for the MCGA and VGA.

You will notice that the valid scan line numbers occupy only four of the bits (bits 0 through 3) placed in these registers. If bit 5 of CH is set on by specifying a value of 20H (decimal 32), the cursor will disappear. This is one of two techniques that you can use to remove the cursor in the text modes. The other technique is to actually move it off the screen, say to row 26, column 1. When a graphics mode is set, bit 5 is automatically set to keep the cursor from being displayed. Because there is no true cursor in the graphics modes, you must simulate one with the solid-block character, DFH (decimal 223), or with a change of background attributes.

Service 02H (decimal 2): Set Cursor Position

Service 02H (decimal 2) sets the position of the cursor using row and column coordinates. In text modes, multiple display pages can exist, each one having an independently recorded cursor position. Even though the graphics modes have no visible cursor, they keep track of the logical cursor position in the same way as the text modes. This logical cursor position is used to control character I/O.

The cursor position is specified by placing a row number in register DH, a column number in DL, and a display page number in BH. The numbering for the rows and columns begins with coordinates 0,0 in the top left corner. The graphics modes also use the character row and column coordinates to identify the cursor location, rather than pixel coordinates. The display page number must be set to 0 in CGA-compatible graphics modes, although the EGA and VGA both support multiple display pages in 16-color graphics modes as well as in text modes.

See Figure 9-3 for a summary of register settings. See page 87 for more on display pages. See service 03H for the reverse operation: Read cursor position.

Service Number	Parameters
AH = 02H	DH = row number
	DL = column number
	BH = page number

Figure 9-3. *Registers values for setting the cursor position using service 02H.*

Service 03H (decimal 3): Read Cursor Position

Service 03H (decimal 3) is the opposite of services 01H and 02H. When you specify the page number in BH, the ROM BIOS reports the cursor size by returning the starting scan line in CH and the ending scan line in CL. In addition, it reports the cursor position by returning the row in DH and the column in DL. (See Figure 9-4.)

Service Number	Returns
AH = 03H	BH = page number (set to 0 in graphics modes)
	DH = row number
	DL = column number
	CH = starting scan line of cursor
	CL = ending scan line of cursor

Figure 9-4. *Values reported by video service 03H.*

Service 04H (decimal 4): Read Light-Pen Position

Service 04H (decimal 4) reports the light-pen status on a CGA or EGA, specifically whether or not the pen has been triggered, and where it is on the screen if it has been triggered.

Register AH is set to indicate triggering: If AH = 01H, the light pen has been triggered; if AH = 00H, it has not been triggered. If the pen has been triggered, the ROM BIOS determines the light pen's character column and pixel row (y-coordinate) from the video hardware. From these, the ROM BIOS computes the character row and pixel column (x-coordinate). The results are returned in registers BX, CX, and DX as shown in Figure 9-5.

Service Number	Returns
AH = 04H	DH = character row number
	DL = character column number
	CH = pixel line number (CGA and EGA video modes 04H, 05H, and 06H)
	CX = pixel line number (all other EGA video modes)
	BX = pixel column number

Figure 9-5. *Light-pen position values returned by service 04H.*

Service 05H (decimal 5): Set Active Display Page

Service 05H (decimal 5) selects the active display page for text modes 0 through 3 and also for 16-color EGA and VGA graphics modes. You specify the page number in register AL. (See Figure 9-6.) In text modes, page numbers range from 0 through 7. Don't forget, however, that the CGA hardware can display only four different 80-column pages, so CGA pages 4 through 7 overlap pages 0 through 3 when you're in 80 × 25 text mode. On the EGA and in the PS/2 video subsystems, you can also select among multiple display pages in 16-color graphics modes.

Service Number	Parameters
AH = 05H	AL = new display page number

Figure 9-6. *The registers used to set the active display page using service 05H.*

In all video modes, page 0 is used by default. Page 0 is located at the beginning of display memory, with higher page numbers in higher memory locations. See page 87 for more on display pages.

Service 06H (decimal 6): Scroll Window Up

Service 06H (decimal 6) and companion service 07H are used to define a rectangular window of text on the screen and to scroll the window's contents up or down one or more lines. To accomplish the scrolling effect, blank lines are inserted at the bottom of the window area with service 06H (at the top with service 07H) and the top lines of the window (the bottom lines with service 07H) are scrolled off and disappear.

The number of lines to be scrolled is specified in AL. If AL = 00H, the entire window is blanked. (The same thing would happen if you scrolled more lines than the window size allowed.) The location or size of the window is specified in the CX and DX registers: CH is the top row, and DH is the bottom row; CL is the left column, and DL is the right column. The display attribute for the new blank lines inserted by the two services is taken from BH. Figure 9-7 summarizes the register settings for both services 06H and 07H.

When you fill a window with lines of text, you'll discover that window scrolling is normally a two-stage process: When a new line is ready to be written in the window, service 06H (or service 07H) scrolls the current window contents. Then the new line is filled with text using the cursor-positioning and character-writing services. The following example demonstrates this window action.

```
DEBUG                    ; invoke DEBUG from DOS utilities
A                        ; ask to assemble instructions
INT 10                   ; create interrupt 10H instruction
[Return]                 ; finish assembling
R AX                     ; ask to see and change contents of AX
0603                     ; specify service 06H (scroll up), using
                         ; 3-line window
R CX                     ; ask to see and change contents of CX
050A                     ; specify top left corner: row 5, column 10
R DX                     ; ask to see and change contents of DX
1020                     ; specify bottom right corner: row 16, column 32
D 0 L 180                ; fill screen with nonsense
G =100 102               ; execute INT 10H, then stop
```

Service Number	Parameters
AH = 06H (scroll up)	AL = number of lines to scroll
AH = 07H (scroll down)	CH = row number of upper-left corner
	CL = column number of upper-left corner
	DH = row number of lower-right corner
	DL = column number of lower-right corner
	BH = display attribute for blank lines

Figure 9-7. *Register values for scrolling using services 06H and 07H.*

See Chapter 8 for more on assembly-language routines. See the *IBM DOS Technical Reference Manual* for more on DEBUG.

Service 07H (decimal 7): Scroll Window Down

Service 07H (decimal 7) is, as we've already mentioned, the mirror image of service 06H. The difference between the two services is the scrolling action. In service 07H, the new blank lines appear at the top of the window and the old lines disappear at the bottom. The opposite scrolling action takes place in service 06H. See Figure 9-7 under service 06H for the register parameter settings.

Service 08H (decimal 8): Read Character and Attribute

Service 08H (decimal 8) is used to read characters ''off the screen,'' that is, directly out of the display memory. This service is unusually spiffy because it works in both text and graphics modes.

In graphics modes, the same character-drawing tables used to write characters are also used to recognize them by a pattern-matching operation.

Even if you create your own character set in graphics mode, this service will be able to recognize them. In text modes, of course, the ASCII character codes are directly available in the display memory.

Service 08H returns the ASCII character code of the character in AL. (See Figure 9-8.) In graphics modes, if the character doesn't match any characters in the graphics character set, the ROM BIOS returns ASCII code 0. In text modes, the service also returns the character's color attributes in AH. Remember to specify a display page number in BH when you call this service.

Service Number	Parameters	Returns
AH = 08H	BH = active display page number	AL = ASCII character read from cursor location
		AH = attribute of text character (text modes only)

Figure 9-8. *The registers used to read a character and attribute with service 08H.*

See page 82 for more on text characters and attribute bytes. See page 89 for more on text- and graphics-mode characters. See Appendix C for more on ASCII characters.

Service 09H (decimal 9): Write Character and Attribute

Service 09H (decimal 9) writes one or more copies of a single character and its color attribute. The character is specified in AL, and the text-mode attribute or graphics-mode color is specified in BL. The number of times the character is to be written (one or more times) is placed in CX, and BH contains the display page number. (See Figure 9-9.)

Service Number	Parameters
AH = 09H	AL = ASCII character to write to screen
	BL = attribute value (text modes) or foreground color (graphics modes)
	BH = background color (video mode 13H only) or display page number (all other modes)
	CX = number of times to write character and attribute

Figure 9-9. *The registers used to write a text character and attribute using service 09H.*

The ROM BIOS writes the character and its color attributes as many times as requested, starting at the current cursor location. Although the cursor is not moved, duplicate characters are written at subsequent screen locations. In text mode, the duplicated characters will successfully wrap around from line to line, which increases the usefulness of this service. In graphics mode, the characters will not wrap around.

Service 09H is quite useful both for writing individual characters and for replicating a character. The repeat operation is most often used to rapidly lay out blanks or other repeated characters, such as the horizontal lines that are part of box drawings. (See Appendix C.) When you want to make a single copy of the character, be sure to set the count in CX to 1. If it's set to 0, the number of repetitions will be a lot more than you want.

Service 09H has an advantage over the similar service 0EH, in that you can control the color attributes. However, its one disadvantage is that the cursor is not automatically advanced.

In graphics modes, the value specified in BL is the foreground color—the color of the pixels that make up the character drawing. Normally the ROM BIOS displays the character with the specified foreground color on a black background. If, however, you set bit 7 of the color value in BL to 1, then the ROM BIOS creates the character's new foreground color by using an exclusive OR operation (XOR) to combine each of the previous foreground pixels with the value in BL. The same feature also applies to the character and pixel writing services, services 0AH and 0CH.

Here's an example of what can happen when the ROM BIOS uses the XOR operation to display a character. Imagine you're in 320 × 200, 4-color graphics mode and the screen is completely filled with white pixels. If you now write a white character in the usual way, with a color value of 03H (white) in register BL, the ROM BIOS displays a white character on a black background. If, however, you write the same character with a color value of 83H (bit 7 set to 1), the ROM BIOS uses XOR to display a black character on a white background.

See page 82 for more on display attributes in text modes. See page 84 for more on color attributes in graphics modes.

Service 0AH (decimal 10): Write Character

Service 0AH (decimal 10) is the same as service 09H (write character and attribute to cursor location) with one exception: Service 09H lets you change the existing screen color attribute in text mode but service 0AH does not.

However, in graphics mode you must still specify a color in BL (see Figure 9-10), which makes the description of this service as only a character-writing service partly incorrect. Service 0AH has the same graphics color rules as services 09H and 0CH: The color can be used directly or used with XOR and the existing color. (See service 09H for an explanation.)

See page 82 for more on display attributes in text modes. See page 84 for more on color attributes in graphics modes.

Service Number	Parameters
AH = 0AH	AL = ASCII character to write to screen
	BL = foreground color (graphics modes only)
	BH = background color (video mode 13H only) or display page number (all other modes)
	CX = number of times to write character

Figure 9-10. *The registers used to write a character using service 0AH.*

Service 0BH (decimal 11): Set 4-Color Palette

Service 0BH (decimal 11) actually consists of two subservices. You select either subservice 00H or subservice 01H by storing the proper value in register BH. (See Figure 9-11.) Subservice 00H lets you set the border color in CGA alphanumeric modes or the background color in CGA 320 × 200, 4-color graphics mode. You designate the border color in BL with a value between 00H and 0FH.

Subservice 01H lets you select one of the two 4-color palettes used in 320 × 200, 4-color mode. The value in BL specifies which of the two hardware palettes to use. A value of 0 designates the red-green-brown palette, and a value of 1 selects the cyan-magenta-white palette. (See page 77 for more on color palettes.)

This service was designed primarily for use with the CGA. Use service 10H to control colors in other video modes on the EGA, MCGA, and VGA.

Service Number	Subservice Number	Parameters
AH = 0BH	BH = 00H	BL = border or background color
	BH = 01H	BL = palette number (0 or 1)

Figure 9-11. *Color control in CGA-compatible video modes using service 0BH.*

Service 0CH (decimal 12): Write Pixel

Service 0CH (decimal 12) writes an individual pixel. You specify the pixel's location on the screen by passing its column (x-coordinate) in register CX and its row (y-coordinate) in DX. Remember that pixel rows and columns are not the same as the character row and column you use in other services to locate the cursor or to display a character. Pixel coordinates correspond to individual dots, not to characters.

If you're using a graphics mode that supports multiple display pages, be sure to specify the display page number in register BH. (See Figure 9-12.) Also, when you specify the pixel's color in register AL, you have the option of setting bit 7 of the color value to 1. As in service 09H, this tells the BIOS to display the pixel with an XORed color value. (See service 09H for an explanation.)

Service Number	Parameters
AH = 0CH	AL = pixel color
	BH = display page number
	DX = row number of pixel
	CX = column number of pixel

Figure 9-12. *The registers used to write a pixel using service 0CH.*

See page 91 for more on pixels in graphics modes.

Service 0DH (decimal 13): Read Pixel

Service 0DH (decimal 13) is the reverse of service 0CH: It reads a pixel's color value rather than writing it. A pixel has only a single color attribute, which is returned through service 0DH. (The read-character service 08H returns both a color and an ASCII character code.) The row is specified in DX, the column in CX, and the display page in BH. The pixel color value is returned in AL. (See Figure 9-13.) All high-order bits of the value returned in AL are set to 0, as you would expect.

Service Number	Parameters	Returns
AH = 0DH	BH = display page number	AL = pixel color value
	DX = row number of pixel	
	CX = column number of pixel	

Figure 9-13. *The registers used to read a pixel using service 0DH.*

Service 0EH (decimal 14): Write Character in Teletype Mode

Service 0EH (decimal 14) is the workhorse service of conventional character output. It writes individual characters to the screen in what is known as *teletype (TTY) mode*. This makes the screen act as the simplest and crudest form of printer—exactly what is needed for routine text output. As such, this service has no regard for such niceties as color, blinking characters, or control over the cursor location.

With this service, the character is written at the current cursor location and the cursor is advanced one position, wrapping to new lines or scrolling the screen as needed. The character to be written is specified in register AL.

In text modes, the character is displayed as in service 0AH; that is, with the color attributes already in use at the screen location where the character is written. In graphics modes, however, you must also specify the foreground color value to be used for the character. (See Figure 9-14.)

There are four characters that service 0EH reacts to according to their ASCII meaning: 07H (decimal 7)—beep, 08H (decimal 8)—backspace, 0AH (decimal 10)—line feed, and 0DH (decimal 13)—carriage return. All other characters are displayed normally.

The primary advantage of this service over service 09H is that the cursor is automatically moved; the advantage of service 09H is that you can control the color attribute. Now, if you could only combine the two....

Service Number	Parameters
AH = 0EH	AL = ASCII character to write
	BL = foreground color (in graphics modes only)
	BH = display page (IBM PC BIOS dated 10/19/81 or earlier)

Figure 9-14. *The registers used to write a character in teletype mode using service 0EH.*

Service 0FH (decimal 15): Get Current Video Mode

Service 0FH (decimal 15) returns the current video mode and two other useful pieces of information: the screen width in characters (80 or 40) and the display page number.

The video mode number, as explained under service 00H, is returned in AL. The screen width is returned in AH as a number of characters per line. The display page number will be returned in BH. (See Figure 9-15.)

Service Number	Returns
AH = 0FH	AL = current display mode
	AH = number of characters per line
	BH = active display page

Figure 9-15. *Information returned by service 0FH.*

See page 72 for more on video modes. See page 58, memory location 0040:0049H, for more on how a record of the mode is kept.

Service 10H (decimal 16): Color Palette Interface

Service 10H (decimal 16) was introduced with the PCjr and carried forward in the EGA and PS/2 ROM BIOS. It consists of a set of subservices (Figure 9-16) that let you control palette colors, blinking, and (on the MCGA and VGA) the video DAC. Be aware that different subservices are supported with different hardware. Before you use these subservices in a program, be sure your program "knows" which subsystem it's running on. (Video service 1AH can provide this information to a program.)

Subservice Number	Description
AL = 00H	Update a specified palette register.
AL = 01H	Specify the border color.
AL = 02H	Update all 16 palette registers plus border.
AL = 03H	Select background intensity or blink attribute.
AL = 07H	Read a specified palette register.
AL = 08H	Read the border color register.
AL = 09H	Read all 16 palette registers plus border.
AL = 10H	Update a specified video DAC color register.
AL = 12H	Update a block of video DAC color registers.
AL = 13H	Set video DAC color paging.
AL = 15H	Read a specified video DAC color register.
AL = 17H	Read a block of video DAC color registers.
AL = 1AH	Get video DAC color paging status.
AL = 1BH	Gray-scale a block of video DAC color registers

Figure 9-16. *Subservices available through video BIOS service 10H.*

Subservice 00H (decimal 0) updates one of the 16 palette registers on an EGA or VGA. You specify the palette register number in BL and a new palette register value in BH when you call this subservice. The VGA BIOS also supports **subservice 07H (decimal 7),** which performs the complementary operation: When you call subservice 07H with a palette register number in BL, the ROM BIOS returns that palette register's current contents in BH. (Subservice 07H isn't available in the EGA BIOS because the EGA has write-only palette registers.)

Subservice 01H (decimal 1) sets the border color on an EGA or VGA. You pass the color value to the BIOS in register BH when you call this subservice. The VGA BIOS supports **subservice 08H**, which returns the current border color value in BH, but again this complementary subservice isn't available on the EGA.

Here are two tips about setting the border color on an EGA or VGA. First, in most EGA video modes the border area is very small, and selecting any border color other than black results in a narrow, smeared border. On the VGA, the border is better. Second, if compatibility with the CGA is important, remember that you can also use video service 0BH (page 180) to set the border color.

Subservice 02H (decimal 2) updates all 16 palette registers, plus the border color, with a single ROM BIOS call. Before you call subservice 02H, you must store all 16 palette register values plus the border color value in a 17-byte table. You then pass the address (segment and offset) of this table to the BIOS in registers ES and DX when you call this subservice. The VGA also provides a subservice that lets you read the palette registers back into a table: When you call **subservice 09H (decimal 9)** with ES:DX pointing to a 17-byte table, the ROM BIOS fills the table with the 16 current palette register values and the border color.

Subservice 03H (decimal 3) lets you selectively enable or disable the blinking attribute. The ROM BIOS uses blinking by default, but if you prefer to have a full range of 16 background colors instead of only 8, you can use subservice 03H to disable blinking. The value you pass in register BL determines whether blinking is enabled (BL = 01H) or disabled (BL = 00H).

Subservices 10H (decimal 16) and **15H (decimal 21)** are supported only by the MCGA and VGA BIOS. These two subservices give you direct access to one of the 256 color registers in the video digital to analog convertor (DAC). To update a video DAC color register, call subservice 10H with the color register number in BX and 6-bit red, green, and blue color values in registers DH, CH, and CL. To read a specified color register, place the color register number in BX and use subservice 15H, which returns the RGB values in DH, CH, and CL.

The related **subservices 12H (decimal 18)** and **17H (decimal 23)** operate on a block of video DAC color registers instead of only one. To use subservice 12H, create a table of 3-byte red-green-blue values. Then place the segment-offset address of the table in ES and DX, the first color register number to update in BX, and the number of registers to update in CX. When you call subservice 12H, the ROM BIOS stores each red-green-blue value in turn into the block of color registers you specified in BX and CX.

The complementary subservice 17H requires you to pass the address of a table in ES:DX, along with a starting register number in BX and a register count in CX. The ROM BIOS fills the table with the red-green-blue values it reads from the block of color registers you specified.

On the VGA, which has both palette registers and video DAC color registers, you can use **subservices 13H (decimal 19)** and **1AH (decimal 26)** to switch rapidly between different palettes. By default, the ROM BIOS configures the VGA hardware so that color decoding is the same as on the EGA: Each of the 16 palette registers contains a 6-bit value that specifies one of the first 64 video DAC registers, and these 64 color registers specify the 64 colors available in the EGA palette.

Subservice 13H lets you use the other three color pages, or groups of 64 video DAC color registers. (See Figure 9-17.) If you call subservice 13H with BH = 01H and BL = 01H, for example, the BIOS configures the VGA hardware to display colors from the second group of 64 color registers (color page 1). To use the first group (color page 0) again, you could call the same subservice with BH = 00H and BL = 01H. If, for example, you used the default, EGA-compatible colors in color page 0, and their gray-scale equivalents in color page 1, you could switch rapidly between the two with a single call to subservice 13H.

If you need to switch rapidly between more than four palettes, you can use subservice 13H with BH = 01H and BL = 00H to configure the VGA color decoding hardware to use 4-bit palette register values instead of 6-bit

Parameters		Description
BL = 00H	BH = 00H	Use four 64-register pages.
	BH = 01H	Use sixteen 16-register pages.
BL = 01H	BH = n	Color page number. (n = 00H–03H if using 64-register pages n = 00H–0FH if using 16-register pages)

Figure 9-17. *Video DAC color paging with service 10H, subservice 13H.*

values. In this case, each palette register value can specify one of only 16 different video DAC registers. This makes 16 color pages available, each comprising 16 color registers. You can select any of the 16 color pages using subservice 13H with BL = 01H.

The VGA ROM BIOS supplements subservice 13H with a complementary function, subservice 1AH. This subservice returns the color page status in BL (16- or 64-register color pages) and BH (current color page number).

With **subservice 1BH (decimal 27)** on the MCGA and VGA, you can convert the color values in a block of consecutive video DAC color registers to corresponding shades of gray. Call this subservice with BX containing the number of the first video DAC register to convert, and with CX containing the number of registers to update.

Service 11H (decimal 17): Character Generator Interface

Service 11H (decimal 17) first appeared in the EGA ROM BIOS. The many subservices available in service 11H were augmented and expanded in the PS/2 ROM BIOS to provide full support for the new video subsystems (MCGA and VGA) introduced with the PS/2s.

To make sense of the many service 11H subservices, it helps to consider them in four groups (Figure 9-18):

- Subservices in the first group (subservices 00H through 04H) change the character set used in text modes.

- Subservices in the second group (subservices 10H through 14H) change the text-mode character set as well as the displayed height of text-mode characters.

- Subservices in the third group (subservices 20H through 24H) update graphics-mode character sets.

- The subservice in the fourth group (subservice 30H) returns information about the character sets currently displayed and about the character sets available to the ROM BIOS.

Subservices 00H (decimal 0), 01H (decimal 1), 02H (decimal 2) and **04H (decimal 4)** all change the character set used to display text-mode characters on the EGA, MCGA, or VGA. Subservices 01H, 02H, and 04H are the easiest to use. You need specify only which available tables in character generator RAM should contain the character set. Thus, for example, a call to service 11H with AL = 02H and BL = 00H instructs the ROM BIOS to use its 8 × 8 characters in the first (default) table in character generator RAM.

If you want to define your own characters you need to use subservice 00H, as follows: Place a table of the bit patterns that define the characters in a buffer. Then call subservice 00H with the address of the table in ES:BP, the number of characters in CX, the ASCII code of the first character in the table in DX, and the number of bytes in each character's bit pattern in BH.

Subservice 03H (decimal 3) lets you select among text-mode character sets once they are loaded into character generator RAM. The EGA and MCGA have four such tables; the VGA has eight. The value in BL specifies which one or two of the tables is to be used to display text-mode characters. On the EGA and MCGA, bits 0 and 1 of BL specify one table, and bits 2 and 3 specify a second table. If the two bit fields specify the same table, that's the table that will be used for all text-mode characters.

Subservice Number	Description
Load a text-mode character set:	
AL = 00H	Load a user-specified character set.
AL = 01H	Load the ROM BIOS 8 × 14 character set.
AL = 02H	Load the ROM BIOS 8 × 8 character set.
AL = 03H	Select displayed character set.
AL = 04H	Load the ROM BIOS 8 × 16 character set (MCGA, VGA only).
Load a text-mode character set and adjust the displayed character height:	
AL = 10H	Load a user-specified character set.
AL = 11H	Load the ROM BIOS 8 × 14 character set.
AL = 12H	Load the ROM BIOS 8 × 8 character set.
AL = 14H	Load the ROM BIOS 8 × 16 character set (MCGA, VGA only).
Load a graphics-mode character set:	
AL = 20H	Load a CGA-compatible, user-specified character set.
AL = 21H	Load a user-specified character set.
AL = 22H	Load the ROM BIOS 8 × 14 character set.
AL = 23H	Load the ROM BIOS 8 × 8 character set.
AL = 24H	Load the ROM BIOS 8 × 16 character set (MCGA, VGA only).
Get character generator information:	
AL = 30H	Get character generator information.

Figure 9-18. *Subservices available through video BIOS service 11H.*

Subservices 10H (decimal 16), 11H (decimal 17), 12H (decimal 18), and 14H (decimal 20) are similar to subservices 00H, 01H, 02H, and 04H. The difference is that with these higher-numbered subservices, the ROM BIOS not only loads a character set but also adjusts the displayed character height appropriately. This difference is obvious if you compare the effect of executing subservice 02H and subservice 12H to load the ROM BIOS 8 × 8 character set. With subservice 02H, the 8 × 8 characters are used without adjusting the displayed character height, so if you're in a default ROM BIOS text mode, you'll see 25 rows of characters. With subservice 12H, the ROM BIOS adjusts the displayed character height so that in a default ROM BIOS text mode you see 43 rows of characters on an EGA or 50 rows of characters on a VGA.

Subservices 20H through 24H (decimal 32 through decimal 36) are related to subservices 00H through 04H in that they also load character sets into memory. However, this third group of subservices is designed for use only in graphics modes. Subservice 20H loads a CGA-compatible set of 8 × 8 characters into RAM. To use subservice 20H, place a table containing the bit patterns for ASCII characters 80H through FFH into memory, and pass the address of this table to the ROM BIOS in registers ES:BP. Subservices 21H through 24H are similar to subservices 00H, 01H, 02H, and 04H. Call them with 00H in BL, the number of displayed character rows in DL, and (for subservice 21H) the number of bytes in each character's bit pattern in CX.

Subservice 30H (decimal 48) returns several pieces of handy information regarding the ROM BIOS character generator. This subservice reports the height of the displayed character matrix in CX and the number of the bottom character row in DL. For example, if you call subservice 30H in the default EGA text mode (80 × 25), the BIOS returns 14 in CX and 24 in DL.

Parameter	Returns
BH = 00H	CGA-compatible 8 × 8 graphics-mode characters (contents of interrupt 1FH vector)
BH = 01H	Current graphics-mode characters (contents of interrupt 43H vector)
BH = 02H	ROM BIOS 8 × 14 characters
BH = 03H	ROM BIOS 8 × 8 characters
BH = 04H	Second half of ROM BIOS 8 × 8 character table
BH = 05H	ROM BIOS 9 × 14 alternate characters
BH = 06H	ROM BIOS 8 × 16 characters (MCGA and VGA only)
BH = 07H	ROM BIOS 9 × 16 alternate characters (VGA only)

Figure 9-19. *Character bit pattern table addresses returned in ES:BP by subservice 30H of video ROM BIOS service 11H.*

Subservice 30H also returns the address of any of several bit pattern tables for the default ROM BIOS character sets. The value you pass in BH when you call this subservice determines which address the ROM BIOS returns in ES:BP. (See Figure 9-19.)

Service 12H (decimal 18): "Alternate Select"

Service 12H (decimal 18) made its debut along with service 11H in the EGA BIOS. It, too, is supported in the ROM BIOS in all PC/2 video subsystems. IBM's name for this service derives from the purpose of one of the subservices of service 12H, namely, to select an alternate print-screen routine for the ROM BIOS Shift-PrtSc function. The name lingers on even though service 12H has been expanded by adding a number of unrelated subservices. (See Figure 9-20.)

Subservice Number	Description
BL = 10H	Return video configuration information.
BL = 20H	Select alternate print-screen routine.
BL = 30H	Select scan lines for VGA text modes.
BL = 31H	Enable/disable default palette loading.
BL = 32H	Enable/disable CPU access to video RAM.
BL = 33H	Enable/disable gray-scale summing.
BL = 34H	Enable/disable ROM BIOS cursor emulation.
BL = 35H	PS/2 display switch interface.
BL = 36H	Enable/disable video refresh.

Figure 9-20. *Subservices available through video BIOS service 12H.*

Subservice 10H (decimal 16) reports on the configuration of an EGA or VGA. The value returned in BH indicates whether the current video mode is color (BH = 00H) or monochrome (BH = 01H). BL contains a number between 0 and 3 that represents the amount of RAM installed on an EGA (0 means 64 KB; 1 means 128 KB; 2 means 192 KB; 3 means 256 KB). The value in CH reflects the status of input from the EGA feature connector, and CL contains the settings of the EGA configuration switches.

Subservice 20H (decimal 32) is provided for the convenience of users of the EGA or a VGA adapter. It replaces the motherboard ROM BIOS print-screen routine with a more flexible routine in the adapter ROM BIOS. Unlike the motherboard ROM BIOS routine, the adapter BIOS routine can print a snapshot of a text-mode screen that has more than 25 rows of characters. In PS/2s, of course, the motherboard routine can already do this, eliminating the need for this subservice.

Subservice 30H (decimal 48) lets you specify how many scan lines to display in VGA text modes. The default ROM BIOS text modes contain 400 scan lines. When you call subservice 30H, the value you pass in register AL can instruct the ROM BIOS to use a different vertical resolution: If AL = 00H, ROM BIOS text modes will display 200 scan lines, as they do on a CGA. If AL = 01H, text modes will display an EGA-compatible 350 scan lines. Finally, when AL = 02H, the ROM BIOS uses its default resolution of 400 scan lines.

When you use subservice 30H, the vertical resolution does not change until the next time a program uses video ROM BIOS service 00H to select a text mode. Thus, changing the vertical resolution actually requires you to make two different ROM BIOS calls: one to specify the resolution and another to set up the text mode.

Subservice 31H (decimal 49) lets you enable or disable palette loading when the ROM BIOS sets up a new MCGA or VGA video mode. Calling subservice 31H with AL = 01H disables palette loading, so you can subsequently change video modes without changing the colors in a previously-loaded palette. A call with AL = 00H enables default palette loading.

Subservices 32H (decimal 50) and **35H (decimal 53)** are provided for programmers who want to use two different video subsystems in the same PS/2 computer. In particular, these routines support the use of a VGA alongside the built-in MCGA subsystem in a PS/2 Model 30.

Subservice 32H enables or disables buffer and port addressing according to the value passed in AL (AL = 00H means enable; AL = 01H means disable). This feature is important if any addresses in the two video subsystems overlap: Before accessing one subsystem, you must disable addressing in the other one.

Subservice 35H provides a complete switching interface that lets you selectively access both an MCGA and a VGA in the same computer. This subservice relies on the function provided through subservice 32H to independently enable and disable each video subsystem. See Chapter 13 and the *IBM BIOS Interface Technical Reference* manual for details.

Subservice 33H (decimal 51) tells the ROM BIOS whether or not to average colors to gray scales when it establishes a new video mode on an MCGA or VGA. A call to this subservice with AL = 01H disables the gray-scaling; a call with AL = 00H enables gray-scaling. You can also use this subservice to force the ROM BIOS to use a gray-scale palette even if you're using a color monitor.

Subservice 34H (decimal 52) enables or disables text-mode cursor emulation on the VGA. When you call this subservice with AL = 00H, the ROM BIOS emulates CGA text-mode cursor sizing whenever you change video modes or update the cursor size. When called with AL = 01H, this subservice disables text-mode cursor emulation.

Subservice 36H (decimal 54) lets you enable or disable VGA video refresh. Calling this subservice with AL = 01H disables refresh, and a call with AL = 00H enables refresh. When you disable refresh, the screen goes blank, but reads and writes to the video buffer are somewhat faster than when refresh is enabled. If you are writing a program that needs to run as fast as possible, and if you don't mind having the screen go blank while you access the video buffer, then consider using subservice 36H to temporarily blank the screen while you update it.

Service 13H (decimal 19): Write Character String

Service 13H (decimal 19), allows you to write a string of characters to the display screen. Through the four subservices that make up this service, you can specify the character attributes individually or as a group. You can also move the cursor to the end of the string or leave it in place, depending on which subservice you choose.

The subservice number is placed in AL, the pointer to the string in ES:BP, the length of the string in CX, the starting position where the string is to be written in DX, and the display page number in BH.

Subservices 00H (decimal 0) and **01H (decimal 1)** write a string of characters to the screen using the attribute specified in register BL. With subservice 00H, the cursor is not moved from the location specified in register DX; with subservice 01H, the cursor is moved to the location following the last character in the string.

Subservices 02H (decimal 2) and **03H (decimal 3)** write a string of characters and attributes to the screen, writing first the character and then the attribute. With subservice 02H, the cursor is not moved from the location specified in register DX; with subservice 03H, the cursor is moved to the location following the last character in the string.

Service 13H is available only in the PC/AT, EGA, PS/2s, and later versions of the PC/XT ROM BIOS.

Service 1AH (decimal 26): Read/Write Display Combination Code

Service 1AH (decimal 26) was introduced in the ROM BIOS in the PS/2s, but it is also part of the ROM BIOS of the VGA. This service returns a 2-byte code that indicates which combination of video subsystems and video displays is found in your computer. The display combination codes recognized by this ROM BIOS service are listed in Figure 9-21. Service 1AH lets you select either of two subservices using the value in register AL; subservice 00H or subservice 01H.

Subservice 00H (decimal 0) returns a 2-byte display combination code in register BX. If your computer has two different video subsystems, the value in BL indicates which one is *active;* that is, which is currently being updated by the video ROM BIOS. The value in BH indicates the inactive subsystem. If your computer has only video subsystem, the value in BH is zero.

Subservice 01H (decimal 1) performs the reverse function of subservice 00H. It lets you change the current display combination code known to the ROM BIOS. Don't use this subservice, however, unless you know exactly what you're doing. It's a rare program indeed that requires you to change the ROM BIOS's idea of what the video hardware actually is.

Code	Video Subsystem
00H	(No display)
01H	MDA
02H	CGA
03H	(Reserved)
04H	EGA with color display
05H	EGA with monochrome display
06H	Professional Graphics Controller
07H	VGA with monochrome display
08H	VGA with color display
09H,0AH	(Reserved)
0BH	MCGA with monochrome display
0CH	MCGA with color display
0FFH	(Unknown)

Figure 9-21. *Display combination codes returned by video BIOS service 1AH.*

Service 1BH (decimal 27): Return Functionality/State Information

Service 1BH (decimal 27) is available in all PS/2s as well as with the VGA. It returns a great deal of detailed information regarding the capabilities of the ROM BIOS as well as the current ROM BIOS and video hardware status.

Service 1BH returns this information in a 64-byte buffer whose address is passed in registers ES:DI. In addition to this address, you must also specify an "implementation type" value of 0 in register BX. (Presumably future IBM video products will recognize implementation type values other than 0.)

The BIOS fills the buffer with information about the current video mode (the mode number, character columns and rows, number of colors available) as well as about the video hardware configuration (total video memory available, display combination code, and so on). See the *IBM BIOS Interface Technical Reference* manual for details on the buffer format.

In the first 4 bytes of the buffer, the ROM BIOS returns a pointer to a table of "static" functionality information. This table lists nearly all of the features the ROM BIOS and the video hardware can support: the video modes available, support for palette switching, RAM-loadable character sets, light-pen support, and many other details.

When you write a program that runs on a PS/2 or in a system with a VGA adapter, service 1BH offers a simple and consistent way for your program to determine what the video subsystem's current and potential capabilities are. Unfortunately, you can't rely on this service if your program must be compatible with non-PS/2 computers. Neither the PC motherboard ROM BIOS nor the EGA BIOS supports this service. A program can determine whether service 1BH is supported by examining the value returned by this service in AL; this value is 1BH if the service is supported.

Service 1CH (decimal 28): Save/Restore Video State

Service 1CH (decimal 28) is provided by the ROM BIOS only in the PS/2 models 50, 60, and 80, and with VGA adapters. (In other words, where you find a VGA you also find service 1CH.) This BIOS service lets you preserve all information that describes the state of the video BIOS and hardware. The ROM BIOS can preserve three types of information: the video DAC state, the BIOS data area in RAM, and the current values in all video control registers.

You can select three different subservices with the value you pass in register AL: subservices 00H, 01H, and 02H.

Subservice 00H (decimal 0) is designed to be called before subservices 01H or 02H. Subservice 00H requires you to specify which of the three types of information you want to preserve, by setting one or more of the three low-order bits of the value in CX. When this service returns, BX contains the size of the buffer you will need to store the information.

Subservice 01H (decimal 1) saves the current video state information in the buffer whose address you pass in ES:BX. Then you can change video modes, reprogram the palette, or otherwise program the ROM BIOS or video hardware.

Subservice 02H (decimal 2) lets you restore the previous video state.

Comments and Example

In cruising through the ROM BIOS video services, you've seen how they work individually. Once you have that information in mind, the next question usually is: Given a choice between using the ROM BIOS services directly or using higher-level services such as the DOS services or the services built into your programming language, which is best? The general advice that we always give is to use the highest-level services that will accomplish what you want to do. In this case, there is no specific reason for you to avoid using the ROM BIOS video services — you can't do any great harm by using them. But in the next chapter on the diskette services, we'll argue the case the other way, advising you to avoid using the ROM BIOS diskette services because more risk is associated with them.

The video capabilities of the PC models are remarkable, and the ROM BIOS services give you full use of them. The DOS services, as you'll see in Chapters 14 through 18, are rather weak and provide only the simplest character services. Likewise, many programming languages (for example, Pascal and C) only provide a dressed-up version of the DOS services and nothing more. So, if you need to use the PC's fancy screen capabilities and if you aren't using a language such as BASIC that provides the services you need, you should be using the ROM BIOS services. Getting control of the display screen is one of the very best reasons for using the ROM BIOS services.

Using the ROM BIOS services directly usually calls for an assembly-language interface, so we'll give you an example of how one can be set up. For the example, we'll set up a module in a format that would be called by C. We'll make the module switch to video mode 1 (40-column text in color) and set the border color to blue.

Here is the assembly module (see Chapter 8, page 161, for general notes on the format):

```
_TEXT           SEGMENT         byte public 'CODE'
                ASSUME          cs:_TEXT

                PUBLIC          _Blue40
_Blue40         PROC            near

                push            bp              ; save previous BP value
                mov             bp,sp           ; use BP to access the stack
```

```
; set video mode

                mov         ah,0        ; BIOS service number
                mov         al,1        ; video mode number
                int         10h         ; call BIOS to set 40x25 text mode

; set border color

                mov         ah,0Bh      ; BIOS service number
                mov         bh,0        ; subservice number
                mov         bl,1        ; color value (blue)
                int         10h         ; call BIOS to set border color

                pop         bp          ; restore previous BP value
                ret

_Blue40         ENDP

_TEXT           ENDS
```

Chapter 10

ROM BIOS Disk Services

We're now going to cover the disk services provided by the ROM BIOS. To understand the logical structure of the contents of a disk, see Chapter 5, particularly pages 106 through 121. For information about the higher-level disk services provided by DOS, see Chapters 15 through 18.

Generally speaking, disk operations are best left to disk operating systems. If you decide to use any of the ROM BIOS disk services, we recommend that you read the section entitled "Comments and Examples" on page 212 of this chapter.

The ROM BIOS Disk Services

The original IBM PC ROM BIOS offered only six different disk services. As the diskette and fixed-disk subsystems of the PC and PS/2 family have become increasingly sophisticated, the number of ROM BIOS services that support disk I/O has increased. To keep the ROM BIOS software modular and flexible, IBM separated the support routines for fixed-disk subsystems from the diskette support routines. Nevertheless, the number of BIOS disk services has grown from six on the original IBM PC to 22 in the PS/2s. (See Figure 10-1.)

All ROM BIOS disk services are invoked with interrupt 13H (decimal 19) and selected by loading the service number into the AH register. Disk drives are identified by a zero-based number passed in DL, with the high-order bit set to 1 to indicate a fixed disk. Thus the first diskette drive in the computer is identified by drive number 00H, and the first fixed disk is designated by drive number 80H.

The ROM BIOS uses a set of descriptive parameter tables called *disk-base tables* to gain information about the capabilities of the disk controller hardware and the disk media. The ROM BIOS maintains the segmented addresses of the disk-base tables it uses in interrupt vectors: The address of the table for the current diskette drive is in the interrupt 1EH vector (0000:0074H); addresses of tables for the first and second fixed drives are in interrupt vectors 41H (0000:0104H) and 46H (0000:0118H).

For most programmers, the disk-base tables are an invisible part of the disk services. However, some disk-base parameters may occasionally need to be changed for special purposes. For this reason we include a brief description of the disk-base table toward the end of this chapter.

The following sections describe each of the ROM BIOS services.

Service	Description	Diskette	Fixed Disk
00H	Reset Disk System.	x	x
01H	Get Disk Status.	x	x
02H	Read Disk Sectors.	x	x
03H	Write Disk Sectors.	x	x
04H	Verify Disk Sectors.	x	x
05H	Format Disk Track.	x	x
06H	Format PC/XT Fixed-Disk Track.		x
07H	Format PC/XT Fixed Disk.		x
08H	Get Disk-Drive Parameters.	x	x
09H	Initialize Fixed-Disk Parameter Tables.		x
0AH	Read Long.		x
0BH	Write Long.		x
0CH	Seek to Cylinder.		x
0DH	Alternate Fixed-Disk Reset.		x
10H	Test for Drive Ready.		x
11H	Recalibrate Drive.		x
15H	Get Disk Type.	x	x
16H	Get Diskette Change Status.	x	
17H	Set Diskette Type.	x	
18H	Set Media Type for Format.	x	
19H	Park Heads.		x
1AH	Format ESDI Unit.		x

Figure 10-1. *The ROM BIOS disk services.*

Service 00H (decimal 0): Reset Disk System

Service 00H resets the disk controller and drive. This service does not affect the disk itself. Instead, a reset through service 00H forces the ROM BIOS disk-support routines to start from scratch for the next disk operation by recalibrating the disk drive's read/write head—an operation that positions the head on a certain track. This reset service is normally used after an error in any other drive operation.

When you call service 00H for a fixed-disk drive, the ROM BIOS also resets the diskette-drive controller. If you want to reset the fixed-disk controller only, use service 0DH. (See page 207.)

Service 01H (decimal 1): Get Disk Status

Service 01H (decimal 1) reports the disk status in register 0AH. The status is preserved after each disk operation, including the read, write, verify, and format operations. By preserving the disk status, an error-handling or error-reporting routine can be completely independent of the routines that operate the disk. This can be very useful. Under the right circumstances, you can rely on DOS or your programming language to drive the disk (a wise choice; see "Comments and Examples" on page 212), and at the same time have your program find out and report the details of what went wrong. See Figure 10-2 for details of the status byte.

Value (hex)	Meaning	Value (hex)	Meaning
00H	No error	10H	Bad CRC or ECC
01H	Bad command	11H	ECC corrected data error (F)
02H	Address mark not found	20H	Controller failed
03H	Write attempted on write-protected disk (D)	40H	Seek failed
		80H	Time out
04H	Sector not found	AAH	Drive not ready (F)
05H	Reset failed (F)	BBH	Undefined error (F)
06H	Diskette removed (D)	CCH	Write fault (F)
07H	Bad parameter table (F)	EOH	Status error (F)
08H	DMA overrun	FFH	Sense operation failed
09H	DMA across 64 KB boundary		
0AH	Bad sector flag (F)		
0BH	Bad cylinder (F)		
0CH	Bad media type (D)		
0DH	Invalid number of sectors on format (F)		
0EH	Control data address mark detected (F)		
0FH	DMA arbitration level out of range (F)		

(F) = fixed disk only
(D) = diskette only

Figure 10-2. *The value of the disk status byte returned in register AH by service 01H.*

Service 02H (decimal 2): Read Disk Sectors

Service 02H (decimal 2) reads one or more disk sectors into memory. If you want to read more than one sector, every sector must be on the same track and read/write head. This is largely because the ROM BIOS doesn't know how many sectors might be on a track, so it can't know when to switch from one head or track to another. Usually, this service is used for reading either individual sectors or an entire trackful of sectors for bulk operations such as DISKCOPY in DOS. Various registers are used for control information in a read operation. They are summarized in Figure 10-3.

Parameters	*Status Results*
DL = drive number	If CF = 0, then no error and AH = 0
DH = head number	If CF = 1, then error and AH contains service 01H status bits
CH = cylinder number (D) low-order 8 bits of cylinder number (F)	
CL = sector number (D) high-order 2 bits of cylinder number plus 6-bit sector number (F)	
AL = number of sectors to be read	
ES:BX = address of buffer	

(F) = fixed disk only
(D) = diskette only

Figure 10-3. *The registers used for control information by the read, write, verify, and format services.*

DL contains the drive number, and **DH** contains the diskette side or fixed-disk read/write head number.

CH and **CL** identify, for diskettes, the cylinder and sector number to be read. CH contains the cylinder number, which should be less than the total number of cylinders on the formatted diskette. (See Chapter 5 for a table of standard IBM formats.) Of course, the cylinder number can be higher with non-IBM formats or with some copy-protection schemes. CL contains the sector number.

For fixed disks, there may be more than 256 cylinders, so the ROM BIOS requires you to specify a 10-bit cylinder number in CH and CL: You must place the 8 low-order bits of the cylinder number in CH. The 2 high-order bits of CL contain the 2 high-order bits of the cylinder number. The 6 low-order bits of CL designate the sector number to be read. Don't forget that sectors are numbered from 1, unlike drives, cylinders, or heads (sides).

AL contains the number of sectors to be read. For diskettes, this is normally either 1, 8, 9, 15, or 18. We are warned by IBM not to request 0 sectors.

ES:BX contains the buffer location. The location of the memory area where the data will be placed is provided by a segmented address given in this register pair.

The data area should be big enough to accommodate as much as is read; keep in mind that while normal DOS sectors are 512 bytes, sectors can be as large as 1024 bytes. (See the format service that follows.) When this service reads more than one sector, it lays the sectors out in memory one right after another.

CF (the carry flag) contains the error status of the operation. The result of the operation is actually reported through a combination of the carry flag and the AH register. If CF = 0, no error occurred, AH will also be 0, and, for a diskette, the number of sectors read will be returned in AL. If CF = 1, an error did occur, and AH will contain the status value detailed under service 01H, the status service.

When using service 02H with a diskette drive or any other active diskette service, remember that the diskette-drive motor takes some time to reach a working speed and that none of these services waits for this to happen. Although our own experience with the ROM BIOS diskette services suggests that this is rarely a problem, IBM recommends that any program using these services try three times before assuming that an error is real and that it use the reset service between tries. The logic of the suggested operation is as follows (partly expressed in BASIC):

```
10 ERROR COUNT = 0
20 WHILE ERROR.COUNT < 3
30 ' do read/write/verify/format operation
40 ' error checking here: if no error goto 90
50   ERROR.COUNT = ERROR.COUNT + 1
60 ' do reset operation
70 WEND
80 ' act on error
90 ' carry on after success
```

Be sure to see the section on page 209 for the effect of the disk-base table on the reset operation.

Service 03H (decimal 3): Write Disk Sectors

Service 03H (decimal 3) writes one or more sectors to a disk — the reverse of service 02H. All registers, details, and comments given for service 02H also apply to service 03H. (Also see Figure 10-3.) The disk sectors must be formatted before they can be written to.

Service 04H (decimal 4) : Verify Disk Sectors

Service 04H (decimal 4) verifies the contents of one or more disk sectors. This operation is not what many people think it is: No comparison is made between the data on the disk and the data in memory. The verification performed by this service simply checks that the sectors can be found and read and that the cyclical redundancy check (CRC) is correct. The CRC acts as a sophisticated parity check for the data in each sector and will detect most errors, such as lost or scrambled bits, very reliably.

Most programmers use the verify service to check the results of a write operation after using service 03H, but you can verify any part of a disk at any time. The DOS FORMAT program, for example, verifies each track after it is formatted. However, many people regard verification as an unnecessary operation because the disk drives are so reliable and because ordinary error reporting works so well. Even DOS doesn't verify a write operation unless you ask it to with the VERIFY ON command.

❑ NOTE: *It's worth pausing here to note that there is nothing unusual or alarming about having "bad tracks" marked on a disk, particularly a fixed disk. In fact, it is quite common for a fixed disk to have a few bad patches on it. The DOS FORMAT program notices bad tracks and marks them as such in the disk's file-allocation table. Later, the bad-track marking tells DOS that these areas should be bypassed. Bad tracks are also common on diskettes; with a diskette, unlike a fixed disk, you have the option of throwing away the defective media and using only perfect disks.*

The verify service operates exactly as do the read and write services and uses the same registers. The only difference between them is that the verify operation does not use any memory area and therefore does not use the register pair ES:BX.

Service 05H (decimal 5) : Format Disk Track

Service 05H (decimal 5) formats one track. The format service operates as do the read and write services except that you need not specify a sector number in CL. All other parameters are as shown in Figure 10-3.

Because formatting is done one full track at a time, you cannot format individual sectors. However, on a diskette you can specify individual characteristics for each sector on a track.

Every sector on a diskette track has 4 descriptive bytes associated with it. You specify these 4 bytes for each sector to be formatted by creating a table of 4-byte groups and passing the table's address in the register pair ES:BX. When you format a disk track, the 4-byte groups are written to the diskette immediately in front of the individual sectors in the track. The 4 bytes of data associated with a sector on the disk are known as *address marks* and are used by the disk controller to identify individual sectors during the read, write, and verify operations. The 4 bytes are referred to as C for cylinder, H for head, R for record (or sector number), and N for number of bytes per sector (also called the *size code*).

When a sector is being read or written, the diskette controller searches the diskette track for the sector's ID, the essential part of which is R, the record or sector number. The cylinder and head parameters are not actually needed in this address mark because the read/write head is positioned mechanically at the proper track and the side is selected electronically, but they are recorded and tested as a safety check.

The size code (N) can take on any one of the four standard values shown in Figure 10-4. The normal setting is code 2 (512 bytes).

Sectors are numbered on the diskette in the order specified by R. On diskettes, the sectors are normally numbered in numeric sequence (unless rearranged for copy protection), but on fixed disks the order of the sectors can be rearranged (interleaved), either for better performance or to create timing differences for copy-protection purposes. The actual interleave used on a fixed disk depends on the capabilities of the disk-controller hardware. For example, the PC/XT's fixed disk has its sectors interleaved so that logically consecutive sectors are physically located six sectors apart.

N	Sector Size (bytes)	Sector Size (KB)
0	128	$\frac{1}{8}$
1	256	$\frac{1}{4}$
2	512	$\frac{1}{2}$
3	1024	1

Figure 10-4. *The four standard sizes of the N size code.*

To format a diskette track using service 05H, perform the following steps:

1. Call service 17H to inform the ROM BIOS what kind of diskette is to be formatted. (See page 208 for more about service 17H.) This service needs to be called only once.

2. Call service 18H to describe the diskette media to the ROM BIOS. (See page 209.)

3. Create a table of address marks for the track. There must be a 4-byte entry in the table for each sector. For example, for track 0, side 1 of a typical nine-sector DOS diskette, the table would contain nine entries:

```
0 1 1 2  0 1 2 2  0 1 3 2  ... 0 1 9 2
```

4. Call service 05H to format the track.

The method for formatting a fixed-disk track is somewhat different. You should omit the calls to services 17H and 18H (steps 1 and 2 above) because there is no need to describe the disk media to the ROM BIOS. Also, with a PC/AT or PS/2, the table whose address you pass in 3 step has a format that consists only of alternating flag bytes (00H = good sector, 80H = bad sector) and sector number (R) bytes. With a PC/XT, you don't need a table at all. Instead, you call service 05H with an interleave value in AL, and the ROM BIOS does the rest.

You may want to verify the formatting process by following each call to service 05H with a call to service 04H.

When a diskette track is formatted, the diskette drive pays attention to the diskette's index hole and uses it as a starting marker to format the track. The index hole is ignored in all other operations (read, write, or verify), and tracks are simply searched for by their address marks.

Nothing in this format service specifies the initial data value written into each formatted sector of a diskette. That is controlled by the disk-base table. (See page 209.)

❑ NOTE: *Service 05H should not be used with ESDI drives in PS/2s. Use service 1AH instead.*

Using Service 05H for Copy Protection

Diskette tracks can be formatted in all sorts of ways, but DOS can only read certain formats. Consequently, some copy-protection schemes are based on an unconventional format that prevents the ROM BIOS or the operating system from successfully reading and copying data. You can choose from several different copy-protection methods:

- You can rearrange the order of the sectors, which alters the access time in a way that the copy-protection scheme can detect.

- You can squeeze more sectors onto a track (10 is about the outside limit for 512-byte sectors on a 360 KB diskette).

- You can simply leave out a sector number.

- You can add a sector with an oddball address mark (for example, you can make C = 45 or R = 22).

- You can specify one or more sectors to be an unconventional size.

Any of these techniques can be used either for copy protection or for changing the operating characteristics of the diskette. Depending on what options are used, a conventionally formatted diskette may have its copy-protection characteristics completely hidden from DOS.

Service 06H (decimal 6): Format PC/XT Fixed-Disk Track

This service is provided only in the PC/XT fixed-disk ROM BIOS. This service commands the XT's fixed-disk controller to format a track in which the disk media is defective. The disk controller records which sectors are defective in a table located in a reserved cylinder. The register parameters are the same as those shown in Figure 10-3, except that register AL contains a sector interleave value and no address need be specified in ES:BX.

Service 07H (decimal 7): Format PC/XT Fixed Disk

This service, like service 06H, is supported only in the PC/XT fixed-disk ROM BIOS. It formats the entire fixed-disk drive, starting at the cylinder number specified in CH and CL. Register parameters for service 07H are the same as for service 05H (Figure 10-3), except that register AL contains a sector interleave value and no head number need be specified in register DH.

Service 08H (decimal 8): Get Disk-Drive Parameters

In the PC/AT and PS/2 BIOS, service 08H (decimal 8) returns disk-drive parameters for the drive whose number you specify in DL. DL reports the number of disk drives attached to the disk controller, so diskette and fixed-disk drive counts are reported separately. DH reports the maximum head number, CH returns the maximum cylinder number, and CL returns the highest valid sector number plus the 2 high-order bits of the maximum cylinder number.

For diskette drives, the PC/AT ROM BIOS (after 1/10/84) and the PS/2 ROM BIOS also report the drive type in BL: 01H = 360 KB, 5¼ inch; 02H = 1.2 MB, 5¼ inch; 03H = 720 KB, 3½ inch; 04H = 1.44 MB, 3½ inch.

Service 09H (decimal 9): Initialize Fixed-Disk Parameter Tables

Service 09H (decimal 9) establishes the disk-base tables for two fixed-disk drives for the PC/AT or PS/2 ROM BIOS. Call this service with a valid fixed-disk drive number in DL and with the interrupt 41H and 46H vectors containing the addresses of disk-base tables for two different fixed-disk drives. Because fixed disks are nonremovable, this service should only be used to install a "foreign" disk drive not recognized by the ROM BIOS or the operating system. For more details, see the *IBM BIOS Interface Technical Reference Manual*.

❏ NOTE: *Do not use service 09H for PS/2 ESDI drives.*

Service 0AH and 0BH (decimal 10 and 11): Read and Write Long

Service 0AH (decimal 10) reads, and service 0BH (decimal 11) writes, "long" sectors on PC/AT or PS/2 fixed disks. A long sector consists of a sector of data plus a 4- or 6-byte error correction code (ECC) that the fixed-disk controller uses for error checking and error correction of the sector's data. These services use the same register parameters as parallel services 02H and 03H.

❑ NOTE: *The* IBM BIOS Interface Technical Reference Manual *states that services 0AH and 0BH are "reserved for diagnostics," so stay away from these services unless you have a very good reason for using them.*

Service 0CH (decimal 12): Seek to Cylinder

Service 0CH (decimal 12) performs a seek operation that positions the disk read/write heads at a particular cylinder on a fixed disk. Register DL provides the drive ID, DH provides the head number, and CH and CL provide the 10-bit cylinder number.

Service 0DH (decimal 13): Alternate Fixed-Disk Reset

For fixed-disk drives, this service is the same as service 00H (reset disk system) except that the ROM BIOS does not automatically reset the diskette-drive controller. This service is available only in the PC/AT and PS/2 ROM BIOS; it should not be used with the PS/2 ESDI drives.

Service 10H (decimal 16): Test for Drive Ready

Service 10H (decimal 16) tests to see if a fixed-disk drive is ready. The drive is specified in register DL and the status is returned in register AH.

Service 11H (decimal 17): Recalibrate Drive

Service 11H (decimal 17) recalibrates a fixed-disk drive. The drive is specified in register DL and the status is returned in register AH.

Service 15H (decimal 21): Get Disk Type

Service 15H (decimal 21) returns information about the type of disk drive installed in a PC/AT or PS/2. Given the drive ID in register DL, it returns in register AH one of four disk-type indicators. If AH = 00H, no drive is present for the specified drive ID; if AH = 01H, a diskette drive that cannot sense when the disk has been changed (typical of many PC and PC/XT disk drives) is installed; if AH = 02H, a diskette drive that can sense a change of disks (drives like the AT's high-capacity diskette drives) is installed; finally, if AH = 03H, a fixed-disk drive is installed. When the drive type is 3, the register pair CX:DX contains a 4-byte integer that gives the total number of disk sectors on the drive.

Service 16H (decimal 22): Diskette Change Status

In the PC/AT and PS/2 ROM BIOS, service 16H (decimal 22) reports whether the diskette in the drive specified in DL was changed. The status is reported in AH (Figure 10-5).

Remember several important points about service 16H. First, before you use this ROM BIOS service, call service 15H to ensure that the diskette-drive hardware can sense when a diskette is changed. Also, you should follow a call to service 16H with a call to service 17H (Set Diskette Type) whenever you detect a diskette change.

Keep in mind that the hardware can only detect whether the diskette-drive door was opened; it cannot tell whether a different physical diskette was placed in the drive. You must still read data from the diskette to determine whether a different diskette is actually in the drive. Data such as a volume label, the root directory, or a file allocation table can help to uniquely identify a diskette.

Value	Meaning
AH = 00H	No diskette change.
AH = 01H	Service called with invalid parameter.
AH = 06H	Diskette has been changed.
AH = 80H	Diskette drive not ready.

Figure 10-5. *Status values returned in AH by diskette service 16H.*

Service 17H (decimal 23): Set Diskette Type

In the PC/AT and PS/2 ROM BIOS, service 17H (decimal 23) describes the type of diskette in use in a specified drive. Call this service with a drive ID in register DL and a diskette-type ID in AL. (See Figure 10-6.) The ROM BIOS resets the diskette change status if it was previously set. It then records the diskette type in an internal status variable that can be referenced by other ROM BIOS services.

Value	Meaning
AL = 01H	320/360 KB diskette in 360 KB drive
AL = 02H	360 KB diskette in 1.2 MB drive
AL = 03H	1.2 MB diskette in 1.2 MB drive
AL = 04H	720 KB diskette in 720 KB drive (PC/AT or PS/2) or 720 KB or 1.44 MB diskette in 1.44 MB drive (PS/2)

Figure 10-6. *Diskette-type ID values for diskette service 17H.*

Service 18H (decimal 24): Set Media Type for Format

Service 18H (decimal 24) describes the number of tracks and sectors per track to the ROM BIOS before it formats a diskette in a specified drive. These values are placed in registers CH, CL, and DL when you call this service (see Figure 10-3). This service is available only in the PC/AT and PS/2 ROM BIOS.

Service 19H (decimal 25): Park Heads

Service 19H (decimal 25) parks the drive heads for the PS/2 fixed disk whose drive ID you specify in register DL. Calling this function causes the disk controller to move the drive heads away from the portion of the disk media where data is stored. This is a good idea if you plan to move the computer because it may prevent mechanical damage to the heads or to the surfaces of the disk media. On the Reference Diskette that accompanies every PS/2, IBM supplies a utility program that uses this ROM BIOS service to park the heads.

Service 1AH (decimal 26): Format ESDI Unit

This service is provided only in the ROM BIOS of the ESDI (Enhanced Small Device Interface) adapter for high-capacity PS/2 fixed disks. It formats a fixed disk attached to this adapter. See the *IBM BIOS Interface Technical Reference Manual* for more details.

Disk-Base Tables

As we mentioned near the beginning of this chapter, the ROM BIOS maintains a set of disk-base tables that describe the capabilities of each diskette drive and fixed-disk drive in the computer. During system startup, the ROM BIOS associates an appropriate disk-base table with each fixed-disk drive. (In the PC/AT and PS/2s, a data byte in the nonvolatile CMOS RAM designates which of several ROM tables to use.) There is no reason to change the parameters in the fixed-disk tables once they have been set up by the ROM BIOS. Doing so may lead to garbled data on the disk.

The situation is different in the case of diskette drives. The parameters in the disk-base table associated with a diskette drive may need to be updated to accommodate different diskette formats. We'll spend the next few pages describing the structure of a disk-base table for a diskette drive and showing how a modified table can be useful.

The disk-base table comprises the 11 bytes shown in Figure 10-7.

Bytes 0 and 1 are referred to as the *specify bytes*. They are part of the command strings sent to the diskette-drive controller, which in IBM's technical reference manuals is also called the *NEC* (Nippon Electric Company) *controller*. The 4 high-order bits of byte 0 specify the *step-rate time* (SRT), which is the time the drive controller allows for the drive heads to move from track to track. The default ROM BIOS SRT value for diskette drives is conservative; for some drives, DOS reduces this value to speed up drive performance.

Byte 2 specifies how long the diskette motor is to be left running after each operation. The motor is left on in case the diskette is needed again. The value is in units of clock ticks (roughly 18.2 ticks per second). All versions of the table have this set to 37 (25H) — meaning that the motor stays on for about 2 seconds.

Offset	Use
00H	Specify byte 1: step-rate time, head-unload time
01H	Specify byte 2: head-load time, DMA mode
02H	Wait time until diskette motor turned off
03H	Bytes per sector: 0 = 128; 1 = 256; 2 = 512; 3 = 1024
04H	Last sector number
05H	Gap length between sectors for read/write operations
06H	Data length when sector length not specified
07H	Gap length between sectors for formatting operations
08H	Data value stored in formatted sectors
09H	Head-settle time
0AH	Motor start-up time

Figure 10-7. *The use of the 11 bytes in the disk-base table for a diskette drive.*

Byte 3 gives the sector length code — the same N code used in the format operation. (See page 203 under service 05H.) This is normally set to 2, representing the customary sector length of 512 bytes. In any read, write, or verify operation, the length code in the disk base must be set to the proper value, especially when working with sectors of unconventional length.

Byte 4 gives the sector number of the last sector on the track.

Byte 5 specifies the gap size between sectors, which is used when reading or writing data. In effect, it tells the diskette-drive controller how long to wait before looking for the next sector's address marking so that it can avoid looking at nonsense on the diskette. This length of time is known as the *search gap*.

Byte 6 is called the *data transfer length* (DTL) and is set to FFH (decimal 255). This byte sets the maximum data length when the sector length is not specified.

Byte 7 sets the gap size between sectors when a track is formatted. Naturally, it is bigger than the search gap at offset 5. The normal format gap-size value varies with the diskette drive. For example, the value is 54H for the PC/AT's 1.2 MB drive and 6CH for 3½-inch PS/2 diskette drives.

Byte 8 provides the data value stored in each byte of the sectors when a diskette track is formatted. The default value is F6H, the division symbol. You can change it to anything you want, if you can think of a good reason to do so.

Byte 9 sets the *head-settle* time, which is how long the system waits for vibration to end after seeking to a new track. This value also depends on the drive hardware. On the original PC, the value was 19H (25 milliseconds), but the ROM BIOS default for the PC/AT 1.2 MB drive and the PS/2 diskette drives is only 0FH (15 milliseconds).

Byte 0AH (decimal 10), the final byte of the disk-base table, sets the amount of time allowed for the diskette-drive motor to get up to speed and is measured in ⅛ seconds.

It's fun to tinker with the disk-base values; there are enough of them to give you an opportunity for all sorts of excitement and mischief. To do this, you need to write a program that builds your customized disk-base table in a buffer in memory. Then tell the ROM BIOS to use your table by carrying out the following steps:

1. Save the segmented address of the current disk base table. (This is the value in the interrupt 1EH vector, 0000:0078H.)

2. Store the segmented address of your modified table in the interrupt 1EH vector.

3. Call ROM BIOS disk service 00H to reset the disk system. The ROM BIOS will reinitialize the diskette-drive controller with parameters from your table.

When you're finished, be sure to restore the address of the previous disk-base table and reset the disk system again.

Comments and Examples

In the last chapter, where we covered the ROM BIOS video services, we were able to recommend that you make direct use of the ROM BIOS services when DOS or your programming language does not provide the support you need. But in the case of the ROM BIOS disk services, things are different.

For the disk operations that a program would normally want performed, the manipulation and supervision of disk input/output should be left to DOS and performed either through the conventional file services of a programming language or through the DOS services. (See Chapters 14 through 18.) There are several reasons for this. The main reason is that it is far easier to let DOS do the work. The DOS facilities take care of all fundamental disk operations, including formatting and labeling disks, cataloging files, and basic read and write operations. Most of the time it isn't necessary to go any deeper into the system software. However, there are times when you may want to work with disk data in an absolute and precise way, usually for copy protection. This is when you should use the ROM BIOS services.

For our example, we'll use C to call a couple of subroutines that use ROM BIOS functions 02H and 03H to read and write absolute disk sectors. We start by defining how we want the interface to look from the C side, which the following program illustrates. If you are not familiar with C and don't want to decipher this routine, you can pass it by and still get the full benefit by studying the assembly-language interface example that follows it.

```
main()
{
        unsigned char Buffer[512];          /* a 512-byte buffer for reading */
                                            /*  or writing one sector */

        int     Drive;
        int     C,H,R;                      /* address mark parameters */
        int     StatusCode;                 /* status value returned by BIOS */

        StatusCode = ReadSector( Drive, C, H, R, (char far *)Buffer );
        StatusCode = WriteSector( Drive, C, H, R, (char far *)Buffer );
}
```

This C fragment shows how you would call the ROM BIOS read and write services from a high-level language. The functions *ReadSector( )* and *WriteSector( )* are two assembly-language routines that use interrupt 13H to interface with the ROM BIOS disk services. The parameters are familiar: C, H, and R are the cylinder, head, and sector numbers we described earlier. The C compiler passes the buffer address as a segment and offset because of the explicit type cast (char far *).

The form of the assembly-language interface should be familiar if you read the general remarks in Chapter 8 on page 161 or studied the example in Chapter 9 on page 194. The assembly-language routines themselves copy the parameters from the stack into the registers. The trick is in how the cylinder number is processed: The 2 high-order bits of the 10-bit cylinder number are combined with the 6-bit sector number in CL.

```
_TEXT           SEGMENT byte public 'CODE'
                ASSUME  cs:_TEXT

                PUBLIC  _ReadSector
_ReadSector     PROC    near            ; routine to read one sector

                push    bp
                mov     bp,sp           ; address the stack through BP

                mov     ah,2            ; AH = ROM BIOS service number 02h
                call    DiskService

                pop     bp              ; restore previous BP
                ret

_ReadSector     ENDP

                PUBLIC  _WriteSector
_WriteSector    PROC    near            ; routine to write one sector

                push    bp
                mov     bp,sp

                mov     ah,3            ; AH = ROM BIOS service number 03h
                call    DiskService

                pop     bp
                ret

_WriteSector    ENDP


DiskService     PROC    near            ; Call with AH = ROM BIOS service number

                push    ax              ; save service number on stack
```

(continued)

213

```
        mov     dl,[bp+4]       ; DL = drive ID
        mov     ax,[bp+6]       ; AX = cylinder number
        mov     dh,[bp+8]       ; DH = head number
        mov     cl,[bp+10]      ; CL = sector number
        and     cl,00111111b    ; limit sector number to 6 bits
        les     bx,[bp+12]      ; ES:BX -> buffer

        ror     ah,1            ; move bits 8 and 9
        ror     ah,1            ;   of cylinder number
                                ;   to bits 6 and 7 of AH
        and     ah,11000000b
        mov     ch,al           ; CH = bits 0-7 of cylinder number
        or      cl,ah           ; copy bits 8 and 9
                                ;   of cylinder number
                                ;   to bits 6 and 7 of CL

        pop     ax              ; AH = ROM BIOS service number
        mov     al,1            ; AL = 1 (# of sectors to read/write)
        int     13h             ; call ROM BIOS service

        mov     al,ah           ; leave return status
        xor     ah,ah           ; # in AX

        ret

DiskService     ENDP

_TEXT           ENDS
```

Note how the code that copies the parameters from the stack to the registers is consolidated in a subroutine, *DiskService*. When you work with the ROM BIOS disk services, you'll find that you can often use subroutines similar to *DiskService* because most of the ROM BIOS disk services use similar parameter register assignments.

Chapter 11

ROM BIOS
Keyboard Services

Although the ROM BIOS services for the keyboard are not as numerous or as complicated as those for the display screen (Chapter 9) and for diskette drives (Chapter 10), the ROM BIOS keyboard services are important enough to warrant their own chapter. All other ROM BIOS services are gathered together in Chapter 12.

Accessing the Keyboard Services

The keyboard services are invoked with interrupt 16H (decimal 22). As with all other ROM BIOS services, the keyboard services are selected according to the value in register AH. Figure 11-1 lists the ROM BIOS keyboard services.

Service	Description
00H	Read Next Keyboard Character.
01H	Report Whether Character Ready.
02H	Get Shift Status.
03H	Set Typematic Rate and Delay.
05H	Keyboard Write.
10H	Extended Keyboard Read.
11H	Get Extended Keystroke Status.
12H	Get Extended Shift Status.

Figure 11-1. *The ROM BIOS keyboard services.*

Service 00H (decimal 0): Read Next Keyboard Character

Service 00H (decimal 0) reports the next keyboard input character. If a character is ready in the ROM BIOS keyboard buffer, it is reported immediately. If not, the service waits until one is ready. As described on page 134, each keyboard character is reported as a pair of bytes, which we call the main and auxiliary bytes. The main byte, returned in AL, is either 0 for special characters (such as the function keys) or else an ASCII code for ordinary ASCII characters. The auxiliary byte, returned in AH, is either the character ID for special characters or the standard PC-keyboard scan code that identifies which key was pressed.

If no character is waiting in the keyboard buffer when service 00H is called, the service waits — essentially freezing the program that called it — until a character does appear. The service we'll discuss next allows a program to test for keyboard input without the risk of suspending program execution.

Contrary to what some versions of the *IBM PC Technical Reference Manual* suggest, services 00H and 01H apply to both ordinary ASCII characters and special characters, such as function keys.

Service 01H (decimal 1): Report Whether Character Ready

Service 01H (decimal 1) reports whether a keyboard input character is ready. This is a sneak-preview or look-ahead operation: Even though the character is reported, it remains in the keyboard input buffer of the ROM BIOS until it is removed by service 00H. The zero flag (ZF) is used as the signal: 1 indicates no input is ready; 0 indicates a character is ready. Take care not to be confused by the apparent reversal of the flag values — 1 means no and 0 means yes, in this instance. When a character is ready (ZF = 0), it is reported in AL and AH, just as it is with service 00H.

This service is particularly useful for two commonly performed program operations. One is *test-and-go,* where a program checks for keyboard action but needs to continue running if there is none. Usually, this is done to allow an ongoing process to be interrupted by a keystroke. The other common operation is clearing the keyboard buffer. Programs can generally allow users to type ahead, entering commands in advance; however, in some operations (for example, at safety-check points, such as "OK to end?") this practice can be unwise. In these circumstances, programs need to be able to flush the keyboard buffer, clearing it of any input. The keyboard buffer is flushed by using services 00H and 01H, as this program outline demonstrates:

```
call service 01H to test whether a character is available in the
keyboard buffer
WHILE (ZF = 0)
        BEGIN
        call service 00H to remove character from keyboard buffer
        call service 01H to test for another character
        END
```

Contrary to what some technical reference manuals suggest, services 00H and 01H apply to both ordinary ASCII characters and special characters, such as function keys.

Service 02H (decimal 2): Get Shift Status

Service 02H (decimal 2) reports the shift status in register AL. The shift status is taken bit by bit from the first keyboard status byte, which is kept at

Bit 7 6 5 4 3 2 1 0	Meaning
X	Insert state: 1 = active
. X	CapsLock: 1 = active
. . X	NumLock: 1 = active
. . . X	ScrollLock: 1 = active
. . . . X . . .	1 = Alt pressed
. . . . . X . .	1 = Ctrl pressed
. . . . . . X .	1 = Left Shift pressed
. . . . X	1 = Right Shift pressed

Figure 11-2. *The keyboard status bits returned to register AL using keyboard service 02H.*

memory location 0040:0017H. Figure 11-2 describes the settings of each bit. (See page 137 for information about the other keyboard status byte at 0040:0018H.)

Generally, service 02H and the status bit information are not particularly useful. If you plan to do some fancy keyboard programming, however, they can come in handy. You'll frequently see them used in programs that do unconventional things, such as differentiating between the left and right Shift keys.

Service 03H (decimal 3): Set Typematic Rate and Delay

Service 03H (decimal 3) was introduced with the PCjr, but has been supported in both the PC/AT (in ROM BIOS versions dated 11/15/85 and later) and in all PS/2s. It lets you adjust the rate at which the keyboard's typematic function operates; that is, the rate at which a keystroke repeats automatically while you hold down a key. This service also lets you to adjust the *typematic delay* (the amount of time you can hold down a key before the typematic repeat function takes effect).

To use this service, call interrupt 16H with AH = 03H, and AL = 05H. BL must contain a value between 00H and 1FH (decimal 31) that indicates the desired typematic rate (Figure 11-3). The value in BH specifies the typematic delay (Figure 11-4). The default typematic rate for the PC/AT is 10 characters per second; for PS/2s it is 10.9 characters per second. The default delay for both the PC/AT and PS/2s is 500 ms.

00H = 30.0	0BH = 10.9	16H = 4.3
01H = 26.7	0CH = 10.0	17H = 4.0
02H = 24.0	0DH = 9.2	18H = 3.7
03H = 21.8	0EH = 8.6	19H = 3.3
04H = 20.0	0FH = 8.0	1AH = 3.0
05H = 18.5	10H = 7.5	1BH = 2.7
06H = 17.1	11H = 6.7	1CH = 2.5
07H = 16.0	12H = 6.0	1DH = 2.3
08H = 15.0	13H = 5.5	1EH = 2.1
09H = 13.3	14H = 5.0	1FH = 2.0
0AH = 12.0	15H = 4.6	20H through FFH - Reserved

Figure 11-3. *Values for register BL in keyboard service 03H. The rates shown are in characters per second.*

00H = 250
01H = 500
02H = 750
03H = 1000
04H through FFH - Reserved

Figure 11-4. *Values for register BH in keyboard service 03H. The delay values shown are in milliseconds.*

Service 05H (decimal 5): Keyboard Write

Service 05H (decimal 5) is handy because it lets you store keystroke data in the keyboard buffer as if a key were pressed. You must supply an ASCII code in register CL and a keyboard scan code in CH. The ROM BIOS places these codes into the keyboard buffer following any keystroke data that may already be present there.

Service 05H lets a program process input as if it were typed at the keyboard. For example, if you call service 05H with the following data, the result is the same as if the keys R-U-N-Enter were pressed:

```
CH = 13H, CL = 52H, call service 05H (the R key)
CH = 16H, CL = 55H, call service 05H (the U key)
CH = 31H, CL = 4EH, call service 05H (the N key)
CH = 1CH, CL = 0DH, call service 05H (the Enter key)
```

If your program did this when it detected that the F2 function key was pressed, the result would be the same as if the word RUN followed by the Enter key had been typed. (If you use BASIC, this should sound familiar.)

Beware: The keyboard buffer can hold only 15 character codes, so you can call service 05H a maximum of 15 consecutive times before the buffer overflows and the function fails.

Service 10H (decimal 16): Extended Keyboard Read

Service 10H (decimal 16) performs the same function as service 00H, but lets you take full advantage of the 101/102-key keyboard: It returns ASCII character codes and keyboard scan codes for keys that don't exist on the older 84-key keyboard. For example, the extra F11 and F12 keys found on the 101/102-key keyboard are ignored by service 00H but can be read using service 10H.

Another example: On the 101/102-key keyboard, an extra Enter key appears to the right of the numeric keypad. When this key is pressed, service 00H returns the same character code (0DH) and scan code (1CH) as it does for the standard Enter key. Service 10H lets you differentiate between the two Enter keys because it returns a different scan code (E0H) for the keypad Enter key.

Service 11H (decimal 17): Get Extended Keystroke Status

Service 11H (decimal 17) is analogous to service 01H, but it, too, lets you use the 101/102-key keyboard to full advantage. The scan codes returned in register AH by this service distinguish between different keys on the 101/102-key keyboard.

Service 12H (decimal 18): Get Extended Shift Status

Like services 10H and 11H, service 12H (decimal 18) provides additional support for the 101/102-key keyboard. Service 12H expands the function of service 02H to provide information on the extra shift keys provided on the 101/102-key keyboard. This service returns the same value in register AL as service 02H (Figure 11-2), but it also returns an additional byte of flags in register AH (Figure 11-5).

This extra byte indicates the status of each individual Ctrl and Alt key. It also indicates whether the Sys Req, Caps Lock, Num Lock, or Scroll Lock keys are currently pressed. This information lets you detect when a user presses any combination of these keys at the same time.

Bit 7 6 5 4 3 2 1 0	Meaning
X	Sys Req pressed
. X	Caps Lock pressed
. . X	Num Lock pressed
. . . X	Scroll Lock pressed
. . . . X . . .	Right Alt pressed
. . . . . X . .	Right Ctrl pressed
. . . . . . X .	Left Alt pressed
. . . . X	Left Ctrl pressed

Figure 11-5. *Extended keyboard status bits returned in register AH by keyboard service 12H.*

Comments and Example

If you are in a position to choose between the keyboard services of your programming language or the ROM BIOS keyboard services, you could safely and wisely use either one. Although in some cases there are arguments against using the ROM BIOS services directly, as with the diskette services, those arguments do not apply as strongly to the keyboard services. However, as always, you should fully examine the potential of the DOS services before resorting to the ROM BIOS services; you may find all you need there, and the DOS services are more long-lived in the ever-changing environments of personal computers.

Most programming languages depend on the DOS services for their keyboard operations, a factor that has some distinct advantages. One advantage is that the DOS services allow the use of the standard DOS editing operations on string input (input that is not acted on until the Enter key is pressed). Provided that you do not need input control of your own, it can save you a great deal of programming effort (and user education) to let DOS handle the string input, either directly through the DOS services or indirectly through your language's services. But if you need full control of keyboard input, you'll probably end up using the ROM BIOS routines in the long run. Either way, the choice is yours.

Another advantage to using the DOS keyboard services is that the DOS services can redirect keyboard input so that characters are read from a file instead of the keyboard. If you rely on the ROM BIOS keyboard services, you can't redirect keyboard input. (Chapters 16 and 17 contain information on input/output redirection.)

For our assembly-language example of the use of keyboard services, we'll get a little fancier than we have in previous examples and show you a complete buffer flusher. This routine will perform the action outlined under keyboard service 01H, the report-whether-character-ready service.

```
_TEXT           SEGMENT byte public 'CODE'
                ASSUME  cs:_TEXT

                PUBLIC  _kbclear
_kbclear        PROC    near

                push    bp
                mov     bp,sp

L01:            mov     ah,1            ; test whether buffer is empty
                int     16h
                jz      L02             ; if so, exit

                mov     ah,0
                int     16h             ; otherwise, discard data
                jmp     L01             ; .. and loop

L02:            pop     bp
                ret

_kbclear        ENDP

_TEXT           ENDS
```

The routine works by using interrupt 16H, service 01H to check whether the keyboard buffer is empty. If no characters exist in the buffer, service 01H sets the zero flag, and executing the instruction JZ L02 causes the routine to exit by branching to the instruction labeled L02. If the buffer still contains characters, however, service 01H clears the zero flag, and the JZ L02 instruction doesn't jump. In this case the routine continues to the instructions that call service 00H to read a character from the buffer. Then the process repeats because the instruction JMP L01 transfers control back to label L01. Sooner or later, of course, the repeated calls to service 00H empty the buffer, service 01H sets the zero flag, and the routine terminates.

Among the new things this buffer-flusher routine illustrates is the use of labels and branching. When we discussed the generalities of assembly-language interface routines in Chapter 8, we mentioned that an ASSUME CS statement is necessary in some circumstances, and you see one in action here.

The ASSUME directive in this example tells the assembler that the labels in the code segment (that is, labels that would normally be addressed using the CS register) do indeed lie in the segment whose name is _TEXT. This may seem obvious, since no other segments appear in this routine.

Nevertheless, it is possible to write assembly-language routines in which labels in one segment are addressed relative to some other segment; in such a case, the ASSUME directive would not necessarily reference the segment within which the labels appear. In later chapters you'll see examples of this technique, but here the only segment to worry about is the _TEXT segment, and the ASSUME directive makes this fact explicit.

Chapter 12

Miscellaneous Services

In this chapter, we'll be covering all ROM BIOS services that are either not important enough or not complex enough to warrant their own chapters: RS-232 serial communications services, system services, ROM BIOS hooks, and printer services. We'll also cover some services that are odd enough to be considered miscellaneous, even in a chapter of miscellany.

RS-232 Serial Communications Services

This section discusses the RS-232 asynchronous serial communications port services in the ROM BIOS. Before we begin describing the ROM BIOS services in detail, you need to know a few important things about the serial communications port, particularly the terminology. We assume you have a basic understanding of data communications, but if you discover that you don't understand the following information, turn to one of the many specialty books on communications for some background information.

Many words are used to describe the RS-232 data path in and out of the computer. One of the most common is *port*. However, this use of the word port is completely different from our previous use of the word. Throughout most of this book, we have used port to refer to the addressable paths used by the 8088 microprocessor to talk to other parts of the computer *within the confines of the computer's circuitry*. All references to port numbers, the BASIC statements INP and OUT, and the assembly-language operations IN and OUT refer to these addressable ports. The RS-232 asynchronous serial communications port differs because it is a general-purpose I/O path, which can be used to interconnect many kinds of information-processing equipment *outside the computer*. Typically, the serial ports are used for telecommunications (meaning a telephone connection through a modem) or to send data to a serial-type printer.

Four serial communications services are common to all IBM models. These services are invoked with interrupt 14H (decimal 20), selected through register AH, and numbered 00H through 03H. (See Figure 12-1.) The PS/2 ROM BIOS contains two additional services that provide extended support for the more capable PS/2 serial port.

The original design of the IBM personal computers allowed up to seven serial ports to be added, although a computer rarely uses more than one or two. The PS/2 ROM BIOS explicitly supports only four serial ports. No matter how many serial ports exist, the serial port number is specified in the DX register for all ROM BIOS serial communications services. The first serial port is indicated by 00H in DX.

Service	Description
00H	Initialize Serial Port.
01H	Send Out One Character.
02H	Receive One Character.
03H	Get Serial Port Status.
04H	Initialize Extended Serial Port.
05H	Control Extended Communication Port.

Figure 12-1. *The RS-232 serial port services available through interrupt 14H (decimal 20).*

Service 00H (decimal 0): Initialize Serial Port

Service 00H (decimal 0) sets the various RS-232 parameters and initializes the serial port. It sets four parameters: the baud rate, the parity, the number of stop bits, and the character size (also called the *word length*). The parameters are combined into one 8-bit code, which is placed in the AL register with the format shown in Figure 12-2. The bit settings for each code are shown in Figure 12-3. When the service is finished, the communication port status is reported in AX, just as it is for service 03H. (See service 03H for the details.)

Bit 7 6 5 4 3 2 1 0	Use
X X X	Baud-rate code
. . . X X . . .	Parity code
. . . . . X . .	Stop-bit code
. . . . . . X X	Character-size code

Figure 12-2. *The bit order of the serial port parameters passed in register AL to service 00H.*

❑ NOTE: *Although it is painfully slow, 300 baud used to be the most commonly used baud rate for personal computers using modems. A rate of 1200 baud is now the most common, particularly for serious applications that require faster transmission, but widespread use of at least 2400 baud communications is inevitable.*

BAUD RATE

Bit 7	6	5	Value	Bits per Second
0	0	0	0	110
0	0	1	1	150
0	1	0	2	300
0	1	1	3	600
1	0	0	4	1200
1	0	1	5	2400
1	1	0	6	4800
1	1	1	7	9600

PARITY

Bit 4	3	Value	Meaning
0	0	0	None
0	1	1	Odd parity
1	0	2	None
1	1	3	Even parity

CHARACTER SIZE

Bit 1	0	Value	Meaning
0	0	0	Not used
0	1	1	Not used
1	0	2	7-bit*
1	1	3	8-bit

STOP BITS

Bit 2	Value	Meaning
0	0	One
1	1	Two

* There are only 128 standard ASCII characters, so they can be transmitted as 7-bit characters, rather than 8-bit characters.

Figure 12-3. *The bit settings for the four serial port parameters for service 00H.*

Service 01H (decimal 1): Send Out One Character

Service 01H (decimal 1) transmits one character out the serial port specified in DX. When you call service 01H, you place the character to be transmitted in AL. When service 01H returns, it reports the status of the communications port. If AH = 00H, then the service was successful. Otherwise bit 7 of AH indicates that an error occurred, and the other bits of AH report the type of error. These bits are outlined in the discussion of service 03H, the status service.

The error report supplied through this service has one anomaly: Because bit 7 reports that an error has occurred, it is not available to indicate a time-out error (as the details in service 03H would suggest). Consequently, when this service or service 02H reports an error, the simplest and most reliable way to check the nature of the error is to use the complete status report given by service 03H, rather than the less-complete status code returned with the error through services 01H and 02H.

Service 02H (decimal 2): Receive One Character

Service 02H (decimal 2) receives one character from the communications line specified in DX and returns it in the AL register. The service waits for a character or any signal that indicates the completion of the service, such as a time-out. AH reports the success or failure of the service in bit 7, as explained in the discussion of service 01H. Again, consider the advice under service 01H for error handling and see service 03H for the error codes.

Service 03H (decimal 3): Get Serial Port Status

Service 03H (decimal 3) returns the complete serial port status in the AX register. The 16 status bits in AX are divided into two groups: AH reports the line status (which is also reported when errors occur with services 01H and 02H), and AL reports the modem status, when applicable. Figure 12-4 contains the bit codings of the status bits. Some codes report errors, and others simply report a condition.

❏ NOTE: *One special bit of information about the time-out error (AH, bit 7) is worth noting: The earliest version of the ROM BIOS for the original PC had a programming error that caused a serial-port time-out to be reported as a transfer-shift-register-empty/break-detect-error combination (bits 01010000 rather than 10000000). This has been corrected on all subsequent versions of the ROM BIOS, but it has caused many communications programs to treat these error codes skeptically. You may want to keep this in mind. See page 62 for details on identifying the ROM BIOS version dates and machine ID codes.*

Bit 7 6 5 4 3 2 1 0	Meaning (when set to 1)	Bit 7 6 5 4 3 2 1 0	Meaning (when set to 1)
AH Register (line status)		*AL Register (modem status)*	
1	Time-out error	1	Received line signal detect
. 1	Transfer shift register empty	. 1	Ring indicator
. . 1	Transfer holding register empty	. . 1	Data-set-ready
. . . 1	Break-detect error	. . . 1	Clear-to-send
. . . . 1 . . .	Framing error	. . . . 1 . . .	Delta receive line signal detect
. . . . . 1 . .	Parity error	. . . . . 1 . .	Trailing-edge ring detector
. . . . . . 1 .	Overrun error	. . . . . . 1 .	Delta data-set-ready
. . . . 1	Data ready	 1	Delta clear-to-send

Figure 12-4. *The bit coding for the status bytes returned in register AX by service 03H.*

Service 04H (decimal 4): Initialize Extended Serial Port

Service 04H (decimal 4) is available only in the PS/2 ROM BIOS. It expands the capabilities of service 00H to provide support for the PS/2's improved serial ports. If you compare service 04H with service 00H, you'll find that the four serial port initialization parameters passed in AL in service 00H are separated into four registers in service 04H (Figure 12-5). Also, service 04H returns both modem and line status in register AX, exactly as service 03H does. Because service 04H has these expanded capabilities, you should generally use it instead of service 00H for PS/2 serial port initialization.

BREAK (register AL)

Value	Meaning
00H	No break
01H	Break

PARITY (register BH)

Value	Meaning
00H	None
01H	Odd
02H	Even
03H	Stick parity odd
04H	Stick parity even

STOP BITS (register BL)

Value	Meaning
00H	One
01H	Two (for word length = 6, 7, or 8) 1 ½ (for word length = 5)

WORD LENGTH (register CH)

Value	Meaning
00H	5 bits
01H	6 bits
02H	7 bits
03H	8 bits

BAUD RATE (register CL)

Value	Meaning	Value	Meaning
00H	110 baud	05H	2400 baud
01H	150 baud	06H	4800 baud
02H	300 baud	07H	9600 baud
03H	600 baud	08H	19,200 baud
04H	1200 baud		

Figure 12-5. *Register values for serial port initialization with interrupt 14H, service 04H. (Register DX contains a serial port number between 0 and 3.)*

Service 05H (decimal 5): Control Extended Communications Port

This service, provided only by the PS/2 ROM BIOS, lets you read from or write to the modem control register of a specified serial communications port. When you call service 05H with AL = 00H and a serial port number in DX, service 05H returns with register BL containing the value in the modem control register of the specified serial port. When you call service 05H with AL = 01H, the ROM BIOS copies the value you pass in register BL into the modem control register for the specified port. In both cases, service 05H returns the modem status and line status in registers AL and AH, as does service 03H.

Miscellaneous System Services

The miscellaneous system services provided through interrupt 15H are indeed miscellaneous. (See Figure 12-6.) Many are intended primarily for writers of operating-system software. Most application programmers will find little use for these services in their programs, because the functions provided are better carried out by calls to the operating system than they are through the ROM BIOS. Some of these services, such as the pointing-device interface (subservice C2H), provide functionality not otherwise available in the ROM BIOS or in DOS; others are obsolete and virtually unusable.

Service	Description
00H	Turn On Cassette Motor.
01H	Turn Off Cassette Motor.
02H	Read Cassette Data Blocks.
03H	Write Cassette Data Blocks.
21H	Read or Write PS/2 Power-On Self-Test Error Log.
4FH	Keyboard Intercept.
80H	Device Open.
81H	Device Close.
82H	Program Termination.
83H	Start or Cancel Interval Timer.
84H	Read Joystick Input.
85H	Sys Req Keystroke.
86H	Wait During a Specified Interval.
87H	Protected-Mode Data Move.
88H	Get Extended Memory Size.
89H	Switch to Protected Mode.

Figure 12-6. *Miscellaneous system services available through interrupt 15H.*　　　　　　　　　　　　　　　*(continued)*

Figure 12-6. *continued*

Service	Description
90H	Device Busy.
91H	Interrupt Complete.
C0H	Get System Configuration Parameters.
C1H	Get Extended BIOS Data Segment.
C2H	Pointing-Device Interface.
C3H	Enable/Disable Watchdog Timer.
C4H	Programmable Option Select.

The four cassette tape services are used when working with the cassette tape connection, which is a part of only two PC models: the original PC and the now-defunct PCjr. The cassette port was created with the original PC on the assumption that a demand might exist for it. None did, and it has remained almost totally unused. Nevertheless, IBM does support the use of the cassette port, both through the ROM BIOS services discussed here and through BASIC, which lets you read and write either data or BASIC programs on standard audio cassette tape.

The cassette port never proved worthwhile, however. Nobody sells PC programs on tape, and nobody has found much use for the cassette port, given the convenience of diskettes and hard disks.

Service 00H (decimal 0): Turn On Cassette Motor

Service 00H (decimal 0) turns on the cassette motor, which is not an automatic operation of the ROM BIOS services as it is with the diskette services. Any program that is using this service can expect a slight delay while the motor starts.

Service 01H (decimal 1): Turn Off Cassette Motor

Service 01H (decimal 1) turns off the cassette motor. This is not an automatic operation of the ROM BIOS services as it is with the diskette services.

Service 02H (decimal 2): Read Cassette Data Blocks

Service 02H (decimal 2) reads one or more cassette *data blocks*. Cassette data is transferred in standard-size 256-byte blocks, just as diskette data normally uses a standard 512-byte sector. The number of bytes to be read is placed in the CX register. Although data is placed on tape in 256-byte blocks, any number of bytes can be read or written. Consequently, the number of bytes placed in the CX register need not be a multiple of 256. The register pair ES:BX is used as a pointer to the memory area where the data is to be placed.

233

After the service is completed, DX contains the actual number of bytes read, ES:BX points to the byte immediately after the last byte transferred, and the carry flag (CF) is set or cleared to report the success or failure of the operation. On failure, AH returns an error code. (See Figure 12-7.)

Code	Meaning
01H	Cyclical redundancy check (CRC) error
02H	Lost data transitions: bit signals scrambled
04H	No data found on tape

Figure 12-7. *The error code returned by service 02H in register AH if the CF indicates a failure to read the data blocks.*

Service 03H (decimal 3): Write Cassette Data Blocks

Service 03H (decimal 3) writes one or more cassette data blocks of 256 bytes each. (See service 02H.) As with service 02H, the CX register gives the count of bytes requested, and ES:BX points to the data area in memory. If the amount of data being written is not a multiple of 256 bytes, the last data block is padded out to full size.

After the service is completed, CX should contain 00H, and ES:BX should point just past the last memory byte that was written.

Curiously, no error signals are provided for this service, essentially because a cassette tape recorder can't inform the computer of any difficulties. This forces the ROM BIOS to write data in blind faith that all is well. Needless to say, it would be a good idea to read back any data written, just to check it.

Service 21H (decimal 33): Read or Write PS/2 POST Error Log

Service 21H (decimal 33) is used internally by the ROM BIOS power-on self-test (POST) routines in PS/2s with the Micro Channel bus to keep track of hardware initialization errors. You will rarely, if ever, find use for this service in your own applications.

Service 83H (decimal 131): Start or Cancel Interval Timer

This service lets a program set a specified time interval and lets the program check a flag to show when the interval expires. The program should call this service with AL = 00H, with the address of a flag byte in registers ES and BX, and with the time interval in microseconds in registers CX and DX. The high-order 16 bits of the interval should be in CX; the low-order 16 bits in DX.

Initially, the flag byte should be 00H. When the time interval elapses, the ROM BIOS sets this byte to 80H. The program can thus inspect the flag byte at its own convenience to determine when the time interval has elapsed:

```
Clear the flag byte
Call service 83H to start the interval timer
WHILE   (flag byte = 00H)
        BEGIN
        (do something useful)
        END
```

The ROM BIOS interval timer uses the system time-of-day clock, which ticks about 1024 times per second, so the timer's resolution is approximately 976 microseconds.

Service 84H (decimal 132): Read Joystick Input

Service 84H (decimal 132) provides a consistent interface for programs that use a joystick or a related input device connected to IBM's Game Control Adapter. When you call this service with DX = 00H, the ROM BIOS reports the adapter's four digital switch input values in bits 4 through 7 of register AL. Calling service 84H with DX = 01H instructs the BIOS to return the adapter's four resistive input values in registers AX, BX, CX, and DX.

Service 84H is not supported on the IBM PC or in the original PC/XT BIOS (dated 11/08/82). Be sure to check the computer's model identification and ROM BIOS revision date before you rely on this BIOS service in a program.

Service 86H (decimal 134): Wait During a Specified Interval

Like service 83H, service 86H (decimal 134) lets a program set a specified time interval to wait. Unlike service 83H, however, service 86H suspends operation of the program that calls it until the specified time interval has elapsed. Control returns to the program only when the wait has completed or if the hardware timer is unavailable.

Service 87H (decimal 135): Protected-Mode Data Move

A program running in real mode can use service 87H to transfer data to or from extended (protected-mode) memory on a PC/AT or PS/2 Model 50, 60, or 80. This service is designed to be used by a protected-mode operating system. The IBM-supplied VDISK utility also uses this function to copy data to and from a virtual disk in extended memory. See the *IBM BIOS Interface Technical Reference Manual* for details.

Service 88H (decimal 136): Get Extended Memory Size

Service 88H (decimal 136) returns the amount of extended (protected-mode) memory installed in a PC/AT or PS/2 Model 50, 60, or 80. The value, in kilobytes, is returned in register AX.

The amount of extended memory is established by the ROM BIOS POST routines. It includes extended memory installed beyond the first megabyte; that is, memory starting at 10000:0000H. Lotus/Intel/Microsoft "expanded" memory is not included in the value returned by service 88H.

Service 89H (decimal 137): Switch to Protected Mode

Service 89H (decimal 137) is provided by the ROM BIOS as an aid to configuring an 80286-based computer (PC/AT, PS/2 Model 50 or 60) or an 80386-based computer (PS/2 Model 80) for protected-mode operation. This ROM BIOS service is intended for operating systems that run in protected mode. To use this service, you must be thoroughly acquainted with protected-mode programming techniques. See the *IBM BIOS Interface Technical Reference Manual* for details.

Service C0H (decimal 192): Get System Configuration Parameters

Service C0H (decimal 192) returns the address of a table of descriptive information pertaining to the hardware and BIOS configuration of a PC/AT (in ROM BIOS versions dated 6/10/85 and later) or PS/2. Figure 12-8 shows the structure of the table. You can find the meaning of the model and submodel bytes in Chapter 3, page 64.

Offset	Size	Contents
0	2 bytes	Size of configuration information table
2	1 byte	Model byte
3	1 byte	Submodel byte
4	1 byte	ROM BIOS revision level
5	1 byte	Feature information byte:
		Bit 7: Fixed-disk BIOS uses DMA Channel 3
		Bit 6: Cascaded interrupt level 2 (IRQ2)
		Bit 5: Real-time clock present
		Bit 4: BIOS keyboard intercept implemented
		Bit 3: Wait for external event supported
		Bit 2: Extended BIOS data area allocated
		Bit 1: Micro Channel bus present
		Bit 0: (Reserved)

Figure 12-8. *System configuration information returned by service C0H.*

Service C1H (decimal 193):
Get ROM BIOS Extended Data Segment

Service C1H (decimal 193) returns the segment address of the ROM BIOS extended data area. The ROM BIOS clears the carry flag and returns the segment value in register ES if an extended BIOS data segment is in use. Otherwise, service C1H returns with the carry flag set.

The ROM BIOS uses the extended data area for transient storage of data. For example, when you pass the address of a pointing-device interface subroutine to the BIOS, the BIOS stores this address in its extended data area.

Service C2H (decimal 194): Pointing-Device Interface

Service C2H (decimal 194) is the ROM BIOS interface to the built-in PS/2 pointing-device controller. This interface makes it easy to use an IBM PS/2 mouse.

To use the interface, you must write a short subroutine to which the ROM BIOS can pass packets of status information about the pointing device. Your subroutine should examine the data in each packet and respond appropriately, for example by moving a cursor on the screen. The subroutine must exit with a far return without changing the contents of the stack.

To use the ROM BIOS pointing-device interface, carry out the following sequence of steps:

1. Pass the address of your subroutine to the BIOS (subservice 07H).

2. Initialize the interface (subservice 05H).

3. Enable the pointing device (subservice 00H).

At this point, the BIOS begins sending packets of status information to your subroutine. The BIOS places each packet on the stack and calls your subroutine with a far CALL so that the stack is formatted when the subroutine gets control as in Figure 12-9. The low-order byte of the X and Y data words contains the number of units the pointing device has moved since the previous packet of data was sent. (The Z data byte is always 0.) The status byte contains sign, overflow, and button information. (See Figure 12-10.)

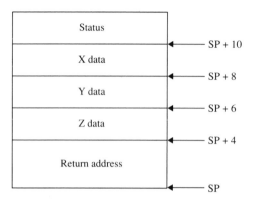

Figure 12-9. *Pointing-device data packet.*

Bit	Meaning
0	Set if left button pressed
1	Set if right button pressed
2–3	(Reserved)
4	Set if X data is negative
5	Set if Y data is negative
6	Set if X data overflows
7	Set if Y data overflows

Figure 12-10. *Status byte in pointing-device data packet.*

When you use service C2H, the value you pass in register AL selects one of eight available subservices. (See Figure 12-11.) The actual register contents for each subservice are in Chapter 13, page 284.

Subservice	Description
00H	Enable/disable pointing device.
01H	Reset pointing device.
02H	Set sample rate.
03H	Set resolution.

Figure 12-11. *Subservices available in the BIOS pointing-device interface*   (continued) *(interrupt 15H, service C2H).*

Figure 12-11. *continued*

Subservice	Description
04H	Get pointing-device type.
05H	Initialize pointing device.
06H	Extended commands.
07H	Pass device-driver address to ROM BIOS.

Service C3H (decimal 195): Enable/Disable Watchdog Timer

Service C3H (decimal 195) provides a consistent interface to the watchdog timer in the PS/2 models 50, 60, and 80. It lets an operating system enable the watchdog timer with a specified timeout interval or disable the timer. Because the watchdog timer is intended specifically for use in operating-system software, this ROM BIOS service will rarely be useful in your applications.

Service C4H (decimal 196): Programmable Option Select

Like many other interrupt 15H services, service C4H (decimal 196) is intended for use by operating system software. This service provides a consistent interface to the Programmable Option Select feature of the Micro Channel architecture in the PS/2 models 50, 60, and 80.

ROM BIOS Hooks

The ROM BIOS in the PC/AT and in the PS/2s provides a number of hooks. These hooks are implemented as interrupt 15H ''services,'' but to use them you must write an interrupt 15H handler that processes only these services and passes all other interrupt 15H service requests to the ROM BIOS. (See Figure 12-12.) This arrangement lets different components of the BIOS communicate with each other and with operating-system or user-written programs in a consistent manner.

The ROM BIOS hooks are intended primarily for use in operating systems and in programs written to augment operating-system or BIOS functions. However, neither DOS nor OS/2 uses these BIOS hooks, and few program applications have reason to. Still, you might find it worthwhile to examine what the ROM BIOS hooks do, if only to get an idea of how the ROM BIOS is put together and how an operating system can interact with it.

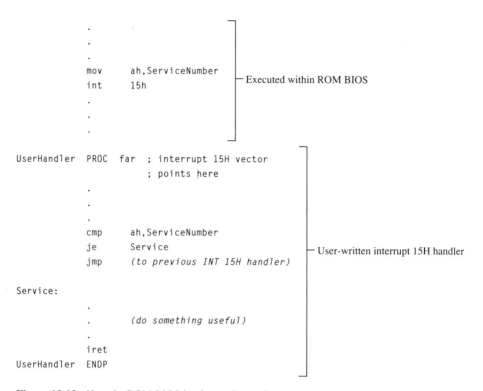

Figure 12-12. *How the ROM BIOS hooks can be used.*

Service 4FH (decimal 79): Keyboard Intercept

In the PC/AT ROM BIOS (dated 06/10/85 and later) and in the PS/2 ROM BIOS, the keyboard interrupt handler (that is, the handler for hardware interrupt 09H) executes interrupt 15H with AH = 4FH and with AL equal to the keyboard scan code. This action has little effect: The ROM BIOS interrupt 15H, service 4FH (decimal 79) handler returns with the carry flag set, and the interrupt 09H handler continues processing the keystroke.

If you write an interrupt handler for interrupt 15H, however, you can hook service 4FH and process keystrokes yourself. Install your handler by storing its segmented address in the interrupt 15H vector. (Be sure to save the previous contents of the interrupt 15H vector.) Your interrupt 15H handler would do the following:

```
IF (AH<>4FH)
        jump to default interrupt 15H handler
ELSE
        process keyboard scan code in AL
        set or reset carry flag
        exit from interrupt handler
```

If your handler processes the scan code in AL, it must either set or reset the carry flag before it returns control to the ROM BIOS interrupt 09H handler. Setting the carry flag indicates that the BIOS interrupt 09H handler should continue processing the scan code in AL: Clearing the carry flag causes the BIOS handler to exit without processing the scan code.

The problem with using the ROM BIOS keyboard intercept is that other programs, including DOS itself, can and do process keystrokes before the ROM BIOS interrupt 09H handler ever has a chance to issue interrupt 15H. (These programs do this by pointing the interrupt 09H vector to their own handlers instead of to the default ROM BIOS handler.) Because your program can't determine if this is happening, you cannot rely on the ROM BIOS keyboard intercept to be called for every keystroke.

Service 80H (decimal 128): Device Open

This hook lets programs determine when a particular hardware device is available for input or output. An installable device driver can issue interrupt 15H with AH = 80H to inform an operating system that the device was opened. The operating system's interrupt 15H handler can inspect BX for an identifying value for the device and CX for an ID value of the program that opened the device.

Service 81H (decimal 129): Device Close

Like service 80H, this service is provided for programs that establish input/ output connections to hardware devices to communicate with an operating system. Service 81H (decimal 129) is called by such a program with a device ID value in register BX and a program ID value in CX. An operating system's interrupt 15H handler can inspect these values to determine that a particular device was closed for input/output by a particular program.

Service 82H (decimal 130): Program Termination

Service 82H (decimal 130) is provided by the ROM BIOS so that a program can signal its own termination to an operating system. When a program executes interrupt 15H with AH = 82H and an ID value in BX, the operating system can handle the interrupt and thus be informed that the program terminated.

Service 85H (decimal 133): Sys Req Keystroke

When you press the Sys Req key on an 84-key keyboard or Alt-Sys Req on a 101/102-key keyboard, the ROM BIOS keyboard interrupt handler executes interrupt 15H with AH = 85H. You can detect when this key is pressed by hooking interrupt 15H and inspecting the value in AH.

When the Sys Req key is first pressed, the ROM BIOS issues interrupt 15H with AH = 85H and AL = 00H. When the key is released, the BIOS executes interrupt 15H with AH = 85H and AL = 01H. Thus the structure of an interrupt 15H handler that detects Sys Req keystrokes would be as follows:

```
IF (AH<>85H)
                    jump to previous interrupt 15H handler
ELSE IF (AL = 00H)
                    process Sys Req keystroke
    ELSE
                    process Sys Req key release
        exit from interrupt handler
```

Service 90H (decimal 144): Device Busy

This service lets a device driver alert an operating system to the beginning of an input or output operation. An operating system's interrupt 15H handler processes this information (for example) by preventing subsequent input/output to the device until the device signals, with service 91H, that it is no longer busy.

The ROM BIOS device drivers for disks, the keyboard, and the printer all issue appropriate service 90H (decimal 144) interrupts. Each device is identified by a value in register AL. (See Figure 12-13.) These ID values are selected according to the following guidelines:

- 00H–7FH: Non-reentrant devices that can process only one I/O request at a time sequentially.

- 80H–BFH: Reentrant devices that can handle multiple I/O requests at once.

- C0H–FFH: Devices that expect the operating system to wait for a predetermined period of time before returning control to the device. The operating system's interrupt 15H handler must set the carry flag to indicate that the wait has been carried out.

Value	Meaning
00H	Fixed disk
01H	Diskette
02H	Keyboard

Figure 12-13. *Device identification values for interrupt 15H,* *services 90H and 91H.* (continued)

Figure 12-13. *continued*

Value	Meaning
03H	Pointing device
80H	Network
FCH	PS/2 fixed-disk reset
FDH	Diskette-drive motor start
FEH	Printer

Service 91H (decimal 145): Interrupt Complete

Devices that use service 90H to notify an operating system that they are busy can subsequently use service 91H (decimal 145) to signal that an input/output operation has been completed. The identification value passed in AL should be the same as the value passed in service 90H.

Printer Services

The ROM BIOS printer services support printer output through the parallel printer adapter. The three ROM BIOS printer services are invoked with interrupt 17H (decimal 23), requested through the AH register, and numbered 00H through 02H. (See Figure 12-14.) The general PC-family design allows more than one printer to be installed, so a printer number must be specified in register DX for all these services.

Service	Description
00H	Send One Byte to Printer.
01H	Initialize Printer.
02H	Get Printer Status.

Figure 12-14. *The three ROM BIOS printer services invoked through interrupt 17H (decimal 23).*

Service 00H (decimal 0): Send 1 Byte to Printer

Service 00H (decimal 0) sends the byte you specify to the printer. When the service is completed, AH is then set to report the printer status (see service 02H), which can be used to determine the success or failure of the operation. See the special notes on printer time-out under service 02H.

Service 01H (decimal 1): Initialize Printer

Service 01H (decimal 1) initializes the printer. To do this, the service simply sends two control codes (08H and 0CH) to the printer control port. As with the other two services, the printer status is reported in AH.

Service 02H (decimal 2): Get Printer Status

Service 02H (decimal 2) reports the printer status in the AH register. The individual bit codes are shown in Figure 12-15.

The printer time-out has caused some difficulty in the IBM personal computers. Any I/O driver needs to set a time limit for a response from the device being controlled. Ideally, this time limit should be short enough to ensure that an unresponsive device can be reported in a timely manner. Unfortunately, one normal printer operation can take a surprisingly long time: a *page eject* ("skip to the top of the next page"). The time allowed varies from version to version of the ROM BIOS. Treat a time-out signal with care.

Bit *7 6 5 4 3 2 1 0*	*Meaning (when set to 1)*
1	Printer *not* busy (0 = busy)
. 1	Acknowledgment from printer
. . 1	Out-of-paper signal
. . . 1	Printer selected
. . . . 1 . . .	I/O error
. . . . . 1 . .	Not used
. . . . . . 1 .	Not used
. . . . 1	Time-out

Figure 12-15. *The printer status bits reported in the AH register by services 00H, 01H, and 02H.*

Other Services

We now come to the grab bag of all other ROM BIOS services. (See Figure 12-16.) Some of these services are intended for use in program applications; others are more likely to be used in operating-system software. The following sections describe these six service interrupts.

Interrupt		
Hex	*Dec*	*Description*
05H	5	Print-Screen Service
11H	17	Equipment-List Service
12H	18	Memory-Size Service
18H	24	ROM BASIC Loader Service
19H	25	Bootstrap Loader Service
1AH	26	Time-of-Day Services

Figure 12-16. *Six miscellaneous ROM BIOS services supported by IBM, and their associated interrupts.*

Interrupt 05H (decimal 5): Print-Screen Service

Interrupt 05H (decimal 5) activates the print-screen service: The keyboard support routines generate interrupt 05H in response to the Shift-PrtSc combination; any other programs that want to perform a print-screen operation can safely and conveniently do so by generating interrupt 05H.

The print-screen service will maintain the current cursor position on the screen and successfully print any printable characters from the screen in either text or graphics mode. It uses both the standard video services (those that waltz the cursor around the screen and read characters from the screen buffer) and the standard printer services.

This service directs all its output to printer number 0, the default printer. There are no input or output registers for this service. However, a status code is available at low-memory location 0050:0000H. (See page 61.) If the byte at that location has a value of FFH (decimal 255), then a previous print-screen operation was not completed successfully. A value of 00H indicates that no error occurred, and that the print-screen operation is ready to go. A value of 01H indicates that a print-screen operation is currently in progress; any request for a second one will be ignored.

The ROM BIOS print-screen routine cannot print images drawn on the screen in graphics modes. If you want to produce a printed screen snapshot in CGA-compatible graphics modes, use the DOS utility program GRAPHICS. This program installs a memory-resident, graphics-mode print-screen routine that hooks interrupt 05H. Once you execute GRAPHICS, pressing Shift-PrtSc or executing interrupt 05H while in a graphics mode will cause the graphics-mode print-screen routine to run.

Interrupt 11H (decimal 17): Equipment-List Service

Interrupt 11H (decimal 17) reports what equipment is installed in the computer. This report contains the same information stored at low-memory location 0040:0010H. (See Chapter 3, page 55.) The report is coded as shown in Figure 12-17, in the bits of a 16-bit word, which is placed in register AX. See interrupt 12H for a related service.

The equipment information is gathered on an as-accurate-as-possible basis and may not be exactly correct. Different methods are used for acquiring the information in the various models.

The equipment list is determined only once at power-up time and is then left in memory. This means that you can change the equipment list under software control. For example, you could take some equipment off line so that it is not used. However, modifying the equipment list is risky business — don't bet on its success. See interrupt 19H for comments on how to modify the equipment list and get reliable results.

Bit 15 14 13 12 11 10 9 8	Bit 7 6 5 4 3 2 1 0	Meaning
X X	. . . .	Number of printers installed
. . X	. . . .	(Reserved)
. . . X	. . . .	Game adapter: 1 = installed
. . . . X X X .	. . . .	Number of RSS-232 serial ports
. . . . X	. . . .	(Not used)
. . . .	X X	Number of diskette drives − 1
. . . .	. . X X	Initial video mode: 11 = monochrome; 10 = 80-column color; 01 = 40-column color
. . . .	. . . . X X . .	PC with 64 KB motherboard: Amount of system board RAM (11 = 64 KB; 10 = 48 KB; 01 = 32 KB; 00 = 16 KB PC/AT: (Not used) PS/2s: Bit 3 = (unused); bit 2: 1 = pointing device installed
. . . .	. . . . . . X .	1 if math co-processor installed
. . . .	 X	1 if any diskette drives exist (if so, see bits 7 and 6)

Figure 12-17. *The bit coding for the equipment list reported in register AX and invoked by interrupt 11H (decimal 17).*

The format of the equipment list was defined for the original IBM PC. As a result, some parts of the list vary, depending on the PC model. For example, bits 2 and 3 originally indicated the amount of RAM installed on the motherboard. (Yes, in those days you could indeed have purchased a PC with as little as 16 KB of RAM.) In PS/2s, these bits have a different significance. (See Figure 12-17.)

Interrupt 12H (decimal 18): Memory-Size Service

Interrupt 12H (decimal 18) invokes the service that reports the available memory size in kilobytes—the same information stored at low-memory location 0040:0013H. (See page 55.) The value is reported in AX. The memory-size value reflects only the amount of base memory available. In a PC/AT or PS/2 with extended (protected-mode) memory, you must use interrupt 15H, service 88H (Get Extended Memory Size), to determine the amount of extended memory installed.

In the standard models of the PC, this value is taken from the setting of the physical switches inside the system unit. These switches are supposed to reflect the actual memory installed, although under some circumstances they are set to less memory than is actually present. In the PC/AT and PS/2s, the ROM BIOS POST determines the amount of memory in the system by exploring available RAM to see what is installed. If the BIOS is using an extended data area, this data area is allocated at the highest memory address available, so the value returned by this service excludes the amount of RAM reserved for the extended data area.

Interrupt 18H (decimal 24): ROM BASIC Loader Service

Interrupt 18H (decimal 24) is normally used to activate ROM BASIC. Any program can activate BASIC (or whatever has replaced it) by generating interrupt 18H. This can be done to intentionally bring up ROM BASIC or also to abruptly shut down, or *dead-end* a program. However, see the next interrupt, number 19H, for a better way to dead-end a program.

Interrupt 19H (decimal 25): Bootstrap Loader Service

Interrupt 19H (decimal 25) activates the standard bootstrap routine for the computer (which produces a similar result to powering on and nearly the same net result as the Ctrl-Alt-Del key combination). However, this bootstrap interrupt bypasses the lengthy memory check of the power-on routines as well as the reset operations of Ctrl-Alt-Del.

The bootstrap loader works by reading the first sector of the first track (the *boot sector*) from the diskette in drive A into memory at 0000:7C00H. If the ROM BIOS cannot read from the diskette, it reads the boot sector from the hard disk in drive C instead. If both attempts fail, the BIOS executes interrupt 18H to bring up ROM BASIC. If the BIOS reads a sector from the disk but the sector doesn't contain an operating-system boot record, the BIOS issues an error message and waits for you to reboot or replace the offending diskette.

We know of two uses for this interrupt service. One is to immediately shut down, or *dead-end,* the operation of the computer. This can be done by a program when it encounters an "illegal" situation, for example, by a copy-protected program that detects an apparent violation of copy protection.

The other use for this service is to reboot the computer without going through the reset and restart operations, which would, for example, recalculate the memory size and equipment list reported by interrupts 11H and 12H. This interrupt is particularly useful for any program that modifies either of these two items. The reasoning is simple: If you want to change the equipment list or the memory size (for example, to set aside some memory for a RAM disk), you cannot reliably count on all programs—including DOS— to check the actual memory or equipment specifications each time they are used. But a program could set aside some memory, change the memory specification, and then use this interrupt to reboot the system. When that is done and DOS is activated, DOS would take its own record of the available memory from the value set by your program. Neither DOS nor any civilized DOS program would be aware of, or interfere with, the memory area that was set aside.

To give you a brief example, here's a fragment of assembler code that will change the ROM BIOS's record of the memory size and then use interrupt 19H to reboot the computer:

```
mov     ax,40H                    ; get BIOS data segment of hex 40...
mov     es,ax                     ; ...into ES segment register
mov     word ptr es:[13h],256     ; set memory to 256 KB
int     19h                       ; reboot system
```

Interrupt 1AH (decimal 26): Time-of-Day Services

Interrupt 1AH (decimal 26) provides the time-of-day services. Unlike other interrupts covered in this section but like all other ROM BIOS services, several services can be activated by this interrupt. When you execute interrupt 1AH, you specify the service number, as usual, in register AH. (See Figure 12-18.)

Service	Description
00H	Get Current Clock Count.
01H	Set Current Clock Count.
02H	Get Real-Time Clock Time.
03H	Set Real-Time Clock Time.
04H	Get Real-Time Clock Date.
05H	Set Real-Time Clock Date.
06H	Set Real-Time Clock Alarm.
07H	Reset Real-Time Clock Alarm.
09H	Get Real-Time Clock Alarm Time and Status.

Figure 12-18. *The ROM-BIOS time-of-day services invoked by interrupt 1AH.*

The ROM BIOS maintains a time-of-day clock based on a count of system-clock ticks since midnight. The system clock "ticks" by generating interrupt 8 at specific intervals. On each clock tick, the ROM BIOS interrupt 08H service routine increments the clock count by 1. When the clock count passes 24 hours' worth of ticks, the count is reset to 0 and a record is made of the fact that midnight has been passed. This record is not in the form of a count, so you can't detect if two midnights have passed.

The clock ticks at a rate that is almost exactly 1,193,180 ÷ 64 KB, or roughly 18.2 times a second. The count is kept as a 4-byte integer at low-memory location 0040:006CH. The midnight count value, used to compare against the rising clock count, is 1800B0H, or 1,573,040; when the clock hits the midnight count value, the byte at location 0040:0070H is set to 01H and the count is reset. When DOS needs to know the time, it reads the clock count through the time-of-day service and calculates the time from this raw count. If it sees that midnight has passed, it also increments the date.

You can use the following BASIC formulas to calculate the current time of day from the clock count:

```
HOURS = INT(CLOCK / 65543)
CLOCK = CLOCK - (HOURS * 65543)
MINUTES = INT(CLOCK / 1092)
CLOCK = CLOCK - (MINUTES * 1092)
SECONDS = CLOCK / 18.2
```

In reverse, we use the following formula to calculate a nearly correct clock count from the time:

```
COUNT = (HOURS * 65543) + (MINUTES * 1092) + (SECONDS * 18.2)
```

The ROM BIOS services in the PC/AT and PS/2s include time-of-day and date services that perform some of these tasks automatically.

Service 00H (decimal 0): Get Current Clock Count

Service 00H (decimal 0) returns the current clock count in two registers: the high-order portion in CX and the low-order portion in DX. AL = 00H if midnight has not passed since the last clock value was read or set; and AL = 01H if midnight has passed. The midnight signal is always reset when the clock is read. Any program using this service must use the midnight signal to keep track of date changes. DOS programs normally should not use this service directly. If they do, they must calculate and set a new date.

❑ NOTE: *It's curious that version 2.0 of DOS did not consistently update the date on the midnight signal. The next version of DOS (2.1) and all other versions of DOS do.*

Service 01H (decimal 1): Set Current Clock Count

Service 01H (decimal 1) sets the clock count in location 0040:006CH using the values you pass in registers CX and DX. This service automatically clears the midnight flag at 0040:0070H.

Service 02H (decimal 2): Get Real-Time Clock Time

The PC/AT and the PS/2s have a real-time clock that maintains the current date and time in nonvolatile memory. This clock runs in parallel to the system timer referenced by services 00H and 01H. When you boot a PC/AT or PS/2, the ROM BIOS initializes the system timer count with the time indicated by the real-time clock.

You can access the real-time clock directly using service 02H (decimal 2). This service returns the time in binary-coded decimal format (BCD) in registers CH (hours), CL (minutes), and DH (seconds). If the real-time clock is defective, the ROM BIOS sets the carry flag.

Service 03H (decimal 3): Set Real-Time Clock Time

This service complements service 02H. It lets you set the real-time clock on a PC/AT or PS/2, using the same register assignments as service 02H. Again, the hours, minutes, and seconds values are in BCD format.

Service 04H (decimal 4): Get Real-Time Clock Date

Service 04H (decimal 4) returns the current date as maintained by the real-time clock in a PC/AT or PS/2. The ROM BIOS returns century (19 or 20) in register CH, the year in CL, the month in DH, and the day in DL. Again, the values are returned in BCD format. As in service 02H, the ROM BIOS sets the carry flag if the real-time clock is not operating.

Service 05H (decimal 5): Set Real-Time Clock Date

Service 05H (decimal 5) complements service 04H. This service sets the real-time clock date, using the same registers as service 04H.

Service 06H (decimal 6): Set Real-Time Clock Alarm

Service 06H (decimal 6) lets you create an "alarm" program that executes at a specific time. This alarm program must be memory-resident at the time the alarm occurs. To use this service, make your alarm program memory-resident using the DOS Terminate-and-Stay-Resident service (see page 302), and be sure that interrupt vector 4AH (0000:0128H) points to the start of your program. Then call service 06H to set the time for the alarm to occur.

Service 06H uses the same register values as service 03H: CH contains hours in BCD format, CL contains minutes, and DH contains seconds. The ROM BIOS sets the carry flag when it returns from this service if the real-time clock is not operating or if the alarm is already in use.

When the real-time clock time matches the alarm time, the BIOS executes interrupt 4AH, which transfers control to your alarm program. Your program can then take appropriate action (display a message, for example). Because the ROM BIOS activates your alarm program by executing an INT 4AH instruction, the program must exit with an IRET instruction.

Service 07H (decimal 7): Reset Real-Time Clock Alarm

Use service 07H (decimal 7) to disable the real-time clock alarm if it has been set by a previous call to service 06H.

Service 09H (decimal 9): Get Real-Time Clock Alarm Time and Status

On PS/2 models 25 and 30, you can determine the current status of the real-time alarm by executing interrupt 1AH, service 09H. This service reports the alarm status in register DL. If DL = 01H, the alarm is active, and the alarm time is returned in CH, CL, and DH. If DL = 00H, the alarm isn't enabled.

Chapter 13

ROM BIOS
Services Summary

This chapter summarizes the ROM BIOS service routines discussed in Chapters 8 through 12 in order to provide you with a quick reference guide.

You can use this chapter to locate the ROM BIOS functions you need and to determine which registers they use. Where a particular service is very detailed or tricky to use, we'll refer you to the discussions in the chapters and to the IBM technical reference manuals.

Short Summary

In this section, we briefly list all the ROM BIOS services so that they can be seen together, at a glance.

Subject	Interrupt Hex	Dec	Service	Description	Notes
Print screen	05H	5	N/A	Send screen contents to printer.	
Video	10H	16	00H	Set video mode.	
Video	10H	16	01H	Set cursor size.	
Video	10H	16	02H	Set cursor position.	
Video	10H	16	03H	Read cursor position.	
Video	10H	16	04H	Read light-pen position.	
Video	10H	16	05H	Set active display page.	
Video	10H	16	06H	Scroll window up.	
Video	10H	16	07H	Scroll window down.	
Video	10H	16	08H	Read character and attribute.	
Video	10H	16	09H	Write character and attribute.	
Video	10H	16	0AH	Write character.	
Video	10H	16	0BH	Set 4-color palette.	
Video	10H	16	0CH	Write pixel.	
Video	10H	16	0DH	Read pixel.	
Video	10H	16	0EH	Write character in teletype mode.	
Video	10H	16	0FH	Get current video mode.	
Video	10H	16	10H	EGA/VGA color palette interface.	
Video	10H	16	11H	EGA/VGA character generator interface.	
Video	10H	16	12H	EGA/VGA "alternate select."	
Video	10H	16	13H	Write character string.	PC/AT, PS/2, EGA, VGA only
Video	10H	16	1AH	Get/Set display combination code.	PS/2 only
Video	10H	16	1BH	Functionality/State information.	PS/2 only

Figure 13-1. *A short summary of the ROM BIOS services.*   *(continued)*

Figure 13-1. *continued*

Subject	Interrupt Hex	Dec	Service	Description	Notes
Video	10H	16	1CH	Save/Restore video state.	VGA only
Equipment	11H	17	N/A	Get list of peripheral equipment.	
Memory	12H	18	N/A	Get base memory size (in KB).	
Disk	13H	19	00H	Reset disk system.	
Disk	13H	19	01H	Get disk status.	
Disk	13H	19	02H	Read disk sectors.	
Disk	13H	19	03H	Write disk sectors.	
Disk	13H	19	04H	Verify disk sectors.	
Disk	13H	19	05H	Format disk track.	
Disk	13H	19	06H	Format disk track and set bad sector flags.	PC/XT fixed disk only
Disk	13H	19	07H	Format drive starting at specified cylinder.	PC/XT fixed disk only
Disk	13H	19	08H	Get current drive parameters.	
Disk	13H	19	09H	Initialize fixed-disk parameter tables.	
Disk	13H	19	0AH	Read long.	
Disk	13H	19	0BH	Write long.	
Disk	13H	19	0CH	Seek to cylinder.	
Disk	13H	19	0DH	Alternate disk reset.	
Disk	13H	19	10H	Test for drive ready.	
Disk	13H	19	11H	Recalibrate drive.	
Disk	13H	19	14H	Controller diagnostics.	
Disk	13H	19	15H	Get disk type.	
Disk	13H	19	16H	Change of diskette status.	
Disk	13H	19	17H	Set diskette type for format.	
Disk	13H	19	18H	Set media type for diskette format.	
Disk	13H	19	19H	Park heads.	PS/2s only
Disk	13H	19	1AH	Format ESDI unit.	PS/2 models 50, 60, 80 only
Serial port	14H	20	00H	Initialize serial port.	
Serial port	14H	20	01H	Send out one character.	
Serial port	14H	20	02H	Receive one character.	
Serial port	14H	20	03H	Get serial port status.	
Serial port	14H	20	04H	Extended serial port initialize.	PS/2s only
Serial port	14H	20	05H	Extended serial port control.	PS/2s only

(continued)

255

Figure 13-1. *continued*

Subject	Interrupt Hex	Dec	Service	Description	Notes
System	15H	21	00H	Turn on cassette motor.	
System	15H	21	01H	Turn off cassette motor.	
System	15H	21	02H	Read data blocks.	
System	15H	21	03H	Write data blocks.	
System	15H	21	21H	Read/write POST error log.	PS/2 models 50, 60, 80 only
System	15H	21	4FH	Keyboard intercept.	PC/AT, PS/2s only
System	15H	21	80H	Device open.	PC/AT, PS/2s only
System	15H	21	81H	Device close.	PC/AT, PS/2s only
System	15H	21	82H	Program termination.	PC/AT, PS/2s only
System	15H	21	83H	Start/stop interval timer.	PC/AT, PS/2s only
System	15H	21	84H	Joystick support.	PC/AT, PS/2s only
System	15H	21	85H	Sys Req keystroke.	PC/AT, PS/2s only
System	15H	21	86H	Wait.	PC/AT, PS/2s only
System	15H	21	87H	Protected-mode data move.	PC/AT, PS/2 models 50, 60, 80
System	15H	21	88H	Get extended memory size.	PC/AT, PS/2 models 50, 60, 80
System	15H	21	89H	Switch to protected mode.	PC/AT, PS/2 models 50, 60, 80
System	15H	21	90H	Device busy.	PC/AT, PS/2s only
System	15H	21	91H	Interrupt complete.	PC/AT, PS/2s only
System	15H	21	C0H	Get system configuration parameters.	
System	15H	21	C1H	Get extended BIOS data segment.	PS/2s only
System	15H	21	C2H	Pointing-device interface.	PS/2s only
System	15H	21	C3H	Enable/disable watchdog timer.	PS/2 models 50, 60, 80
System	15H	21	C4H	Programmable Option Select interface.	PS/2 models 50, 60, 80
Keyboard	16H	22	00H	Read next keystroke.	
Keyboard	16H	22	01H	Report whether keystroke ready.	
Keyboard	16H	22	02H	Get shift status.	
Keyboard	16H	22	03H	Set typematic rate and delay.	PC/AT, PS/2s only
Keyboard	16H	22	05H	Write to keyboard buffer.	PC/AT, PS/2s only
Keyboard	16H	22	10H	Extended keyboard read.	PC/AT, PS/2s only

(continued)

Figure 13-1. *continued*

Subject	Interrupt Hex	Dec	Service	Description	Notes
Keyboard	16H	22	11H	Extended keyboard status.	PC/AT, PS/2s only
Keyboard	16H	22	12H	Extended shift status.	PC/AT, PS/2s only
Printer	17H	23	00H	Send 1 byte to printer.	
Printer	17H	23	01H	Initialize printer.	
Printer	17H	23	02H	Get printer status.	
BASIC	18H	24	N/A	Switch control to ROM BASIC.	
Bootstrap	19H	25	N/A	Reboot computer.	
Time	1AH	26	00H	Read current clock count.	
Time	1AH	26	01H	Set current clock count.	
Time	1AH	26	02H	Read real-time clock.	PC/AT, PS/2s only
Time	1AH	26	03H	Set real-time clock.	PC/AT, PS/2s only
Time	1AH	26	04H	Read date from real-time clock.	PC/AT, PS/2s only
Time	1AH	26	05H	Set date in real-time clock.	PC/AT, PS/2s only
Time	1AH	26	06H	Set alarm.	PC/AT, PS/2s only
Time	1AH	26	07H	Reset alarm.	PC/AT, PS/2s only
Time	1AH	26	09H	Get alarm time and status.	PS/2 Model 30 only

Long Summary

In this section, we expand the previous summary table to show the register usage for input and output parameters. The preceding section is best used to quickly find *which* service you need; this section is best used to quickly find *how* to use each service.

Service	Interrupt	Register Input	Output	Notes
Print screen.	05H	N/A	N/A	Send screen contents to printer. Status and result byte at 0050:0000H.

Video Services

Service	Interrupt	Register Input	Output	Notes
Set video mode.	10H	AH = 00H AL = video mode	None	*Video modes in AL:* 00H: 40 × 25 16-color text (gray-scaled on composite monitors). 01H: 40 × 25 16-color text. 02H: 80 × 25 16-color text (gray-scaled on composite monitors). 03H: 80 × 25 16-color text. 04H: 320 × 200 4-color graphics. 05H: 320 × 200 4-color graphics (gray-scaled on composite monitors). 06H: 640 × 200 2-color graphics. 07H: 80 × 25 monochrome text (MDA, EGA, VGA). 0DH: 320 × 200 16-color graphics (EGA, VGA). 0EH: 640 × 200 16-color graphics (EGA, VGA). 0FH: 640 × 350 monochrome graphics (EGA, VGA). 10H: 640 × 350 16-color graphics (EGA, VGA). 11H: 640 × 480 2-color graphics (MCGA, VGA). 12H: 640 × 480 16-color graphics (VGA). 13H: 320 × 200 256-color graphics (MCGA, VGA).

Figure 13-2. *A complete summary of the ROM BIOS services.* *(continued)*

Figure 13-2. *continued*

Service	Interrupt	Register Input	Output	Notes
Set cursor size.	10H	AH = 01H CH = starting scan line CL = ending scan line	None	Useful values for CH and CL depend on video mode.
Set cursor position.	10H	AH = 02H BH = display page DH = row DL = column	None	
Read cursor position.	10H	AH = 03H BH = display page	CH = starting scan line CL = ending scan line DH = row DL = column	
Read light-pen position.	10H	AH = 04H	AH = pen trigger signal BX = pixel column CH = pixel row (CGA and EGA video modes 4, 5, and 6) CX = pixel row (EGA except modes 4, 5, and 6) DH = character row DL = character column	
Set active display page.	10H	AH = 05H AL = page number	None	
Scroll window up.	10H	AH = 06H AL = lines to scroll up BH = fill attribute CH = upper row CL = left column DH = lower row DL = right column	None	

(continued)

259

Figure 13-2. *continued*

Service	Interrupt	Register Input	Output	Notes
Scroll window down.	10H	AH = 07H AL = lines to scroll down BH = fill attribute CH = upper row CL = left column DH = lower row DL = right column	None	
Read character and attribute.	10H	AH = 08H BH = display page	AH = attribute AL = character	
Write character and attribute.	10H	AH = 09H AL = character BH = display page BL = attribute CX = number of characters to repeat	None	
Write character.	10H	AH = 0AH AL = character BH = page number BL = color in graphics mode CX = number of characters to repeat	None	
Set color palette.	10H	AH = 0BH BH = palette color ID BL = color to be used with palette ID	None	
Write pixel.	10H	AH = 0CH AL = color BH = display page CX = pixel column DX = pixel row	None	

(continued)

Figure 13-2. *continued*

Service	Interrupt	*Register* Input	Output	Notes
Read pixel.	10H	AH = 0DH BH = display page CX = pixel column DX = pixel row	AL = pixel value	
Write character in teletype mode.	10H	AH = 0EH AL = character BH = display page BL = color for graphics mode	None	Display page number required only for IBM PC ROM BIOS dated 10/19/81 and earlier.
Get current video mode.	10H	AH = 0FH	AH = width in characters AL = video mode BH = display page	
Set one palette register.	10H	AH = 10H AL = 00H BH = palette register value BL = palette register number	None	EGA, VGA.
Set border register.	10H	AH = 10H AL = 01H BH = border color	None	EGA, VGA.
Set all palette registers.	10H	AH = 10H AL = 02H ES:DX → table of palette values	None	EGA, VGA.
Select background intensity or blink attribute.	10H	AH = 10H AL = 03H *To enable background intensity:* BL = 00H *To enable blinking:* BL = 01H	None	EGA, VGA.

(continued)

261

Figure 13-2. *continued*

Service	Interrupt	Register Input	Output	Notes
Read one palette register.	10H	AH = 10H AL = 07H BL = palette register number	BH = palette register value	VGA only.
Read border register.	10H	AH = 10H AL = 08H	BH = border color value	VGA only.
Read all palette registers.	10H	AH = 10H AL = 09H	ES:DX → table of palette register values	VGA only.
Update one video DAC color register.	10H	AH = 10H AL = 10H BX = color register number DH = red value CH = green value CL = blue value	None	MCGA, VGA.
Update block of video DAC color registers.	10H	AH = 10H AL = 12H BX = first register to update CX = number of registers to update ES:DX → table of red-green-blue values		MCGA, VGA.
Set video DAC color page.	10H	AH = 10H AL = 13H *To select paging mode:* BL = 00H BH = 00H selects 4 pages of 64 registers, *or* BH = 01H selects 16 pages of 16 registers	None	VGA only.

(continued)

Figure 13-2. *continued*

Service	Interrupt	Register Input	Output	Notes
Set video DAC color page, *continued.*		*To select page:* BL = 01H BH = page number		
Read one video DAC color register.	10H	AH = 10H AL = 15H BX = color register number	DH = red value CH = green value CL = blue value	MCGA, VGA.
Read block of video DAC color registers.	10H	AH = 10H AL = 17H BX = first register number CX = number of registers ES:DX → table of red-green-blue values	Table at ES:DX updated	MCGA, VGA.
Get video DAC color page.	10H	AH = 10H AL = 1AH BH = current page BL = current paging mode	None	VGA only.
Sum video DAC color values to gray shades.	10H	AH = 10H AL = 1BH BX = first color register CX = number of color registers	None	MCGA, VGA.
Load user-specified alphanumeric character set.	10H	AH = 11H AL = 00H BH = bytes per character in table BL = character generator RAM block	None	EGA, MCGA, VGA.

(continued)

263

Figure 13-2. *continued*

		Register		
Service	*Interrupt*	*Input*	*Output*	*Notes*
Load user-specified alphanumeric character set, *continued.*		CX = number of characters DX = first character ES:BP → character definition table		
Load ROM BIOS 8 × 14 alphanumeric character set.	10H	AH = 11H AL = 01H BL = character generator RAM block	None	EGA, VGA.
Load ROM BIOS 8 × 8 alphanumeric character set.	10H	AH = 11H AL = 02H BL = character generator RAM block	None	EGA, MCGA, VGA.
Select displayed alphanumeric character sets.	10H	AH = 11H AL = 03H BL = character block generator RAM	None	EGA, MCGA, VGA.
Load ROM BIOS 8 × 16 alphanumeric character set.	10H	AH = 11H AL = 04H BL = character generator RAM block	None	MCGA, VGA.
Load user-specified alphanumeric character set and adjust displayed character height.	10H	AH = 11H AL = 10H BH = bytes per character definition BL = character generator RAM block	None	EGA, MCGA, VGA.

(continued)

Figure 13-2. *continued*

		Register		
Service	**Interrupt**	**Input**	**Output**	**Notes**
Load user-specified alphanumeric character set and adjust displayed character height. *(continued)*		CX = number of characters DX = first character ES:BP → character definition table		
Load ROM BIOS 8 × 14 alphanumeric character set and adjust displayed character height.	10H	AH = 11H AL = 11H BL = character generator RAM block	None	EGA, VGA.
Load ROM BIOS 8 × 8 alphanumeric character set and adjust displayed character height.	10H	AH = 11H AL = 12H BL = character generator RAM block	None	EGA, VGA.
Load ROM BIOS 8 × 16 alphanumeric character set and adjust displayed character height.	10H	AH = 11H AL = 14H BL = character generator RAM block	None	VGA only.
Load user-specified 8 × 8 graphics character set.	10H	AH = 11H AL = 20H ES:BP → character definition table	None	EGA, MCGA, VGA. Copies ES:BP into the interrupt 1FH vector. Only characters 80H through FFH should be defined.

(continued)

Figure 13-2. *continued*

Service	Interrupt	Register		Notes
		Input	*Output*	
Load user-specified graphics character set.	10H	AH = 11H AL = 21H CX = bytes per character definition ES:BP → character definition table *User-specified number of character rows:* BL = 00H DL = number of character rows *14 character rows:* BL = 01H *25 character rows:* BL = 02H *43 character rows:* BL = 03H	None	EGA, MCGA, VGA.
Load ROM BIOS 8 × 14 graphics character set.	10H	AH = 11H AL = 22H BL = (as for AL = 21H) DL = (as for AL = 21H)	None	EGA, VGA.
Load ROM BIOS 8 × 8 graphics character set.	10H	AH = 11H AL = 23H BL = (as for AL = 21H) DL = (as for AL = 21H)	None	EGA, MCGA, VGA.
Load ROM BIOS 8 × 16 graphics character set.	10H	AH = 11H AL = 24H BL = (as for AL = 21H) DL = (as for AL = 21H)	None	MCGA, VGA.

(continued)

Figure 13-2. *continued*

		Register		
Service	*Interrupt*	*Input*	*Output*	*Notes*
Get character generator information.	10H	AH = 11H AL = 30H *Contents of interrupt 1FH vector:* BH = 00H *Contents of interrupt 43H vector:* BH = 01H *Address of ROM 8 × 14 characters:* BH = 02H *Address of ROM 8 × 8 characters:* 1BH = 03H *Address of second half of ROM 8 × 8 table:* BH = 04H *Address of ROM 9 × 14 alternate characters:* BH = 05H *Address of ROM 8 × 16 characters:* BH = 06H *Address of ROM 9 × 16 alternate characters:* BH = 07H	CX = points DL = displayed character rows − 1 ES:BP → character table	EGA, MCGA, VGA.
Return video configuration information.	10H	AH = 12H BL = 10H	BH = default BIOS video mode (00H = color, 01H = monochrome) BL = amount of video RAM (00H = 64 KB, 01H = 128 KB, 02H = 192 KB, 03H = 256 KB)	EGA, VGA.

(continued)

Figure 13-2. *continued*

		Register		
Service	*Interrupt*	*Input*	*Output*	*Notes*
Return video configuration information. *(continued)*			CH = feature bits CL = configuration switches	
Select alternate print screen routine.	10H	AH = 12H BL = 20H	None	EGA, MCGA, VGA. Updates INT 05H vector.
Select scan lines for alphanumeric modes.	10H	AH = 12H BL = 30H *200 scan lines:* AL = 00H *350 scan lines:* AL = 01H *400 scan lines:* AL = 02H	AL = 12H	VGA only.
Select default palette loading.	10H	AH = 12H BL = 31H *Enable default palette loading:* AL = 00H *Disable default palette loading:* AL = 01H	AL = 12H	MCGA, VGA.
Enable/disable video addressing.	10H	AH = 12H BL = 32H *Enable video addressing:* AL = 00H *Disable video addressing:* AL = 01H	AL = 12H	MCGA, VGA.

(continued)

Figure 13-2. *continued*

Service	Interrupt	Register Input	Output	Notes
Enable/disable gray-scale summing.	10H	AH = 12H BL = 33H *Enable gray-scale summing:* AL = 00H *Disable gray-scale summing:* AL = 01H	AL = 12H	MCGA, VGA.
Enable/disable BIOS cursor emulation.	10H	AH = 12H BL = 34H *Enable cursor emulation:* AL = 00H *Disable cursor emulation:* AL = 01H	AL = 12H	VGA only.
Display switch interface.	10H	AH = 12H BL = 35H *Initial adapter video off:* AL = 00H *Initial planar video on:* AL = 01H *Switch active video off:* AL = 02H *Switch inactive video on:* AL = 03H ES:DX→128-byte save area	AL = 12H	MCGA, VGA.
Enable/disable video refresh.	10H	AH = 12H BL = 36H *Enable refresh:* AL = 00H *Disable refresh:* AL = 01H	AL = 12H	VGA only.

(continued)

Figure 13-2. *continued*

		Register		
Service	*Interrupt*	*Input*	*Output*	*Notes*
Write string; don't move cursor.	10H	AH = 13H AL = 00H BL = attribute BH = display page DX = starting cursor position CX = length of string ES:BP → start of string	None	PC/AT, EGA, MCGA, VGA.
Write string; move cursor after string.	10H	AH = 13H AL = 01H BL = attribute BH = display page DX = starting cursor position CX = length of string ES:BP → start of string	None	PC/AT, EGA, MCGA, VGA.
Write string of alternating characters and attributes; don't move cursor.	10H	AH = 13H AL = 02H BH = display page DX = starting cursor position CX = length of string ES:BP → start of string	None	PC/AT, EGA, MCGA, VGA.
Write string of alternating characters and attributes; move cursor.	10H	AH = 13H AL = 03H BH = display page DX = starting cursor position CX = length of string ES:BP → start of string	None	PC/AT, EGA, MCGA, VGA.

(continued)

Figure 13-2. *continued*

Service	Interrupt	Register Input	Output	Notes
Get display combination code.	10H	AH = 1AH AL = 00H	AL = 1AH BL = active display BH = inactive display	MCGA, VGA. *Values returned in BL and BH:* 00H: no display. 01H: MDA or compatible. 02H: CGA or compatible. 04H: EGA with color display. 05H: EGA with monochrome display. 06H: Professional Graphics Controller. 07H: VGA with monochrome display. 08H: VGA with color display. 0BH: MCGA with monochrome display. 0CH: MCGA with color display. FFH: unknown.
Set display combination code.	10H	AH = 1AH AL = 01H BL = active display BH = inactive display	AL = 1AH	MCGA, VGA. See table above for values in BL and BH.
BIOS functionality/state information.	10H	AH = 1BH BX = 00H ES:DI → 64-byte buffer	AL = 1BH Buffer at ES:DI updated	MCGA, VGA. See the *IBM BIOS Interface Technical Reference Manual* for table format.
Return save/ restore buffer size.	10H	AH = 1CH AL = 00H CX = requested states (bit 0 = video hardware state; bit 1 = video BIOS data area; bit 2 = video DAC and color registers)	AL = 1CH (if function supported) BX = save/restore buffer size in 64-byte blocks	VGA only. Use this service before saving the current video state.

(continued)

271

Figure 13-2. *continued*

Service	Interrupt	Register Input	Output	Notes
Save current video state.	10H	AH = 1CH AL = 01H CX = requested states ES:BX → save/restore buffer		VGA only. May disrupt current video state, so follow a call to this service with a call to the "Restore Current Video State" service.
Restore current video state.	10H	AH = 1CH AL = 02H CX = requested states ES:BX → save/restore buffer	None	VGA only.

Equipment-List Service

Service	Interrupt	Register Input	Output	Notes
Get list of peripheral attached equipment.	11H	None	AX = equipment list, bit-coded	*Bit settings in AX:* 00 = diskette drive installed. 01 = math coprocessor installed. 02, 03 = system board RAM in 16 KB blocks (PCs with 64 KB motherboard only). 02 = pointing device installed (PS/2s only). 04, 05 = initial video mode: 00 = unused; 01 = 40 × 25 color; 10 = 80 × 25 color; 11 = 80 × 25 monochrome. 06, 07 = number of diskette drives − 1. 08 = (not used). 09, 10, 11 = number of RS-232 cards in system. 12 = game I/O attached (PC and PC/XT only). 13 = internal modem installed. 14, 15 = number of parallel printers attached.

(continued)

272

Figure 13-2. *continued*

Service	Interrupt	Register Input	Output	Notes
Memory Service				
Get base memory size.	12H	None	AX = memory size (KB)	See also "Get extended memory size" (INT 15H, AH = 88H).
Disk Services				
Reset disk system.	13H	AH = 00H DL = drive number	CF = success/ failure flag AH = status code	See INT 13H, service 01H, for status code values.
Get disk status.	13H	AH = 01H DL = drive number	AH = status code *Status values (hex):* AH = 00H: no error AH = 01H: bad command AH = 02H: address mark not found AH = 03H: write attempted on write-protected disk (D) AH = 04H: sector not found AH = 05H: reset failed (F) AH = 06H: diskette removed (D) AH = 07H: bad parameter table (F) AH = 08H: DMA overrun AH = 09H: DMA across 64 KB boundary AH = 0AH: bad sector flag (F) AH = 0BH: bad cylinder (F) AH = 0CH: bad media type (D) AH = 0DH: invalid number of sectors on format (F)	(F) = fixed disk only. (D) = diskette only.

(continued)

273

Figure 13-2. *continued*

Service	Interrupt	Register Input	Output	Notes
Get disk status, *continued*.			AH = 0EH: control data address mark detected (F) AH = 0FH: DMA arbitration level out of range (F) AH = 10H: bad CRC or ECC AH = 11H: ECC corrected data error (F) AH = 20H: controller failed AH = 40H: seek failed AH = 80H: time out (F) or drive not ready (D) AH = AAH: drive not ready (F) AH = BBH: undefined error (F) AH = CCH: write fault (F) AH = E0H: status error (F) AH = FFH: sense operation failed (F)	
Read disk sectors.	13H	AH = 02H AL = number of sectors CH = track number CL = sector number DH = head number DL = drive number ES:BX = pointer to buffer	CF = success/ failure flag AH = status code AL = number of sectors read	*Status codes in AH:* See INT 13H, service 01H.

(continued)

Figure 13-2. *continued*

Service	Interrupt	Register Input	Output	Notes
Write disk sectors.	13H	AH = 03H AL = number of sectors CH = track number CL = sector number DH = head number DL = drive number ES:BX = pointer to buffer	CF = success/ failure flag AH = status code AL = number of sectors written	*Status codes in AH:* See INT 13H, service 01H.
Verify disk sectors.	13H	AH = 04H AL = number of sectors CH = track number CL = sector number DH = head number DL = drive number	CF = success/ failure flag AH = status code AL = number of sectors verified	*Status codes in AH:* See INT 13H, service 01H.
Format disk track (cylinder).	13H	AH = 05H AL = interleave value (PC/XT only) CH = cylinder number (bits 0–7) CL = cylinder number (bits 8–9) DH = head number DL = drive number ES:BX → table of sector format information	CF = success/ failure flag AH = status code	*Status codes in AH:* See INT 13H, service 01H. See Chapter 10 for contents of table.

(continued)

Figure 13-2. *continued*

Service	Interrupt	Register		Notes
		Input	*Output*	
Format disk track and set bad sector flags.	13H	AH = 06H AL = interleave value CH = cylinder number (bits 0–7) CL = cylinder number (bits 8–9) DH = head number DL = drive number	CF = success/ failure flag AH = status code	PC/XT fixed disk only.
Format drive starting at specified cylinder.	13H	AH = 07H AL = interleave value CH = cylinder number (bits 0–7) CL = cylinder number (bits 8–9) DH = head number DL = drive number	CF = success/ failure flag AH = status code	PC/XT fixed disk only.
Get current drive parameters.	13H	AH = 08H	CF = success/ failure flag AH = status code DL = number of drives DH = max. read/write head number CL (bits 6–7) = max. cylinder number (bits 8–9) CL (bits 0–5) = max. sector number CH = max. number of cylinders (bits 0–7)	*Status codes in AH:* See INT 13H, service 01H.
Initialize fixed-disk base tables.	13H	AH = 09H DL = drive number	CF = success/ failure flag AH = status code	Interrupt 41H points to table for drive 0. Interrupt 46H points to table for drive 1. *Status codes in AH:* See INT 13H, service 01H.

(continued)

Figure 13-2. *continued*

		Register		
Service	*Interrupt*	*Input*	*Output*	*Notes*
Read long.	13H	AH = 0AH DL = drive number DH = head number CH = cylinder number CL = sector number ES:BX → buffer	CF = success/ failure flag AH = status code	*Status codes in AH:* See INT 13H, service 01H.
Write long.	13H	AH = 0BH DL = drive number DH = head number CH = cylinder number CL = sector number ES:BX → buffer	CF = success/ failure flag AH = status code	*Status codes in AH:* See INT 13H, service 01H.
Seek to cylinder.	13H	AH = 0CH DL = drive number DH = head number CH = cylinder number	CF = success/ failure flag AH = status code	*Status codes in AH:* See INT 13H, service 01H.
Alternate disk reset.	13H	AH = 0DH DL = drive number	CF = success/ failure flag AH = status code	*Status codes in AH:* See INT 13H, service 01H.
Test for drive ready.	13H	AH = 10H DL = drive number	CF = success/ failure flag AH = status code	*Status codes in AH:* See INT 13H, service 01H.
Recalibrate drive.	13H	AH = 11H DL = drive number	CF = success/ failure flag AH = status code	*Status codes in AH:* See INT 13H, service 01H.

(continued)

Figure 13-2. *continued*

Service	Interrupt	Register Input	Output	Notes
Controller diagnostics.	13H	AH = 14H	CF = success/ failure flag AH = status code	Status codes in AH: See INT 13H, service 01H.
Get disk type.	13H	AH = 15H DL = drive number	CF = success/ failure flag AH = disk type CX, DX = number of 512-byte sectors (fixed-disk only)	*Disk types:* AH = 00H: disk not there. AH = 01H: diskette, no change detection present. AH = 02H: diskette, change detection present. AH = 03H: fixed disk.
Change of diskette status.	13H	AH = 16H DL = drive number	AH = diskette change status: 00H = no diskette change 01H = invalid parameter 06H = diskette changed 80H = drive not ready	
Set diskette type for format.	13H	AH = 17H AL = diskette type DL = drive number	CF = success/ failure flag AH = status code	*Diskette type set in AL:* AL = 01H: 360 KB diskette in 360 KB drive. AL = 02H: 360 KB diskette in 1.2 MB drive. AL = 03H: 1.2 MB diskette in 1.2 MB drive. AL = 04H: 720 KB diskette in 720 KB drive.
Set media type for diskette format.	13H	AH = 18H CH = number of tracks (bits 0–7) CL (bits 6–7) = number of tracks (bits 8–9) CL (bits 0–5) = sectors per track DL = drive number	CF = success/ failure flag AH = status code ES:DI → 11-byte parameter table (disk-base table)	Only in PC/AT BIOS dated 11/15/85 and later, PC/XT BIOS dated 1/10/86 and later, and PS/2s.

(continued)

278

Figure 13-2. *continued*

Service	Interrupt	Register Input	Output	Notes
Park heads.	13H	AH = 19H DL = drive number	CF = success/ failure flag AH = status code	PS/2s only.
Format Unit.	13H	AH = 1AH	None	For PS/2 fixed disks used with IBM Enhanced Small Device Interface (ESDI) adapter. See the *IBM BIOS Interface Technical Reference Manual.*

Serial Port Services

Service	Interrupt	Register Input	Output	Notes
Initialize serial port.	14H	AH = 00H AL = serial port parameters DX = serial port number	AX = serial port status	*Serial port parameter bit settings:* bits 0–1 = word length: 10 = 7 bits; 11 = 8 bits. bit 2 = stop bits: 0 = 1; 1 = 2. bits 3–4 = parity: 00, 10 = none; 01 = odd; 11 = even. bits 5–7 = baud rate: 000 = 110; 001 = 150; 010 = 300; 011 = 600; 100 = 1200; 101 = 2400; 110 = 4800; 111 = 9600. For PC/XT/AT family only. For PS/2s, use subservice 04H, ''Extended serial port initialize.'' See page 280.
Send one character to serial port.	14H	AH = 01H AL = character DX = serial port number	AH = status code	*Status bit settings:* See INT 14H, service 03H.

(continued)

Figure 13-2. *continued*

Service	Interrupt	Register Input	Output	Notes
Receive one character from serial port.	14H	AH = 02H DX = serial port number	AH = status code AL = character	*Status bit settings:* See INT 14H, service 03H.
Get serial port status.	14H	AH = 03H DX = serial port number	AX = status code	Status code bit settings: *AH bit settings:* bit 0 = data ready. bit 1 = overrun error. bit 2 = parity error. bit 3 = framing error. bit 4 = break detected. bit 5 = transmission buffer register empty. bit 6 = transmission shift register empty. bit 7 = time out. *AL bit settings:* bit 0 = delta clear-to-send. bit 1 = delta data-set-ready. bit 2 = trailing-edge ring detected. bit 3 = change, receive line signal detected. bit 4 = clear-to-send. bit 5 = data-set-ready. bit 6 = ring detected. bit 7 = receive line signal detected.
Extended serial port initialize.	14H	AH = 04H AL = break BH = parity BL = stop bit CH = word length CL = baud rate DX = serial port number (0–3)	AH = line status AL = modem status	PS/2s only. See Chapter 12 for details.

(continued)

Figure 13-2. *continued*

Service	Interrupt	Register Input	Output	Notes
Extended serial port control.	14H	AH = 05H DX = serial port number (0, 1, 2, 3) *To read modem control register:* AL = 00H *To write modem control register:* AL = 01H BL = value for modem control register	AH = line status AL = modem status *If called with* *AL = 00H:* BL = modem control register value	For PS/2s only. See Chapter 12 for details.

System Services*

Service	Interrupt	Register Input	Output	Notes
Turn on cassette motor.	15H	AH = 00H	AH = 00H CF = 0	IBM PC only.
Turn off cassette motor.	15H	AH = 01H	AH = 00H CF = 0	IBM PC only.
Read cassette data blocks.	15H	AH = 02H CX = number of bytes ES:BX → data area	ES:BX → last byte read + 1 DX = number of bytes read CF = 0 (no error) or 1 (error)	IBM PC only.
Write cassette data blocks.	15H	AH = 03H CX = number of bytes ES:BX → data area	CF = success/ failure flag ES:BX → last byte written + 1 CX = 00H	IBM PC only.
Read/Write power-on self-test error log.	15H	AH = 21H	AH = 00H	PS/2 models 50, 60, 80.

* For interrupt 15H service numbers not supported in the ROM BIOS, the PC/XT BIOS
returns AH = 80H and CF = 1; the AT or PS/2 BIOS returns AH = 86H and CF = 1.

(continued)

Figure 13-2. *continued*

Service	Interrupt	Register Input	Output	Notes
Read/Write power-on self-test error log, *continued.*		*To read error log:* AL = 00H *To write error log:* AL = 01H BH = device code BL = error code	*If called with AL = 00H:* BX = number of POST error codes logged ES:DI → POST error log *If called with AL = 01H:* CF = status (0: no error; 1: log full)	
Keyboard intercept.	15H	AH = 4FH		See Chapter 12 for details.
Device open.	15H	AH = 80H		See Chapter 12 for details.
Device close.	15H	AH = 81H		See Chapter 12 for details.
Program termination.	15H	AH = 82H		See Chapter 12 for details.
Start/stop interval timer (event wait).	15H	AH = 83H *To start interval timer:* AL = 00H CX,DX = time in microseconds ES:BX → 1-byte flag *To stop interval timer:* AL = 01H	*If called with AL = 00H:* CF = 0 (if timer started) *or* CF = 1 (if timer already running or function not supported) *If called with AL = 01H:* CF = 0 (if timer canceled) CF = 1 (if function not supported)	PC/AT and PS/2 models 50, 60, 80. At completion of specified interval, the high-order bit of the byte at ES:BX is set to 1.
Joystick support.	15H	AH = 84H *To read switches:* DX = 00H *To read resistive inputs:* DX = 00H	*If called with DX = 00H:* AL = switch settings (bits 4–7)	Not supported by PC or XT BIOS prior to 01/10/86.

(continued)

Figure 13-2. *continued*

Service	Interrupt	Register Input	Output	Notes
Joystick support, *continued*.			CF = 0 (if switches successfully read) *or* CF = 1 (if unsuccessful) *If called with DX = 01H:* AX = stick A *x*-value BX = stick A *y*-value CX = stick B *x*-value DX = stick B *y*-value	
Sys Req keystroke.	15H	AH = 85H AL = key status		See Chapter 12 for details.
Wait during a specified interval.	15H	AH = 86H CX,DX = time in microseconds	CF = 0 (if successful) CF = 1 (timer already running or function not supported)	PC/AT and PS/2s only.
Protected-mode data move.	15H	AH = 87H		PC/AT and PS/2 models 50, 60, 80. See the *IBM BIOS Technical Reference Manual* for details.
Get extended memory size.	15H	AH = 88H	AX = memory size (KB)	PC/AT and PS/2 models 50, 60, 80.
Switch to protected mode.	15H	AH = 89H		PC/AT and PS/2 models 50, 60, 80. See the *IBM BIOS Technical Reference Manual* for details.
Device busy.	15H	AH = 90H		See Chapter 12 for details.
Interrupt complete.	15H	AH = 91H		See Chapter 12 for details.

(continued)

Figure 13-2. *continued*

		Register		
Service	*Interrupt*	*Input*	*Output*	*Notes*
Get system configuration parameters.	15H	AH = C0H	AH = 0 CF = 0 ES:BX → ROM BIOS system configuration parameters	See Chapter 12 for details. Not supported in PC, XT BIOS prior to 01/10/86, or AT prior to 06/10/85.
Get extended BIOS data segment.	15H	AH = C1H	CF = 0 ES = extended BIOS data segment address	PS/2s only.
Enable/disable pointing device.	15H	AH = C2H AL = 00H *To enable:* BH = 00H *To disable:* BH = 01H	CF = 0 if successful; 1 if error AH = status: 00H: no error 01H: invalid function call 02H: invalid input 03H: interface error 04H: resend 05H: no device driver installed	PS/2s only.
Reset pointing device.	15H	AH = C2H AL = 01H	CF = 0 if successful; 1 if error AH = status (as above) BH = 00H (device ID) BL = undefined	PS/2s only.
Set pointing-device sample rate.	15H	AH = C2H AL = 02H BH = sample rate: 00H: 10/second 01H: 20/second 02H: 40/second 03H: 60/second 04H: 80/second 05H: 100/second 06H: 200/second	CF = 0 if successful; 1 if error AH = status (as above)	PS/2s only.

(continued)

Figure 13-2. *continued*

Service	Interrupt	Register Input	Output	Notes
Set pointing-device resolution.	15H	AH = C2H AL = 03H BH = resolution: 00H: 1 count/ millimeter 01H: 2 count/ millimeter 02H: 4 count/ millimeter 03H: 8 count/ millimeter	CF = 0 if successful; 1 if error AH = status (as above)	PS/2s only.
Get pointing-device type.	15H	AH = C2H AL = 04H	CF = 0 if successful; 1 if error AH = status (as above) BH = device ID	PS/2s only.
Initialize pointing device.	15H	AH = C2H AL = 05H BH = data packet size (1–8 bytes)	CF = 0 if successful; 1 if error AH = status (as above)	PS/2s only.
Extended pointing-device commands.	15H	AH = C2H AL = 06H *To get status:* BH = 00H *To set scaling to 1:1:* BH = 01H *To set scaling to 2:1:* BH = 02H	CF = 0 if successful; 1 if error AH = status (as above) *If called with BH = 00H:* BL = status byte 1 CL = status byte 2 DL = status byte 3	PS/2s only. See Chapter 12 for contents of status bytes.
Pass pointing-device driver address to BIOS.	15H	AH = C2H AL = 07H ES:BX → device driver	CF = 0 if successful; 1 if error AH = status (as above)	PS/2s only.

(continued)

Figure 13-2. *continued*

Service	Interrupt	Register Input	Output	Notes
Enable/disable watchdog timer.	15H	AH = C3H BX = timer count (01H–FFH) *To enable:* AL = 01H *To disable:* AL = 00H	CF = 0 if successful	PS/2 models 50, 60, 80 only.
Programmable Option Select (POS) interface.	15H	AH = C4H *To get POS register base address:* AL = 00H *To enable slot for POS setup:* AL = 01H *To enable an adapter:* AL = 02H	*If called with AL = 00H:* AL = 00H DX = base POS register address *If called with AL = 01H:* AL = 01H BL = slot number *If called with AL = 02H:* AL = 02H	PS/2 models 50, 60, 80 only.

Keyboard Services

Service	Interrupt	Register Input	Output	Notes
Read next keystroke.	16H	AH = 00H	AH = scan code AL = ASCII character code	
Report whether keystroke ready.	16H	AH = 01H	ZF = 0 if keystroke available AH = scan code (if ZF = 0) AL = ASCII character code (if ZF = 0)	
Get shift status.	16H	AH = 02H	AL = shift status bits	*Shift status bits:* bit 7 = 1: Insert state active bit 6 = 1: Caps Lock active bit 5 = 1: Num Lock active bit 4 = 1: Scroll Lock active bit 3 = 1: Alt pressed bit 2 = 1: Ctrl pressed bit 1 = 1: left Shift pressed bit 0 = 1: right Shift pressed

(continued)

Figure 13-2. *continued*

Service	Interrupt	Register Input	Output	Notes
Set typematic rate and delay.	16H	AH = 03H AL = 05H BL = typematic rate BH = delay value	None	PC/AT (BIOS dated 11/15/85 and later) and PS/2s only. See Chapter 11 for rate and values.
Write to keyboard buffer.	16H	AH = 05H CH = scan code CL = ASCII character code	AL = 00H (success); AL = 01H (keyboard buffer full)	PC/XT (BIOS dated 01/10/86 and later), PC/AT (BIOS dated 11/15/85 and later), and PS/2s only.
Extended keyboard read.	16H	AH = 10H	AH = scan code AL = ASCII character code	PC/XT (BIOS dated 01/10/86 and later), PC/AT (BIOS dated 11/15/85 and later), and PS/2s only.
Extended keyboard status.	16H	AH = 11H	*If no keystroke available:* ZF = 1 *If keystroke available:* ZF = 0 AH = scan code AL = ASCII character code	PC/XT (BIOS dated 01/10/86 and later), PC/AT (BIOS dated 11/15/85 and later), and PS/2s only.
Extended shift status.	16H	AH = 12H	AL = shift status (as above) AH = extended shift status: bit 7: Sys Req is pressed bit 6: CapsLock is pressed bit 5: NumLock is pressed bit 4: ScrollLock is pressed bit 3: right Alt is pressed bit 2: right Ctrl is pressed	PC/XT (BIOS dated 01/10/86 and later), PC/AT (BIOS dated 11/15/85 and later), and PS/2s only.

(continued)

287

Figure 13-2. *continued*

Service	Interrupt	Register Input	Output	Notes
Extended shift status, *continued*.			bit 1: left Alt is pressed bit 0: left Ctrl is pressed	

Printer Services

Service	Interrupt	Register Input	Output	Notes
Send 1 byte to printer.	17H	AH = 00H AL = character DX = printer number	AH = success/ failure status flags	*Status bit settings:* bit 7 = 1: not busy bit 6 = 1: acknowledge bit 5 = 1: out of paper bit 4 = 1: selected bit 3 = 1: I/O error bit 2 = unused bit 1 = unused bit 0 = time out
Initialize printer.	17H	AH = 01H DX = printer number	AH = status code	Status code bit settings as above.
Get printer status.	17H	AH = 02H DX = printer number	AH = status code	Status code bit settings as above.

Miscellaneous Services

Service	Interrupt	Register Input	Output	Notes
Switch control to ROM BASIC.	18H	None	N/A	No return, so no possible output.
Reboot computer.	19H	None	N/A	No return, so no possible output.

Time-of-Day Services

Service	Interrupt	Register Input	Output	Notes
Read current clock count.	1AH	AH = 00H	AL > 00H if time of day has passed midnight CX = tick count, high word DX = tick count, low word	Timer-tick frequency is about 18.2 ticks/second, or about 65,543 ticks/hour.

(continued)

Figure 13-2. *continued*

Service	Interrupt	Register Input	Output	Notes
Set current clock count.	1AH	AH = 01H CX = tick count, high word DX = tick count, low word	None	
Read real-time clock.	1AH	AH = 02H	CH = hours (in BCD) CL = minutes (in BCD) DH = seconds (in BCD) CF = 1 if clock not operating DL = 01H if daylight savings time option set	PC/AT and PS/2s only. Daylight savings option not available in PC/AT BIOS dated 01/10/84.
Set real-time clock.	1AH	AH = 03H CH = hours CL = minutes DH = seconds DL = 01H for automatic adjustment for daylight savings time		Input values in BCD. PC/AT and PS/2s only. Daylight savings option not available in PC/AT BIOS dated 01/10/84.
Read date from real-time clock.	1AH	AH = 04H	DL = day (in BCD) DH = month (in BCD) CL = year (in BCD) CH = century (19 or 20 in BCD) CF = 1 if clock not operating	PC/AT and PS/2s only.
Set date in real-time clock.	1AH	AH = 05H DL = day (in BCD) DH = month (in BCD) CL = year (in BCD) CH = century (19 or 20, in BCD)		PC/AT and PS/2s only.

(continued)

Figure 13-2. *continued*

Service	Interrupt	Register Input	Output	Notes
Set alarm.	1AH	AH = 06H CH = hours (in BCD) CL = minutes (in BCD) DH = seconds (in BCD)	CF = 1 if clock not operating or alarm already set	Place address for alarm routine in interrupt 4AH vector before using this service.
Reset alarm.	1AH	AH = 07H	None	Disables alarm previously set with INT 1AH, service 06H.
Get alarm time and status.	1AH	AH = 09H	CH = hours (in BCD) CL = minutes (in BCD) DH = seconds (in BCD) DL = alarm status: 00H: alarm not enabled 01H: alarm enabled	PS/2 models 25, 30 only.

Chapter 14

DOS Basics

Chapters 15 through 18 focus on the program support services provided by DOS. These *DOS services* are the entire set of operations that DOS provides to programs. The last chapter in the series, Chapter 18, summarizes their technical details. In this chapter, we introduce some of the main concerns a programmer often faces when working with the DOS services.

Programs access DOS services through a set of interrupts. Interrupt numbers 20H through 3FH (decimal 32 through 63) are reserved for use by DOS. Although 10 of these interrupts can be used in programs, most DOS services are invoked in much the same way as the ROM BIOS services: through one umbrella interrupt, interrupt 21H (decimal 33). You can access a variety of DOS functions by specifying a function number in register AH at the time you call interrupt 21H.

The Pros and Cons of Using the DOS Services

The question of whether or not to use the DOS services arises naturally during the design and development of sophisticated programs. Our general advice, echoed throughout this book, is for you to use the highest available services that will accomplish what you need. This means that, whenever possible, you should use the built-in services of your programming language first, resorting only when necessary to direct use of the DOS services or the ROM BIOS services, and resorting only in extreme circumstances to direct programming of the computer's hardware.

In practical terms, either a program can be written entirely within the confines of the programming language's facilities or nearly all of its I/O work must be done outside the programming language, at a lower level. When a lower level of programming is needed, with very few exceptions the DOS services are best suited for disk operations. When you are working with the keyboard or other I/O devices, either the DOS routines or the ROM BIOS routines will be adequate, depending on the application. But for low-level video-display programming, the situation is more complex. Satisfactory screen output almost always seems to call for the ROM BIOS services and direct hardware programming, even though in some cases screen output is best left in the hands of DOS. We'll see why in a moment.

DOS: A Disk-Service Cornucopia

When you inspect the full range of tools and services placed in your hands by programming languages, by DOS, by the ROM BIOS, and by the computer's hardware, it becomes quite clear that the richest concentration of disk-oriented services exists at the DOS level. This almost goes without saying, because DOS, as a disk operating system, is inherently strongest in its support of disk operations.

As discussed in Chapters 16 and 17, the majority of services that DOS performs are directly connected to the manipulation of disk files. Even some services that are nominally controlled by a program, such as loading and executing another program (interrupt 21H, function 4BH), involve disk-file operations. From this perspective, DOS is not so much a disk operating system as it is a system of disk services designed for use by your programs. When you are developing programs for the IBM personal computer family, you should approach DOS from this standpoint: Think of DOS as a cornucopia of disk operations placed at your service.

DOS and Video: A Difficult Match

Unfortunately, DOS does not provide much in the way of video output services. In fact, the available DOS services are limited to a character-only, "glass teletype" interface that is rapidly becoming an anachronism in these days of high-resolution color graphics.

To achieve attractive, high-performance video output, you must rely on the ROM BIOS or on direct programming of the video hardware. As we have seen, IBM has maintained a fairly consistent programming interface to its video hardware, so many programmers make a practice of bypassing DOS and using lower-level video programming techniques.

But when you bypass DOS, you encounter a problem: Two different programs can't reliably share the video hardware. Consider what can happen, for example, if you write a program that configures the video hardware in a way that conflicts with the configuration used by a memory-resident "pop-up" program like SideKick. If your program runs in a video mode that the pop-up program doesn't recognize, the pop-up program's output may appear incomprehensible on the screen. Worse, the pop-up program may reconfigure the video subsystem for its own purposes and leave your program's video output in limbo.

The problem is amplified in multitasking operating environments, such as Microsoft Windows or OS/2, where programs generally share access to the screen. In these environments, a program can bypass the operating system and gain complete control of the screen only if the operating system suspends video output from all other concurrently executing programs. Thus a program that ties up the video hardware can delay the multitasking execution of background programs.

The designers of OS/2 and Microsoft Windows attacked this problem by providing a sophisticated gamut of video output services. These video output services not only resolve conflicts between programs that want to access the video display, but they also provide very good performance. To get the best video performance in the world of DOS, however, you must either resort to ROM BIOS calls and direct hardware programming or else rely on the video output services provided by your programming language (which themselves bypass DOS).

When trying to decide which method to use, you should consider the probable lifetime of your programs and the range of machines they might be used on. For a PC-specific game program with an expected life of a few months (common for games), you have little reason to worry about these issues. This is not the case for a generalized business or professional application, which should be usable for many years and in many environments. Make your choice and place your bets.

DOS Version Differences

DOS has evolved since the release of version 1.0 in 1981. Even though each new release has contained both improvements and bug-fixes, the driving force behind each release has been a hardware change, and a hardware change has usually involved a disk-drive change. (See Figure 14-1.)

In all but versions 2.1 and 3.1, changes to DOS involved significant modifications to disk support (including new disk-storage formats). The main change to 2.1 was relatively minor, but was disk-related: The diskette

Version	Release Date	Hardware Change
1.0	August 1981	Original IBM PC (single-sided diskette drive)
1.1	May 1982	Double-sided diskette drive
2.0	March 1983	PC/XT
2.1	October 1983	PCjr and Portable PC
3.0	August 1984	PC/AT
3.1	March 1985	PC Network
3.2	January 1986	Support for 3½-inch diskette drives
3.3	April 1987	PS/2s

Figure 14-1. *DOS releases and associated changes to hardware.*

control head-settle time was adjusted to allow for differences in the performance of the half-height drives used in the PCjr and Portable PC. Version 2.1 also corrected a few of the known bugs in 2.0. Version 3.1 incorporated networking functions that were designed for version 3.0, but not ready when 3.0 was released. The following list summarizes the main differences between these versions:

Version 1.0 supported the single-sided, 8-sector diskette format. All basic DOS services were included in this release.

Version 1.1 added support for double-sided diskettes. The DOS services remained the same.

Version 2.0 added support for 9-sector diskettes (both single- and double-sided) and for the PC/XT fixed disk. The DOS services were enhanced extensively in this version. (See Chapter 17.)

Version 2.1 added neither new disk formats nor new DOS services; it did, however, adjust its disk operation timing to benefit the PCjr and the Portable PC.

Version 3.0 added support for the PC/AT's 1.2 MB diskette drive and additional fixed-disk formats. It also laid the groundwork for network disks.

Version 3.1 added network disks, which include a file-sharing capability.

Version 3.2 introduced support for 3½-inch diskette drives.

Version 3.3 was announced concurrently with IBM's introduction of the PS/2s. Several new commands and functions were included specifically to support the PS/2 hardware.

❑ NOTE: *Each version of DOS is compatible with prior versions, except in some very detailed respects (these sorts of details always seem to be unavoidable).*

With each release of DOS, there has been a question among software developers about which version of DOS to target.

In particular, DOS versions 2.0 and later supported a much wider variety of disk hardware and provided significantly more programming services than did versions 1.0 and 1.1, so programs that used the more advanced features of the later DOS versions wouldn't run at all on versions 1.0 and 1.1. Fortunately, the number of people still using version 1.0 or 1.1 is very small, so most software developers target their applications toward versions 2.0 and later. The differences between these later DOS versions are relatively minor and can usually be accommodated in software that verifies which version of DOS is running.

Far-sighted software developers must also tackle the question of compatibility with future versions of DOS. Both IBM and Microsoft are looking toward OS/2 as the logical successor to DOS. In this view, DOS is considered a "mature" product; that is, enhancements to future versions aren't likely to affect existing DOS programs.

Microsoft has published guidelines to help DOS software developers write programs that can later be converted for use under OS/2. In our discussions of DOS services in the next few chapters, we'll point out several techniques that can help ensure the future compatibility of your DOS programs.

In any case, a program can detect which version of DOS it is running under by using DOS function 30H (decimal 48). Unless you can be sure of your audience, you should include this safeguard in your programs and always check to be certain that the correct DOS version is installed.

Diskette Format Considerations

If you're planning to share or sell your programs, you must decide which diskette format you'll use to distribute your software. Initially, most software vendors used single-sided 5¼-inch diskettes with eight sectors per track, because this format was the lowest common denominator that could be read by all versions of DOS. Later, as single-sided diskette drives became virtually extinct, software publishers adopted the double-sided 5¼-inch diskette format as an acceptable medium.

If you sell software for both PCs and PS/2s, however, you must contend with 3½-inch as well as 5¼-inch diskette formats. In this case, you should probably stick to the 720 KB format for 3½-inch disks. You should also offer a choice of diskette sizes, because both 5¼-inch and 3½-inch formats are in widespread use and will be for some time to come.

Comments

Technical information about DOS has become much easier to find since the early days, when the only reliable sources of information were the DOS technical reference manuals. Nowadays, many PC programming magazines discuss DOS programming techniques. Several good reference books on various detailed aspects of DOS programming, including memory-resident programs, installable device drivers, and exception handlers, are also available.

❑ NOTE: *Two "official" sources of detailed information about DOS are the DOS technical reference manuals distributed by IBM and* The MS-DOS Encyclopedia *(published by Microsoft Press).*

Chapter 15

DOS Interrupts

In this chapter we'll describe how to communicate with DOS through interrupts. (See Figure 15-1.) DOS reserves all 32 interrupt numbers from 20H through 3FH (decimal 32 through decimal 63) for its own use. DOS provides system services through five of these interrupts (20H, 21H, 25H, 26H, and 27H). These interrupts can be called directly from a program with the INT instruction. DOS uses the interrupt vectors for four others (22H, 23H, 24H, and 28H) to contain the addresses of routines called by DOS itself; you can substitute your own routines for the default DOS routines by updating one of these interrupt vectors. Interrupt 2FH is reserved for communication between memory-resident programs. The other 22 interrupts reserved by DOS are not intended for use in your programs.

Interrupt Number		
Hex	*Dec*	*Description*
20H	32	Program Terminate
21H	33	General DOS Services
22H	34	Terminate Address
23H	35	Ctrl-C Handler Address
24H	36	Critical Error-Handler Address
25H	37	Absolute Disk Read
26H	38	Absolute Disk Write
27H	39	Terminate and Stay Resident
28H	40	DOS Idle Interrupt
2FH	47	Multiplex Interrupt

Figure 15-1. *DOS interrupts.*

❑ NOTE: *You can use any of the 10 interrupts described in this chapter in your programs. Nevertheless, there is some overlap between the services provided through the separate interrupts described in this chapter and the functions available through interrupt 21H. When you have a choice, use the interrupt 21H functions described in Chapters 16 and 17. We'll point out why as we describe each DOS interrupt.*

The Five Main DOS Interrupts

Of the DOS interrupts described in this chapter, five have built-in interrupt-handling programs, each of which performs a particular task.

Interrupt 20H (decimal 32): Program Terminate

Interrupt 20H (decimal 32) is used to exit from a program and pass control back to DOS. It is similar to interrupt 21H, function 00H. (See page 325.) These services can be used interchangeably with any version of DOS to end a program.

Interrupt 20H does not automatically close files opened with interrupt 21H, functions 0FH or 16H when it terminates a program, so you should always use interrupt 21H, function 10H to close such files before exiting. If a modified file is not formally closed, its new length will not be recorded in the file directory.

A program can set three operational addresses through DOS interrupts 22H, 23H, and 24H, as we will see shortly. As part of the clean-up operations performed by DOS for interrupt 20H, these addresses are restored to the values they had before the program was executed. Resetting these addresses is essential if the program that invoked interrupt 20H was executed as the "child" of another program. It serves to protect the "parent" program from using routines intended for the "child." (See DOS function 4BH [decimal 75] in Chapter 17.)

❏ NOTE: *When DOS executes a program, it constructs a* program segment prefix *(PSP), a 256-byte block of memory that contains control information that, among other things, is referenced by DOS when a program is terminated. (We discuss the PSP in detail at the end of this chapter.) DOS depends on the CS register to point to the PSP when the interrupt 20H terminate service is invoked. If the CS register points elsewhere, DOS may crash.*

In practice, we recommend that you terminate your programs with interrupt 21H, function 4CH, which is more flexible and less restrictive than interrupt 20H. The only reason to use interrupt 20H is to maintain compatibility with DOS version 1.0.

Interrupt 21H (decimal 33): General DOS Services

You can take advantage of a wide range of DOS functions through interrupt 21H (decimal 33). Each function has a unique number you specify when you execute interrupt 21H. Chapters 16 and 17 cover the gamut of interrupt 21H services in detail.

Interrupts 25H and 26H (decimal 37 and 38): Absolute Disk Read and Write

Interrupt 25H (decimal 37) and its companion, interrupt 26H (decimal 38), are used to read and write specific disk sectors. They are the only DOS services that ignore the logical structure of a disk and work only with individual sectors, paying no attention to the locations of files, file directories, or the File Allocation Table.

Interrupts 25H and 26H are similar to the corresponding ROM BIOS disk services, except that the sectors are located by a different numbering method. With the ROM BIOS services, the sectors are selected by their three-dimensional coordinate locations (cylinder, head, and sector), whereas with interrupts 25H and 26H, the sectors are selected by their sequential logical sector numbers. (DOS's sector-numbering system is discussed on page 109.)

The following BASIC formula converts three-dimensional coordinates used by the ROM BIOS to logical sector numbers used by DOS:

```
LOGICAL.SECTOR = (SECTOR - 1) + (HEAD * SECTORS.PER.TRACK) +
(CYLINDER * SECTORS.PER.TRACK * NUMBER.OF.HEADS)
```

And here are the formulas for converting logical sector numbers to three-dimensional coordinates:

```
SECTOR = 1 + LOGICAL.SECTOR MOD SECTORS.PER.TRACK
HEAD = (LOGICAL.SECTOR \ SECTORS.PER.TRACK) MOD NUMBER.OF.HEADS
CYLINDER = LOGICAL.SECTOR \ (SECTORS.PER.TRACK * NUMBER.OF.HEADS)
```

❑ NOTE: *Don't forget that the ROM BIOS counts heads and cylinders from 0 but counts sectors from 1; DOS logical sectors are numbered from 0.*

To use interrupt 25H or 26H to read or write a block of logical sectors, load the necessary parameters into the CPU registers and execute the interrupt. The number of sectors is specified in the CX register, the starting sector number is specified in DX, and the memory address for data transfer is specified in DS:BX. The disk drive is selected by placing a number in the AL register: Drive A is 0, drive B is 1, and so on.

Although ROM BIOS services work with true physical drives, DOS services work with logical drive numbers. DOS assumes every computer has at least two logical drives. If no physical drive B exists, DOS will simulate it by using the one physical drive as either A or B, whichever is needed. You can then remap these logical drives by using the DOS ASSIGN command.

The results of interrupts 25H and 26H are reported in the carry flag (CF) and the AL and AH registers. If no error occurred, CF = 0. If an error did occur (CF = 1), AL and AH contain the error codes in two somewhat redundant groups. The AL codes in Figure 15-2 are based on those used by the DOS critical-error handler through interrupt 24H (see page 308), and the AH codes in Figure 15-3 are based on the error codes reported by the ROM BIOS (see page 201).

Error Code		
Hex	Dec	Meaning
00H	0	Write-protect error: attempt to write on protected diskette
01H	1	Unknown unit: invalid drive number
02H	2	Drive not ready (e.g. no disk, or door open)
04H	4	CRC (cyclical redundancy check) error: parity error
06H	6	Seek error: move to requested cylinder failed
07H	7	Unknown media: disk format not recognized
08H	8	Sector not found
0AH	10	Write error
0BH	11	Read error
0CH	12	General, nonspecific error
0FH	15	Invalid disk change

Figure 15-2. *The error-code values and meanings returned in the AL register following an error in a disk read or write through DOS interrupt 25H or 26H.*

Error Code		
Hex	Dec	Meaning
02H	2	Bad address mark: sector ID marking invalid or not found
03H	3	Write-protect error: attempt to write on protected disk
04H	4	Bad sector: requested sector not on disk
08H	8	DMA (direct memory access) failure
10H	16	Bad CRC: read found invalid parity check of data
20H	32	Controller failed: disk drive controller malfunction
40H	64	Bad seek: move to requested track failed
80H	128	Time out: drive did not respond

Figure 15-3. *The error-code values and meanings returned in the AH register following an error in a disk read or write through DOS interrupt 25H or 26H.*

Normally, interrupt handlers and other service routines leave the stack clean when they exit, returning it to its original size and contents. DOS interrupts 25H and 26H deliberately do not clean up the stack. Instead, they finish and return to the program with one word left on the stack. This word holds the contents of the flag register, showing how the flags were set when the program invoked the service. This is purportedly done to preserve the program's flag status before the service was used, because interrupts 25H and 26H use the flags for their return codes. We think this is a silly precaution because any program that needs to preserve the flags can simply do what programs normally do when they need something saved: PUSH them onto the stack themselves. Any program that uses interrupts 25H and 26H should POP the two extra flag-status bytes off the stack after the interrupt returns. These bytes can either be placed in the flags register with a POPF command (which should be done after testing CF for an error) or be discarded by incrementing the stack pointer register by 2 (ADD SP,2).

Interrupt 27H (decimal 39): Terminate and Stay Resident

Interrupt 27H (decimal 39) invokes one of the most interesting of all the services provided by DOS.

Like interrupt 20H, interrupt 27H ends a program, but does not erase it from memory. Instead, it leaves a specified portion of the program in memory (the program *stays resident*). The program and data that are made resident using interrupt 27H become, in effect, an extension of DOS and will not be overwritten by other programs.

❑ NOTE: *As with interrupt 20H, DOS versions 2.0 and later provide a more flexible alternative to interrupt 27H. This is interrupt 21H, function 31H, which we recommend instead of interrupt 27H unless you are concerned about compatibility with DOS version 1.0. See Chapter 17 for more about interrupt 21H, function 31H.*

Interrupt 27H (or its function-call equivalent) is used by a number of sophisticated "pop-up" programs like SideKick. Terminate-and-stay-resident (TSR) programs typically use this service to establish new interrupt-handling routines that are meant to stay in effect indefinitely. Most often, these interrupt-handling routines replace existing DOS or ROM BIOS interrupt handlers in order to change or extend their operation. But the resident item is not limited to interrupt handlers and program instructions; it could just as easily be data. For example, the same programming technique could be used to load status information into a common area that various programs would share, allowing them to communicate indirectly.

Normally, a TSR program is designed in two parts: a *resident portion* that remains in memory and a *transient portion* that installs the resident portion by updating interrupt vectors, initializing data, and calling the Terminate-and-Stay-Resident service. The transient portion does not remain in memory after interrupt 27H is executed.

To accommodate this process, TSR programs are designed with the resident portion first (that is, at lower addresses). The transient portion computes the size of the resident portion and places this value in register DX when it executes interrupt 27H. DOS then leaves the resident portion in memory but reclaims the memory occupied by the transient portion for executing other programs.

Anything left resident by this service normally remains resident as long as DOS is also resident. It is not unusual for several different programs to leave part of themselves resident. Programs that use this technique are usually sophisticated and complicated, so it is also not unusual for them to interfere with each other. To operate such a group of resident programs successfully, you must sometimes load them in a particular order — an order you may have to discover through experimentation (an unfair trick to play on an unsuspecting user).

As with interrupt 20H, the ordinary terminate service, DOS resets the address vectors for interrupts 22H through 24H when it performs this terminate-and-stay-resident service. Therefore, you can't use this service to create resident interrupt handlers for the address interrupts. Although seemingly a limitation, this is actually fairly reasonable: The address interrupts are not meant to be used globally; they are meant to be used only by individual programs. (See the DOS address interrupts section that follows for further discussion.)

The Multiplex Interrupt

The *multiplex interrupt*, interrupt 2FH (decimal 47), is used to communicate with memory-resident programs. This interrupt wasn't used in DOS version 1, but in version 2 the RAM-resident print spooler PRINT used it. In DOS versions 3.0 and later, the protocol for using interrupt 2FH was standardized to allow multiple memory-resident programs to share the interrupt. (That's why this interrupt is called the multiplex interrupt.)

❑ NOTE: *Most of the material in this chapter applies to all versions of DOS; however, interrupt 2FH is available only with DOS versions 3.0 and later.*

To use the multiplex interrupt, you must write a memory-resident TSR program that contains an interrupt handler for interrupt 2FH. (Use the DOS Terminate-and-Stay-Resident service to do this.) The transient portion of the TSR program must copy the address of the previous interrupt 2FH handler from the interrupt 2FH vector (0000:00BCH) to a variable in the resident portion. The transient portion then updates the interrupt 2FH vector with the address of the resident portion's interrupt 2FH handler so that when interrupt 2FH is subsequently executed, the TSR's handler gets control.

When interrupt 2FH is executed, the resident interrupt 2FH handler does the following:

```
IF      AH=IDnumber
THEN    process the value in AL
        return from the interrupt (IRET)
ELSE    jump to the previous interrupt 2FH handler
```

This simple logic lets several memory-resident programs use the multiplex interrupt to communicate. The key is that every memory-resident program must have a unique ID number. Your program's interrupt 2FH handler should recognize one of the 64 values between C0H and FFH. (There are 256 possible ID numbers, of course, but Microsoft and IBM reserve numbers 00H through BFH for use by DOS utilities.)

When your program's interrupt 2FH handler gains control, it must first check the value in register AH. If the value in AH matches the program's ID number, the handler looks in AL to decide what to do next. If the values don't match, the handler simply jumps to the address of the previous interrupt 2FH handler.

The interrupt 2FH handler considers the value in AL to be a function number and processes it accordingly, as described in the following paragraphs:

Function 00H has a special meaning. It instructs the interrupt handler to return one of two values in AL:

- A value of FFH indicates that an interrupt 2FH handler is resident in memory and available to process other function numbers.

- A value of 01H indicates that the ID number in AH is in use.

So, to detect whether a particular TSR program is installed in memory, a program executes interrupt 2FH with the TSR's ID number in AH and with AL = 00H. If the TSR is present in memory, it returns AL = FFH. If another TSR is using the ID number for its own purposes, that TSR returns

AL = 01H. Otherwise, any interrupt 2FH handlers in memory simply ignore the interrupt, causing the interrupt to return AL = 00H.

The best-documented example of how to use the multiplex interrupt is the PRINT program supplied with DOS versions 3.0 and later. By examining how PRINT uses the multiplex interrupt, you can make better use of this interrupt in your own memory-resident programs.

PRINT's multiplex ID number is 1. Any time interrupt 2FH is executed with this ID number in AH, PRINT's memory-resident interrupt handler processes the interrupt. Because six different functions are defined by PRINT (see Figure 15-4), a call to PRINT consists of executing interrupt 2FH with AH = 01H and a function number in AL.

Each time you run PRINT, the program executes interrupt 2FH with AH = 01H and AL = 00H. The first time you run the program, the value returned in AL by the interrupt is 00H, so the program installs itself in memory. When you invoke PRINT a second time, the value returned in AL as a result of executing the multiplex interrupt with AH = 01H is FFH. This value is placed there by the memory-resident copy of PRINT, so the second invocation of the program knows not to install itself in memory.

The second and subsequent invocations of PRINT can request any of five different functions by passing a function number to the first, memory-resident copy of the program. You could also use these functions in your own programs by placing the value 01H (PRINT's multiplex ID) in register AH, the function number in register AL, and then issuing interrupt 2FH.

Function Number	Description
00H	Get installed status.
01H	Submit file to print.
02H	Remove file from print queue.
03H	Cancel all files in print queue.
04H	Hold print queue.
05H	Release print queue.

Figure 15-4. *PRINT functions defined through the multiplex interrupt.*

Function 01H submits a file to the print spooler for printing. To tell PRINT what is to be printed, you set the register pair DS:DX to point to a 5-byte area called a *submit packet*. The first byte of the submit packet is a level code (which should be 0). The remaining 4 bytes of the submit packet are the segmented address of an ASCIIZ string (see page 350) that defines the pathname of the file to be printed. The pathname must be a single file. The global filename characters * and ? are not allowed.

When a file is submitted using this function, it is added to the end of the queue, or list, of files to be printed. The files are printed in turn and are dropped from the queue after they're printed.

Function 02H cancels individual files queued for printing. The register pair DS:DX points to the ASCIIZ string that defines which file is to be removed from the queue. In this case, the global filename characters * and ? can be used. In function 02H, DS:DX points directly to the filename string, rather than to a submit packet that points to the string.

Function 03H cancels all files queued for printing. For both functions 02H and 03H, if the file currently being printed is canceled, PRINT stops printing the file and prints a short message to that effect.

Function 04H gives programs access to the print queue so they can inspect it. The queue is frozen when this function is requested, so you don't have to worry about the list changing while you inspect it. Issuing any other PRINT function call will unfreeze the queue. Function 04H returns a pointer in the register pair DS:SI that points to a list of filenames queued for printing. Entries in the list are strings with a fixed length of 64 bytes. The end of the list is indicated by an entry that begins with a zero byte.

The queue freeze imposed by function 04H doesn't need to halt the printing operation. But function 04H will suspend the removal from the queue of a file that is finished printing.

Function 05H is essentially a null function that does nothing but unfreeze the queue of filenames frozen by function 04H. (The other four functions can do this, too.)

The Three DOS Address Interrupts

DOS uses three interrupts, 22H through 24H (decimal 34 through 36), to handle three exceptional circumstances: the end of a program, a ''break'' keyboard action (Ctrl-Break or Ctrl-C on the standard PC keyboard), and any ''critical error'' (usually a disk error of some kind). Your programs can affect the action taken in each of these three circumstances by changing the corresponding interrupt vector to point to any operation you choose. This is why we call these interrupts the *address interrupts*.

DOS maintains a default address setting for each of these interrupts, which is preserved at the beginning of a program's operation and restored after the program is finished. This allows your programs to freely change these vectors according to their needs without disturbing the operation of subsequent programs or the operation of DOS itself.

Interrupt 22H (decimal 34): Terminate Address

The address associated with interrupt 22H (decimal 34) specifies where control of the computer will be passed when a program's execution ends with a call to DOS interrupt 20H or 27H, or with interrupt 21H, function 00H, 31H, or 4CH. Interrupt 22H isn't designed to be executed directly by a program using the INT instruction. Instead, DOS uses the interrupt 22H vector to store the address of its own program termination routine.

It's not a good idea to manipulate the DOS terminate address. The inner workings of the default DOS program termination routine are not documented, so writing a substitute routine that terminates a program cleanly without confounding DOS is difficult. If you are qualified to use this feature, then you probably understand it better than we can explain it.

Interrupt 23H (decimal 35): Ctrl-C Handler Address

The address associated with interrupt 23H (decimal 35) points to the interrupt-handling routine that DOS invokes in response to the Ctrl-C key combination. Thus interrupt 23H is intended to be executed only by DOS, not by an application program. A few old-fashioned programs, such as the DOS editor EDLIN, use Ctrl-C as a command keystroke, but in most applications the Ctrl-C combination signals that the user wants to interrupt an ongoing process.

DOS is a bit quirky about when it will respond to a Ctrl-C keystroke. Normally, DOS acts on a break only when it is reading from or writing to a character I/O device (the screen, keyboard, printer, or communications port). However, the BREAK ON command allows DOS versions 2.0 and later to act on Ctrl-C at the time of most other DOS system calls.

DOS's default Ctrl-C handler terminates the program or batch file you are executing. However, if your program provides its own interrupt 23H handler, it can have DOS take any action you want.

In general, a Ctrl-C handler can take three different courses of action:

- It can perform some useful action, such as setting a flag, and then return to DOS with an interrupt return (IRET) instruction. In this case, DOS picks up where it left off, without terminating your program's execution.

- It can set or clear the carry flag and then return to DOS with a far return instruction (RET 2) that discards the flags pushed on the stack when the interrupt 23H handler was called by DOS. If the carry flag is set, DOS terminates the interrupted program. If the carry flag is clear, DOS continues execution.

- It can keep control without returning to DOS. This option is tricky, however, because you don't usually know what was on the stack at the moment DOS detected the Ctrl-C keystroke. An interrupt 23H handler that doesn't return to DOS should generally restore the stack pointer register (SP) to a predetermined value. It should also execute interrupt 21H, function 0DH, to flush DOS file buffers so that the DOS disk I/O system will be in a known state.

The usual reason to write your own Ctrl-C handler is to let your program handle a keyboard break itself. Even if you want your program to terminate immediately after Ctrl-C is pressed, you may still need to clean up before your program terminates. For example, if you use interrupt 21H, functions 0FH or 16H, to open a file, you should write your own Ctrl-C handler to close it because the default DOS Ctrl-C handler won't do so. Also, if you installed your own interrupt handlers for ROM BIOS or hardware interrupts, the DOS Ctrl-C handler won't restore them before it terminates your program. Again, your Ctrl-C handler should do this if necessary.

If you do write your own Ctrl-C handler, don't forget the relationship between Ctrl-C and the keyboard Ctrl-Break combination. When you press Ctrl-Break, the ROM BIOS keyboard interrupt handler generates interrupt 1BH. DOS's interrupt 1BH handler inserts a Ctrl-C key code into the keyboard input buffer. The next time DOS checks the keyboard buffer, it finds Ctrl-C and executes interrupt 23H. Thus, in effect, pressing Ctrl-Break has the same effect as pressing Ctrl-C, except that DOS detects the break generated by Ctrl-Break without first processing the intervening characters in the keyboard buffer.

Interrupt 24H (decimal 36): Critical Error-Handler Address

The address associated with interrupt 24H (decimal 36) points to the interrupt-handling routine invoked whenever DOS detects a "critical error" — an emergency situation that prevents DOS from continuing with normal processing. Typically, the critical error is a disk error, but other errors are also reported, as we'll see.

Like interrupt 23H, interrupt 24H is intended to be invoked only by DOS, not by an application program. However, an application can substitute its own interrupt 24H handler for the default DOS handler. The DOS default handler produces a familiar message (shown on the following page).

```
Abort, Retry, Ignore?        (in DOS versions prior to 3.3)
```

or

```
Abort, Retry, Fail?          (in DOS versions 3.3 and later)
```

If you substitute a customized interrupt 24H handler for the one DOS provides, you can tailor critical-error handling to the needs of your program.

When DOS transfers control to a critical-error handler, it provides several sources of information about the error itself, and about the state of the system before the error occurred. These sources include the register pair BP:SI, the stack, the AH register, and the DI register. We will cover them one by one because this process is quite complicated.

If you are operating under DOS version 2.0 or later, the register pair BP:SI is set to point to a device-header control block. Your critical-error handler can inspect the device header to learn more about the device (disk drive, printer, and so forth) that experienced the error. (See the DOS technical reference manuals for more about the device header.)

When the critical-error handler gains control, the stack contains the complete register set of the program that issued the DOS function call that ended in the critical error. This information can be quite useful to an error handler that is intimately integrated with the active program. The usual method of accessing the information on the stack is to address the stack through register BP. You can access the stack as shown in Figure 15-5 on the following page if the first two instructions in your critical-error handler are

```
PUSH    BP
MOV     BP,SP
```

DOS indicates the nature of a critical error primarily through a combination of the high-order bit of the AH register and the low-order byte of the DI register (a curious choice, for sure). If the high-order bit of AH is 0, the error is related to a disk operation. If the same bit (bit 7 of AH) is 1, the error is something other than a disk error, as we shall discuss shortly.

When the error is a disk-device error (high-order bit of AH is 0), register AL identifies the drive number (0 is drive A, 1 is drive B, and so on). Bits 0 through 5 of AH indicate further information about the error, as shown in Figure 15-6.

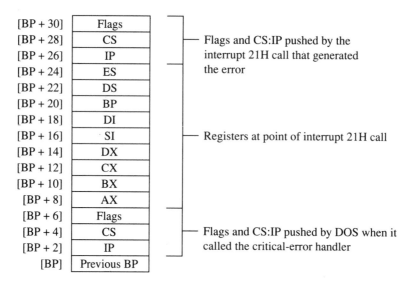

[BP + 30]	Flags	
[BP + 28]	CS	Flags and CS:IP pushed by the
[BP + 26]	IP	interrupt 21H call that generated
[BP + 24]	ES	the error
[BP + 22]	DS	
[BP + 20]	BP	
[BP + 18]	DI	
[BP + 16]	SI	Registers at point of interrupt 21H call
[BP + 14]	DX	
[BP + 12]	CX	
[BP + 10]	BX	
[BP + 8]	AX	
[BP + 6]	Flags	
[BP + 4]	CS	Flags and CS:IP pushed by DOS when it
[BP + 2]	IP	called the critical-error handler
[BP]	Previous BP	

Figure 15-5. *Information passed on the stack to an interrupt 24H (critical-error) handler.*

Bit 5 4 3 2 1 0	Value	Meaning
. 0	0	Read error
. 1	1	Write error
. . . 0 0 .	0	Error involved DOS system files
. . . 0 1 .	1	Error involved file allocation table
. . . 1 0 .	2	Error involved root directory
. . . 1 1 .	3	Error involved files area of disk
. . 1 . . .	1	Fail response allowed
. 1	1	Retry response allowed
1	1	Ignore response allowed

Figure 15-6. *The bit values and associated errors indicated in bits 0 through 5 of the AH register when DOS invokes interrupt 24H.*

DOS returns additional information about the error in the low-order byte of register DI (Figure 15-7). The error codes in DI cover a variety of input/output devices, so you must rely on a combination of the information in AH and in DI to determine the exact nature of the critical error.

If bit 7 of AH is set, the error is probably not a disk error, though it may be disk related. One disk-related error normally reported when bit 7 of AH is set is an error in the disk's FAT. In DOS version 1, this is always the case. For versions 2.0 and later, the error handler should inspect bit 15 of the word that is offset 4 bytes into the device header (BP: [SI + 4]). If this bit is clear, the device is a block device (disk) and the error is a FAT error. If this bit is set, the device is a character device, in which case the low-order byte of DI defines the exact problem (the high-order byte should be ignored). DI error-code values shown in Figure 15-7 are essentially the same as those reported in AL for interrupts 25H and 26H (decimal 37 and 38).

You can use the following interrupt 21H functions in your critical-error handler to report what's going on to the program's user:

- Functions 01H through 0CH, which provide simple keyboard and display services

- Function 30H, which returns the DOS version number

- Function 59H, which returns extended error information in DOS versions 3.0 and later

Error Code		
Hex	*Dec*	*Description*
00H	0	Write-protect error; attempt to write on protected diskette
01H	1	Unknown unit (invalid drive number)
02H	2	Drive not ready (no diskette or drive door open)
03H	3	Unknown command requested
04H	4	Data error (CRC)
05H	5	Bad request structure length
06H	6	Seek error; move to requested cylinder failed
07H	7	Unknown disk format
08H	8	Sector not found
09H	9	Printer out of paper
0AH	10	Write fault
0BH	11	Read fault
0CH	12	General, nonspecific error
0FH	15	Invalid disk change (DOS version 3.0 or later)

Figure 15-7. *Errors indicated in the low-order byte of register DI when DOS invokes interrupt 24H.*

Don't call other DOS services within your critical-error handler, however, because other services may overwrite internal buffers or stacks that DOS will need when the error handler returns.

Normally, an error-handler routine returns to DOS after doing whatever it chooses to do. DOS can then take one of four courses of action: It can ignore the error, try the operation again, terminate the program, or fail the requested operation and return to the program (DOS versions 3.1 and later). You tell DOS which course you want it to take by loading a value from Figure 15-8 into the AL register before executing an IRET to return to DOS.

If you use a custom critical-error handler, it will remain in effect only as long as the program that installs it is running. When the program terminates, DOS replaces the contents of the interrupt 24H vector with the address of the default critical-error handler.

AL	Description
00H	Ignore the error and press onward.
01H	Retry the operation.
02H	Terminate the program.
03H	Fail the operation (DOS versions 3.1 and later).

Figure 15-8. *Values that can be returned to DOS in register AL by an interrupt 24H (critical-error) handler.*

The DOS Idle Interrupt

DOS executes interrupt 28H (decimal 40) within interrupt 21H services that loop while waiting for an expected event, such as a keystroke. For example, if you execute the DOS keyboard-input service (interrupt 21H, service 01H), DOS executes interrupt 28H within an idle loop that waits for the next keystroke.

The default DOS handler for interrupt 28H is merely an IRET instruction; that is, executing interrupt 28H normally does nothing at all. You can substitute your own interrupt 28H handler, however, that does something useful while DOS is otherwise idle. In particular, a memory-resident program can contain an interrupt 28H handler that is executed repeatedly whenever DOS is waiting for keyboard output.

The biggest problem with installing your own interrupt 28H handler is that the handler can execute interrupt 21H to access DOS services only under very specific circumstances. Unfortunately, you must know many details about the way DOS internally processes interrupt 21H requests in order to use these safely within an interrupt 28H handler.

The Program Segment Prefix (PSP)

When DOS loads a program, it sets aside a 256-byte block of memory for the program: the *program segment prefix* (PSP). The PSP contains a hodgepodge of information that DOS uses to help run the program. A PSP is associated with every DOS program, no matter what language the program is written in. However, for programming purposes, the information stored in the PSP is more relevant to programs written in assembly language than to programs written in high-level languages. This is because with high-level languages, the language is normally in charge of the program's working environment, memory usage, and file control — all the information that the PSP is concerned with. Therefore, you can normally make good use of the PSP only if your program is assembly-language based.

Before we describe the different elements of the PSP, we need to look at the relationship between the PSP and the program it supports.

DOS always builds a program's PSP in memory just below the memory area allocated to the program itself. When the program receives control from DOS, segment registers DS and ES point to the beginning of the PSP. Because it sometimes needs to locate PSP information, DOS keeps a copy of the PSP segment value internally.

The best way to explain how the PSP and the program work together is to jump right into the PSP's internal structure. We will reveal the purpose and potential use of each element as we explain it.

The Internal Structure of the PSP

As you will soon discover, the PSP contains a rather confusing mixture of items. (See Figure 15-9.) The background and history of DOS pull it in different directions — backward to the earlier CP/M system and forward to UNIX-type operating environments. As a result, the PSP contains elements that serve different purposes and are oriented to different programming methods. We'll discuss the elements in the order in which they appear.

The field at offset 00H (2 bytes) contains bytes CDH and 20H, the interrupt 20H instruction. As we saw in the discussion of interrupt 20H in this chapter, this interrupt is only one of several standard ways for a program to terminate. This instruction is placed at the beginning of the PSP (at offset 00H) so that a program can end itself simply by jumping to this location when the CS points to the PSP. As you might guess, this is not the most sensible thing for a program to do; it's always best to go through the appropriate interrupt or function call. This odd method of terminating a program is a relic of the days when CP/M compatibility was important.

Offset Hex	Dec	Length (bytes)	Description
00H	0	2	INT 20H instruction
02H	2	2	Size of memory (in paragraphs)
04H	4	1	(Reserved; normally 0)
05H	5	5	Call to DOS function dispatcher
0AH	10	4	Interrupt 22H (Terminate) address
0EH	14	4	Interrupt 23H (Ctrl-C) address
12H	18	4	Interrupt 24H (Critical Error) address
16H	22	22	(Reserved)
2CH	44	2	Environment segment address
2EH	46	34	Reserved
50H	80	3	INT 21H, RETF instructions
53H	83	9	(Reserved)
5CH	92	16	FCB #1
6CH	108	20	FCB #2
80H	128	128	Command-line parameters and default Disk Transfer Area (DTA)

Figure 15-9. *The parts of the program segment prefix (PSP).*

The field at offset 02H (2 bytes) contains the segment address of the last paragraph of memory allocated to the program. DOS normally loads a program in the first free area of memory large enough to contain the program. A program can use this field to determine the actual size of the memory area allocated to it.

In practice, there's a better way to determine the amount of memory allocated to a program. Interrupt 21H, function 4AH can return the size of any block of memory, not just the block into which a program is loaded. (See Chapter 17 for more on this DOS service.)

The field at offset 05H (5 bytes) contains a long call to the *DOS function dispatcher,* the internal DOS routine that examines the function number you pass to DOS and executes the corresponding service routine. This field, too, is a remnant of the days when CP/M compatibility was important to DOS programmers. A program can make a near CALL to offset 05H in the PSP with a function number in register CL and get the same result as if it had loaded AH with the function number and executed interrupt 21H.

Needless to say, this technique is not very useful in real-world DOS programs.

The fields at offsets 0AH, 0EH, and 12H (4 bytes each) contain the segmented addresses of the default handlers for interrupt 22H (Terminate), 23H (Ctrl-C), and 24H (Critical Error). These addresses are stored in the PSP for your convenience. If you substitute a customized interrupt handler for one of the DOS handlers, you can restore the default handler by copying its address from the PSP into the corresponding interrupt vector.

In DOS versions 2.0 and later, the field at offset 2CH (2 bytes) contains the paragraph address of the program's *environment block*. The environment block contains a list of ASCIIZ strings (strings of ASCII characters, each terminated with a zero byte) that define various kinds of information. The end of the environment block is marked by a zero-length string (a single zero byte) where you would expect to find the first byte of the next string. Environment blocks that begin with a zero-length string contain no strings.

Each environment string is of the form *NAME = value*, where NAME is capitalized and of any reasonable length and *value* can be almost anything. The environment thus consists of a list of global variables, each of which contains information that your program may be able to use. For example, if the environment block contains the PATH environment variable (that is, a string that starts with PATH=), any program — including DOS itself — can examine its environment block to determine which directories to search for executable files (and in what order). In this way the environment block provides a simple means of passing information to any program that examines it. (You can change the contents of the environment block with the DOS SET command.)

DOS makes a copy of the environment block whenever it loads a program to be executed, and places the copy's paragraph address (segment) in the program's PSP. To obtain information from the environment block, a program must first obtain its segment from the PSP and then examine each of the zero-terminated strings. Some high-level languages contain functions that do this for you. For example, in C, the *getenv()* library function does all the work.

Many sophisticated DOS programs rely on information in the environment block. Also, the concept of the environment is found in other powerful operating systems, including UNIX and OS/2. Whenever you need to pass user-configurable information to a program, we highly recommend the use of the environment block.

The field at offset 50H contains two executable 8086 instructions: INT 21H and RETF (far return).

This is another kludge that lets you invoke DOS functions somewhat indirectly. To use this feature, set up everything necessary to invoke a DOS interrupt 21H function (selecting the function in AH, and so forth). Then, instead of bravely performing an interrupt 21H (a 2-byte instruction), do a far call to offset 50H in the PSP (a 5-byte instruction).

You might expect that this feature is another flash from the past, a bit of CP/M compatibility, but actually it was introduced with DOS version 2.0 and will not work with previous versions of DOS. You might find that making a far call to offset 50H in the PSP is handy if you intend to patch the address of a different function dispatcher into your code, but in most cases, a simple INT 21H will suffice.

The fields at offsets 5CH and 6CH support old-fashioned file processing, using file control blocks, or FCBs. FCBs can be used for file I/O with any version of DOS, but their use is discouraged with DOS versions 2.0 and later, where more modern file I/O is available through the use of file handles. See page 341 for more on file control blocks, and see page 350 for more on file handles.

This area of the PSP was designed to make life easier for programs that receive one or two filenames as parameters. The basic idea, and a good one we think, is to let DOS construct the necessary FCBs out of the first two command-line parameters (the parameters given on the command line, following the program name). If a program needs either or both FCBs, it can open and use them without having to decode the command-line parameters and construct the FCBs itself.

If you use this feature of the PSP, you should be aware of three potential complications: First, the two FCBs overlap where they are placed. If your program needs only the first, fine; but if it needs the second FCB as well, one or both of them should be moved elsewhere before they are used. Second, these FCBs can involve FCB extensions, a fact overlooked in most DOS documentation for the PSP. Finally, if you use a DOS function that requires an extended FCB, you should be careful to copy the default FCBs to another area of memory where the FCB extensions won't overlap other data in the PSP.

Keep in mind that the use of FCBs is considered obsolete, but if you want to use them, this information should help.

The field at offset 80H serves two purposes: When DOS first builds the PSP, it fills this field with the command-line parameters typed by the user when the program was invoked. The length of the command line is in the byte at offset 80H. A string containing the command-line parameters follows at offset 81H.

This string has some peculiarities: It does not contain the name of the program that was invoked. Instead, it begins with the character that immediately follows the program name, which is usually a blank. Separators, such as blanks or commas, are not stripped out or compressed. If you use the command line, you have to be prepared to scan through it, recognizing standard separators. Fortunately, high-level languages often provide functions that parse the command parameter string for you. In C, for example, the values *argc* and *argv* are passed to the main startup routine in every C program. These two values contain the number of command-line parameters and the address of a list of individual parameters. It's usually easier to rely on your high-level language to extract command-line parameters from the PSP than it is to do it yourself in assembly language.

Starting with DOS version 2.0, the command line is modified in a particular way: DOS strips any redirection parameters (such as < or >) and reconstructs the parameter line as if these items were not there. As a result of these two operations on the command string, a program can neither find out if its standard I/O is being redirected nor find out its own name.

The other purpose served by the field at offset 80H in the PSP is that of the default Disk Transfer Area. This default buffer area is established by DOS just in case you use a DOS service that calls for a DTA and haven't yet set up your own DTA buffer. See Chapters 16 and 17 for descriptions of the services that use or manipulate the DTA.

An Example

This chapter's interface example shows how you can use an interrupt handler to process Ctrl-C keystrokes. The example consists of two assembly-language routines.

The first routine, *INT23Handler*, gains control when DOS executes INT 23H in response to a Ctrl-C keystroke. This handler simply increments the value in a flag and then returns to DOS with an IRET instruction.

Note how the flag *_INT23Flag* is addressed through the segment group DGROUP. In many languages, segments with different names are grouped together in one logical group so that they can all be addressed with the same segment register. In the case of Microsoft C, this group of segments is named DGROUP, and it includes the data segment (*_DATA*) used by the compiled C program.

The second assembly-language routine, *_Install()* is designed to be called by a C program. This short routine calls a DOS interrupt 21H function that updates the interrupt 23H vector with the address of the interrupt handler. (The next few chapters contain more about this DOS function and about interrupt 21H services in general.)

317

```
DGROUP          GROUP   _DATA

_TEXT           SEGMENT byte public 'CODE'
                ASSUME  cs:_TEXT,ds:DGROUP

;
; the interrupt 23H handler:

INT23Handler    PROC    far
                push    ds                      ; preserve all registers used
                push    ax                      ; ... in this interrupt handler

                mov     ax,seg DGROUP           ; set DS to the segment where
                mov     ds,ax                   ; ... the flag is located
                inc     word ptr _INT23flag     ; increment the flag

                pop     ax                      ; restore regs and return
                pop     ds
                iret

INT23Handler    ENDP

;
; the C-callable installation routine:

                PUBLIC  _Install
_Install        PROC    near

                push    bp                      ; the usual C prologue
                mov     bp,sp
                push    ds                      ; preserve DS

                push    cs                      ; set DS:DX to point to ...
                pop     ds
                mov     dx,offset INT23Handler   ; ... the interrupt handler
                mov     ax,2523h                ; AH = DOS function number
                                                ; AL = interrupt number
                int     21h                     ; call DOS to update the ...
                                                ; ... interrupt vector
                pop     ds
                pop     bp                      ; restore regs and return
                ret

_Install        ENDP

_TEXT           ENDS
```

```
;
; the flag set by the interrupt 23H handler when Ctrl-C is pressed:

_DATA           SEGMENT word public 'DATA'

                PUBLIC  _INT23flag
_INT23flag      DW      0                   ; flag (initial value = 0)
_DATA           ENDS
```

The snippet of C code that follows shows how you could use this interrupt 23H handler in a program. This C program does nothing but wait for you to press Ctrl-C. When you do, the assembly-language interrupt 23H handler increments the flag. When the loop in the C program sees that the flag is nonzero, it displays a message and decrements the flag.

```
extern int INT23flag;                       /* flag set when Ctrl-C is pressed */

main()
{
        int     KeyCode;


        Install();                          /* install the interrupt 23H handler */

        do
        {
          while( INT23flag > 0 )
          {
            printf( "\nCtrl-C was pressed" );  /* ... show a message ... */
            --INT23flag;                        /* ... and decrement the flag */
          }

          if( kbhit() )                     /* look for a keypress */
            KeyCode = getch();
          else
            KeyCode = 0;
        }
        while( KeyCode != 0x0D );          /* loop until Enter is pressed */
}
```

Although the C code is short, it suggests two important points. One is that you must give DOS the chance to detect a Ctrl-C keystroke each time you test your interrupt 23H flag. (Remember that DOS is guaranteed to check for Ctrl-C only when it reads or writes to a character input/output device.) In this program, C's *kbhit()* function calls DOS to check for keyboard activity and, at the same time, lets DOS check for Ctrl-C as well.

Also, note how the interrupt handler increments the flag instead of merely setting it to ''true'' or ''false.'' This lets the loop in the C program process rapid, successive interrupts without losing track of how many interrupts have occurred.

Chapter 16

DOS Functions: Version 1

The File Control Block   341

An Example   345

The next three chapters describe the DOS functions accessed through interrupt 21H. DOS version 1 had 42 interrupt 21H functions. This variety of functions was strongly rooted in the 8-bit microcomputer tradition typified by the CP/M operating system, whose services many of the DOS functions resembled.

DOS version 1 was adequate for diskette-based microcomputers with keyboards and video displays, but the advent of high-capacity fixed disks and a wider variety of diskette formats called for a new set of sophisticated disk file-management functions. These were supplied in DOS version 2, and roughly patterned after the disk file-management services used in the UNIX operating system. In version 3, DOS continued to evolve, but offered only a few new functions, primarily in support of new hardware such as the PC/AT, networks, and the PS/2s.

Although some interrupt 21H functions introduced in later versions of DOS provide services similar to those in earlier versions, all version 1 functions continue to be supported in later versions. When you have a choice between two similar functions, you should, in general, use the higher-numbered, more recent function. We'll point out why as we go along.

Interrupt 21H Functions: DOS Version 1

All DOS function calls are invoked by interrupt 21H (decimal 33). Individual functions are selected by placing the appropriate function number in the AH register.

The interrupt 21H function calls in DOS version 1 are organized into the logical groups shown in Figure 16-1. In an effort to make this figure as clear as possible, we have organized and described these function calls in a slightly different manner than does the DOS technical reference manual. Figure 16-2 lists the individual function calls.

Function		
Hex	Dec	Group
00H	0	Nondevice function
01H–0CH	1–12	Character device I/O
0DH–24H	13–36	File management
25H–26H	37–38	More nondevice functions
27H–29H, 2EH	39–41, 46	More file management
2AH–2DH	42–45	More nondevice functions

Figure 16-1. *The logical groups of DOS version 1 function calls.*

Function		
Hex	Dec	Description
00H	0	Terminate
02H	1	Character Input with Echo
02H	2	Character Output
03H	3	Auxiliary Input
04H	4	Auxiliary Output
05H	5	Printer Output
06H	6	Direct Character Input/Output
07H	7	Direct Character Input Without Echo
08H	8	Character Input Without Echo
09H	9	String Output
0AH	10	Buffered Keyboard Input
0BH	11	Check Keyboard Status
0CH	12	Flush Keyboard Buffer, Read Keyboard
0DH	13	Flush Disk Buffers
0EH	14	Select Disk Drive
0FH	15	Open File
10H	16	Close File
11H	17	Find First Matching Directory Entry
12H	18	Find Next Matching Directory Entry
13H	19	Delete File
14H	20	Sequential Read
15H	21	Sequential Write
16H	22	Create File
17H	23	Rename File
19H	25	Get Current Disk
1AH	26	Set Disk Transfer Area
1BH	27	Get Default Drive Information
1CH	28	Get Specified Drive Information
21H	33	Read Random Record
22H	34	Write Random Record
23H	35	Get File Size
24H	36	Set FCB Random Record Field
25H	37	Set Interrupt Vector
26H	38	Create New Program Segment Prefix
27H	39	Read Random Records

Figure 16-2. *DOS version 1 functions available through interrupt 21H.*   *(continued)*

Figure 16-2. *continued*

| Function | | Description |
Hex	Dec	
28H	40	Write Random Records
29H	41	Parse Filename
2AH	42	Get Date
2BH	43	Set Date
2CH	44	Get Time
2DH	45	Set Time
2EH	46	Set Verify Flag

The design and organization of a few of these functions, particularly numbers 01H through 0CH, are screwball — to put it mildly. They are this way for historical reasons. Many details of DOS, and especially the details of DOS function calls, were designed to closely mimic the services provided by CP/M. This was an important and deliberate choice, made to make it much easier for 8-bit CP/M software to be converted to the 16-bit IBM PC and DOS. Although the creation of DOS provided a timely opportunity to break with and clean up the mistakes of the past, the real departure from the 8-bit tradition came with DOS version 2, as you will see in Chapter 17.

The following pages describe the 42 original DOS function calls, universally used in all versions of DOS.

Function 00H (decimal 0): Terminate

Function 00H (decimal 0) ends a program and passes control back to DOS. It is functionally identical to DOS interrupt 20H, discussed on page 299. Either can be used interchangeably to exit a program.

DOS versions 2.0 and later provide an enhanced terminate service through function 4CH, which leaves a return code (an error code) in register AL when a program ends. DOS batch files can act on the return codes with the DOS subcommand ERRORLEVEL. Use function 4CH instead of function 00H if you want to use a return code to record errors that occur when a program ends. (See page 377.)

Like DOS interrupt 20H, function 00H does not close files opened with functions 0FH or 16H. To ensure that the proper length of such files is recorded in the file directory, use function 10H to close them before calling function 00H. Also, as with interrupt 20H, you must be sure the PSP segment address is in the CS register before exiting.

Function 01H (decimal 1): Character Input with Echo

Function 01H (decimal 1) waits for character input from the standard input device and returns it in the AL register when available. This function should be compared with the other keyboard function calls, particularly functions 06H, 07H, and 08H.

❏ NOTE: *In DOS version 1, the standard input device is always the keyboard; the standard output device is always the video screen. In later DOS versions, however, standard input and output can be redirected to other devices such as files. DOS processes characters from the standard input device without distinguishing whether the actual input source is the keyboard or a stream of characters redirected from a file.*

Here is how function 01H works: Keystrokes that result in an ASCII character are returned as 1 byte in AL and immediately reported by this function. The keystrokes that result in something other than an ASCII character (see page 135) generate 2 bytes, which must be obtained through two consecutive calls to this function.

The usual way to use this function is to test whether it returns 00H in AL. If AL is not 00H, you have an ASCII character. If AL = 00H, you have a non-ASCII keystroke (which should be recorded), and this function should be repeated immediately to get the pseudo-scan code that represents the special key action. (See page 135 for a list of the actions, codes, and their meanings.) As with all the DOS keyboard input services, the scan code for ASCII characters is not available, even if the corresponding ROM BIOS keyboard services make it available. (See page 135.)

The various DOS keyboard service functions are distinguished primarily by three criteria: whether they wait for input (or report no input when none is available); whether they echo input onto the display screen; and whether the standard break-key operation is active for that service. Function 01H performs all three operations: It waits for input, echoes input to the screen, and lets DOS execute interrupt 23H if Ctrl-C is pressed.

Remember, function 01H always waits for the user to press a key before it returns to a program. If you don't want to wait, either use function 0BH—before you call function 01H—to test whether a key was pressed, or use function 06H. Also, see functions 08H and 0CH for related services.

Function 02H (decimal 2): Character Output

Function 02H (decimal 2) copies a single ASCII character from register DL to the standard output device. In DOS version 1, the standard output device is always the video screen; in later DOS versions, output can also be redirected to a file.

In general, this function treats the ASCII control characters, such as backspace or carriage return, as commands. In the case of the backspace character, the display screen cursor is moved backward one column without erasing the previous character.

Function 03H (decimal 3): Auxiliary Input

Function 03H (decimal 3) reads one character into AL from AUX the standard auxiliary device. The default auxiliary device is COM1, the first RS-232 serial communications port. You can, however, use the DOS MODE command to assign other devices, such as COM2, to the auxiliary device.

❑ NOTE: *This function waits for input. It does not report status information about the many miseries that a serial port can suffer. If you want to know the status of the serial port, use the ROM BIOS communications-port services.*

Function 04H (decimal 4): Auxiliary Output

Function 04H (decimal 4) writes one character from register DL to the standard auxiliary device. See the remarks under function 03H.

Function 05H (decimal 5): Printer Output

Function 05H (decimal 5) writes 1 byte from DL to the standard printer device, which is normally known as PRN: or LPT1: (although printer output can be redirected with the DOS MODE command to other devices). The default standard printer is always the first parallel printer, even if a serial port is used for printer output.

Function 06H (decimal 6): Direct Console Input/Output

Function 06H (decimal 6) is a complex function that combines the operations of keyboard input and display output into one untidy package. As with everything else in DOS versions 2.0 and later, the I/O is not connected to the keyboard and display, but rather to the standard input and output devices (which default to the keyboard and display).

Here is how this function works: The AL register is used for input and the DL register for output. If you call function 06H with DL = FFH (decimal 255), the function performs input:

- If a key was pressed, function 06H returns the corresponding ASCII code in AL and clears the zero flag.

- If no key was pressed, function 06H sets the zero flag.

If you call function 06H with any other value in DL, the function performs output: The character in DL is copied to the standard output device.

Function 06H does not wait for keyboard input, and it does not echo input to the display screen. In addition, function 06H does not interpret Ctrl-C as a keyboard break; instead, it returns the value 03H (the ASCII value of Ctrl-C) in AL.

Compare this function with functions 01H, 07H, and 08H. See function 0CH for a variation of this service.

Function 07H (decimal 7): Direct Console Input Without Echo

Function 07H (decimal 7) waits for character input from the standard input device and returns it in the AL register when available. It does not echo input to the display screen, and it does not recognize Ctrl-C as a keyboard break character.

Function 07H works in the same way as function 01H: ASCII character key actions are returned as single bytes in AL and are immediately reported by this function. The non-ASCII function keystrokes (see page 135) generate 2 bytes, which must be obtained through two consecutive calls to function 07H.

Compare this function with functions 01H, 06H, and 08H. If you want to use this function but don't want to wait when input is not ready, see function 0BH, which reports whether or not input is ready. See function 0CH for a variation of this function.

Function 08H (decimal 8): Console Input Without Echo

Function 08H (decimal 8) waits for input, does not echo, and breaks on a Ctrl-C. It is identical to function 01H, except it does not echo the input to the display screen (or standard output device).

See the discussion under function 01H for a description of this function. Compare this function with functions 01H, 06H, and 07H. If you want to use this function but don't want to wait when input is not ready, see function 0BH, which reports whether or not input is ready. See function 0CH for a variation of this function.

Function 09H (decimal 9): String Output

Function 09H (decimal 9) sends a string of characters to the standard output device (which defaults to the display screen). The register pair DS:DX provides the address of the string. A $ character, ASCII 24H (decimal 36), marks the end of the string.

Although this function can be far more convenient than the byte-by-byte display services (functions 02H and 06H), it is flawed by the use of a real, displayable character, $, as its string delimiter. This is not a recent mistake; it's another by-product of CP/M compatibility. You should never use this function with programs that output dollar signs.

Function 0AH (decimal 10): Buffered Keyboard Input

Function 0AH (decimal 10) puts the power of the DOS editing keys to work in your programs. The function gets a complete string of input, which is presented to your programs whole, rather than character by character. If you assume that the input is actually from live keyboard action and is not redirected elsewhere, the full use of the DOS editing keys is available to the person who is typing the input string. When the Enter key is pressed (or a carriage return, ASCII 0DH (decimal 13), is encountered in the input file), the input operation is complete and the entire string is presented to your program.

This function provides many advantages, particularly to those programs needing complete, coherent strings of keyboard input, rather than byte-by-byte input. The two foremost benefits are that you are spared the effort of writing detailed input-handling code, and your programs' users are given a familiar set of input editing tools: the DOS editing conventions.

To use this function, you must provide DOS with an input buffer area where the input string will be built. The register pair DS:DX points to this buffer when you call the function. The first 3 bytes of this buffer have specific purposes:

- The first byte indicates the *working size* of the buffer (the number of bytes that DOS can use for input).

- The second byte is updated by DOS to indicate the actual number of bytes input.

- The third byte is the beginning of the input string, which consists entirely of ASCII characters. The end of the input string is signaled by the carriage-return character, ASCII 0DH. Although the carriage return is placed in the buffer, it is not included in the character count that DOS returns in the second byte.

329

By these rules, the longest buffer you can give DOS is 255 working bytes, and the longest string that DOS can return is 1 byte less than the working length. Because the first 2 bytes of the buffer are used for status information, the actual working size of the buffer is 2 bytes less than the buffer's overall size. This may explain some of the mysteries of the input conventions in both DOS and BASIC.

If input continues beyond what DOS can place in the buffer (which is 1 byte short of its working length), then DOS will discard any further input, beeping all the while, until a carriage return is encountered.

See function 0CH for a variation of this function.

Function 0BH (decimal 11): Check Keyboard Status

Function 0BH (decimal 11) reports whether input is ready from the keyboard (or standard input device). If a character is ready, AL = FFH (decimal 255). If no input is ready, AL = 00H.

DOS checks for Ctrl-C when you execute function 0BH, so a loop that contains a call to this function can be interrupted by a keyboard break.

Function 0CH (decimal 12):
Flush Keyboard Buffer, Read Keyboard

Function 0CH (decimal 12) clears the keyboard buffer in RAM and then invokes one of five DOS functions: function 01H, 06H, 07H, 08H, or 0AH. The AL register is used to select which of these functions will be performed after the keyboard buffer is flushed. With the keyboard buffer clear of extraneous characters, function 0CH forces the system to wait for new input before it acts on the invoked function.

Because function 06H is supported, the follow-up service need not be keyboard input: It can be display output.

Function 0DH (decimal 13): Flush Disk Buffers

Function 0DH (decimal 13) flushes (writes to disk) all internal DOS file buffers. However, this function does not update directory entries or close any open files. To ensure that the proper length of a changed file is recorded in the file directory, use the close-file functions 10H or 3EH.

Function 0EH (decimal 14): Select Disk Drive

Function 0EH (decimal 14) selects a new current default drive. It also reports the number of drives installed. The drive is specified in DL, with 00H indicating drive A, 01H drive B, and so on. The number of drives is reported in AL.

Keep a few things in mind when using this function:

- The drive IDs used by DOS are consecutively numbered.

- If only one physical diskette drive exists, DOS will simulate a second drive, drive number 1 (drive B). Thus the first fixed-disk drive is always drive number 2, corresponding to drive letter C.

- If you use the value in AL to determine the number of drives in your system, beware: In DOS versions 3.0 and later, the minimum value returned by this function is 05H.

Function 0FH (decimal 15): Open File

Function 0FH (decimal 15) opens a file using a file control block (FCB). An FCB is a data structure used by DOS to track input and output for a particular file. Among other things, an FCB contains a file's name and disk drive number. (See page 341 in this chapter for details on the contents of FCBs.)

❑ NOTE: *Function 0FH is one of 15 DOS functions that use an FCB to track file input and output. You should avoid the DOS functions that use FCBs. These functions were made obsolete by the more powerful handle-based file functions introduced in DOS version 2.0. Furthermore, unlike handle-based functions, FCB-based functions are not supported in OS/2 protected mode. Use the FCB-based functions only if compatibility with DOS version 1 is important.*

To use an FCB to open a file, you must reserve memory for the FCB and place the file's name and disk drive number in the proper fields in the data structure. Then call function 0FH with the segmented address of the FCB in the register pair DS:DX. DOS attempts to open the file, using the drive and filename you specified in the FCB. If the file is opened, AL = 00H; if the file cannot be opened, AL = FFH.

If the file is opened successfully, DOS initializes several fields in the FCB, including the drive number field (with a value of 1 for drive A, 2 for drive B, and so on), the date and time fields, and the logical record-size field (which is set to 128). You can either use this record size or change it, depending on your application.

Function 10H (decimal 16): Close File

Function 10H (decimal 16) closes a file and updates the file's directory entry. Call this function with the segmented address of the file's FCB in DS:DX. DOS returns AL = 00H if the function successfully closed the file or AL = FFH if an error occurred.

It is good practice to use function 10H to explicitly close all files you opened with function 0FH or 16H. This ensures that the file contents are updated from DOS internal file buffers and that the corresponding directory entries are current.

Function 11H (decimal 17): Find First Matching Directory Entry

Function 11H (decimal 17) searches the current directory for a specified directory entry. The name you specify to function 11H can contain the wildcard characters ? and *. The ? character matches any single ASCII character (as a wild card in a poker game matches any other card) and the * matches any string of characters, so DOS can match a name that contains one or more wildcard characters with several different directory entries. If more than one directory entry matches, DOS reports only the first match. You must then use function 12H to continue the search for subsequent matching directory entries.

Before you call function 11H, store the address of an FCB in DS:DX. The filename field of this FCB must contain the name you want DOS to search for. DOS reports a successful match by returning AL = 00H; if no directory entries match the specified name, DOS returns AL = FFH. When DOS finds a matching directory entry, it creates a new FCB in the current disk transfer area (DTA) and copies the matching name from the directory entry into the new FCB's filename field.

If the FCB has an FCB extension (see page 344), then you can specify the attributes of the file that you wish to search for. If you specify any combination of the hidden, system, or directory attribute bits, the search matches normal files and also any files with those attributes. If you specify the volume-label attribute, this function searches only for a directory entry with that attribute. With DOS versions prior to 2.0, neither the directory nor the volume-label attributes can be used in the file search operation. The archive and read-only attributes cannot be used as search criteria in any DOS release.

Function 12H (decimal 18): Find Next Matching Directory Entry

Function 12H (decimal 18) finds the next of a series of files, following the set-up preparation performed by function 11H. As with function 11H, you must call function 12H with the address of an FCB in DS:DX. For function 12H, the FCB should be the same as the one you used for a successful call to function 11H.

DOS reports a successful match by returning AL = 00H; if no match exists, DOS returns AL = FFH. This lets you combine functions 11H and 12H to perform a complete directory search by using the following logic:

```
initialize FCB
call function 11H
WHILE AL = 0
        use current contents of DTA
        call function 12H
```

Function 13H (decimal 19): Delete File

Function 13H (decimal 19) deletes all files that match the name specified in the FCB pointed to by the register pair DS:DX. The filename in the FCB can contain wildcard characters so that multiple files can be deleted with a single call to function 13H. The function returns AL = 00H if the operation is a success and all matching file directory entries are deleted. AL = FFH if the operation is a failure, meaning that no directory entries matched.

Function 14H (decimal 20): Sequential Read

Function 14H (decimal 20) reads records sequentially from a file. To use this function, open a file using function 0FH. Then initialize the current-record and record-size fields of the FCB. For example, to read the first 256-byte record from a file, set the record-size field to 100H (decimal 256) and the current-record field to 00H before you call function 14H.

After the FCB is initialized, you can call function 14H once for each record you want to read. Each time you call function 14H, pass the address of the file's FCB in DS:DX. DOS reads the next record from the file and stores the data in the current disk transfer area (DTA). At the same time, DOS tracks its current position in the file by updating the current-block and current-record fields in the FCB.

AL reports the results of the read. Complete success is signaled when AL = 00H; AL = 01H signals an end-of-file, indicating that no data was read; AL = 02H signals that data could have been read, but wasn't, because insufficient memory remained in the DTA segment; AL = 03H signals an end-of-file with a partial record read (the record is padded with zero bytes).

Function 15H (decimal 21): Sequential Write

Function 15H (decimal 21) writes a sequential record and is the companion to function 14H. As with function 14H, DOS tracks its current position in the file by updating the FCB whose address you pass in DS:DX. DOS copies the data from the current DTA to the file and reports the status of the write operation in AL.

If AL = 00H, the write operation was a success. If AL = 01H, the disk was full and the record was not written. If AL = 02H, the amount of memory remaining in the DTA's segment was less than the record size, so DOS aborted the write operation.

It's important to note that data is logically written by this function, but not necessarily physically written. DOS buffers output data until it has a complete disk sector to write—only then does DOS actually transfer the data to the disk.

Function 16H (decimal 22): Create File

Function 16H (decimal 22) opens an empty file with a specified name. If the file exists in the current directory, function 16H truncates it to zero length. If the file does not exist, function 16H creates a directory entry for the new file. As with the other FCB-based file functions, you call function 16H with DS:DX pointing to an FCB containing the name of the file. The function returns AL = 00H to indicate successful operation. If AL = FFH, the function failed, possibly because the filename you specified in the FCB is not valid.

If you want to avoid inadvertently losing the contents of an existing file, you should determine if the file already exists by calling function 11H before you use function 16H.

Function 17H (decimal 23): Rename File

Function 17H (decimal 23) renames files or subdirectories in a modified FCB pointed to by DS:DX. For the rename operation, the FCB has a special format. The drive and original name are located in their usual positions, but the new name and extension are placed at offsets 11H through 1BH in the FCB.

AL = 00H signals complete success, and AL = FFH signals that the original name wasn't found or the new name is already in use.

If the new name contains wildcard characters (?), they are interpreted as *ditto-from-old-name,* and the characters in the original name that correspond to the positions of the wildcard characters are not changed.

Function 19H (decimal 25): Get Current Disk

Function 19H (decimal 25) reports the current drive number in AL, using the standard numeric code of drive A = 00H, drive B = 01H, and so forth.

Function 1AH (decimal 26): Set Disk Transfer Area

Function 1AH (decimal 26) establishes the disk transfer area that DOS will use for file I/O. The location of the DTA is specified by the register pair DS:DX. Normally, you should specify a DTA address before you use any of the interrupt 21H functions that access a DTA. If you do not, DOS uses the default 128-byte DTA at offset 80H in the program segment prefix.

Function 1BH (decimal 27): Get Default Drive Information

Function 1BH (decimal 27) returns important information about the disk in the current drive. Function 1CH performs the identical service for any drive. Function 36H performs a nearly identical service. (See Chapter 17.)

The following information is returned through this function call:

- AL contains the number of sectors per cluster.

- CX contains the size, in bytes, of the disk sectors (512 bytes for all standard PC formats).

- DX contains the total number of clusters on the disk.

- DS:BX points to a byte in DOS's work area containing the DOS media descriptor. Prior to DOS version 2.0, the DS:BX register pair pointed to the complete disk FAT (which could be guaranteed to be in memory, complete), whose first byte would be the ID byte. In later DOS versions, DS:BX points only to the single ID byte.

Beware: Function 1BH uses the DS register to return the address of the media descriptor byte. If your program relies on the DS register to point to data — and most high-level and assembly-language programs do — then you should be careful to preserve the contents of the DS register while you call function 1BH.

The following example shows how to do this:

```
push    ds              ; preserve DS
mov     ah,1Bh
int     21h             ; call function 1BH; DS:BX -> media descriptor
mov     ah,[bx]         ; get a copy of the media descriptor byte
pop     ds              ; restore DS
```

Function 1CH (decimal 28): Get Specified Drive Information

Function 1CH works in the same way as function 1BH except that it reports on any drive, not only the current drive. Before calling this function, set DL to the drive ID number, where 0 = the current drive, 1 = drive A, 2 = drive B, and so forth.

Function 21H (decimal 33): Read Random Record

Function 21H (decimal 33) reads one record from a random location in a file. To use this function, open a file with an FCB. Then store the record number of the record you want to read in the random-record field of the FCB. When you call function 21H with DS:DX pointing to the FCB, DOS reads the specified record into the DTA.

AL is set with the same codes as it is for a sequential read: AL = 00H indicates a successful read; AL = 01H indicates end-of-file, with no more data available; AL = 02H means that insufficient space exists in the DTA segment; and AL = 03H indicates an end-of-file, with a partial data record available.

Contrast this function with function 27H, which can read more than one random record at a time, or with function 14H, which reads sequential records. See function 24H for more on setting the random-record field.

Function 22H (decimal 34): Write Random Record

Function 22H (decimal 34) writes one record to a random location in a file. As with function 21H, you must initialize the random-record field in the file's FCB and then call this function with DS:DX pointing to the FCB. DOS then writes data from the DTA to the file at the position specified in the FCB.

AL is set with the same codes used for a sequential write: AL = 00H indicates a successful write; AL = 01H means the disk is full; AL = 02H indicates insufficient space in the DTA segment.

Contrast this function with function 28H, which can write more than one random record, or with function 15H, which writes sequential records. See function 24H for more on setting the random-record field.

Function 23H (decimal 35): Get File Size

Function 23H (decimal 35) reports the size of a file in terms of the number of records in the file. DS:DX points to the FCB of the file you want to know about. Before calling the function, the FCB should be left unopened and the record-size field in the FCB filled in. If you set the record size to 1, the file size is reported in bytes, which is most likely what you want.

If the operation is successful, AL = 00H and the file size is inserted into the FCB. If the file is not found, AL = FFH.

Function 24H (decimal 36): Set FCB Random Record Field

Function 24H (decimal 36) sets the random-record field to correspond to the current sequential block and record fields in an FCB. This facilitates switching from sequential to random I/O. The DS:DX registers point to the FCB of an open file.

Function 25H (decimal 37): Set Interrupt Vector

Function 25H (decimal 37) sets an interrupt vector. Before you call function 25H, place the segmented address of an interrupt handler in DS:DX and an interrupt number in AL. DOS stores the segment and offset of your interrupt handler in the proper interrupt vector.

When updating an interrupt vector, you should use function 25H instead of simply computing the address of the vector and updating it directly. Not only is it simpler to call this function than to do the work yourself, but this function gives the operating system the chance to detect when an important interrupt vector is modified.

To examine the contents of an interrupt vector, see function 35H in the next chapter.

Function 26H (decimal 38): Create New Program Segment Prefix

Function 26H is used within a program to prepare for loading and executing another subprogram, or overlay. When you call function 26H, DX must contain the paragraph address of the start of the memory area where you want DOS to build the new PSP. DOS builds a new PSP at the location you specify. You can then load an executable program from a file into the memory above the new PSP and transfer control to it.

❏ NOTE: *Function 26H is obsolete. You should use function 4BH (Chapter 17) to load and execute a new program from within another executing program.*

Function 27H (decimal 39): Read Random Records

Unlike function 21H, function 27H reads one or more records, starting at a random file location. DS:DX points to the FCB for the file to be read and the random-record number is then taken from this FCB. CX contains the number of records desired, which should be more than 0.

The return codes are the same as they are for function 21H: AL = 00H means the read was successful; AL = 01H indicates end-of-file, with no more data (if the records were read, the last record is complete); AL = 02H indicates that the DTA segment was too small; and AL = 03H indicates the end-of-file, where the last record read is incomplete and padded with zeros.

No matter what the result, CX is set to the number of records read, including any partial record, and the random-record field in the FCB is set to the next sequential record.

Contrast this with function 21H, which reads only one record.

Function 28H (decimal 40): Write Random Records

Unlike function 22H, function 28H (decimal 40) writes one or more records, starting at a specified random file location. DS:DX points to the FCB for the file to be written, and the random record number is then taken from this FCB. CX contains the number of records desired and in this case, CX can be 00H. CX = 00H signals DOS to adjust the file's length to the position of the specified random record. This adjustment makes it easier for a program to manage random files: If you have logically deleted records at the end of a file, this service allows you to truncate the file at that point by setting the file's length in CX, thereby freeing disk space.

The return codes are the same as they are for function 22H: AL = 00H indicates a successful write; AL = 01H means that no more disk space is available; and AL = 02H indicates that the DTA segment was too small. No matter what the result, CX is always set to the number of records written.

Contrast this function with function 22H, which writes only one random record.

Function 29H (decimal 41): Parse Filename

Function 29H (decimal 41) parses a string for a filename with the form DRIVE:FILENAME.EXT. Call this function with DS:SI pointing to a text string and ES:DI pointing to the drive-identifier byte in an unopened FCB. Function 29H attempts to extract the drive and filename information from the string, and to use it to initialize the drive and name fields of the FCB. If the function executes successfully, it returns AL = 00H if the string contains no wildcard characters or AL = 01H if the string contains at least one * or ? wildcard character. If the drive letter specifies an invalid drive, the function returns AL = FFH.

Function 29H also updates DS:SI to point to the byte after the end of the filename in the string. This facilitates processing a string that contains multiple filenames. Also, if the parsing was unsuccessful, the FCB contains a blank filename.

Function 29H lets you control four different aspects of the filename parsing. When you call the function, the 4 low-order bits of the value in AL specify how function 29H parses the string:

- If bit 0 is set, the function scans past separator characters (for example, leading blank spaces) to find the file specification. If bit 0 is 0, the scan operation is not performed, and the file specification is expected to start in the first byte of the string.

- If bit 1 is set, then the drive byte in the FCB will be set only if it is specified in the file specification being scanned. This allows the FCB to specify a default drive.

- If bit 2 is set, the filename in the FCB is changed only if a valid filename is found in the string. This lets the FCB specify a default filename, which can be overridden by the filename in the string.

- If bit 3 is set, the filename extension in the FCB is changed only if a valid extension is found in the file specification. This allows the FCB to specify a default extension.

❏ NOTE: *Although this service can be handy, it is intended for use only with FCB-based file functions. You don't need this function if you rely on the handle-based file functions described in Chapter 17.*

Function 2AH (decimal 42): Get Date

Function 2AH (decimal 42) reports DOS's record of the current date. The date is reported in CX and DX. DH contains the month number (1 through 12); DL contains the day of the month (1 through 28, 29, 30, or 31, as appropriate); and CX contains the year (1980 through 2099).

This function reports the day of the week by returning a value from 0 through 6, which signifies Sunday through Saturday, in register AL. This day-of-the-week feature is somewhat of an orphan. It has been present in DOS since version 1.1, but was not even mentioned until DOS version 2.0. In both the 2.0 and 2.1 manuals, it is incorrectly described as a part of the get-time function and not as part of the get-date function. Starting with DOS 3.0, the manual tells it as it is. Turn to the example on page 345 to see how this function can be used.

Function 2BH (decimal 43): Set Date

Function 2BH (decimal 43) sets DOS's record of the current date, using the same registers as function 2AH. The date is set in CX and DX. DH contains the month number (1 through 12); DL contains the day of the month (1 through 28, 29, 30, or 31, as appropriate); CX contains the year (1980 through 2099). This function returns AL = 00H if the date is successfully updated, or AL = FFH if you specified an invalid date.

Starting in DOS version 3.3, this function also updates the real-time clock/calendar in the PC/AT and PS/2. In earlier versions, you must still use ROM BIOS interrupt 1AH services to change the real-time clock date.

Function 2CH (decimal 44): Get Time

Function 2CH (decimal 44) reports the time of day. The time is calculated from the ROM BIOS timer-tick count. (See page 59.) DOS responds to the ROM BIOS's midnight-passed signal and updates the date every 24 hours.

The timer-tick count is converted into a meaningful time and placed in registers CX and DX. CH contains the hour (0 through 23, on a 24-hour clock); CL contains the minutes (0 through 59); DH contains the seconds (0 through 59); and DL contains hundredths of seconds (0 through 99). This function returns AL = 00H if the time is successfully updated, or AL = FFH if you specified an invalid time.

The IBM PC timer ticks 18.2 times per second, so the time of day reported by DOS is only as accurate as the timer tick — roughly 5.4 hundredths of a second. Nevertheless, even with this relatively low accuracy, you can use DOS function 2CH to measure time intervals in many applications.

Function 2DH (decimal 45): Set Time

Function 2DH (decimal 45) sets the time of day. The time is specified in registers CX and DX. CH contains the hour (0 through 23, on a 24-hour clock); CL contains the minutes (0 through 59); DH contains the seconds (0 through 59); DL contains hundredths of seconds (0 through 99).

Starting in DOS version 3.3, this function also updates the real-time clock in the PC/AT and PS/2. In earlier versions, you must still use ROM BIOS interrupt 1AH services to change the real-time clock time.

Function 2EH (decimal 46): Set Verify Flag

Function 2EH (decimal 46) controls verification of disk-write operations. Call this function with AL = 01H to set DOS's internal verify flag and enable verification; call it with AL = 00H to turn off the flag and verification. Also, in DOS versions 1 and 2, you must zero DL before you call function 2EH.

The disk-verify operation requires the disk controller to perform a cyclical redundancy check (CRC) each time it writes data to the disk. This process involves reading the data just written, which significantly decreases the speed of disk writes.

With DOS versions 2.0 and later, function 54H can be used to report the current setting of the verify flag. (See page 379.)

The File Control Block

As mentioned several times in this chapter, file control blocks and the DOS functions that use them are obsolete. We recommend that you use the handle-based file I/O functions introduced in DOS version 2.0 and described in the next chapter. Usually, the only reason to concern yourself with FCBs is when compatibility with DOS version 1 is an issue.

With that in mind, let's take a look at the structure of the FCB. The usual FCB is a 37-byte data structure that contains a variety of information DOS can use to control file input/output. (See Figure 16-3.) A 44-byte, extended FCB is also used in some DOS functions: 7 extra bytes are tacked onto the beginning of the usual FCB data structure. (See Figure 16-4.)

The situation with the FCB extension is more than a little peculiar. The extension is used only when you work with the attribute field in a directory entry in which read-only files, hidden files, system files, volume

Offset	Field Width	Description
00H	1	Drive identifier
01H	8	Filename
09H	3	File extension
0CH	2	Current-block number
0EH	2	Record size in bytes
10H	4	File size in bytes
14H	2	Date
16H	2	Time
18H	8	(Reserved)
20H	1*	Current-record number
21H	4	Random-record number

*Only the low-order 7 bits are used.

Figure 16-3. *Structure of a file control block.*

Offset	Field Width	Description
00H	1	Extended FCB flag (always FFH)
01H	5	(Reserved)
06H	1	Attribute
07H	1	Drive identifier
08H	8	Filename
10H	3	File extension
13H	2	Current-block number
15H	2	Record size in bytes
17H	4	File size in bytes
1BH	2	Date
1DH	2	Time
1FH	8	(Reserved)
27H	1*	Current-record number
28H	4	Random-record number

*Only the low-order 7 bits are used.

Figure 16-4. *Structure of an extended file control block. The first three fields distinguish this data structure from a normal FCB.*

labels, and subdirectories are identified. In general, you need to use extended FCBs only if you are performing directory searches or otherwise working with directory entries rather than the contents of files. However, all FCB-based functions recognize the extended FCB format if you should choose to use it.

With two exceptions, all fields in an extended FCB are identical to those in a normal FCB. Only the offsets are different: In an extended FCB, the offset of a particular field is 7 bytes greater than the offset of the same field in a normal FCB.

The following sections describe the fields in normal extended FCBs.

FCB Fields

Offset 00H. The first field in a normal (nonextended) FCB is the *disk drive identifier*. Values for the drive identifier start at 1; a value of 1 indicates drive A, 2 indicates drive B, and so on. If this field contains 0 at the time an FCB is opened, DOS uses the current default drive and updates this field with the corresponding drive identifier.

Offsets 01H and 09H. The two fields at offsets 01H and 09H contain an 8-byte name and a 3-byte extension. These fields are left-justified and padded on the right with blanks. Following DOS convention, either upper- or lowercase letters may be used. If the filename is a device name that DOS recognizes, such as CON, AUX, COM1, COM2, LPT1, LPT2, PRN, or NUL, DOS will use that device rather than a disk file.

❑ NOTE: *This is a reasonably good place to point out that the FCB mechanism has no provision for working with pathnames. Whenever you use FCBs, they always apply to the current directory in any drive. For flexible use of paths and subdirectories, see the new, extended functions in Chapter 17.*

Offsets 0CH and 20H. For sequential file operations, the current-block and current-record fields keep track of the location in the file. The use of these fields is rather odd. Instead of using one integrated record number, the record number is divided into a high and low portion, referred to as the *block number* and *record number*. The record number is a 7-bit value, so record numbers range from 0 through 127. Thus the first record in a file is block 0, record 0; the 128th record is block 1, record 0.

Before you use the sequential read and write functions 14H and 15H, be sure to initialize the current block and record fields to the desired starting location in the file.

Offset 0EH. The record-size field contains a 2-byte value that specifies the size, in bytes, of the logical records in the file. When DOS reads or writes a record, the *logical size* of the record is the number of bytes transferred between DOS's disk buffers and the DTA.

The same file data can be worked on using a variety of record sizes. When a file is opened through functions 0FH or 16H, DOS sets the record size to 128 bytes by default. If you want another size, such as 1 for single-byte operations, you must change the record-size field *after* the file is opened.

Offset 10H. The file-size field at offset 10H indicates the file size in bytes. The value is taken from a file's directory entry and is placed in the FCB when DOS opens the file. For an output file, this field is changed by DOS as the file grows. When the file is closed, the value is copied from the FCB to the file's directory entry.

By changing this field, you can gain some last-minute control over the size of an output file, but be careful when doing this. You can, for example, truncate a file you have updated by decreasing the file-size value in this field. Also, be careful not to use function 17H to rename an open file: This function requires that you specify the file's new name in the same part of the FCB used for the file size.

Offsets 14H and **16H.** The 2-byte fields at offset 14H (date) and offset 16H (time) record when a file was last updated. These fields use the same format as the corresponding fields in a directory entry. (See Chapter 5.) The initial values in these fields are copied from a file's directory entry when the file is opened. They are subsequently updated each time you write to the file. If the file was updated, DOS copies the values from the FCB to the directory entry when the file is closed.

Offset 21H. The random-record field is used during random read and write operations, just as the current record and block numbers are used during sequential operations. This field is in the form of a 4-byte, 32-bit integer. Records are numbered from 0, which makes it easy to calculate the file offset to any record by multiplying the random-record number by the record size. You must set this field before any random file operation. DOS leaves it undisturbed.

Extended FCB Fields

An extended FCB has two additional fields not found in a normal FCB:

- The first field of an extended FCB is a flag byte whose contents must be FFH. DOS distinguishes between normal and extended FCBs by examining this byte. (In a normal FCB, the first field is the disk-drive specifier, which should never be FFH.)

- Offset 06H in an extended FCB is a 1-byte field that consists of an attribute byte whose bits signify file, volume label, and subdirectory attributes. This byte's format is identical to the attribute byte in a directory entry. (See Chapter 5.)

❑ NOTE: *One rare situation in which you would use FCB-based functions instead of handle-based functions is when you work with a disk's volume label. DOS versions 2.0 and later do not provide any special services for manipulating a volume label. You must use function 16H with an extended FCB to create a volume label, function 17H to rename it, and function 13H to rename it.*

An Example

For our assembly-language example in this section, we've chosen something rather interesting. It's a routine used within the Norton Utility programs, so you'll be seeing some actual production code.

The purpose of this routine is to calculate the day of the week for any day within DOS's working range, which is stated to be from Tuesday, January 1, 1980, through Thursday, December 31, 2099. Occasionally, it's valuable for a program to be able to report the day of the week, either for the current date or for any other date that may be in question. For example, DOS keeps track of the date and time each file was last changed. Because people often use this information to find out when they last worked with a file, it can be handy to know the day of the week as well. In fact, the day of the week is often more immediately meaningful than the actual date.

Although several interesting and clever algorithms let you calculate the day of the week, the actual work of writing a day-of-the-week program is usually rather tedious. Beginning with version 1.10, DOS incorporated a day-of-the-week calculation, which spared us the chore of writing our own. DOS's routine is available only in a form that reports the current day of the week, but that is no obstacle: We can temporarily change DOS's date to the date we're interested in and then have DOS report the day of the week. That is what the following assembly-language routine does for us.

Besides being slightly foxy, this routine is interesting because it illustrates how three DOS function calls operate together to produce one result. It also illustrates the minor intricacies involved in saving and restoring things on the stack. As we will see here, stack use occasionally has to be carefully orchestrated so that different values don't get in each others' way.

This particular subroutine, named *Weekday*, is set up in the form needed for use with the Microsoft C compiler. The routine is called with three integer variables, which specify the month, day, and year we are interested in. The routine returns the day of the week in the form of an integer in the range of 0 through 6 (signifying Sunday through Saturday). This conforms to the C language convention for arrays, providing an index to an array of strings that give the names of the days. Therefore, we could use this subroutine in this way:

```
DayName[ Weekday( month, day, year ) ]
```

It is important to note that this routine works blindly with the date, checking neither for a valid date nor for the range of dates accepted by DOS. Here is the subroutine:

```
_TEXT           SEGMENT byte public 'CODE'
                ASSUME  cs:_TEXT

                PUBLIC  _Weekday
_Weekday        PROC    near

                push    bp              ; establish stack addressing ..
                mov     bp,sp           ; .. through BP

                mov     ah,2Ah          ; get current date
                int     21h

                push    cx              ; save current date on the stack
                push    dx

                mov     cx,[bp+8]       ; CX = year
                mov     dl,[bp+6]       ; DL = day
                mov     dh,[bp+4]       ; DH = month

                mov     ah,2Bh          ; set the date specified
                int     21h

                mov     ah,2Ah          ; get the date back from DOS
                int     21h             ; (AL = day of the week)

                pop     dx              ; restore the current date ..
                pop     cx              ; .. in CX and DX
                push    ax              ; save day of week on the stack

                mov     ah,2Bh          ; set the current date
                int     21h

                pop     ax              ; AL = day of week
                mov     ah,0            ; AX = day of week

                pop     bp              ; restore BP and return
                ret

_Weekday        ENDP

_TEXT           ENDS
```

Chapter 17

DOS Functions: Versions 2.0 and Later

In this chapter we'll discuss the interrupt 21H functions introduced in DOS versions 2.0 and later. These functions provide a wide range of operating system services within a more sophisticated and flexible framework than the original 42 functions we described in Chapter 16.

Almost every DOS upgrade has increased the number of services provided to programmers. DOS 2.0 initiated the most dramatic changes: It added 33 new functions to the existing 42; it changed the way you access file information as a result of these new functions; and it made it possible to adapt DOS to work with almost any hardware device through the use of programs called *installable device drivers.* Before discussing the newer DOS functions in detail, we'll briefly cover how some of these enhancements can affect your programming practices.

Enhancements in DOS Versions 2 and 3

The services introduced with DOS versions 2 and 3 have three important new features that directly affect the way you use the services:

- Most of the functions return a set of consistent error codes in the AX register.

- All functions that use string input require a special string format known as the *ASCIIZ format*—a string of ASCII characters terminated by a single zero byte.

- The newer DOS functions use a 16-bit number called a *handle,* instead of an FCB, to identify the files and I/O devices that a program communicates with.

We'll discuss each of these enhancements on the next few pages.

Consistent Error Codes

When you call an interrupt 21H function in DOS versions 2.0 and later, the function returns an error status code in the AX register. These functions also set the carry flag to signal that an error has occurred. You should generally follow each call to these interrupt 21H functions with a test of the carry flag; if the flag is set, the value in AX describes what caused the error.

In DOS versions 3.0 and later, you can also use interrupt 21H, function 59H, to obtain extended error information from DOS. You can call function 59H after any interrupt 21H function reports an error; you can also use it inside a critical-error (interrupt 24H) handler to determine the nature of a DOS critical error. In both situations, function 59H returns an extended error code and also suggests possible actions to alleviate the problem.

For a complete list of extended error codes and how to use them, see the discussion of function 59H on page 381.

ASCIIZ Strings

Many interrupt 21H functions introduced in DOS versions 2 and 3 require you to pass file and directory names in the form of *ASCIIZ strings*. An ASCIIZ string is simply a string of ASCII characters terminated by a single zero byte that marks the end of the string. For example, the ASCIIZ representation of the pathname C:\COMMAND.COM would consist of the following 15 hexadecimal bytes:

The ASCIIZ string format is commonly used within the UNIX operating system and the C programming language; it is only one of many new elements with a C/UNIX flavor introduced in DOS version 2.0.

File Handles

The newer interrupt 21H functions in DOS versions 2.0 and later rely on the notion of *handles*. Handles are 16-bit numbers that DOS uses to identify open files. Handles can also identify other sources of input and output for a program, including the keyboard and the video display. (They're also another example of the UNIX influence: In UNIX, file handles are called "file descriptors" but are used in essentially the same way as they are in DOS.)

The use of handles allows DOS to be more flexible in its file management services than it was with FCB-based file services. In particular, capabilities such as file redirection and support for hierarchical directories would have been very difficult to graft onto the fixed-format FCB data structure. Furthermore, the use of handles actually simplifies file management by making the mechanics of file input/output — parsing filenames, keeping track of the current file position, and so on — the responsibility of DOS instead of your programs.

DOS assigns a new handle number whenever you create or open a file. Five standard handles, numbered 0 through 4, are automatically available to every program. (See Figure 17-1.) Other handles, with higher handle numbers, are issued by DOS as needed.

Handle	Use	Default Device
0	Standard input (normally keyboard input)	CON
1	Standard output (normally screen output)	CON
2	Standard error output (always to the screen)	CON
3	Standard auxiliary device (AUX device)	AUX
4	Standard printer (LPT1 or PRN device)	PRN

Figure 17-1. *The five standard DOS handles.*

❑ NOTE: *Of the five standard DOS handles, only the first three are supported in OS/2 protected mode. If you are programming with upward compatibility in mind, you should avoid using handles 3 and 4 by default. Instead, open the serial port and printer devices explicitly, as you would any other file or input/output device.*

DOS limits the use of handles in regard to how many files or devices your program can open at one time:

- DOS maintains an internal data structure that controls I/O for each file or other input/output device associated with a handle. The default size of this data structure allows for only 8 handles. Fortunately, the FILES command in the CONFIG.SYS file lets you increase the number of possible handles (99 in DOS versions prior to 3.0; 255 in versions 3.0 and later).

- DOS uses a reserved area in each program's PSP to maintain a table of handles associated with the program. This table has room for a maximum of 20 handles. Thus, even if you specify FILES = 30 in your CONFIG.SYS file, your programs will still be able to use only 20 handles at a time. (DOS 3.3 provides a way around this through interrupt 21H, function 67H. See page 392 for details.) Fortunately, few applications require more than 20 different files to be open at once, so these limitations are not usually important.

Installable Device Drivers

In DOS versions 2.0 and later, you can write a routine that provides a consistent interface between DOS's handle-based I/O functions and almost any I/O device that can input or output a stream of data. Such a routine is called a *device driver.* DOS comes with several built-in device drivers for the keyboard, video display, printer, communications port, and disks. You can also install device drivers for other devices by including their names in DEVICE commands in the CONFIG.SYS file.

DOS I/O device drivers allow handles to be associated not only with disk files but with any input/output device. When you use a handle-based DOS function to open a device, DOS searches its list of device drivers before it searches for a disk filename. Familiar names like ''CON'', ''LPT1'', and ''NUL'' are all part of the default list of device drivers. Opening a device for input/output thus consists only of passing a name to a DOS function and receiving a handle from DOS in return, regardless of whether the device is a disk file or is associated with some other type of hardware.

❏ NOTE: *Incidentally, this explains why you can't open a file named ''CON'' or ''PRN'': DOS searches for device names before it searches for filenames, so it always finds a named device before it finds a file with the same name.*

You don't have to know much about the implementation of device drivers to use the handle-based DOS functions, so we will save a more detailed discussion of device drivers for Appendix A. Keep in mind that by placing the discussion of device drivers at the end of the book, we in no way mean to diminish their importance. All programmers concerned with the range and longevity of their programs should at least be familiar with the use and operation of DOS device drivers.

Interrupt 21H Functions: DOS Versions 2.0 and Later

All DOS function calls described in this chapter are invoked through interrupt 21H (decimal 33). The individual functions are selected by placing the function number in the AH register. Any program that uses these functions should test the DOS version number first to be sure the functions are supported. (Function 30H provides this service.)

The functions can be organized into the groups shown in Figure 17-2. In an effort to make the logical groupings of the function calls as clear as possible, we organized and described them in a slightly different manner than that in IBM's DOS technical reference manuals. You may want to compare this organization with IBM's, to be sure you understand. Figure 17-3 lists the individual function calls.

Function		Group
Hex	*Dec*	*Group*
2FH–38H	47–56	Miscellaneous functions
39H–3BH	57–59	Directory functions
3CH–46H	60–70	File-management functions
47H	71	Directory function
48H–4BH	72–75	Memory-management functions
4CH–5BH	76–91	Miscellaneous functions
5CH–5FH	92–95	Network support
62H–68H	98–104	Miscellaneous functions

Figure 17-2. *The logical groups of extended DOS function calls.*

Function		Description	DOS
Hex	*Dec*	*Description*	*Version*
2FH	47	Get DTA Address	2.0
30H	48	Get DOS Version Number	2.0
31H	49	Terminate and Stay Resident	2.0
33H	51	Get/Set Ctrl-C Flag	2.0
35H	53	Get Interrupt Vector	2.0
36H	54	Get Disk Free Space	2.0
38H	56	Get/Set Country-Dependent Information	2.0
39H	57	Create Directory	2.0
3AH	58	Remove Directory	2.0
3BH	59	Change Current Directory	2.0
3CH	60	Create File	2.0
3DH	61	Open Handle	2.0
3EH	62	Close Handle	2.0
3FH	63	Read from File or Device	2.0
40H	64	Write to File or Device	2.0
41H	65	Delete File	2.0
42H	66	Move File Pointer	2.0
43H	67	Get/Set File Attributes	2.0
44H	68	IOCTL — I/O Control for Devices	2.0
45H	69	Duplicate File Handle	2.0
46H	70	Force Duplicate File Handle	2.0
47H	71	Get Current Directory	2.0

Figure 17-3. *Interrupt 21H functions available in DOS versions 2.0 and later. (continued)*

Figure 17-3. *continued*

Function		Description	DOS
Hex	*Dec*		*Version*
48H	72	Allocate Memory Block	2.0
49H	73	Free Memory Block	2.0
4AH	74	Resize Memory Block	2.0
4BH	75	EXEC—Load and Execute a Program	2.0
4CH	76	Terminate with Return Code	2.0
4DH	77	Get Return Code	2.0
4EH	78	Find First Matching Directory Entry	2.0
4FH	79	Find Next Matching Directory Entry	2.0
54H	84	Get Verify Flag	2.0
56H	86	Rename File	2.0
57H	87	Get/Set File Date and Time	2.0
58H	88	Get/Set Memory Allocation Strategy	3.0
59H	89	Get Extended Error Information	3.0
5AH	90	Create Temporary File	3.0
5BH	91	Create New File	3.0
5CH	92	Lock/Unlock File Region	3.0
5EH	94	Network Machine Name and Printer Setup	3.1
5FH	95	Network Redirection	3.1
62H	98	Get PSP Address	3.0
65H	101	Get Extended Country Information	3.3
66H	102	Get/Set Global Code Page	3.3
67H	103	Set Handle Count	3.3
68H	104	Commit File	3.3

Function 2FH (decimal 47): Get DTA Address

Function 2FH (decimal 47) returns the address of the disk transfer area (DTA) currently used by DOS. The address is returned in the register pair ES:BX. Contrast this with function 1AH, discussed on page 335.

Function 30H (decimal 48): Get DOS Version Number

Function 30H (decimal 48) returns the DOS major and minor version numbers. The major version number is in AL, and the minor version number is in AH; BX and CX contain a serial number (0 in IBM's versions of DOS; other possible values in non-IBM versions). For example, if you execute function 30H in DOS version 3.3, the function returns AL = 03H (the major version number), AH = 1EH (30, the minor version number), BX = 00H, and CX = 00H. In the OS/2 compatibility box, function 30H returns AL = 0AH; that is, the major version number is 10.

In DOS version 1, function 30H was unsupported. Nevertheless, you can still test for DOS version 1 by executing function 30H; in DOS version 1, function 30H is guaranteed to return AL = 00H. Thus, a simple test of the value returned in AL is sufficient to distinguish between version 1 and later versions:

```
mov ah,30h         ; AH = 30H (interrupt 21H function number)
int 21h            ; get DOS version number
cmp al,2
jl  EarlyVersion   ; jump if DOS version 1
```

Any program that uses interrupt 21H functions with numbers above 2EH can use function 30H to determine if the appropriate DOS version is being used.

Function 31H (decimal 49): Terminate and Stay Resident

Function 31H (decimal 49) terminates a program and leaves part of the program resident in memory. Except for the fact that function 31H lets you reserve memory for a memory-resident program, its function is the same as that of the program termination function (function 4CH). You call function 31H with a return code value in AL and with the number of paragraphs of memory to reserve for the program in DX.

Before you use function 31H, you should generally carry out the following steps:

1. Call function 30H to verify that the DOS version is 2.0 or later. Function 31H isn't supported in DOS version 1.

2. Call function 49H to free the memory allocated to the program's environment block. (The word at offset 2CH in the program's PSP contains the paragraph address of the environment block.)

3. Determine the amount of memory to reserve for the resident program. This value must include the 16 paragraphs reserved for the program's PSP in addition to contiguous memory reserved for the program itself. This value does not include memory allocated dynamically by the program using function 48H.

4. Call function 31H to terminate the program.

Like function 4CH, function 31H restores the interrupt vectors for interrupts 22H (Terminate Address), 23H (Ctrl-C Handler), and 24H (Critical Error Handler) to the DOS default values; therefore, you cannot use this function to install memory-resident handlers for these interrupts.

Function 31H is much more flexible than the Terminate-and-Stay-Resident service supported through interrupt 27H. You should always use function 31H in your TSR programs unless you are concerned about maintaining compatibility with DOS version 1.

Function 33H (decimal 51): Get/Set Ctrl-C Flag

Function 33H (decimal 51) lets you test or update DOS's internal Ctrl-C flag. When you call function 33H with AL = 00H, DOS reports the current state of the Ctrl-C flag in DL:

- If the flag is clear (DL = 00H), DOS checks for Ctrl-C keystrokes only when transmitting a character to or from a character device (interrupt 21H functions 00H through 0CH).

- If the flag is set (DL = 01H), DOS also checks for Ctrl-C when it responds to other service requests, such as file I/O operators.

When you call function 33H with AL = 01H, DOS expects DL to contain the desired value for the break flag:

- DL = 00H disables the break check.

- DL = 01H enables the break check.

Function 35H (decimal 53): Get Interrupt Vector

Function 35H (decimal 53) returns the interrupt vector for the interrupt number you specify in register AL. The vector is returned in the register pair ES:BX.

Function 35H provides a complementary service to function 25H, which updates an interrupt vector. (See Chapter 16.)

Function 36H (decimal 54): Get Disk Free Space

Function 36H (decimal 54) is similar to function 1CH (which gets disk information), but also provides information about unused disk space, which function 1CH does not. Before calling this function, select the drive that you are interested in with the DL register: DL = 00H indicates the default drive, DL = 01H indicates drive A, DL = 02H indicates drive B, and so on.

If you specify an invalid drive, function 36H returns FFFFH in the AX register. Otherwise, AX contains the number of sectors per cluster, CX contains the number of bytes per sector, BX contains the number of available clusters, and DX contains the total number of clusters.

From these numbers you can make many interesting calculations, as follows:

CX ∗ AX = bytes per cluster
CX ∗ AX ∗ BX = total number of free bytes
CX ∗ AX ∗ DX = total storage space in bytes
(BX ∗ 100) / DX = percentage of free space

If S were the size of a file in bytes, you could calculate the number of occupied clusters in this way:

$(S + CX ∗ AX − 1) \backslash (CX ∗ AX)$

Similar formulas would give you the number of sectors and the amount and proportion of space allocated to a file but not used (the *slack space*).

Function 38H (decimal 56): Get/Set Country-Dependent Information

Function 38H (decimal 56) allows DOS to adjust to different international currency and date format conventions. In DOS version 2, this function reports a very small set of country-dependent information. In DOS version 3, function 38H reports a more detailed list of country-dependent items; in this version of DOS, a program can also change the country-dependent information with a call to function 38H.

To get country-dependent information from DOS, call function 38H with DS:DX containing the address of a 32-byte buffer. (In DOS versions 3.0 and later, the size of the buffer must be 34 bytes.) Register AL must be set to 00H to get the current country information. For DOS versions 3.0 and later, register AL can also be set to a predefined *country code*. (The country code is the same 3-digit code used as the country's international telephone access code.) To specify a country code of 255 or greater, AL can be set to FFH (decimal 255), and the country code can be put into register BX.

If the requested country code is invalid, DOS sets the carry flag (CF) and places an error code in AX. Otherwise, register BX contains the country code, and the buffer at DS:DX is filled in with the country-specific information shown in Figures 17-4 and 17-5.

To set the current country code in DOS version 3, set DX equal to FFFFH and call function 38H with AL equal to the country code (or if the code is greater than 254, set AL equal to FFH and register BX equal to the country code).

The country-dependent information is used by DOS utilities like DATE and TIME. A program can call function 38H to obtain the information DOS uses to configure itself for country-dependent conventions.

The *date format* is an integer word whose value specifies the display format for the date. This word has three predefined values and three corresponding date formats. (See Figure 17-6.) Room is reserved so that others might be added in the future.

The *currency symbol* is the symbol used in displaying an amount of money: In the United States, the currency symbol is a dollar sign ($); in the United Kingdom, it's the pound symbol (£); in Japan, it's the yen symbol (¥). In DOS versions 2.0 and 2.1, the currency symbol can only be a single character, but in DOS version 3, a string up to four characters in length can be used. For example, one of the currency strings that could be used in DOS version 3.3 is DKR, which stands for Danish kroner.

Offset Hex	Offset Dec	Size (bytes)	Description
00H	0	2	Date format
02H	2	2	Currency symbol string (ASCIIZ format)
04H	4	2	Thousands separator string (ASCIIZ format)
06H	6	2	Decimal separator string (ASCIIZ format)
08H	8	24	(Reserved)

Figure 17-4. *The country-dependent information reported by function 38H in DOS version 2.*

Offset		Size	
Hex	Dec	(bytes)	Description
00H	0	2	Date format
02H	2	5	Currency symbol string (ASCIIZ format)
07H	7	2	Thousands separator string (ASCIIZ format)
09H	9	2	Decimal separator string (ASCIIZ format)
0BH	11	2	Date separator string (ASCIIZ format)
0DH	13	2	Time separator string (ASCIIZ format)
0FH	15	1	Currency symbol location
10H	16	1	Currency decimal places
11H	17	1	Time format: 1 = 24-hour clock; 0 = 12-hour
12H	18	4	Extended ASCII map call address
16H	22	2	List separator string (ASCIIZ format)
18H	24	10	(Reserved)

Figure 17-5. *The country-dependent information returned by function 38H in DOS version 3.*

Value	Use	Date
00H	American	month day year
01H	European	day month year
02H	Japanese	year month day

Figure 17-6. *The three predefined date formats returned by function 38H.*

The *thousands separator* is the symbol used to punctuate the thousands mark in numbers. The U.S. uses a comma as a thousands separator, as in the number 12,345; other countries use a period or a blank.

The *decimal separator* is the symbol used to punctuate decimal places. The U.S. uses a period as a decimal separator, as in 3.0; other countries use a comma.

The *date separator* and *time separator* are the punctuation used in displaying the date (for example, – as in 7–4–1988) and in displaying the time (for example, : as in 12:34).

The *currency symbol location* indicates where the currency symbol should be placed. A value of 00H places the currency symbol immediately before the amount (¥1500); 01H places the symbol immediately after the amount (15¢); 02H places the symbol before the amount with an intervening space (FFr 15); 03H places the symbol after the amount with an intervening space (15 DKR); and 04H replaces the decimal separator with the currency symbol.

The *currency decimal places value* specifies how many decimal places are used in the currency. For example, the value would be 02H for U.S. currency (dollars and cents) and 00H for Italian currency (lire).

The *time format field* specifies whether time appears in a 12-hour or 24-hour format. Only the low-order bit (bit 0) is currently used; if the bit is set to 0, a 12-hour clock is used; if it is set to 1, a 24-hour clock is used.

The *extended ASCII map call address* is the segmented address of a routine that maps ASCII characters 80H through FFH to characters in the range 00H through 7FH. Not all printers or plotters can display extended ASCII characters in the range 80H–FFH, so the routine at this address is called when it is necessary to map such characters into the usual range of ASCII characters (00H–7FH).

The *list separator* indicates the symbol used to separate items in a list, such as the commas in the list A, B, C, and D.

Function 39H (decimal 57): Create Directory

Function 39H (decimal 57) creates a subdirectory, just as the DOS command MKDIR does. To invoke this service, create an ASCIIZ string containing the pathname of the new directory. The register pair DS:DX contains the address of the ASCIIZ string. If an error occurs, function 39H sets the carry flag and returns an error code in AX. The possible error codes are 03H (path not found) and 05H (access denied).

Function 3AH (decimal 58): Remove Directory

Function 3AH (decimal 58) removes (deletes) a subdirectory exactly as the DOS command RMDIR does. To invoke this function, create an ASCIIZ string containing the pathname of the directory you want to remove. The register pair DS:DX points to the ASCIIZ string. If an error occurs, function 3AH sets the carry flag and returns an error code in AX. The possible error codes are 03H (path not found), 05H (access denied), and 10H (attempt to remove current directory).

Function 3BH (decimal 59): Change Current Directory

Function 3BH (decimal 59) changes the current directory exactly as the DOS command CHDIR does. To invoke this function, create an ASCIIZ string containing the pathname of the new directory. DS:DX contains the address of the ASCIIZ string. If an error occurs, function 3BH sets the carry flag and returns an error code in AX. The one possible error code is 03H (path not found).

Function 3CH (decimal 60): Create File

Function 3CH (decimal 60) opens an empty file using a specified name. If the file exists, function 3CH truncates it to zero length. If the file does not exist, function 3CH creates a new file. This function parallels function 16H (discussed on page 334).

To invoke this function, create an ASCIIZ string containing the pathname and filename. The register pair DS:DX contains the address of the ASCIIZ string. CX contains the file attribute. (See page 113 for more on file attributes and attribute bit settings.) When function 3CH executes successfully, it clears the carry flag and returns a handle in AX. Otherwise, this function sets the carry flag and leaves an error code in AX. Possible error codes are 03H (path not found), 04H (no handle available), and 05H (access denied). Code 05H can indicate either that there is no room for a new directory entry or that the existing file is marked read-only and can't be opened for output.

Be aware that by using function 3CH you can accidentally truncate an existing file to zero length. The best way to avoid this mistake is simply to call function 4EH to search the directory for an existing file before you call function 3CH. Or, if you are using DOS 3.0 or later, you have two other alternatives: You can call function 5BH, which works like function 3CH but won't open an existing file, or you can use function 5AH to create a temporary file with a unique filename.

Function 3DH (decimal 61): Open Handle

Function 3DH (decimal 61) opens an existing file or device. You provide the pathname and filename in the form of an ASCIIZ string. As with all other file I/O functions, DS:DX points to this string. You also indicate how you want to use the file by placing a file-access code in register AL. The 8 bits of AL are divided into the four fields shown in Figure 17-7 on the following page.

Bit								Use
7	6	5	4	3	2	1	0	
I	.	.	.	.	.	.	.	Inheritance flag (DOS version 3 only)
.	S	S	S	.	.	.	.	Sharing mode (DOS version 3 only)
.	.	.	.	R	.	.	.	(Reserved)
.	.	.	.	.	A	A	A	Access code

Figure 17-7. *File-access and sharing codes for function 3DH.*

The file-access code for DOS version 2 is simple: Only the access bits (bits 0–2) are used; all other bits are set to 0. The three access-code settings are defined in Figure 17-8.

Bit			Use
2	1	0	
0	0	0	Read (only) access
0	0	1	Write (only) access
0	1	0	Read or write access

Figure 17-8. *File-access modes for function 3DH.*

DOS version 3 uses the *inheritance* and *sharing codes* as well as the access code. The inheritance and sharing codes give you control over how different programs access the same file at the same time.

Bit 7, the inheritance bit, indicates whether or not a child process can inherit the use of this file. (For more about parent and child processes, see the discussion of function 4BH later in this chapter.) When a child process inherits a handle, it inherits the file's access and sharing codes: If bit 7 = 0, a child process can use the same handle to access the file as the parent process; if bit 7 = 1, the child process must itself open the file to obtain a different handle.

Bits 4 through **6,** the sharing-mode bits (SSS in Figure 17-7), define what will happen when more than one program tries to open the same file. There are five sharing modes: compatibility mode (SSS = 000), deny read/ write mode (SSS = 001), deny write mode (SSS = 010), deny read mode (SSS = 011), and deny none mode (SSS = 100). When a second attempt is made to open the file, DOS compares the file's sharing code with the access requested in the second open operation. DOS allows the second open operation to succeed only if the sharing mode and the requested access mode are compatible.

❏ NOTE: *DOS performs this file-sharing validation only if it is running on a network or if the SHARE utility is installed. See the DOS technical reference manual for more details on networking and the SHARE utility.*

Bit 3, marked as "Reserved" in Figure 17-7, should be set to 0.

Like function 3CH, function 3DH clears the carry flag and returns a handle in AX when it successfully opens a file or device. Otherwise, this function sets the carry flag and leaves an error code in AX. The possible return codes from function 3DH are 02H (file not found), 03H (path not found), 04H (no handles available), 05H (access denied), and 0CH (invalid access code).

If SHARE or network file sharing is in force in DOS version 3, DOS signals a sharing violation by executing interrupt 24H.

Function 3EH (decimal 62): Close Handle

Function 3EH (decimal 62) closes a file or device associated with the handle in BX. This function flushes all file buffers and updates the directory if necessary. The only error code this function can return is 06H (invalid handle).

Function 3FH (decimal 63): Read from File or Device

Function 3FH (decimal 63) reads the file or device associated with the handle in BX. The CX register specifies the number of bytes to read; DS:DX points to the buffer where data that is read will be placed. If the read operation is successful, function 3FH clears the carry flag and returns the number of bytes read in AX. If this value is 0, the function has tried to read from the end of a file. If the read operation fails, this function sets the carry flag and leaves an error code in AX. The possible error codes are 05H (access denied) and 06H (invalid handle).

Function 40H (decimal 64): Write to File or Device

Function 40H (decimal 64) writes to the file or device associated with the handle in BX. CX specifies the number of bytes to be written; DS:DX points to the address of the data bytes.

When the write operation is complete, function 40H updates the file pointer to point past the data just written.

You must examine both the carry flag and the value in AX returned by function 40H to determine the success of the write operation:

- If the carry flag is clear and AX = CX, the operation completed successfully.

- If the carry flag is clear but AX < CX, then the output was written to a disk file that had insufficient disk space to complete the write operation.

- If the carry flag is set, AX contains an error code of 05H (access denied) or 06H (invalid handle).

The fact that function 40H updates the file pointer has an interesting side effect: You can set the size of a file to any arbitrary value by executing function 40H with CX = 00H. The usual technique is to call function 42H to set the file pointer location and then to immediately call function 40H with CX = 00H to update the file size.

Function 41H (decimal 65): Delete File

Function 41H (decimal 65) deletes the directory entry of a file. The file is specified by an ASCIIZ string containing the path and filename. The register pair DS:DX points to the string. Unlike function 13H, function 41H does not support wildcard characters in the file specification: With function 41H you can delete only one file at a time.

You cannot delete read-only files with this function. To delete a read-only file, first remove the read-only attribute using function 43H, and then use function 41H.

Function 41H can return three error codes in AX: 02H (file not found), 03H (path not found), and 05H (access denied).

Function 42H (decimal 66): Move File Pointer

Function 42H (decimal 66) changes the logical read/write position in a file. To invoke this service, load BX with a handle and then specify the new pointer location by placing a reference location in AL and an offset relative to the reference location in register pair CX:DX. The byte offset in CX:DX is a 32-bit, long integer. CX is the high-order part of the offset (which is 0, unless the offset amount is more than 65,535) and DX is the low-order part.

You can specify the reference location in AL in three different ways: If AL = 00H, the offset is taken relative to the beginning of the file and the file pointer is moved CX:DX bytes from that point; if AL = 01H, the offset is taken relative to the current file pointer location; if AL = 02H, the offset is taken from the current end of file.

If the function executes successfully, it clears the carry flag and returns in the register pair DX:AX the current file pointer location relative to the beginning of the file. The pointer is returned as a 32-bit long integer, with the high-order part in DX and the low-order part in AX. If the function fails, it sets the carry flag and returns an error code in AX. Possible error codes are 01H (invalid function number, which means AL did not contain 00H, 01H, or 02H) and 06H (invalid handle).

You can use function 42H in several different ways:

- To place the file pointer at an arbitrary location in the file, call function 42H with AL = 00H and CX:DX specifying the desired offset relative to the start of the file.

- To position the file pointer at the end of the file, call function 42H with AL = 02H and 00H in CX:DX.

- To determine the current location of the file pointer, use AL = 01H and 00H in CX:DX; the value returned in DX:AX is the current file pointer location.

DOS does not validate the resulting location of the file pointer. In particular, you can end with a *negative file pointer offset* (that is, a file pointer at a position before the logical start of the file). However, it's not a good idea to use negative file pointers for two reasons: If you perform a subsequent read or write operation, you'll be in error; and your program will be harder to adapt for OS/2, where an attempt to move a file pointer to a negative offset generates an error.

❑ NOTE: *The operation of moving a logical file pointer to a specified location in a file is sometimes called a "seek," but the same word is also used in the sense of moving the read/write heads of a disk drive to a specified cylinder on a disk. The two operations aren't the same.*

Function 43H (decimal 67): Get/Set File Attributes

Function 43H (decimal 67) gets or sets the attributes of a file. (See page 113 for details about file attributes.) DS:DX points to an ASCIIZ string that specifies the file in question. (Global filename characters ? and * cannot be used.) Calling function 43H with AL = 00H returns the file's attributes in CX; AL = 01H sets the attribute values you specify in CX.

If function 43H fails, the carry flag is set and AX contains one of four error codes: 01H (invalid function), 02H (file not found), 03H (path not found), and 05H (access denied).

Function 44H (decimal 68): IOCTL — I/O Control for Devices

Function 44H (decimal 68) performs input/output control operations, mostly for devices. (See Figure 17-9.) AL selects one of 16 subfunctions, numbered 00H through 0FH; some of these subfunctions have sub-subfunctions you specify with a "minor code" in CL.

The main purpose of the IOCTL function is to provide a consistent interface between DOS programs and device drivers. In general, you shouldn't use IOCTL calls unless you know something about how device drivers are structured — a topic we'll cover in Appendix A. A few IOCTL calls, however, are useful even if you don't understand the details of device-driver operations. We'll point these out as we summarize the various IOCTL calls.

❏ NOTE: *Not all IOCTL subfunctions are supported in earlier versions of DOS. Figure 17-9 indicates the DOS versions in which the various IOCTL subfunctions were introduced.*

| Subfunction | | | DOS |
Hex	Dec	Description	Version
00H	0	Get device data.	2.0
01H	1	Set device data.	2.0
02H	2	Receive control data from character device.	2.0
03H	3	Send control data to character device.	2.0
04H	4	Receive control data from block device.	2.0
05H	5	Send control data to block device.	2.0
06H	6	Check input status.	2.0
07H	7	Check output status.	2.0
08H	8	Check if block device is removable.	3.0
09H	9	Check if block device is remote.	3.1
0AH	10	Check if handle is remote.	3.1
0BH	11	Change sharing retry count.	3.0
0CH	12	Generic I/O control for handles.	3.2
0DH	13	Generic I/O control for block devices.	3.2
0EH	14	Get logical drive map.	3.2
0FH	15	Set logical drive map.	3.2

Figure 17-9. *Subfunctions available under interrupt 21H, function 44H (IOCTL).*

Subfunctions 00H and **01H.** These subfunctions get and set device information formatted in DX by a complicated set of bit coding. Bit 7 is set to 1 for devices and to 0 for disk files. For devices, bits 0 through 5 are specified as shown in Figure 17-10. For disk files, bits 0 through 5 provide the disk-drive number: A value of 0 represents drive A, a value of 1 represents drive B, and so on. Both subfunctions should be called with a file or device handle in BX. Subfunction 00H can be called for both disk files and devices; subfunction 01H can be called only for character devices.

15	14	13	12	11	10	9	8	*Bit* 7	6	5	4	3	2	1	0	Use
.	.	.	.	.	.	.	.	.	.	.	.	.	.	.	X	1 = standard input device
.	.	.	.	.	.	.	.	.	.	.	.	.	.	X	.	1 = standard output device
.	.	.	.	.	.	.	.	.	.	.	.	.	X	.	.	1 = null device
.	.	.	.	.	.	.	.	.	.	.	.	X	.	.	.	1 = clock device
.	.	.	.	.	.	.	.	.	.	.	X	.	.	.	.	(Reserved)
.	.	.	.	.	.	.	.	.	.	X	.	.	.	.	.	1 = data is "raw" (without control-character checking); 0 = data is "cooked" (with control-character checking)
.	.	.	.	.	.	.	.	.	X	.	.	.	.	.	.	0 = end of file; 1 = not end of file (for input)
.	.	.	.	.	.	.	.	X	.	.	.	.	.	.	.	1 = device; 0 = disk-drive file
.	.	.	.	.	.	R	.	.	.	.	.	.	.	.	.	(Reserved)
.	.	.	.	.	R	.	.	.	.	.	.	.	.	.	.	(Reserved)
.	.	.	.	R	.	.	.	.	.	.	.	.	.	.	.	(Reserved)
.	.	.	R	.	.	.	.	.	.	.	.	.	.	.	.	(Reserved)
.	.	R	.	.	.	.	.	.	.	.	.	.	.	.	.	(Reserved)
.	R	.	.	.	.	.	.	.	.	.	.	.	.	.	.	(Reserved)
.	X	.	.	.	.	.	.	.	.	.	.	.	.	.	.	1 = device can process control strings transferred by IOCTL subfunctions 02H through 05H
R	.	.	.	.	.	.	.	.	.	.	.	.	.	.	.	(Reserved)

Figure 17-10. *The bit settings of the device data word DX for subfunction 00H or 01H of interrupt 21H, function 44H.*

You can modify how DOS processes I/O for the CON device (the keyboard/video display combination) by setting "raw" input/output mode for the device. Do this by clearing bit 5 of the device data word in DX and calling subfunction 01H:

```
mov     ax,4400h        ; AH = 44H (interrupt 21H function number)
                        ; AL = 0 (subfunction number)
mov     bx,0            ; BX = 0 (handle for CON device)
int     21h             ; get device data into DX
or      dx,0020h        ; set bit 5 ("raw" mode)
and     dx,00FFh        ; zero reserved bits 8-15
mov     ax,4401h        ; set up for subfunction 1
mov     bx,0            ; BX = CON device handle
int     21h             ; set device data for CON
```

After you execute this sequence of code, DOS no longer recognizes Ctrl-P and Ctrl-S characters, nor does it expand tabs on output.

Subfunctions 02H through **05H.** These subfunctions transfer control data between your program and a device driver. Subfunctions 02H and 03H get and send control data for character-oriented devices; subfunctions 04H and 05H get and send control data for block-oriented devices. In all four subfunctions you specify the subfunction number in AL, the address of a data buffer in DS:DX, and the number of bytes to transfer in CX. For subfunctions 02H and 03H, you must specify a handle in BX; for subfunctions 04H and 05H, you must specify a drive number in BL (00H = default drive, 01H = drive A, and so on).

The control data you transfer to or from a device driver is not necessarily part of the device's input/output data stream: The control data is often used to obtain the device status or to control hardware-specific features such as printer font characteristics or tape drive rewind.

These subfunctions can be used only if the device can process control strings. This capability is indicated by bit 14 in the device data word returned by subfunction 00H.

Subfunctions 06H and **07H.** These subfunctions return the current input or output status of a device or file. Call them with a handle in BX: Subfunction 06H returns the current input status; subfunction 07H returns the current output status.

Both of these subfunctions use the carry flag to indicate a successful call. If the carry flag is clear, AL contains the status: AL = 00H means the device is not ready for input or output; AL = FFH means the device is ready. (For a file, input status AL = 00H means end-of-file; output status is always "ready" regardless of the value in AL.) If the carry flag is set, AX contains an error code: 01H (invalid function), 05H (access denied), 06H (invalid handle), or 0DH (invalid data).

Subfunction 08H. This subfunction, supported only in DOS versions 3.0 and later, indicates whether a block-oriented device has removable media or not. (The floppy diskettes in a diskette drive are removable; the fixed disk in a fixed-disk drive is not.) Subfunction 08H can be extremely useful because it lets a program know if it has to check for a disk change or if it can rely on the same disk always being there. Call subfunction 08H with a drive number in BL (00H = default drive, 01H = drive A, and so on). The subfunction clears the carry flag on a successful return and leaves AX = 00H if the storage medium is removable or AX = 01H if the storage medium is nonremovable. If the carry flag is set, AX contains an error code: 01H (invalid function) or 0FH (invalid drive).

Subfunction 09H. In a network configuration, this subfunction determines whether a particular block device is local (attached to the computer running the program) or remote (redirected to a network server). You must specify a drive number in BL when you call this subfunction.

Subfunction 09H clears the carry flag to indicate a successful call. In this case, bit 12 of the value in DX indicates whether the device is remote (bit 12 = 1) or local (bit 12 = 0). If the carry flag is set, AX contains an error code: 01H (invalid function) or 0FH (invalid drive). Subfunction 09H is available in DOS 3.1 and later.

Subfunction 0AH (decimal 10). This subfunction is similar to subfunction 09H but is used with a device handle instead of a drive number. Specify the handle in BX when you call this subfunction.

Like subfunction 09H, subfunction 0AH clears the carry flag and returns a value in DX that indicates whether the device is local or remote. Bit 15 of DX indicates whether the device is remote (bit 15 = 1) or local (bit 15 = 0). If an error occurs, the function sets the carry flag and returns an error code in AX: 01H (invalid function) or 06H (invalid handle). Subfunction 09H is available in DOS 3.1 and later.

Subfunction 0BH (decimal 11). This subfunction, which is supported only in DOS versions 3.0 and later, controls the way DOS attempts to resolve file-sharing conflicts. Because some programs lock files only briefly, file-sharing conflicts can be very transitory. DOS can try more than once to gain access to a shared file before reporting a conflict, in the hope that the lock condition goes away in the meantime.

Subfunction 0BH can help you empirically tune a network in which you expect transient file-sharing conflicts to occur. Call this subfunction with DX containing the number of times you want DOS to retry access to a shared file before it gives up and reports an error. CX should specify the delay value between retries. DOS creates a delay by executing an empty loop 65,536 times; the value in CX indicates the number of times you want DOS to execute the empty delay loop. (The DOS defaults are three retries and one delay loop between retries.)

If the subfunction executes successfully, it clears the carry flag. If the carry flag is set, AX contains an error code of 01H (invalid function).

Subfunction 0CH (decimal 12). This subfunction provides miscellaneous control functions for character-oriented devices. Each control function is designated by a minor code in CL and a major code (also called a category code) in CH. The various major and minor codes are listed in Figure 17-11.

Minor codes 45H and 65H were introduced in DOS version 3.2. They apply only to print devices (major code 05H). They deal with the number of times DOS attempts to send a character to a printer before it assumes the printer is busy. The remaining minor codes were introduced in DOS version

Hex	Dec	Description
Major Code (specified in CH)		
00H	0	Unknown
01H	1	Serial port (COM1, COM2, COM3, COM4)
03H	3	Console (CON)
05H	5	Printer (LPT1, LPT2, LPT3)
Minor Code (specified in CL)		
45H	69	Set iteration count.
4AH	74	Select code page.
4CH	76	Start code page preparation.
4DH	77	End code page preparation.
65H	101	Get iteration count.
6AH	106	Query selected code page.
6BH	107	Query prepare list.

Figure 17-11. *Major and minor codes for IOCTL subfunction 0CH (generic I/O control for handles).*

3.3. They provide detailed support for defining and loading code pages for output devices that can use multiple character sets or fonts.

For details on the use of the services provided in this IOCTL subfunction, see the DOS technical reference manual.

Subfunction 0DH (decimal 13). Subfunction 0DH provides six generic services for block-oriented devices. Each service is designated by a major code in CH and a minor code in CL. (See Figure 17-12.) In general, these services are similar to services provided by the ROM BIOS for diskettes and fixed disks, but these IOCTL services provide a consistent interface to *any* block-oriented device with a device driver that supports these IOCTL calls.

Subfunction 0DH is available in DOS 3.2 and later. See the DOS technical reference manual for details on subfunction 0DH services.

Hex	Dec	Description
Major Code (specified in CH)		
08H	8	Disk drive
Minor Code (specified in CL)		
40H	64	Set parameters for block device.
41H	65	Write track on logical drive.
42H	66	Format and verify track on logical drive.
60H	96	Get parameters for block device.
61H	97	Read track on logical drive.
62H	98	Verify track on logical drive.

Figure 17-12. *Major and minor codes for IOCTL subfunction 0DH (generic I/O control for block devices).*

Subfunctions 0EH and 0FH (decimal 14 and 15). These two subfunctions relate logical mapping of drive letter assignments to physical drives. For example, in systems with only one diskette drive, DOS maps drive letter B to physical drive A.

Call these subfunctions with a logical drive ID in BL (01H represents drive A, 02H represents drive B, and so on). Subfunction 0EH returns a logical drive ID that is currently mapped to the drive you specified in BL. Subfunction 0FH also updates DOS's internal logical map so that the drive ID you specified becomes the new logical drive ID. Both subfunctions use AL to return the logical drive ID; if AL = 00H, only one logical drive is associated with the drive ID you specified in BL. If an error occurs, the carry flag is set and AX contains an error code: 01H (invalid function) or 0FH (invalid drive).

For example, if you execute the following instructions on a system with only one diskette drive, DOS associates drive B with the diskette drive:

```
mov bl,2                ; BL = logical drive number
mov ax,440Fh            ; set logical drive map
int 21h                 ; update the logical drive ID
                        ; (DOS returns AL = 02H)
```

Function 45H (decimal 69): Duplicate Handle

Function 45H (decimal 69) duplicates an open file handle and returns a new handle number that refers to the same file or device. All actions performed with one handle will be reflected in the other handle — the new handle does not act independently in any way.

Call function 45H with an open handle in BX. If the function executes successfully, it clears the carry flag and leaves a new handle number in AX. If an error occurs, the carry flag is set and AX contains an error code: 04H (no more handles) or 06H (invalid handle).

You can use function 45H along with function 46H to implement input/output redirection. You can also use it to commit an open file to disk by duplicating the open file's handle and then closing the duplicate handle. This has the effect of flushing the file's disk buffers and updating the directory, without the overhead of closing the file, reopening it (which involves a directory search), and repositioning the file pointer:

```
mov bx,Handle           ; BX = handle of open file
mov ah,45h
int 21h                 ; get duplicate handle into AX
jc  Error
mov bx,ax               ; BX = duplicate handle
mov ah,3Eh
int 21h                 ; close duplicate handle
                        ;    (original handle remains open)
```

Function 46H (decimal 70): Force Duplicate Handle

Function 46H (decimal 70) has a somewhat misleading name because it really does not create a duplicate handle as does function 45H. Instead, function 46H associates an existing open handle with a different device. This is the key to implementing input/output redirection in DOS.

Call function 46H with an open handle in BX and a second handle in CX. When function 46H returns, the handle in CX is associated with the same device as the open handle in BX. If the handle in CX was previously associated with an open device, function 46H closes the device (which might otherwise be without a handle). If no errors occur, the function clears the carry flag. Otherwise, the carry flag is set, and AX contains an error code: 04H (no more handles) or 06H (invalid handle).

To see how function 46H works, consider how you would redirect output from the standard output device (the video screen) to a file:

```
mov bx,stdout          ; BX = handle of standard output device
mov ah,45h             ; AH = function number ("Duplicate Handle")
int 21h                ; get duplicate handle into AX
jc  Error              ; (trap errors)
mov stdoutDup,ax       ; save the duplicate handle in a memory variable

mov bx,FileHandle      ; BX = handle of open file
mov cx,stdout          ; CX = handle to be redirected
mov ah,46h             ; AH = function number ("Force Duplicate Handle")
int 21h                ; redirect stdout to the file
jc  Error

                       ; at this point, all output to stdout
                       ;   goes into the file
```

To undo this redirection, associate the standard output device with the saved duplicate:

```
mov bx,stdoutDup       ; BX = duplicate of previous stdout
mov cx,stdout          ; CX = handle to be redirected
mov ah,46h             ; AH = function number ("Force Duplicate Handle")
int 21h                ; restore stdout to what it was
jc  Error

mov bx,stdoutDup       ; BX = duplicate
mov ah,3Eh             ; AH = function number ("Close")
int 21h                ; discard duplicate handle
```

Function 47H (decimal 71): Get Current Directory

Function 47H (decimal 71) reports the current directory in the form of an ASCIIZ string. Call function 47H with a drive number in DL (00H = default drive, 01H = drive A, and so on) and the address of a 64-byte buffer in DS:SI. The function normally clears the carry flag and fills the buffer with an ASCIIZ string indicating the path from the root to the current directory. If you specify an invalid drive number, the function sets the carry flag and returns an error code of 0FH in AX.

Because the path returned by this function starts at the root directory, the string at DS:SI includes neither the drive letter (as in A:) nor the start-from-the-root backslash (as in A:\). By these rules, if the current directory is the root directory, then this function returns a null string. If you want an intelligible display of the current directory, you can prefix the information returned by this function with the drive-and-root indicators (as in A:\).

Function 48H (decimal 72): Allocate Memory Block

Function 48H (decimal 72) dynamically allocates memory. You request the number of paragraphs (16-byte units) you want allocated in BX. On return, AX contains the segment of the allocated memory block.

If an error occurs, the carry flag is set and AX contains an error code: 07H (memory control blocks destroyed) or 08H (insufficient memory). If there is insufficient memory to satisfy your request, BX contains the size, in paragraphs, of the largest available block of memory.

Memory blocks allocated to a program using function 48H are freed by DOS when the program terminates with function 00H or 4CH, but they remain allocated to a memory-resident program that terminates with the Terminate-and-Stay-Resident function, 31H.

Function 49H (decimal 73): Free Memory Block

Function 49H (decimal 73) frees a block of memory for subsequent reuse by DOS or by other programs. Call function 49H with ES containing the paragraph address (segment) of the start of the memory block. If the memory is successfully freed, the function clears the carry flag. Otherwise, the carry flag is set, and AX contains an error code: 07H (memory control blocks destroyed) or 09H (invalid memory-block address).

Although function 49H is usually used to free memory previously allocated through function 48H, it will free any memory block. For example, a Terminate-and-Stay-Resident program can free its environment block by calling function 49H with ES containing the paragraph address of the environment block. (See the discussion of function 31H in this chapter.)

Function 4AH (decimal 74): Resize Memory Block

Function 4AH (decimal 74) is used to increase or decrease the size of a block of memory that was allocated by function 48H. Register ES contains the segment address of the block that will be changed. Register BX contains the desired size of the block in paragraphs (units of 16 bytes).

The function clears the carry flag if the memory block can be resized as requested. If an error occurs, the carry flag is set, and AX contains an error code: 07H (memory control blocks destroyed), 08H (insufficient memory), or 09H (invalid memory-block address). If DOS reported that there was insufficient memory to increase the size of a memory block, BX contains the maximum size, in paragraphs, of the memory block.

Function 4BH (decimal 75): EXEC—Load and Execute a Program

Function 4BH (decimal 75) lets a parent program load a "child" program into memory and execute it. This function can also be used to load executable code or data into memory without executing it. In both cases, you call function 4BH with DS:DX pointing to an ASCIIZ string with the path and filename of the file to be loaded. The register pair ES:BX points to a parameter block that contains control information for the load operation. AL specifies whether the child program is to be executed after it is loaded.

If AL = 00H, DOS allocates memory for the child program, creates a new program segment prefix at the start of the newly allocated memory, loads the child program into memory immediately above the PSP, and transfers control to it. The parent program regains control only when the child program terminates. If AL = 03H, DOS does not allocate memory, create a PSP for the child program, or transfer control to the program after it is loaded. For these reasons, the AL = 03H variation is normally used to load a program overlay. It is also an effective way to load data into memory.

When AL = 00H, ES:BX points to a block 14 bytes long, which contains the information shown in Figure 17-13. When AL = 03H, ES:BX points to a block 4 bytes long, which contains the information shown in Figure 17-14 on the following page.

| Offset | | Size | |
Hex	Dec	(bytes)	Description
00H	0	2	Segment address of environment string
02H	2	4	Segmented pointer to command line
06H	6	4	Segmented pointer to first default FCB
0AH	10	4	Segmented pointer to second default FCB

Figure 17-13. *The information in the EXEC parameter block that is pointed to by ES:BX when AL = 00H. DOS builds this information into the PSP of the program that is being loaded.*

| Offset | | Size | |
Hex	Dec	(bytes)	Description
00H	0	2	Segment address where file is to be loaded
02H	2	2	Relocation factor for program (applies only to EXE-format programs)

Figure 17-14. *The information in the EXEC parameter block that is pointed to by ES:BX when AL = 03H.*

Function 4BH clears the carry flag if it successfully loads a program. However, in DOS version 2, this function changes all registers, including SS:SP. For this reason, you should save the current SS and SP values in the code segment before you call function 4BH.

If function 4BH fails, it sets the carry flag and returns one of the following error codes in AX: 01H (invalid function), 02H (file not found), 03H (path not found), 05H (access denied), 08H (insufficient memory), 0AH (invalid environment block), or 0BH (invalid format).

When a child program is loaded and executed, it inherits any handles opened by the parent program. (The only exception, in DOS versions 3.0 and later, is when a handle opened by the parent had the inheritance bit of its file-access code set to 1.) Because a child program inherits its parent's open handles, the parent program can redirect the standard I/O handles and use this technique to influence the operation of the child program. For example, a parent program might redirect the standard input and output devices to files and then use the DOS SORT filter to sort the data in one file and copy it to another.

More commonly, however, a parent program uses EXEC to execute a copy of the DOS command interpreter, COMMAND.COM. The parent program can carry out any DOS command by passing the command to COMMAND.COM through the EXEC parameter block. You can even get fancy by making COMMAND.COM execute a batch file — one that the parent program might well have constructed dynamically. This batch file could, in turn, invoke other programs and then perform the EXIT command, which would end the execution of the command interpreter. At that point, the parent program would be back in control. This opens up vast and complicated possibilities.

❏ NOTE: *Strangely enough, you can't use function 4BH to load overlays created with the DOS LINK program's overlay option: LINK builds all program overlays into a single executable file, not into separate files as would be needed with function 4BH.*

Function 4CH (decimal 76): Terminate with Return Code

Function 4CH (decimal 76) ends a program and passes back the return code you specify in AL. If the program was invoked as a child program, the parent program can retrieve the return code through function 4DH. If the program was invoked as a DOS command, then the return code can be tested in a batch file using the DOS ERRORLEVEL option.

When this function is performed, DOS does some cleanup work in case your program neglected to do so: It restores the interrupt 22H, 23H, and 24H vectors to default values, flushes the file buffers and closes all open files, and frees all memory allocated to the program.

Because function 4CH is more flexible and easier to use than interrupt 20H or interrupt 21H, function 00H, you should normally use function 4CH to terminate your programs. The only exception to this rule is if you need to maintain compatibility with DOS version 1, which does not support function 4CH. In that case, you should use either interrupt 20H or function 00H of interrupt 21H.

Function 4DH (decimal 77): Get Return Code

Function 4DH (decimal 77) gets the return code of a child program invoked with function 4BH and terminated with function 31H or 4CH. The information is returned in two parts. AL reports the return code issued by the child program; AH reports how the child program ended and has four possible values:

- AH = 00H indicates a normal voluntary end.

- AH = 01H indicates termination by DOS due to a keyboard break (Ctrl-C).

- AH = 02H indicates termination by DOS within a critical-error handler.

- AH = 03H indicates a voluntary end using a terminate-and-stay-resident service (interrupt 27H or function 31H).

You should call this function only after you call function 4BH. Function 4DH does not indicate an error if you call it when no previous child program has terminated. Also, you can call this function only once for each EXEC call. The second time you call it, you'll get garbage in AH and AL instead of return codes.

Function 4EH (decimal 78): Find First Matching Directory Entry

Function 4EH (decimal 78) searches a directory for a specified name and attribute. Call function 4EH with DS:DX pointing to an ASCIIZ string containing the path and name to be matched. (You can use both * and ? wildcard characters in the search name you specify.) In addition, you must place a directory attribute for the search in CX. You can search for hidden, system, subdirectory, and volume-label directory entries by setting the appropriate bits in CX. (See page 113 for a table of attribute bits.)

❑ NOTE: *Before you call function 4EH, be sure that the current disk transfer area (DTA) is at least 43 bytes in size.*

If this function successfully matches the name you specify to a directory entry, it clears the carry flag and fills the DTA with the data shown in Figure 17-15. If the function fails, it sets the carry flag and returns an error code in AX: 02H (file not found), 03H (path not found), or 12H (no more files; no match found).

This function is similar to function 11H. The file attributes in this search function are the same as they are with an extended FCB in function 11H. (See page 332.)

The attribute search follows a particular logic. If you specify any combination of the hidden, system, or directory attribute bits, the search matches normal files and also any files with the specified attributes. If you specify the volume-label attribute, the search matches only a directory entry with that attribute. The archive and read-only bits do not apply to the search operations.

Offset		*Size*	
Hex	*Dec*	*(bytes)*	*Description*
00H	0	21	Area used by DOS for find-next function 4FH
15H	21	1	Attribute of file found
16H	22	2	Time stamp of file (see page 116)
18H	24	2	Date stamp of file (see page 116)
1AH	26	4	File size in bytes
1EH	30	13	Filename and extension (ASCIIZ string)

Figure 17-15. *The information returned in the DTA by function 4EH.*

Function 4FH (decimal 79): Find Next Matching Directory Entry

Function 4FH (decimal 79) continues a directory search with a name that may match more than one directory entry because it contains wildcard characters. When you call this function, the DTA must contain the data returned by a previous call to function 4EH or 4FH.

If this function finds a matching directory entry, it clears the carry flag and updates the DTA accordingly. If it fails to find a match, it sets the carry flag and returns error code 12H (no more files) in AX.

The usual logic for a wildcard search with functions 4EH and 4FH follows this pattern:

```
initialize DTA address with function 1AH
call function 4EH
WHILE carry flag = 0
    use current contents of DTA
    call function 4FH
```

Function 54H (decimal 84): Get Verify Flag

Function 54H (decimal 84) reports the current state of the verify flag, which controls whether or not DOS verifies disk-write operations. AL = 00H indicates that disk writes will not be verified; AL = 01H indicates that they will be. This function complements function 2EH, which sets or resets the verify flag.

This function brings up an annoying inconsistency in DOS services: While some get/set service pairs are integrated into one function (like function 57H), others are split into two separate functions, like function 54H and function 2EH.

Function 56H (decimal 86): Rename File

Like the standard DOS RENAME command, function 56H (decimal 86) changes the name of a file. But it can also move a file's directory entry from one directory to another. The file itself is not moved, only the directory entry, which means the new and old directory paths must be on the same drive. This is a truly fabulous and useful feature, and it is rather disappointing that it's not a part of the RENAME command.

This function needs two pieces of information: the old and new path and filenames. These can be full-blown file specifications, with drive and path components. The specified or implied drives must be the same so that the new directory entry will be on the same drive as the file. The wildcard characters * and ? cannot be used, because this function works on single files only.

As usual, both file specifications are supplied in the form of ASCIIZ strings. The register pair DS:DX points to the old name string and ES:DI points to the new string.

Function 56H clears the carry flag when it successfully renames a file. If an error occurs, the carry flag is set, and AX contains an error code: 02H (file not found), 03H (path not found), 05H (access denied), or 11H (not the same device). One error that might not be reported occurs if you use function 56H to rename an open file. Be sure to close an open file with function 10H or 3EH before you use function 56H to rename it.

Function 57H (decimal 87): Get/Set File Date and Time

Function 57H (decimal 87) gets or sets a file's date and time. Normally a file's directory entry contains the date and time the file was created or last changed. This function lets you inspect or explicitly update the recorded date and time. AL selects the operation: AL = 00H gets the date and time, and AL = 01H sets the date and time.

The file is selected by placing the file handle in BX, which makes this function applicable only to files that were opened using the handle-based DOS functions covered in this chapter. Thus, setting a file's time stamp with this function will take effect only if the file is successfully closed.

The date and time are placed in registers CX and DX in the same format used in the disk directory entries, though in a slightly different order. In this function, the time is placed in CX and the date in DX.

Use the following formulas to build or break down the date and time:

$$CX = HOUR * 2048 + MINUTE * 32 + SECOND / 2$$
$$DX = (YEAR - 1980) * 512 + MONTH * 32 + DAY$$

If this function fails, it returns an error code in AX: 01H (invalid function number — based on the subfunction selected in AL, not the main function number) or 06H (invalid handle).

Function 58H (decimal 88): Get/Set Memory Allocation Strategy

Function 58H (decimal 88) gets or sets the method DOS uses to allocate free memory to programs. You can choose from three different memory allocation strategies. (See Figure 17-16.) Each strategy assumes that memory resources are broken into blocks of various sizes and that each block can be randomly allocated to a program or freed, depending on the specific requirements of DOS and of each program. You might think that all free

Value in Function 58H	Strategy
0	First fit
1	Best fit
2	Last fit

Figure 17-16. *DOS memory allocation strategies.*

memory would be located in one large block just above where a program ends, but terminate-and-stay-resident programs and device drivers can reserve memory blocks and thereby fragment available memory into two or more smaller blocks.

When DOS responds to a request for memory allocation, it searches through a list of free-memory blocks, starting at the lowest available address and working upward. With the first-fit strategy, DOS allocates the first free block of memory large enough to accommodate the memory-allocation request. With the last-fit strategy, DOS allocates the last free block in the list that is large enough. With the best-fit strategy, DOS searches the entire list and allocates the smallest block that is large enough. DOS uses the first-fit strategy by default.

To obtain the allocation strategy from DOS, call function 58H with AL = 00H. DOS reports the current allocation strategy (00H, 01H, or 02H) in AX. To set the allocation strategy, call this function with AL = 01H and the desired strategy (00H, 01H, or 02H) in BX. The only error detected by this function occurs when you call it with AL > 01H, in which case the carry flag is set and AX contains an error code of 01H (invalid function). This function does not validate the value you pass in BX, so be careful to use a valid value (00H, 01H, or 02H) when you set the allocation strategy.

Function 59H (decimal 89): Get Extended Error Information

Function 59H (decimal 89) is used after an error occurs. It provides detailed information about the errors that occur under these circumstances: inside a critical-error (interrupt 24H) handler, after a DOS function call invoked with interrupt 21H reports an error by setting the carry flag (CF), and after old-style FCB file operations report a return code of FFH. It will not work with other DOS functions that do not report errors in CF, even though they may have ended in an error.

This function is called in the standard way, by placing function code 59H in register AH. You must also specify a version code in the BX register. For DOS version 3, set the version code to 0.

Four types of information are returned on completion of this service:

- AX contains the extended error code.

- BH indicates the class of error.

- BL gives the code of any suggested action that your program should take.

- CH gives a *locus code,* which attempts to show where the error occurred.

Beware: Registers CL, DX, SI, DI, ES, and DS are also changed by function 59H. Save these registers as necessary before you make a call to this function.

The extended error codes can be organized into three groups: Codes 01H through 12H are returned by interrupt 21H functions. Codes 13H through 1FH are used in critical-error (interrupt 24H) handlers. The remaining error codes were introduced in DOS 3.0 and generally report network-related errors. Figure 17-17 lists the extended error codes, Figure 17-18 lists the error classes, Figure 17-19 lists the action codes, and Figure 17-20 lists the locus codes.

Error Code		
Hex	*Dec*	*Description*
Returned by interrupt 21H functions:		
00H	0	(No error)
01H	1	Invalid function number
02H	2	File not found
03H	3	Path not found
04H	4	No more handles (too many open files)
05H	5	Access denied (e.g., attempt to write to read-only file)
06H	6	Invalid handle
07H	7	Memory control blocks destroyed
08H	8	Not enough memory
09H	9	Invalid memory-block address
0AH	10	Invalid environment block
0BH	11	Invalid format
0CH	12	Invalid file-access code

Figure 17-17. *DOS extended error codes.* (*continued*)

Figure 17-17. *continued*

| Error Code | | Description |
Hex	Dec	

Returned by interrupt 21H functions: *(continued)*

0DH	13	Invalid data
0EH	14	(Reserved)
0FH	15	Invalid drive specification
10H	16	Attempt to remove the current directory
11H	17	Not the same device
12H	18	No more files

Used in critical-error (interrupt 24H) handlers:

13H	19	Disk is write-protected
14H	20	Unknown disk unit ID
15H	21	Disk drive not ready
16H	22	Unknown disk command
17H	23	Disk data error
18H	24	Bad disk request structure length
19H	25	Disk seek error
1AH	26	Non-DOS disk
1BH	27	Disk sector not found
1CH	28	Printer out of paper
1DH	29	Write error
1EH	30	Read error
1FH	31	General failure

Used in DOS versions 3.0 and later:

20H	32	File-sharing violation
21H	33	File-locking violation
22H	34	Invalid disk change
23H	35	No FCB available
24H	36	Sharing buffer overflow
25H–31H	37–49	(Reserved)
32H	50	Network request not supported
33H	51	Remote computer not listening

(continued)

Figure 17-17. *continued*

Error Code		
Hex	*Dec*	*Description*

Used in DOS versions 3.0 and later: *(continued)*

34H	52	Duplicate name on network
35H	53	Network name not found
36H	54	Network busy
37H	55	Network device no longer exists
38H	56	Network BIOS command limit exceeded
39H	57	Network adapter hardware error
3AH	58	Incorrect response from network
3BH	59	Unexpected network error
3CH	60	Incompatible remote adapter
3DH	61	Print queue full
3EH	62	Not enough space for print file
3FH	63	Print file was deleted
40H	64	Network name was deleted
41H	65	Access denied
42H	66	Network device type incorrect
43H	67	Network name not found
44H	68	Network name limit exceeded
45H	69	Net BIOS session limit exceeded
46H	70	Sharing temporarily paused
47H	71	Network request not accepted
48H	72	Print or disk redirection is paused
49H–4FH	73–79	(Reserved)
50H	80	File already exists
51H	81	(Reserved)
52H	82	Cannot create directory entry
53H	83	Fail on interrupt 24H
54H	84	Out of network structures
55H	85	Network device already assigned
56H	86	Invalid password
57H	87	Invalid parameter
58H	88	Network data fault

Code		
Hex	**Dec**	**Meaning**
01H	1	Out of resource: no more of whatever you asked for
02H	2	Temporary situation: Try again later
03H	3	Authorization: You aren't allowed; someone else might be
04H	4	Internal error in DOS: not your fault
05H	5	Hardware failure
06H	6	System software error: other DOS problems
07H	7	Application software error: It's your fault
08H	8	Item requested not found
09H	9	Bad format (e.g., unrecognizable disk)
0AH	10	Item locked
0BH	11	Media error (e.g., disk reports CRC error)
0CH	12	Already exists
0DH	13	Error class is unknown

Figure 17-18. *The error classes returned in register BH by function 59H.*

Code		
Hex	**Dec**	**Meaning**
01H	1	Try again several times, then issue ''Abort or Ignore'' prompt.
02H	2	Try again after a pause, then issue ''Abort or Ignore'' prompt.
03H	3	Ask the user to change incorrect information (e.g., bad filename).
04H	4	Shut down the program, but OK to clean up (e.g., close files).
05H	5	Shut down immediately; don't try to clean up.
06H	6	Ignore the error: It's for information only.
07H	7	Retry after user action (e.g., change diskettes).

Figure 17-19. *The suggested action codes returned in register BL by function 59H.*

Code		
Hex	*Dec*	*Meaning*
01H	1	Unknown: sorry
02H	2	Block device (e.g., disk drive)
03H	3	Network
04H	4	Serial device (e.g., printer)
05H	5	Memory

Figure 17-20. *The locus codes returned in register CH by function 59H.*

Function 5AH (decimal 90): Create Temporary File

Function 5AH (decimal 90) was introduced in DOS version 3.0. It creates a file for temporary use. It generates a unique filename for the file by building the name from the current time of day. You provide two parameters: the file attribute, placed in the CX register, and the pathname of the directory where the file will be created. The pathname must be an ASCIIZ string and is pointed to by the register pair DS:DX.

The pathname string must be ready to have the filename of the created file appended to it: The string must end with a backslash character and be followed by 13 bytes to allow enough room for DOS to add a filename to the string. If you don't want to specify a particular path, you can give DOS a null string, which tells it to use the current directory of the current drive.

If function 5AH successfully creates a file, it clears the carry flag and returns the name of the file appended to the pathname you specified in DS:DX. If the function fails, it sets the carry flag and returns an error code in AX: 03H (path not found), 04H (no more handles), or 05H (access denied).

This function is called "create temporary file" only to suggest its intended purpose. Actually, there is nothing temporary about the file that is created because DOS does not automatically delete it; your programs must look after that chore.

Function 5BH (decimal 91): Create New File

Function 5BH (decimal 91) was introduced in DOS version 3.0. It is similar to function 3CH, which is (inaccurately) called the "create-file function." Function 3CH is actually designed to find a file or to create one if the requested file does not exist. By contrast, function 5BH is a pure create-file function and will fail if the file already exists.

As with function 3CH, the CX register is set to the file attribute, and DS:DX contains the address of the pathname and filename (which is stored as an ASCIIZ string). On return, if CF = 0, then AX = file handle for the new file. If CF = 1, then AX contains the error code: 03H (path not found), 04H (no more handles), 05H (access denied), or 50H (file already exists).

You should use function 3CH if you want to reuse a file with a particular filename if it exists or create a file with that name if it doesn't exist. If, however, you simply want to open a file that does not already exist, use function 5BH.

Function 5CH (decimal 92): Lock/Unlock File Region

Function 5CH (decimal 92) locks certain parts of a file so that the file can be shared by several programs without one program interfering with the operations of another. If one program locks one part of a file, it can use or change that part of the file while it is locked, safe in the knowledge that no other program will be able to use that part while it remains locked. As you may guess, file locking is used only in conjunction with file-sharing operations, like those that can occur in a network.

When you call function 5CH, AL indicates whether you are locking (AL = 00H) or unlocking (AL = 01H) a portion of a file. BX gives the file handle. CX and DX are treated as a 4-byte integer that specifies the byte offset of the start of the locked portion of the file. SI and DI also form a 4-byte integer that specifies the length of the locked portion. The first register in each of these register pairs (CX or SI) gives the high-order part of the integer. When function 5CH successfully locks a portion of a file, it clears the carry flag. If an error occurs, the carry flag is set, and AX contains an error code: 01H (invalid function), 06H (invalid handle), 21H (file-locking violation), or 24H (sharing buffer overflow).

You are not allowed to unlock file portions piecemeal or in combination; an unlock request should exactly match a previous lock request. You must also explicitly remove all locks before closing a file or terminating a program that does file locking.

Use function 5CH to lock a file region before you read or write a file that may have been locked by another program; use function 5CH again to unlock the region after the read or write operation is complete. The first call to function 5CH tells you if the part of the file you intend to access is already locked; you should not rely on the read and write functions to return error codes if they access a previously locked region.

Function 5CH is supported only in DOS versions 3.0 and later.

Function 5EH (decimal 94):
Network Machine Name and Printer Setup

Function 5EH (decimal 94) first appeared in DOS version 3.1. It comprises several subfunctions that are useful only to programs running in a network. (See Figure 17-21.) You must specify a subfunction number in AL when you call function 5EH.

| Subfunction | | Description |
Hex	Dec	
00H	0	Get machine name.
02H	2	Set printer setup string.
03H	3	Get printer setup string.

Figure 17-21. *Subfunctions available through interrupt 21H, function 5EH.*

Subfunction 00H. This subfunction retrieves the network name of the computer on which the program is running. Call it with DS:DX pointing to an empty 16-byte buffer. If the function returns successfully, the buffer contains the machine name as an ASCIIZ string; CH contains a flag that, if nonzero, indicates that the machine name is a valid network name; and CL contains the NETBIOS number associated with the machine name.

Subfunction 02H. This subfunction passes a printer setup string to DOS. DOS adds this string to the beginning of any files it sends to a network printer. Call this function with an assign-list index number in BX, the length of the setup string in CX, and DS:SI pointing to the string itself. The assign-list number identifies a particular printer on the network. (See function 5FH.) The maximum length of the string is 64 bytes.

Subfunction 03H. This subfunction complements subfunction 02H. Call it with an assign-list index number in BX and with ES:DI pointing to an empty 64-byte buffer. The subfunction places the requested printer setup string in the buffer and returns the length of the string in CX.

Function 5FH (decimal 95): Network Redirection

Like function 5EH, function 5FH (decimal 95) consists of subfunctions used by programs running in a network. (See Figure 17-22.) In a network environment, DOS maintains an internal table of devices that can be shared across the network; this is called an *assign list* or *redirection list*. The table associates local logical names for such devices with their network names. These subfunctions give a program access to the table.

| Subfunction | | Description |
Hex	Dec	
02H	2	Get assign-list entry.
03H	3	Make assign-list entry.
04H	4	Cancel assign-list entry.

Figure 17-22. *Subfunctions available through interrupt 21H, function 5FH.*

Subfunction 02H. This subfunction obtains the local name and network name for one of the devices in the assign-list table. Call this subfunction with an assign-list index number in BX, with DS:SI pointing to an empty 16-bit buffer, and with ES:DI pointing to an empty 128-byte buffer. The subfunction returns the local device name in the 16-bit buffer and the network name in the 128-byte buffer. The subfunction also indicates the device status in BH (00H = valid device, 01H = invalid device) and the device type in BL (03H = printer, 04H = disk drive), and it updates CX with the user parameter associated with the device through subfunction 03H.

Subfunction 02H is designed to let you step through the assign-list table. The first table entry's assign-list index is 0. By incrementing the assign-list index each time you call this subfunction, you can examine each table entry in turn. When you request a table entry past the end of the table, subfunction 02H sets the carry flag and returns an error code of 12H (no more files) in AX.

Beware: A successful call to subfunction 02H changes DX and BP.

Subfunction 03H. This subfunction redirects a local device to a network device. Call this subfunction with DS:SI containing the address of a 16-byte buffer that contains an ASCIIZ local device name (e.g., PRN or E) and ES:DI pointing to a 128-byte buffer containing an ASCIIZ network device name followed by an ASCIIZ password. You must also specify the device type in BL (03H = printer, 04H = drive) and place a user parameter in CX. (This parameter should be 00H if you are using IBM's Local Area Network software.)

If subfunction 03H successfully establishes redirection of input/output to the network device, it adds a corresponding entry to its assign-list table and clears the carry flag. If the operation fails, the carry flag is set, and AX contains an error code.

Subfunction 04H. This subfunction cancels network redirection of a device and removes the corresponding assign-list table entry. Call it with DS:SI pointing to an ASCIIZ string that specifies the local device whose redirection you want canceled. If the operation is successful, subfunction 04H clears the carry flag.

Function 5FH is supported only in DOS versions 3.1 and later.

Function 62H (decimal 98): Get PSP Address

Function 62H (decimal 98) returns the segment (paragraph address) of the program segment prefix in BX.

When DOS transfers control to a program, registers DS and ES always contain the segment of the program's PSP. Function 62H provides an alternative method of determining this address in DOS versions 3.0 and later.

Function 65H (decimal 101): Get Extended Country Information

Function 65H (decimal 101) was introduced in DOS version 3.3 along with support for global code pages (user-configurable character sets for output devices). It returns a superset of the country information available through function 38H. Function 65H has subfunctions, each of which returns a different type of information. (See Figure 17-23.)

Call function 65H with a subfunction number in AL, a code page number in BX, a buffer size in CX, a country ID in DX, and the address of an empty buffer in ES:DI. Calls with BX = −1 refer to the active code page; calls with DX = −1 return information for the default country ID.

The size of the buffer you supply to this function depends on which subfunction you call. The function clears the carry flag and fills the buffer with the information you requested.

| Subfunction | | Description |
Hex	Dec	
01H	1	Get extended country information.
02H	2	Get pointer to character translation table.
04H	4	Get pointer to filename character translation table.
05H	5	(Reserved)
06H	6	Get pointer to collating sequence.

Figure 17-23. *Subfunctions available through interrupt 21H, function 65H.*

Subfunction 01H. This subfunction returns the same information as function 38H, but also includes the current code page and country ID (Figure 17-24).

Offset Hex	Offset Dec	Size (bytes)	Description
00H	0	1	Subfunction ID (always 01H)
01H	1	2	Size of following information (38 bytes or less)
03H	3	2	Country ID
05H	5	2	Code page
07H	7	2	Date format
09H	9	5	Currency symbol string (ASCIIZ format)
0EH	14	2	Thousands separator string (ASCIIZ format)
10H	16	2	Decimal separator string (ASCIIZ format)
12H	18	2	Date separator string (ASCIIZ format)
14H	20	2	Time separator string (ASCIIZ format)
16H	22	1	Currency symbol location
17H	23	1	Currency decimal places
18H	24	1	Time format
19H	25	4	Extended ASCII map call address
1DH	29	2	List separator string (ASCIIZ format)
1FH	31	10	(Reserved)

Figure 17-24. *Format of extended country information returned by function 65H, subfunction 01H. The information starting at offset 7 is the same as that returned by interrupt 21H, function 38H.*

Subfunction 02H. This subfunction returns 5 bytes of data in the buffer at ES:DI. The first byte always has the value 02H (the subfunction number). The 4 remaining bytes contain the segmented address of a translation table used to convert extended ASCII characters (ASCII codes 80H through FFH) to characters with ASCII codes 00H through FFH. This table is used by the character-mapping routine whose address is returned by subfunction 01H.

Subfunction 04H. This subfunction also fills the buffer at ES:DI with a single subfunction ID byte followed by the 4-byte segmented address of a translation table. This table serves the same purpose as the table whose address is returned by subfunction 02H, but this table is used for filenames.

Subfunction 06H. Like subfunctions 02H and 04H, this subfunction fills the buffer at ES:DI with a subfunction ID byte followed by a segmented address. In this case, the address points to a table that specifies the collating sequence for the character set defined in the code page.

Function 66H (decimal 102): Get/Set Global Code Page

Function 66H (decimal 102), also introduced with DOS version 3.3, consists of two subfunctions that provide support for code page switching within a program. Call this function with a subfunction number (01H or 02H) in AL.

Subfunction 01H. This subfunction returns the number of the active code page in BX. It also reports (in DX) the number of the default code page used when the system is first booted.

Subfunction 02H. Call this subfunction with a new code page number in BX. DOS copies the new code page information from the COUNTRY.SYS file and uses it to update all devices configured for code page switching. For this subfunction to operate successfully, you must include the appropriate DEVICE and COUNTRY commands in your CONFIG.SYS file and also execute the MODE CP PREPARE and NLSFUNC commands. (See your DOS reference manual for details.)

Function 67H (decimal 103): Set Handle Count

Function 67H (decimal 103), introduced in DOS version 3.3, lets a program specify the maximum number of handles it can keep open at any one time. DOS maintains a table of the handles used by a program in a reserved area in the program's PSP. Normally, the limit is 20 handles, of which 5 are automatically opened by DOS for the standard input, output, error, auxiliary, and printer devices.

To increase the maximum number of open handles, call function 67H with the maximum number of desired handles in BX. DOS will allocate a new block of memory and use it to store an expanded table of handles. The function clears the carry flag to indicate success; if the carry flag is set, AX contains an error code.

Remember two points about function 67H:

- If you are running a COM program that uses all available memory, it must call function 4AH to shrink its memory allocation before DOS can allocate a memory block for the handle table.

- The size of DOS's internal file table imposes an upper limit on the number of handles you can open. You can increase the size of that table with the FILES command in your CONFIG.SYS file.

Function 68H (decimal 104): Commit File

Function 68H (decimal 104) was first supported in DOS version 3.3. When you call this function with an open file handle in BX, DOS flushes the disk buffer associated with the handle and updates the disk directory accordingly. This ensures that data written to the disk buffer but not yet physically written on a disk will not be lost should a power failure or other mishap occur.

By executing function 68H, you obtain the same result that you would by using function 45H to duplicate a file handle and then using function 3EH to close the duplicate handle.

Chapter 18

DOS Functions Summary

This chapter summarizes the DOS functions and is designed to be used as a quick reference guide. For details about the specific operation of each function, see Chapters 15 through 17. Once you understand the DOS functions, these tables should provide you with most of the programming information you'll need.

Short Summary

Figure 18-1 lists the five interrupts that can be executed to obtain various DOS functions. Of these, interrupt 21H is by far the most useful — it is the function-call interrupt that provides general access to nearly all DOS functions. Interrupts 25H and 26H, the absolute disk read/write interface, may occasionally be needed to bypass the usual DOS file interface. The remaining interrupts, 20H and 27H, provide program-termination services in DOS version 1 that were made obsolete by interrupt 21H functions introduced in DOS version 2.0. Chapter 15 covers the DOS interrupts in detail.

| *Interrupt* | | |
Hex	*Dec*	*Description*
20H	32	Program terminate: Come to a normal ending.
21H	33	General DOS functions.
25H	37	Absolute disk read.
26H	38	Absolute disk write.
27H	39	Terminate and stay resident.

Figure 18-1. *The five main DOS interrupts.*

Figure 18-2 lists the interrupt 21H functions introduced with DOS version 1 and supported in all versions of DOS. These functions are discussed in Chapter 16.

Figure 18-3 lists the expanded set of interrupt 21H functions introduced in DOS version 2.0 and augmented in later DOS versions. Chapter 17 describes these functions.

All interrupt 21H functions are called by executing interrupt 21H with a function number in the AH register and other parameters as needed in the other 8086 registers. Most DOS functions return a completion code in the AL or AX register; most of the functions introduced in DOS versions 2.0 and later also use the carry flag to report the success of a function call. See Chapters 16 and 17 for several program examples of interrupt 21H calls.

Function		Description
Hex	Dec	
00H	0	Terminate.
01H	1	Character Input with Echo.
02H	2	Character Output.
03H	3	Auxiliary Input.
04H	4	Auxiliary Output.
05H	5	Printer Output.
06H	6	Direct Character Input/Output.
07H	7	Direct Character Input Without Echo.
08H	8	Character Input Without Echo.
09H	9	String Output.
0AH	10	Buffered Keyboard Input.
0BH	11	Check Keyboard Status.
0CH	12	Flush Keyboard Buffer, Read Keyboard.
0DH	13	Flush Disk Buffers.
0EH	14	Select Disk Drive.
0FH	15	Open File.
10H	16	Close File.
11H	17	Find First Matching Directory Entry.
12H	18	Find Next Matching Directory Entry.
13H	19	Delete File.
14H	20	Sequential Read.
15H	21	Sequential Write.
16H	22	Create File.
17H	23	Rename File.
19H	25	Get Current Disk.
1AH	26	Set DTA Address.
1BH	27	Get Default Drive Information.
1CH	28	Get Specified Drive Information.
21H	33	Read Random Record.
22H	34	Write Random Record.
23H	35	Get File Size.
24H	36	Set FCB Random Record Field.
25H	37	Set Interrupt Vector.
26H	38	Create New PSP.
27H	39	Read Random Records.

Figure 18-2. *Interrupt 21H functions available in all DOS versions.*   *(continued)*

Figure 18-2. *continued*

| Function | | Description |
Hex	Dec	Description
28H	40	Write Random Records.
29H	41	Parse Filename.
2AH	42	Get Date.
2BH	43	Set Date.
2CH	44	Get Time.
2DH	45	Set Time.
2EH	46	Set Verify Flag.

| Function | | Description | DOS |
Hex	Dec	Description	Version
2FH	47	Get DTA Address.	2.0
30H	48	Get DOS Version Number.	2.0
31H	49	Terminate and Stay Resident.	2.0
33H	51	Get/Set Ctrl-C Flag.	2.0
35H	53	Get Interrupt Vector.	2.0
36H	54	Get Disk Free Space.	2.0
38H	56	Get/Set Country-Dependent Information.	2.0
39H	57	Create Directory.	2.0
3AH	58	Remove Directory.	2.0
3BH	59	Change Current Directory.	2.0
3CH	60	Create File.	2.0
3DH	61	Open File.	2.0
3EH	62	Close File.	2.0
3FH	63	Read from File or Device.	2.0
40H	64	Write to File or Device.	2.0
41H	65	Delete File.	2.0
42H	66	Move File Pointer.	2.0
43H	67	Get/Set File Attributes.	2.0
44H	68	IOCTL — I/O Control for Devices.	2.0
45H	69	Duplicate File Handle.	2.0
46H	70	Force Duplicate File Handle.	2.0

Figure 18-3. *Interrupt 21H functions available in DOS versions 2.0 and later.* *(continued)*

Figure 18-3. *continued*

| Function | | Description | DOS |
Hex	Dec		Version
47H	71	Get Current Directory.	2.0
48H	72	Allocate Memory Block.	2.0
49H	73	Free Memory Block.	2.0
4AH	74	Resize Memory Block.	2.0
4BH	75	Load and Execute a Program.	2.0
4CH	76	Terminate with Return Code.	2.0
4DH	77	Get Return Code.	2.0
4EH	78	Find First Matching Directory Entry.	2.0
4FH	79	Find Next Matching Directory Entry.	2.0
54H	84	Get Verify Flag.	2.0
56H	86	Rename File.	2.0
57H	87	Get/Set File Date and Time.	2.0
58H	88	Get/Set Memory Allocation Strategy.	3.0
59H	89	Get Extended Error Information.	3.0
5AH	90	Create Temporary File.	3.0
5BH	91	Create New File.	3.0
5CH	92	Lock/Unlock File Region.	3.0
5EH	94	Network Machine Name and Printer Setup.	3.1
5FH	95	Network Redirection.	3.1
62H	98	Get PSP Address.	3.0
65H	101	Get Extended Country Information.	3.3
66H	102	Get/Set Global Code Page.	3.3
67H	103	Set Handle Count.	3.3
68H	104	Commit File.	3.3

Long Summary

In the last section, we briefly listed all the DOS functions so that individual functions could be found by their function number. In this section, we have expanded the listing to show the register values passed to and returned from interrupt 21H functions.

Since most new versions of DOS have introduced new functions that cannot be used with earlier versions, we have included the DOS version number in which each function was introduced.

Service	Function (hex)	Register Input	Output	DOS Version	Notes
Program Control Functions					
Terminate: End program.	00H	AH = 00H CS = segment of PSP		1.0	Obsolete: Use function 4CH instead.
Create new program segment.	26H	AH = 26H DX = segment where new PSP starts		1.0	Obsolete: Use function 4BH instead.
Terminate and stay resident.	31H	AH = 31H AL = return code DX = # of paragraphs to keep resident		2.0	
Get/set Ctrl-C flag.	33H	AH = 33H *To set flag:* AL = 01H DL = value *To get flag:* AL = 00H	AL = result code *If called with AL = 01H:* DL = current value of flag (0 = off, 1 = on)	2.0	
EXEC: Load and execute a program.	4BH	AH = 4BH DS:DX → ASCIIZ command line ES:BX → control block *To execute child program:* AL = 00H	*If no error:* CF clear *If error:* CF set AX = error code	2.0	Changes all registers, including SS:SP.

Figure 18-4. *A summary of the DOS interrupt 21H functions.*   *(continued)*

Figure 18-4. *continued*

Service	Function (hex)	Register Input	Output	DOS Version	Notes
EXEC: Load and execute a program. *(continued)*		*To load without executing:* AL = 03H			
Terminate with return code.	4CH	AH = 4CH AL = return code		2.0	
Get return code.	4DH	AH = 4DH	AL = return code AH = termination method	2.0	Call only once after calling function 4CH.
Get PSP address.	62H	AH = 62H	BX = PSP segment	3.0	

Standard Input Functions

Service	Function (hex)	Register Input	Output	DOS Version	Notes
Character input with echo.	01H	AH = 01H	AL = 8-bit character	1.0	
Direct character input without echo.	07H	AH = 07H	AL = 8-bit character	1.0	
Character input without echo.	08H	AH = 08H	AL = 8-bit character	1.0	
Buffered keyboard input.	0AH	AH = 0AH DS:DX → input buffer	Buffer contains keyboard input.	1.0	See Chapter 16 for input buffer format.
Check keyboard status.	0BH	AH = 0BH	*If character available:* AL = FFH *If no character available:* AL = 00H	1.0	
Flush keyboard buffer, read keyboard.	0CH	AH = 0CH AL = function number (01H, 06H, 07H, 08H, or 0AH)	*(Depends on function specified in AL)*	1.0	

(continued)

Figure 18-4. *continued*

Service	Function (hex)	Register Input	Output	DOS Version	Notes
Standard Output Functions					
Character output.	02H	AH = 02H DL = 8-bit character		1.0	
String output.	09H	AH = 09H DS:DX → string terminated with '$'		1.0	
Console I/O Functions					
Direct character input/output.	06H	AH = 06H *To input a character:* DL = FFH *To output a character:* DL = 8-bit character (00H–FEH)	*If called with* *DL = FFH:* AL = 8-bit character	1.0	
Miscellaneous I/O Functions					
Auxiliary input.	03H	AH = 03H	AL = 8-bit character	1.0	
Auxiliary output.	04H	AH = 04H DL = character		1.0	
Printer output.	05H	AH = 05H DL = character		1.0	
Disk Functions					
Flush disk buffers.	0DH	AH = 0DH		1.0	See also function 68H
Select disk drive.	0EH	AH = 0EH DL = drive ID	AL = number of drives in system	1.0	In DOS 3.0 and later, AL >= 05H.

(continued)

Figure 18-4. *continued*

Service	Function (hex)	Register Input	Output	DOS Version	Notes
Get current disk.	19H	AH = 19H	AL = drive ID	1.0	
Set DTA address.	1AH	AH = 1AH DS:DX → DTA		1.0	
Get default drive information.	1BH	AH = 1BH	AL = sectors per cluster CX = bytes per sector DX = total clusters on disk DS:BX → media ID byte	1.0	Obsolete: Use function 36H instead.
Get specified drive information.	1CH	AH = 1CH DL = drive ID	AL = sectors per cluster CX = bytes per sector DX = total clusters on disk DS:BX → media ID byte	1.0	Obsolete: Use function 36H instead.
Set verify flag.	2EH	AH = 2EH AL = value for flag (0 = off, 1 = on) DL = 00H		1.0	Call with DL = 00H in DOS versions prior to 3.0.
Get DTA address.	2FH	AH = 2FH	ES:BX → DTA	2.0	
Get disk free space.	36H	AH = 36H DL = drive ID	*If bad drive ID:* AX = FFFFH *If no error:* AX = sectors per cluster BX = unused clusters CX = bytes per sector DX = total clusters on disk	2.0	

(continued)

Figure 18-4. *continued*

Service	Function (hex)	Register Input	Output	DOS Version	Notes
Get verify flag.	54H	AH = 54H	AL = value of flag (0 = off, 1 = on)	2.0	

File Management Functions

Service	Function (hex)	Register Input	Output	DOS Version	Notes
Delete file.	13H	AH = 13H DS:DX → FCB	*If error:* AL = FFH *If no error:* AL = 0	1.0	Obsolete: Use function 41H instead.
Create file.	16H	AH = 16H DS:DX → FCB	*If error:* AL = FFH *If no error:* AL = 00H	1.0	Obsolete: Use function 3CH, 5AH, or 5BH instead.
Rename file.	17H	AH = 17H DS:DX → modified FCB	*If error:* AL = FFH *If no error:* AL = 00H	1.0	Obsolete: Use function 56H instead.
Get file size.	23H	AH = 23H DS:DX → FCB	*If error:* AL = FFH *If no error:* AL = 00H FCB contains file size.	1.0	Obsolete: Use function 42H instead.
Parse filename.	29H	AH = 29H AL = control bits DS:SI → string to parse ES:DI → FCB	AL = error code DS:SI → byte past parsed string ES:DI → FCB	1.0	Cannot parse pathnames.

(continued)

Figure 18-4. *continued*

Service	Function (hex)	Register Input	Output	DOS Version	Notes
Create file.	3CH	AH = 3CH CX = attribute DS:DX → ASCIIZ file specification	*If error:* CF set AX = error code *If no error:* CF clear AX = handle	2.0	
Delete file.	41H	AH = 41H DS:DX → ASCIIZ file specification	*If error:* CF set AX = error code *If no error:* CF clear	2.0	
Get/set file attributes.	43H	AH = 43H DS:DX → ASCIIZ file specification *To get attributes:* AL = 00H *To set attributes:* AL = 01H CX = attributes	*If error:* CF set AX = error code *If no error:* CF clear CX = attributes (if called with AL = 00H)	2.0	
Rename file.	56H	AH = 56H DS:DX → old ASCIIZ file specification ES:DI → new ASCIIZ file specification	*If error:* CF set AX = error code *If no error:* CF clear	2.0	May be used to move a file from one directory to another.
Get/set file date and time.	57H	AH = 57H BX = handle *To get date and time:* AL = 00H *To set date and time:* AL = 01H CX = time DX = date	*If error:* CF set AX = error code *If no error:* CF clear *If called with AL = 00H:* CX = time DX = date	2.0	

(continued)

Figure 18-4. *continued*

Service	Function (hex)	Register Input	Output	DOS Version	Notes
Create temporary file.	5AH	AH = 5AH CX = attribute DS:DX → ASCIIZ path followed by 13 empty bytes	*If error:* CF set AX = error code *If no error:* CF clear AX = handle DS:DX → ASCIIZ file specification	3.0	
Create new file.	5BH	AH = 5BH CX = attribute DS:DX → ASCIIZ file specification	*If error:* CF set AX = error code *If no error:* CF clear AX = handle	3.0	

File I/O Functions

Service	Function (hex)	Register Input	Output	DOS Version	Notes
Open file.	0FH	AH = 0FH DS:DX → FCB	AL = result code	1.0	Obsolete: Use function 3DH instead.
Close file.	10H	AH = 10H DS:DX → FCB	*If no error:* AL = result code	1.0	Obsolete: Use function 3EH instead.
Sequential read.	14H	AH = 14H DS:DX → FCB	AL = result code DTA contains data read.	1.0	Obsolete: Use function 3FH instead.
Sequential write.	15H	AH = 15H DS:DX → FCB DTA contains data to write.	AL = result code	1.0	Obsolete: Use function 40H instead.
Read random record.	21H	AH = 21H DS:DX → FCB	AL = result code DTA contains data read.	1.0	Obsolete: Use function 3FH instead.

(continued)

Figure 18-4. *continued*

Service	Function (hex)	Register Input	Output	DOS Version	Notes
Write random record.	22H	AH = 22H DS:DX → FCB DTA contains data to write.	AL = result code	1.0	Obsolete: Use function 40H instead.
Set FCB random record field.	24H	AH = 24H DS:DX → FCB	AL = 00H FCB contains updated random record field.	1.0	Obsolete: Use function 42H instead.
Read random records.	27H	AH = 27H CX = record count DS:DX → FCB	AL = result code CX = number of records read DTA contains data read.	1.0	Obsolete: Use function 3FH instead.
Write random records.	28H	AH = 28H CX = record count DS:DX → FCB DTA contains data to write.	AL = result code CX = number of records written	1.0	Obsolete: Use function 40H instead.
Open handle.	3DH	AH = 3DH AL = file access code DS:DX → ASCIIZ file specification	*If error:* CF set AX = error code *If no error:* CF clear AX = handle	2.0	
Close handle.	3EH	AH = 3EH BX = handle	*If error:* CF set AX = error code *If no error:* CF clear	2.0	

(continued)

Figure 18-4. *continued*

Service	Function (hex)	Register Input	Output	DOS Version	Notes
Read from file or device.	3FH	AH = 3FH BX = handle CX = number of bytes to read DS:DX → buffer	*If error:* CF set AX = error code *If no error:* CF clear AX = number of bytes read DS:DX → buffer	2.0	
Write to file or device.	40H	AH = 40H BX = handle CX = number of bytes to write DS:DX → buffer	*If error:* CF set AX = error code *If no error:* CF clear AX = number of bytes written	2.0	
Move file pointer.	42H	AH = 42H BX = handle CX:DX = offset to move pointer *Move relative to start of file:* AL = 00H *Move relative to current location:* AL = 01H *Move relative to end of file:* AL = 02H	*If error:* CF set AX = error code *If no error:* CF clear DX:AX = new file pointer	2.0	
Duplicate file handle.	45H	AH = 45H BX = handle	*If error:* CF set AX = error code *If no error:* CF clear AX = new handle	2.0	See Chapter 17 for details.

(continued)

Figure 18-4. *continued*

Service	Function (hex)	Register Input	Output	DOS Version	Notes
Force duplicate file handle.	46H	AH = 46H BX = handle CX = handle to be forced	*If error:* CF set AX = error code *If no error:* CF clear	2.0	See Chapter 17 for details.
Lock/Unlock file region.	5CH	AH = 5CH BX = handle CX:DX = start of region to lock/unlock SI:DI = size of region to lock/unlock *To lock region:* AL = 00H *To unlock region:* AL = 01H	*If error:* CF set AX = error code *If no error:* CF clear	3.0	Use with SHARE or in network environment.
Set handle count.	67H	AH = 67H BX = number of handles	*If error:* CF set AX = error code *If no error:* CF clear	3.3	
Commit file.	68H	AH = 68H BX = handle	*If error:* CF set AX = error code *If no error:* CF clear	3.3	

Directory Functions

Service	Function (hex)	Register Input	Output	DOS Version	Notes
Find first matching directory entry.	11H	AH = 11H DS:DX → FCB	*If error:* AL = FFH *If no error:* AL = 00H DTA contains directory information.	1.0	Obsolete: Use function 4EH instead.

(continued)

Figure 18-4. *continued*

Service	Function (hex)	Register Input	Output	DOS Version	Notes
Find next matching directory entry.	12H	AH = 12H DS:DX → FCB	*If error:* AL = FFH *If no error:* AL = 00H DTA contains directory information.	1.0	Obsolete: Use function 4FH instead.
Create directory.	39H	AH = 39H DS:DX → ASCIIZ path	*If error:* CF set AX = error code *If no error:* CF clear	2.0	
Remove directory.	3AH	AH = 3AH DS:DX → ASCIIZ path	*If error:* CF set AX = error code *If no error:* CF clear	2.0	
Change current directory.	3BH	AH = 3BH DS:DX → ASCIIZ path	*If error:* CF set AX = error code *If no error:* CF clear	2.0	
Get current directory.	47H	AH = 47H DL = drive ID DS:SI → empty 64-byte buffer	*If error:* CF set AX = error code *If no error:* CF clear DS:SI → ASCIIZ path	2.0	
Find first matching directory entry.	4EH	AH = 4EH CX = attribute DS:DX → ASCIIZ file specification	*If error:* CF set AX = error code	2.0	

(continued)

Figure 18-4. *continued*

Service	Function (hex)	Register Input	Output	DOS Version	Notes
Find first matching directory entry. *(continued)*			*If no error:* CF clear DTA contains directory information.		
Find next matching directory entry.	4FH	AH = 4FH DTA contains information from previous call to function 4EH or 4FH.	*If error:* CF set AX = error code *If no error:* CF clear DTA contains directory information.	2.0	

Date/Time Functions

Service	Function (hex)	Register Input	Output	DOS Version	Notes
Get date.	2AH	AH = 2AH	AL = day of week CX = year DH = month DL = day	1.0	
Set date.	2BH	AH = 2BH CX = year DH = month DL = day	*If error:* AL = FFH *If no error:* AL = 00H	1.0	
Get time.	2CH	AH = 2CH	CH = hours CL = minutes DH = seconds DL = 100ths of seconds	1.0	
Set time.	2DH	AH = 2DH CH = hours CL = minutes DH = seconds DL = 100ths of seconds	*If error:* AL = FFH *If no error:* AL = 00H	1.0	

(continued)

Figure 18-4. *continued*

Service	Function (hex)	Register Input	Output	DOS Version	Notes
Miscellaneous Functions					
Set interrupt vector.	25H	AH = 25H AL = interrupt number DS:DX = segmented address for specified interrupt vector		1.0	
Get DOS version number.	30H	AH = 30H	AH = minor version number AL = major version number BX, CX = serial number	2.0	DOS version 1.0 returns AL = 00H. OS/2 com- patibility box returns AL = 0AH.
Get interrupt vector.	35H	AH = 35H AL = interrupt number	ES:BX = contents of specified interrupt vector	2.0	
Get/set country-dependent information.	38H	AH = 38H AL = country code *or* FFH BX = country code (if AL = FFH) *To get country information:* DS:DX → empty 34-byte buffer *To set country information:* DX = FFFFH	*If error:* CF set AX = error code *If no error:* CF clear *If called with DX <> FFFFH:* BX = country code DS:DX → country information	2.0	Calls with DX = FFFFH or AL = FFH are supported only in DOS versions 3.0 and later. See also function 65H.
IOCTL.	44H	AH = 44H AL = subfunction number	*If error:* CF set AX = error code	2.0	See Chapter 17 for details.

(continued)

Figure 18-4. *continued*

Service	Function (hex)	Register Input	Output	DOS Version	Notes
IOCTL. (continued)		*(Other registers depend on subfunction.)*	*If no error:* CF clear *(Other registers depend on subfunction.)*		
Get extended error information.	59H	AH = 59H BX = 00H	AX = extended error code BH = error class BL = suggested action CH = location of error	3.0	Alters CL, DX, SI, DI, ES, and DS. See Chapter 17 for details.
Network machine name and printer setup.	5EH	AH = 5EH AL = subfunction number *(Other registers depend on subfunction.)*	*If error:* CF set AX = error code *If no error:* CF clear *(Other registers depend on subfunction.)*	3.1	Use in network environment only. See Chapter 17 for details.
Network redirection.	5FH	AH = 5FH AL = subfunction number *(Other registers depend on subfunction.)*	*If error:* CF set AX = error code *If no error:* CF clear *(Other registers depend on subfunction.)*	3.1	Use in network environment only. See Chapter 17 for details.
Get extended country information.	65H	AH = 65H AL = information ID code BX = code page number CX = buffer length DX = country ID ES:DI → buffer	*If error:* CF set AX = error code *If no error:* CF clear ES:DI → extended country information	3.3	See Chapter 17 for details.

(continued)

Figure 18-4. *continued*

Service	Function (hex)	Register Input	Output	DOS Version	Notes
Get/set global code page.	66H	AH = 66H *To get current code page:* AL = 01H *To set code page:* AL = 02H BX = code page number	*If error:* CF set AX = error code *If no error:* CF clear *If called with AL = 01H:* BX = current code page DX = default code page	3.3	

Memory Functions

Service	Function (hex)	Register Input	Output	DOS Version	Notes
Allocate memory block.	48H	AH = 48H BX = size of block in paragraphs	*If error:* CF set AX = error code BX = size of largest available block *If no error:* CF clear AX = paragraph address of allocated block	2.0	
Free memory block.	49H	AH = 49H ES = paragraph address of memory block	*If error:* CF set AX = error code *If no error:* CF clear	2.0	
Resize memory block.	4AH	AH = 4AH BX = new size of memory block in paragraphs ES = paragraph address of memory block	*If error:* CF set AX = error code BX = size of largest available block (if increased size was requested)	2.0	

(continued)

Figure 18-4. *continued*

Service	Function (hex)	Register Input	Output	DOS Version	Notes
Resize memory block. *(continued)*			*If no error:* CF clear		
Get/set memory allocation strategy.	58H	AH = 58H *To get allocation strategy:* AL = 00H *To set allocation strategy:* AL = 01H BX = strategy code	*If error:* CF set AX = error code *If no error:* CF clear *If called with AL = 00H:* AX = strategy code	3.0	See Chapter 17 for details.

Chapter 19

Program Building

As we've mentioned before, the wisest approach to programming the PC family is to write nearly all your programs in a high-level language (such as BASIC, Pascal, or C) and when necessary use the DOS or ROM BIOS services for whatever the high-level languages don't provide. On occasion, you may also want to create your own assembly-language routines to perform specialized tasks not available through your programming language or system services.

When creating programs within the confines of a single programming language, you really don't need to know anything more about a language than what you can find in the manuals that come with it. However, if you need to break out of the bounds of a single language to access DOS or ROM BIOS routines, or perhaps to tie into a program that's written in a different language, you'll need to dig deeper into the technical aspects of both DOS (to learn how to link programs together) and the programming languages (to learn the requirements for program interfaces, which let the different languages communicate with each other).

This chapter presents some overall considerations that apply to the advanced use of most programming languages. We'll start by describing the structure of the executable programs generated by compilers and assemblers. Later we'll consider the details of combining separate program modules into a unified program.

Structure of an Executable Program

Every language translator imposes a certain structure on each executable program it generates. This structure is partly determined by the structure of the source code, but it also reflects the way the 8086 addresses memory.

The Memory Map

DOS loads an executable program by reading the contents of a .COM or .EXE file directly into an area of free memory. The layout of executable code and data in memory — the *memory map* — reflects the structure of the executable file, which in turn is primarily determined by the language translator you use to compile or assemble your program. Although language translators differ, most of them produce executable programs in which logically separate portions of the program are mapped in different blocks of memory. (See Figure 19-1.)

This memory map fits comfortably into the addressing schemes that are natural to the 8086: The executable code is addressed through the CS register; the program data is accessed through the DS and ES registers; and the SS register points to the stack.

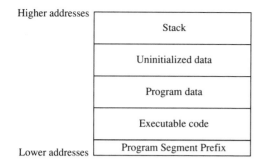

Higher addresses

Stack

Uninitialized data

Program data

Executable code

Program Segment Prefix

Lower addresses

Figure 19-1. *Memory usage in a typical DOS program.*

❏ NOTE: *This memory map is also practical because it conforms to the memory conventions for programs that run in a protected-mode environment like OS/2. In protected mode, the 80286 and 80386 require you to use particular segment registers to address executable code and data. When you write a program to run in protected mode, you must avoid storing data values in a code segment or branching to executable code in a data segment.*

The Use of Registers

An executable program whose code, data, and stack are mapped to distinct areas of memory can make efficient use of the 8086 registers. This is because the 8086's segment registers can each address a different portion of the memory map:

- The CS and IP registers point to the currently executing instruction.

- The DS register is used in combination with BX, SI, or DI to access program data.

- The SS register is used in combination with the SP and BP registers to point to data in the program's stack. The SS:SP combination points to the top of the stack, and SS:BP can be used to access data above or below the top of the stack.

These aren't hard-and-fast rules for register usage. They are a natural consequence of the way the 8086 register set is designed.

Memory Models

There are various ways to produce an executable program whose memory map comprises separate code, data, and stack segments. The way a particular program addresses the different areas of its memory map is determined by the program's *memory model*.

A memory model specifically describes how executable code and data are addressed within a program. For example, the 8086 imposes a limit of 64 KB in any given segment, so a program with more than 64 KB of executable code must be mapped into more than one executable code segment. Similarly, a program with more than 64 KB of data must store that data in at least two different data segments. Thus the simple memory model shown in Figure 19-1 can be elaborated upon—into four different memory models. (See Figure 19-2.)

The memory model you use affects how your program uses segment registers. In a small-model program, the CS and DS registers can be initialized at the start of a program and left undisturbed for the duration. Contrast this with a large-model program, where the CS register must be changed whenever the program branches from one code segment to another, and the DS or ES registers must often be updated whenever data from different segments must be accessed.

Some high-level language compilers let you specify which memory model to use. (See your compiler documentation for more information.) If you know your program contains fewer than 64 KB of executable code and fewer than 64 KB of data, you can explicitly request such a compiler to generate a small-model executable program. (This is the memory model we have used in all the assembly-language examples in previous chapters.) Other compilers can use a compact, medium, or large model, regardless of the program size. Whatever the case, you should know what memory model your compiler uses if you want to understand how the different parts of an executable program fit together.

Model	*Number of Code Segments*	*Number of Data Segments*
Small	1	1
Compact	1	More than 1
Medium	More than 1	1
Large	More than 1	More than 1

Figure 19-2. *Four common memory models.*

Subroutine Interfaces

A *subroutine interface* is a layer of assembly-language code that lets a program written in a high-level language communicate with an assembly-language subroutine. A subroutine interface has two main parts: a control interface and a data interface.

The control interface handles the business of *calling and returning;* that is, of passing control of the computer from the calling program to a subroutine and back again. The control interface, by the way, can be tricky to program. It is remarkably simple if you know how to program properly, but you can create incredible messes if you make even minor programming errors.

The data interface lets the calling program and a subroutine share data. In order to share successfully, you need to know how each side of the interface finds and works with data, and you must understand how data is formatted so that each side can interpret it in the same way. We'll be covering these topics in more detail in the next chapter.

All three program elements — the calling program, the called subroutine, and the interface — must accomplish the following in order to work together successfully:

The program must be able to find its way to the subroutine. In the 8086-based system of the standard PC family, a subroutine is called through a CALL instruction. There are two kinds of CALL instruction:

- The near CALL locates a subroutine within the current 64 KB code segment (CS) and does not require the CS register to be changed.

- The far CALL locates a subroutine outside the current CS using a complete segmented address in the CALL instruction (which changes the CS setting). Because it needs to access only one executable code segment, a small-model or compact-model program uses near CALLs to call subroutines. A medium-model or large-model program uses far CALLs so that it can change CS and access multiple code segments.

The subroutine must know what to do when finished. A subroutine typically returns to the calling program with an instruction that corresponds to the way it was called (that is, with a near or far RET instruction). Occasionally, however, a subroutine does something unusual — for example, you may want to terminate a program and return to DOS from a subroutine.

The subroutine must know what supporting framework is provided by the caller. A typical supporting framework describes how the segment registers are set and whether a stack is available for use. In general, the segment registers are exactly as they should be: CS has the right code segment, DS points to the location of the calling program's data, and SS and SP are set up with the caller's stack.

The called subroutine usually can continue to use the caller's stack, but there is no practical way to know how much working space is available. If the subroutine's needs are reasonable — say, fewer than 64 bytes — the caller's stack space should be adequate. However, if the subroutine should need more working space, it can set up its own stack space in memory.

If the program needs to pass information (parameters) to the subroutine, both the program and the subroutine must know how many parameters exist, where they are, and what they are. Programs and subroutines typically work with a fixed number of parameters, although some languages, including C, can handle a variable number of parameters. The parameters are usually passed to the subroutine through the stack, either directly or indirectly. The direct method, known as *pass-by-value,* passes the actual value of the parameter through the stack; the indirect method, known as *pass-by-reference,* passes the parameter's address through the stack.

The parameter-passing method used depends primarily on the language; some languages place only addresses — never parameter values — on the stack. With languages that can handle both addresses and values, you have a lot more freedom to decide which method to use, and the method you use lets you control how the parameters are dealt with as they are passed from one program to another.

For example, if you want to protect a caller's parameter from being changed by the called subroutine, you'll use the pass-by-value method to pass a copy of the parameter's value on the stack. But if you want the parameter's value to be changed by the called subroutine, you must use the pass-by-reference method so that the subroutine can change the parameter's value by modifying the contents of memory at the specified address.

Parameter passing is the most complicated part of the subroutine interface, made even more complicated by the different ways programming languages deal with data and stack information. Because of its complexity and variability from one language to another, parameter passing is the main issue we'll discuss in our language comparisons in the next chapter.

The subroutine must preserve certain information. Although requirements may vary in different situations, a few ground rules govern what information should be preserved, and what can and cannot be done when calling a subroutine.

- Interrupts can be suspended briefly when segment registers are changed; they must be turned back on before returning. (See page 52.)

- The contents of any CPU registers used by the calling program as well as the subroutine are preserved by being pushed on the stack.

- The BP and DS registers should usually be saved and restored if they are changed within a subroutine.

Register usage varies: One compiler may rely on the contents of ES being constant, and another might require you to preserve SI and DI if you use them in a subroutine. See your compiler manual for specific information.

The stack must be cleaned up after the subroutine is finished. Four things might clutter the stack when a subroutine is finished: some parameters, the return address from the CALL instruction, register values saved from before the CALL, and some working storage from the subroutine.

Three of these leftovers are not problems: Subroutines are expected to remove their own working storage from the stack, saved registers are removed by POP instructions, and the return address is removed by the RET instruction. The parameters, however, usually complicate the clean-up process, because the method of removal varies in different languages. Some languages expect the subroutine to remove the parameters by specifying in the RET instruction the number of bytes to remove from the stack. Other languages expect the caller to remove them. We'll point out these differences as we discuss some languages in detail in Chapter 20.

With all these program design elements in mind, let's step back a bit farther and see how the whole process works—from creating a program or subroutine to combining it with others.

Combining Program Modules

In this section, we're going to describe the general process of putting a program together from two or more program modules. Programming languages—and programmers—vary in the way they perform this process, but in general, the tools you use and the sequence of operations you carry out are the same for most language translators. (See Figure 19-3.)

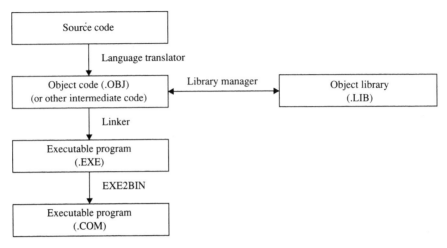

Figure 19-3. *Building an executable program. By convention, object filenames use the .OBJ extension; object libraries use .LIB; executable files use .EXE or .COM.*

Step 1: Writing the Source Code

To begin with, you have to write your program using the commands and syntax of your programming language. This form of the program is known as the *source code*. For programming languages that use the standard DOS conventions, the source code must be in the form of an ASCII text file. (See Appendix C.) Interpreted BASIC does not normally use the ASCII text file format for its source files, but it can. (To create ASCII text files with the BASIC interpreter, use the A option of the SAVE command.)

By convention, source-code files have a filename extension that reflects the name of the programming language used, such as BAS or C.

Step 2: Translating the Source Code

The next step in creating an executable program is to process the source code with a language translator. For assembly language, the translator is called an *assembler;* for high-level languages like Pascal and C, the translator is called a *compiler*. A translator converts source code into machine-language instructions, in a form known as *object code*. Object code contains executable machine code, but also includes additional information about the structure of the executable program. The object-code format is designed so that separate object modules can be combined into a single, unified program. Object-code files, by convention, have a filename extension of .OBJ.

You can also use an interpreter to translate a program built from separate source-code modules. Interpreters, however, are rarely capable of generating object code, so binding separate program modules together generally relies on improvised language-specific programming, as we'll see in Chapter 20.

Step 3: Linking

The next basic step is to link the object modules together. The *linker,* or link-editor program (known as LINK in DOS) performs two main tasks: It combines separate object modules (as needed), making all the necessary connections between them; and it converts the modules from an object-code format to a loadable program in the .EXE format.

The actual combining, or linking, of program modules to create an .EXE file is the most important aspect of this discussion. We'll take it up again later in this chapter, after we've covered two other steps that are involved in preparing programs.

Step 4: Converting File Formats

A program that uses one of the memory models we described earlier is ready to run after you use LINK to create an .EXE file. But if you have a fairly simple program, or if you long for the good old days of CP/M compatibility and an absolute maximum program size of 64 KB, you can convert your .EXE program into a .COM file. Before you do, however, be sure your program conforms to the restrictions imposed by the .COM format.

The memory model used in a .COM file places everything—executable code, program data, uninitialized memory, stack, and PSP—into the same segment. Consequently, the source code for a .COM program is simpler than the source code for an .EXE program. There is only one segment, with code and data at the bottom (starting at offset 100H). A .COM program doesn't contain a stack segment; instead, DOS automatically loads the .COM program into 64 KB of memory and locates the stack at the top.

If your program is constructed in .COM format, you can run the DOS EXE2BIN utility to transform the .EXE file generated by LINK into a .COM file. Be forewarned, however: Few high-level language compilers use the .COM format because of its limitations. You can very simply and safely find out if a program can be converted from .EXE format to .COM format by trying to do it. If it works, it works. If EXE2BIN says it can't be done, however, it can't be done.

Step 5: Creating Object Libraries

Most high-level programming languages use dozens of prepared subroutines that support the operation of your programs. Naturally, these subroutines are in the translated, object-code form. It is very inconvenient, however, to have dozens or hundreds of these object files taking up space on your disks. It is also inconvenient to have to determine which ones need to be combined with your own program's object files. To solve this problem, we have *object libraries,* which are collections of object modules gathered together into one file. By convention, libraries have the filename extension .LIB.

Most high-level programming languages come with a ready-to-use library of standard supporting subroutines. Some compilers have several libraries that provide different versions of standard routines. For example, a compiler might have two libraries of equivalent floating-point math routines: one with subroutines that use the 8087 coprocessor and the other with subroutines that emulate the same floating-point operations in software.

The DOS linker can search through a library to find and use the subroutines it needs in order to create a complete, executable program. Without this library mechanism, you would be faced with the annoying task of telling the linker which object files were needed. If you omitted any, the link-editing would fail; if you included any unnecessarily, your program would become too large. Libraries let you avoid these problems.

To manipulate the contents of an object library, you need a special utility program called a *library manager.* (DOS version 3.3. is distributed with a library manager called LIB, but earlier versions did not include this utility.) Luckily, when you purchase a language translator that relies on object libraries, you'll almost always find that a library manager accompanies the compiler. The following discussion pertains to the Microsoft/IBM library manager, LIB.

You can use LIB for three main purposes: simply to explore the contents of existing libraries (which can be a very illuminating experience), to selectively replace modules in existing libraries, or to create new libraries.

The documentation for LIB in the IBM and Microsoft manuals will fully explain its operation, but to give you a taste of the ways LIB can be used, we have included a few examples to try out. To create a new library named TESTLIB, enter this command:

```
LIB TESTLIB;
```

To list the contents of an existing library, directing the listing to the printer LPT1:, enter the following command:

```
LIB TESTLIB,LPT1;
```

To add the module X.OBJ to a library, enter the following:

```
LIB TESTLIB +X;
```

To replace an existing module with a new version, enter the following:

```
LIB TESTLIB -+X;
```

To extract a module for disassembly or other separate use, enter the following:

```
LIB TESTLIB M *X;
```

Most programs call a number of subroutines. The way you organize these subroutines determines how much value you'll obtain from LIB:

- If you prefer to combine the source code for your subroutines into one source file, which means they will all be compiled together, then you have little need for LIB.

- If you prefer to compile your subroutines separately into separate object files, then LIB performs a valuable service: It gathers together and organizes your object files. We have no absolute recommendation for either style of operation, although many programmers prefer to break a large program into separate source code files that can be compiled into separate object files and linked together. Such a modular approach can be more convenient than maintaining one large source code file that must be completely recompiled with each change.

Using LINK

We're now ready to return to our discussion of combining program modules and using the LINK program. The LINK documentation in the *IBM DOS Technical Reference Manual* fully explains its operation, including the complexity of its control switches. Here we'll summarize the most common and useful operations, particularly where they pertain to the programming languages discussed in the following chapter.

Just to give you some background information, the LINK program command might be written like this:

```
LINK 1,2,3,4;
```

The first parameter lists object modules (such as PROG1 + PROG2 + PROG3), the second contains the name of the finished program, the third tells where to send the linker's display output (for example, to the printer or display screen), and the fourth lists libraries, if they are used.

Linking a Self-contained Program

Now for some practical examples. To start with, let's consider a completely self-contained program, such as the BEEP program shown on page 437. To link it, simply type

```
LINK BEEP;
```

Linking a single program such as this creates an .EXE file.

Linking a Program to a Library

Next, let's consider what is surely the most common linking circumstance. Say you've compiled a program in a high-level language, such as Microsoft C. As you know, every compiled C program needs to be linked with one or more standard object libraries that contain all the usual C functions. Consider what happens when you compile even a simple C program like this one:

```
main()
{
        printf( "Hello, world" );
}
```

If your source code is stored in a file called HELLO.C, the compiler generates an object file called HELLO.OBJ. This object module isn't yet ready to execute. You must use LINK to combine HELLO.OBJ with another object module that contains the *printf()* function. The *printf()* object module is in one of the C compiler's standard libraries; if you use the C compiler's small memory model, the name of the standard subroutine library is SLIBC.LIB.

To link the two object modules and generate an executable file, simply specify the name of the program's object module and the name of library that contains *printf()*'s object module:

```
LINK HELLO,,,SLIBC;
```

LINK then searches through SLIBC.LIB for *printf()*, links *printf()* to HELLO.OBJ, and leaves the resulting executable file in HELLO.EXE.

Even this simple example is more complicated than it has to be. Most modern compilers, including the Microsoft C compiler in this example, can include the names of their standard libraries in the object modules they generate. This means that LINK can do its job without being told explicitly about standard libraries:

```
LINK HELLO;
```

Of course, if you want LINK to use a nonstandard library, you still need to specify its name.

Linking Object Files

You can use LINK to combine two or more object files as well as to use object libraries. Do this by listing each object filename:

```
LINK ALPHA+BETA+GAMMA;
```

You can also link several object files and one or more object libraries at the same time:

```
LINK HELLO+GOODBYE,,,MYLIB;
```

Thus, the exact method you use to link a program depends on your language translator as well as on how many object files and object libraries you need to build a complete executable program.

Chapter 20

Programming Languages

In the last chapter, we briefly discussed the general principles of building and linking program modules. In this chapter, we're going to discuss some specific programming languages. We'll focus on those aspects of the languages that you need to be concerned with when you link modules written in high-level languages to assembly-language subroutines.

The title of this chapter implies that we are going to discuss programming languages in general, but that's really not the case. It's all very well to discuss any topic in the abstract, but to get anything done, you have to get down to specifics. If you want to create computer programs, you have to work with a specific programming language — and a programming language is much more specific than many people are led to believe.

First of all, there is no such thing as a generic programming language. You can create working programs only with a compiler or interpreter for a programming language designed for a particular machine. Although academic experts on computers would like to pretend otherwise, the general definitions of programming languages lack many of the essential features that you need to create real programs that work on real computers. So, when a compiler or an interpreter is created for a particular programming language (such as BASIC) to run on a particular computer (such as the IBM PC), the fundamental language is altered and extended to provide specific features. The alterations are often quite significant, and in every case, they create a programming language that is related to, but distinct from, all other programming languages of the same name.

What we're trying to say is that this chapter does not and could not possibly cover every PC programming language that exists or that might be created in the future. Because each compiler, in effect, creates a unique programming language, we've chosen not to discuss programming languages in general. Instead, we will examine several real-world implementations: Microsoft/IBM Macro Assembler, Microsoft C, IBM interpreted BASIC, Microsoft QuickBASIC, and Borland's Turbo Pascal.

Language Specifics

The five programming languages that we chose are really families in themselves. Various versions of each exist, and most are available from several sources. Fortunately, the differences between the versions are minor — minor enough that we don't need to think of them as separate languages in the same sense that BASIC and Pascal are separate languages.

Assembly language. Our discussion of assembly languages will be based on version 5.0 of Microsoft's Macro Assembler. A number of other versions are available from Microsoft, from IBM, and from other computer manufacturers who have licensed the use of Microsoft's basic assembler. Newer versions of the assembler have many features not implemented in earlier versions, but in our discussion we'll stick to the fundamental features common to most, if not all, versions of this assembler.

The C language. For our discussion of C, we will use the Microsoft C compiler version 5.0.

Interpreted BASIC. The interpreted BASIC described in this chapter has taken on a thousand faces and minor variations. To IBM PC users, the version we'll discuss is known simply as BASIC or BASICA, and is further defined by version names associated with a DOS version number (such as C1.10, A2.10, or A3.30). Outside the IBM world, it may be known as BASIC, Microsoft BASIC, or GW-BASIC. We're not concerned with the differences here; we're concerned with the common elements.

Compiled BASIC. For our discussion of compiled BASIC, we'll be guided by version 4.0 of Microsoft QuickBASIC.

Pascal. For Pascal, we'll use Borland's Turbo Pascal version 4.0, a popular load-and-go Pascal compiler.

Assembly Language

As with any programming language, you can use assembly language in two different ways: to write stand-alone programs and to write subroutines that can be called by other programs. Subroutines depend largely on the calling program to provide their structure and support, but a stand-alone assembly-language program must provide its own structure and support and must cope with all the fundamental operating issues that stand-alone programs face. Assembler subroutines are relatively easy to construct, but stand-alone assembler programs can be quite complicated. Subroutines have more immediate appeal to those who need to build interface routines between a high-level language and some of the system's ROM BIOS or DOS services, but stand-alone programs appeal to programmers who must accomplish a task that neither conventional programming languages nor system services provide.

In this brief discussion of assembly language, we'll demonstrate techniques that will help you figure out the high-level-language interface conventions for your assembly-language subroutines. We'll also lead you through the process of creating a stand-alone assembler program. However, we will not even try to teach you how to use assembly language — that is far too large and complex a subject.

If you are not particularly proficient at assembly language, one way to learn about it is to study some of the readily available sources of assembly-language coding. One place to look is in the ROM BIOS listings that are part of IBM's technical reference manuals. Another source, available with most compilers, is the assembler-like listing that many compilers can be asked to produce. This is useful both for learning how the compiler handles particular coding problems (which you can control by selecting appropriate statements in the high-level language) and for learning the subroutine interface conventions the compiler uses. A related, but less useful, way to learn about assembly language is to load an existing program using the DOS DEBUG program and then use DEBUG's U (Unassemble) command to look through sections of the program. Each method can help you learn different programming techniques and tricks.

Logical Organization

The elements of an assembly-language subroutine are easy to understand if they are laid out in the order they occur. As you may recall, the logical organization was fully explained in Chapter 8, where we described an interface routine as five nested parts:

Level 1: General assembler overhead
  Level 2: Subroutine assembler overhead
    Level 3: Entry code
      Level 4: Get parameter data from caller
        Level 5: Invoke ROM BIOS service
      Level 4: Pass results back to caller
    Level 3: Exit code
  Level 2: Finishing subroutine assembler overhead
Level 1: Finishing general assembler overhead

You can follow this basic organization for most interface routines written for system services or conventional assembly-language subroutines, but be aware that the actual coding will vary with every programming language.

Learning About Interface Conventions

Once you have your assembly language in hand, you'll need to examine the assembly-language conventions and interface customs that apply to your programming language. Your assembly-language interface will have to know how to gain access to the parameters passed by the calling program, how to interpret the data format, and how to send the parameters back—among other things. Even if your language documentation doesn't provide such information, you can obtain it from the language itself.

To learn the conventions for both a calling and a called program—that is, to see both sides of the program-call interface—you can study your compiler's assembler-style listing, as we mentioned earlier. You can also study the assembly-language subroutines provided with the language compiler for a somewhat different perspective. This technique not only provides the interface conventions for assembly-language routines but also gives you specific programming examples that can serve as models.

The most accessible subroutines are often part of the libraries that accompany your compiler. Usually, it is easiest to simply choose a compiler feature that you're interested in, such as I/O, screen control, or arithmetic, and then determine which subroutines are invoked for that feature.

A few compiler vendors sell source code for their subroutine libraries. If source code isn't available, however, you'll have to resort to disassembling the actual subroutines by extracting them from your compiler's object libraries. You can locate a particular subroutine in an object library by using a library manager like LIB to list the contents of the library. Let's assume there's a library named SLIBC.LIB on your disk. You can direct the library listing to another file named LISTING.TXT with the following DOS instruction:

```
LIB SLIBC,LISTING.TXT;
```

Look over the library listing to find the subroutine you're interested in and the name of the module that it's a part of; let's say the subroutine's name is _abs and the name of the library module containing it is ABS. You can use LIB to extract ABS from the library and create a separate object file, ABS.OBJ:

```
LIB SLIBC *ABS;
```

At this point, you could try to look inside ABS.OBJ. But because this file contains extraneous link-editor information that would only get in your way, it's easier to convert the object module into an executable file (even though it's only a subroutine and not a complete program). Use the linker utility, LINK, to do this:

```
LINK ABS;
```

LINK generates an executable file, ABS.EXE. In the process, you'll probably see a few error messages, because the subroutine you're linking isn't a complete program and lacks such necessities as a stack. That's not important in this case, because you really only want to examine the subroutine's executable code.

To disassemble the subroutine, use DEBUG:

```
DEBUG ABS.EXE
```

You can now use DEBUG's U command to convert the executable code into readable assembly-language instructions. First, note the size of your .EXE file, and subtract 512 bytes to determine the actual size of the subroutine. (The 512 bytes contain information that is used by DOS to load an executable program, but that is not part of the subroutine itself.) For example, if the size of ABS.EXE is 535 bytes, the size of the subroutine is actually only 23 (hexadecimal 17) bytes. The DEBUG command to use would then be

```
U 0 L17
```

These steps may seem overly elaborate and cumbersome, but once you learn them, you can perform them quickly and easily, and they will give you an inside look at how your own programming language uses assembly-language interface routines.

The next section will repeat the key steps of this exercise as we demonstrate the mechanics of creating a small but complete assembly-language program.

Writing and Linking Assembler Programs

To illustrate the process involved in writing and linking an assembler program, we will show you how to create an incredibly simple and yet useful program that sounds a tone on the computer's speaker. To do this on any PC-family computer or any DOS computer, you write the bell character, ASCII 07H, to the screen. In this example, we do this by using DOS interrupt 21H, function 02H. Then we end the program and return program control to DOS using interrupt 21H, function 4CH. Follow this example and you'll learn quite a bit about creating self-contained assembly-language programs. The source code for this little program is on the following page.

```
; DOS generic beep program

CodeSeg         SEGMENT byte
                ASSUME  cs:CodeSeg

Beep            PROC

                mov     dl,7     ; bell character
                mov     ah,2     ; interrupt 21H function number
                int     21h      ; call DOS to write the character

                mov     ax,4C00h ; AH = 4CH (interrupt 21H function number)
                                 ; AL = 00H (return code)
                int     21h      ; call DOS to terminate the program

Beep            ENDP

CodeSeg         ENDS

                END              Beep
```

As you see, the program is only five instructions long, filling only 11 bytes. If you save this program's source code in a file named BEEP.ASM, you can use the assembler to translate it into object code with a simple command:

```
MASM BEEP;
```

The resulting object file is ready for linking. In this case, you can link the program without subroutines, libraries, or other object files, like this:

```
LINK BEEP;
```

The linker program usually expects to find a stack segment in the programs it links, but our very simple program doesn't have one — a key characteristic that requires us to convert it into a .COM file, as we shall soon see. The linker will complain about the missing stack, but you can ignore its complaint.

Linking will give you an executable program called BEEP.EXE. If you run BEEP.EXE, however, DOS won't know where to locate the program's stack. You can solve this problem by converting BEEP.EXE into a .COM program with EXE2BIN:

```
EXE2BIN BEEP BEEP.COM
```

When you run BEEP.COM, DOS automatically locates the stack for you. Now you have a finished beeper program that can be used on any computer that runs DOS. You can safely delete the intermediate files BEEP.OBJ and BEEP.EXE.

Note what happens to the size of the BEEP program as it is transformed from an idea to an executable .COM file. The source code for this program is approximately 400 bytes (depending on such factors as the use of spaces in the comments). When you assemble and link it, you'll discover that only 11 bytes of working machine-language instructions are created. However, the object file, which includes some standard linker information as overhead, is 71 bytes — much smaller than the source file, but much larger than the 11 bytes of actual machine code. After linking, the 71-byte object file swells to a 523-byte .EXE file. (Remember, the .EXE file contains a 512-byte header that contains program-loading information.) Converting the program to .COM format eliminates the 512 bytes of overhead, and you end up with a .COM file that's only 11 bytes of pure machine code.

The C Language

We'll start our discussion of specific high-level languages with the C language. In previous chapters we've already shown you several examples of the C subroutine interface. Now we'll show how to adapt that interface to different parameter-passing methods and memory models. Although the examples we'll give you here pertain specifically to the Microsoft C compiler, you'll find that essentially the same subroutine interface design can be used not only in other vendors' compiler implementations, but in other programming languages as well.

The C subroutines presented in previous chapters used a small memory model and the pass-by-value convention. The subroutine on the following page which computes the absolute value of an integer, uses the same conventions.

The subroutine uses a near call-return sequence because the program uses a small memory model with all executable code in the same segment. The parameter value is passed to the subroutine on the stack and accessed through BP in the usual way. The parameter value is found at [BP + 4] because the first 4 bytes of the stack are used by the calling program's return address (2 bytes) and the saved value of BP (2 bytes).

```
_TEXT           SEGMENT byte public 'CODE'
                ASSUME  cs:_TEXT

                PUBLIC  _AbsValue
_AbsValue       PROC    near            ; call with near CALL

                push    bp
                mov     bp,sp

                mov     ax,[bp+4]       ; AX = value of 1st parameter

                cwd
                xor     ax,dx
                sub     ax,dx           ; leave result in AX

                pop     bp
                ret                     ; near RETurn

_AbsValue       ENDP

_TEXT           ENDS
```

The subroutine uses register AX to return its result to the calling program. If the return value had been a 4-byte value, the register pair DX:AX would have been used, with the high-order word of the value in DX.

If this subroutine had used more than one parameter, the second and subsequent parameters would have been found at higher addresses on the stack. For example, the second parameter would have been located at [BP + 6]. (See the *Weekday()* subroutine in Chapter 16 for an example.) In effect, the C compiler pushes parameters on the stack in reverse of their declared order. Because of this, a subroutine always knows where to find the first parameter on the stack. A C function like *printf()* can use a variable number of parameters if the first parameter specifies the actual number of parameters.

When it returns, the subroutine leaves the value of the parameter on the stack. In C, the calling program must clean up the stack after a subroutine call. For example, consider the way a C compiler generates executable code for a simple C statement that calls *AbsValue()*:

```
x = AbsValue( y );      /* x and y are integers */
```

439

The executable code generated by the C compiler for this statement looks something like this:

```
push Y                    ; push the value at address Y
call _AbsValue            ; call the subroutine (near call)
add  sp,2                 ; discard the value from the stack
mov  X,ax                 ; store the returned value at address X
```

Parameter Passing

Let's look more closely at the difference between the pass-by-value and pass-by-reference methods of parameter passing. The pass-by-value method works by passing a copy of a parameter's current value to the subroutine. In contrast, the pass-by-reference method passes a parameter's address. This affects the subroutine interface in two different ways.

First, the value of a parameter passed by reference cannot be accessed directly. Instead, you must first copy the parameter's address from the stack and then obtain the parameter's value through the address. For example:

```
_TEXT           SEGMENT byte public 'CODE'
                ASSUME  cs:_TEXT

                PUBLIC  _SmallAbs
_SmallAbs       PROC    near            ; call with near CALL

                push    bp
                mov     bp,sp

                mov     bx,[bp+4]       ; BX = address of 1st parameter
                mov     ax,[bx]         ; AX = value of 1st parameter

                cwd
                xor     ax,dx
                sub     ax,dx

                mov     [bx],ax         ; leave result at parameter address

                pop     bp
                ret                     ; near RETurn

_SmallAbs       ENDP

_TEXT           ENDS
```

SmallAbs(), which uses pass-by-reference, obtains the value of its parameter in two steps. First, it copies the parameter's address from the stack (MOV BX,[BP + 4]). Then it obtains the parameter's value from that address (MOV AX,[BX]). Once the parameter's value is in AX, the computation of its absolute value proceeds as before.

To pass a parameter from a C program to *SmallAbs()*, you need to pass its address instead of its value:

```
SmallAbs( &x );          /* pass the address of x */
```

The corresponding executable code would look something like this:

```
mov ax,offset X          ; push the address of X
push ax
call _SmallAbs           ; call the subroutine (near call)
add  sp,2                ; discard the address from the stack
```

The way *SmallAbs()* returns its result points out the key reason to use the pass-by-reference method: *SmallAbs()* actually changes the value of its parameter. Instead of simply returning a result in AX, *SmallAbs()* stores its return value at the parameter's address (MOV [BX],AX).

In high-level programming languages, both the pass-by-reference and pass-by-value methods can be used. In some languages, the method of passing parameters defaults to one method or the other. For example, BASIC uses pass-by-reference by default, but C uses the pass-by-value method as the default. In many languages, the default method can vary, depending on a parameter's data type. You can usually determine which method is used to call a subroutine by specifying a method in your source code (if your compiler supports such specifications) or by using a data type associated with a particular parameter-passing method.

Memory Model Variations

A simple rule of thumb can help you determine how a program's memory model affects the design of its subroutines: If you have multiple segments, use far (intersegment) addressing; if you have a single segment, use near (intrasegment) addressing. Let's see how this simple rule can be applied in a pair of real subroutines.

The following variation of our absolute-value subroutine is designed for a medium-model C program. A medium-model program has multiple code segments but only one data segment. Subroutines in separate segments must be accessed through far jumps and far call-return sequences, but the single data segment can be accessed with near addresses:

```
MEDABS_TEXT     SEGMENT byte public 'CODE'
                ASSUME  cs:MEDABS_TEXT

                PUBLIC  _MedAbs
_MedAbs         PROC    far             ; call with far CALL

                push    bp
                mov     bp,sp

                mov     bx,[bp+6]       ; BX = address of 1st parameter
                mov     ax,[bx]

                cwd
                xor     ax,dx
                sub     ax,dx

                mov     [bx],ax         ; leave result at parameter address

                pop     bp
                ret                     ; far RETurn

_MedAbs         ENDP

MEDABS_TEXT     ENDS
```

This medium-model version (*MedAbs()*), looks very much like *SmallAbs()*. In *MedAbs()*, the PROC statement declares that the routine is to be called with a far CALL and instructs the assembler to generate a far RETurn instruction instead of a near RETurn. Because *MedAbs()* is called with a far CALL, the stack contains a segmented return address (4 bytes) as well as the saved value of BP (2 bytes), so the subroutine looks for its parameter at [BP + 6] instead of [BP + 4].

A large-model program introduces one more variation in subroutine design. Because a large-model program uses multiple data segments, the addresses of subroutine parameters are far (segmented) addresses.

```
LARGEABS_TEXT    SEGMENT byte public 'CODE'
                 ASSUME  cs:LARGEABS_TEXT

                 PUBLIC  _LargeAbs
_LargeAbs        PROC    far                 ; call with far CALL

                 push    bp
                 mov     bp,sp

                 les     bx,[bp+6]           ; ES:BX = segmented address
                                             ; of first parameter
                 mov     ax,es:[bx]          ; AX = value of first parameter
                 cwd
                 xor     ax,dx
                 sub     ax,dx

                 mov     es:[bx],ax          ; leave result at parameter address

                 pop     bp
                 ret                         ; far RETurn

_LargeAbs        ENDP

LARGEABS_TEXT    ENDS
```

Because it conforms to a large memory model, *LargeAbs( )* is designed to obtain both segment and offset from the stack (LES BX,[BP + 6]). The segment part of the parameter's address goes into ES; the offset goes into BX. The subroutine uses this register pair to obtain the parameter's value (MOV AX,ES:[BX]) and to return a result (MOV ES:[BX],AX).

If you call *LargeAbs( )* like this:

```
LargeAbs( &x );
```

a C compiler generates executable code that looks something like this:

```
push ds                 ; push the parameter's segment
mov ax,offset X         ; push the parameter's offset
push ax
call _LargeAbs          ; call the subroutine (far call)
add  sp,4               ; discard the address from the stack
```

Naming Conventions

As we mentioned earlier, the parameter-passing and memory-model methods used in your program determine how a subroutine interface is implemented, regardless of which language or compiler you use. Unfortunately, other differences between languages and compilers can make the design of a subroutine interface tricky and somewhat tedious.

One problem is that different languages and compilers use different names for the subroutines, segments, segment groups, and variables that crop up in a program written in a high-level language. For example, the names used in Microsoft C (_TEXT, _DATA, DGROUP, and so on) are different not only in other vendors' C compilers, but also in earlier versions of Microsoft's C compiler.

Other differences in naming appear when you compare different languages. C is case-sensitive, but interpreted BASIC and Pascal convert all lowercase letters to upper case. C compilers generally prefix all names declared in a C program with an underscore, so a name like *printf* in C must be referenced as *_printf* in assembly language. The surest way to know exactly what naming conventions your language translator uses is to look at your compiler's manuals.

Data Representation

Before we leave our discussion of C, let's look at the way C represents different data types. When you write a routine that shares data with a C program, you must know how the C compiler stores data in memory.

The data types available in C can be divided into three general categories: *integer types, floating-point types,* and *other types.*

- Integer types, including *char, int, short,* and *long,* are stored with their low-order bytes first in the familiar "back-words" 8086 format. In 8086 C implementations, *char* is 1 byte in size, *int* and *short* are 2 bytes, and *long* is 4 bytes. The integer data types may be specified as either *signed* or *unsigned.*

- In Microsoft C, representations of floating-point data types (*float* and *double*) are based on the IEEE standard for floating-point data representation used in the 8087 math coprocessor. With this representation, a *float* value is 4 bytes long and a *double* is 8 bytes long. Despite the difference in size, a simple relationship exists between *float* and *double*: You can convert a *float* to a *double* by appending 4 bytes of zeros.

- Other C data types include *pointers* and *strings*. Pointers are address values; near pointers are 2 bytes long and far pointers are 4 bytes long. Strings are defined as arrays of type *char*. However, all strings in C are stored as ASCIIZ strings; that is, as a string of bytes terminated with a single zero byte. In a C program, you must accommodate the extra byte when you declare a string. For example, you would reserve storage for 64 bytes of string data plus the terminating null byte like this:

```
char s[65];
```

In C, the value of the name *s* would be the address of the string data associated with it. A subroutine called with *s* as a parameter can obtain the value of *s* (the address of the string data) directly from the stack and access the string data by reference to this address.

Interpreted BASIC

To be candid and blunt, let us admit right away that we can't give you everything you need here. Working with BASIC and interfacing to BASIC are very, very complicated subjects — complex enough to fill several books by themselves. Frankly, interfacing with interpreted BASIC is a particularly messy area, made even messier by the number of BASIC versions used with the different models of the extended PC family. The specific techniques we describe here apply to the most popular interpreted BASICs: the BASIC distributed by IBM with every PC and PS/2; and Microsoft's GW-BASIC.

In this section we describe the interface between assembly-language subroutines and interpreted BASIC programs. We discuss only those subroutines accessed through BASIC's CALL statement.

❑ NOTE: *Interpreted BASIC supports a second subroutine-call mechanism through the USR statement, but in our opinion, USR functions involve annoying and unnecessary complications. We recommend that you stick to the CALL interface instead.*

The Subroutine Interface

Interpreted BASIC uses a medium memory model, so subroutines are accessed through a far call-return sequence, and data is accessed with near addresses. Also, interpreted BASIC passes all parameters by reference.

Knowing this, you can easily design assembly-language subroutines that can be accessed within an interpreted BASIC program.

Be aware, however, that interpreted BASIC knows nothing about object files, object libraries, or linkers: You must explicitly instruct BASIC to load and link your subroutine. Although several loading techniques have been developed, the most straightforward uses BASIC's own BLOAD command to make a subroutine accessible to a high-level interpreted BASIC program.

The BLOAD command loads binary data from a disk file into BASIC's default data segment. If you build a subroutine in the format that BLOAD will recognize, you can use BLOAD to place the subroutine anywhere in memory. In particular, you can load a subroutine into an integer array whose address you can call with interpreted BASIC's CALL statement.

BLOAD loads files that are prefixed with a 7-byte header containing a signature byte (FDH), two words (4 bytes) of zeros, and a word that contains the number of bytes of data to load. Simply adding this header to a medium-model subroutine makes it loadable by BLOAD:

```
CodeSeg         SEGMENT byte
                ASSUME  cs:CodeSeg

; header for BASIC BLOAD

                DB      0FDh            ; signature byte
                DW      2 dup(0)        ; two 16-bit zeros
                DW      SubroutineSize  ; size of this subroutine

MedAbs          PROC    far             ; call with far CALL

                push    bp
                mov     bp,sp

                mov     bx,[bp+6]       ; BX = address of first parameter
                mov     ax,[bx]

                cwd
                xor     ax,dx
                sub     ax,dx

                mov     [bx],ax         ; leave result at parameter address

                pop     bp
                ret     2               ; far RETurn, discard
                                        ; parameter address
```

```
MedAbs           ENDP

SubroutineSize EQU      $-MedAbs

CodeSeg          ENDS
```

Apart from the BLOAD header, the only difference between this version of *MedAbs()* and the earlier version is in the naming conventions: Interpreted BASIC doesn't use symbolic names to link a subroutine loaded with the BLOAD command, so you can use any names you choose.

To convert the assembly-language source code into a form readable by BLOAD, use LINK and EXE2BIN. For example, if this subroutine's source file is named MEDABS.ASM, the following two commands convert it into MEDABS.BIN, a file that BLOAD can use:

```
LINK MEDABS.ASM;
EXE2BIN MEDABS;
```

To link the subroutine into a high-level BASIC program, do this:

1. Allocate a block of memory for the subroutine by using a DIM statement to declare an integer variable.

2. Use the VARPTR function to store the memory block's address in a variable.

3. Use BLOAD to copy the subroutine into memory.

4. Use the CALL statement to call the subroutine through the variable that contains its address.

Here's an example:

```
100 DEFINT A-Z                       ' default all variables to integer type
110 '
120 X = 0 : Y = 0                    ' reserve RAM for all variables used
130 SUBADDR = 0
140 '
150 DIM SUBAREA(16)                  ' reserve RAM for the subroutine
160 SUBADDR = VARPTR(SUBAREA(1))     ' save the address of the subroutine
170 BLOAD "medabs.bin",SUBADDR
180 '
190 FOR X=-10 TO 10
200   Y = X
210   CALL SUBADDR(Y)                ' call the subroutine
220   PRINT"ABS(";X;")=";Y
230   NEXT
240 END
```

447

Note how the four steps of linking are carried out. The statement DIM SUBAREA(16) reserves 32 bytes of memory, more than enough for the subroutine. Then SUBADDR = VARPTR(SUBAREA(1)) stores the address of the memory block in the variable SUBADDR. At this point, the BLOAD command can load the subroutine from the binary file, and the CALL statement can call the subroutine through the variable SUBADDR.

There is one tricky thing to remember about this process: Interpreted BASIC allocates variables and strings dynamically. Because of this, you should define all variables in your BASIC program before you use BLOAD to load the subroutine. (Lines 120 and 130 do this in our example.) If you don't, you may find that the address returned by VARPTR doesn't reflect the final location of the subroutine in memory.

If you pass more than one parameter to a BASIC subroutine through a CALL statement, the parameters appear with the last parameter at [BP + 6], the next-to-last at [BP + 8], and so on. This is the reverse of the order used in C. The advantage to using this parameter order is that the subroutine can clean up the stack with a single RET instruction. Instead of using a simple far RETurn, a BASIC subroutine uses a return-and-pop instruction to discard the parameters. In the BASIC version of *MedAbs()*, for example, the instruction is RET 2; the value 2 is the number of bytes occupied by the subroutine's parameter on the stack.

Data Representation

BASIC uses four data formats: *integers, variable-length strings,* and *floating-point numbers* in long and short form (known in BASIC terminology as *single-precision* and *double-precision* numbers). BASIC variables can be explicitly given one of these four format types by appending an identifying suffix to the variable name: % for integer, $ for string, ! for single-precision (short floating point), and # for double-precision (long floating point). Numeric constants can be similarly classified. Implicit typing can be controlled with the DEF statement and defaults to single-precision. For reference, here are some simple examples:

```
A%      Integer variable
A!      Single-precision variable
A#      Double-precision variable
A$      String variable
1%      Integer constant
1!      Single-precision constant
1#      Double-precision constant
"1"     String constant
```

Interpreted BASIC supports one integer data format: 2-byte (16-bit) integers. See page 23 for a general discussion of this data format.

The distinction between signed and unsigned integers in BASIC is a bit blurry. BASIC regards integers as signed when it performs arithmetic, compares integers, or displays them with the PRINT statement. However, BASIC disregards the sign when it performs bitwise logical operations (AND, OR, XOR, and so on) and when processing hexadecimal values (values prefixed with &H or converted with the HEX$ function.)

If you want to display unsigned decimal integers, convert them to floating-point:

```
IF I% < 0 THEN D# = I% + 65536# ELSE D# = I%
```

where *I%* is an integer and *D#* is its equivalent in double-precision. To convert values from double-precision to unsigned integers, you can use this method:

```
IF D# > 32767 THEN I% = D# - 65536 ELSE I% = D#
```

In interpreted BASIC, single-precision floating-point numbers are 4 bytes in size; double-precision values are 8 bytes. However, BASIC stores floating-point values in its own peculiar format. Not only is interpreted BASIC's floating-point format different from that used by most other programming languages for the PC family, it is also incompatible with the formats used by the 8087 and 80287 math coprocessors.

String values in interpreted BASIC are stored in two parts: a string descriptor that holds the length and address of the string; and the string itself, which is a series of ASCII characters. (See Figure 20-1.)

The string descriptor is 3 bytes long. The first byte contains the string length, which limits the maximum size of a string to 255 bytes. The next 2 bytes are the near address of the actual string data. String data has no special format; it is simply stored as a series of bytes at the indicated address.

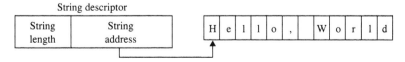

Figure 20-1. *String data representation in interpreted BASIC.*

When the VARPTR function is applied to a string, it returns the address of the string descriptor. From the string descriptor, you can obtain the offset address of the string itself. The following program demonstrates the process of finding and decoding this information:

```
100 INPUT "Enter any string: ",OUR.STRING$
110 DESCRIPTOR.ADDRESS = VARPTR (OUR.STRING$)
120 PRINT "The string pointer is at hex ";
130 PRINT HEX$ (DESCRIPTOR.ADDRESS)
140 STRING.LENGTH = PEEK (DESCRIPTOR.ADDRESS)
150 PRINT "The length of the string is";
160 PRINT STRING.LENGTH
170 STRING.ADDRESS = PEEK (DESCRIPTOR.ADDRESS + 1)
      + 256 * PEEK (DESCRIPTOR.ADDRESS + 2)
180 PRINT "The string value is at hex ";
190 PRINT HEX$ (STRING.ADDRESS)
200 PRINT "The string value is: ";
210 FOR I = 0 TO STRING.LENGTH - 1
220   PRINT CHR$ (PEEK (I + STRING.ADDRESS));
230 NEXT I
240 PRINT : PRINT
250 GOTO 100
```

Compiled BASIC

When you use a BASIC compiler to translate your BASIC source code into object files, you avoid all the improvised programming required to link a subroutine to an interpreted BASIC program. A good example of a BASIC compiler that generates object files is Microsoft's QuickBASIC.

The Subroutine Interface

QuickBASIC's default is a medium memory model, with multiple executable code segments and one default data segment. As in interpreted BASIC, you must design your subroutines to use a far call-return sequence, but you can access the single default data segment with near addresses. Also, like interpreted BASIC, compiled QuickBASIC passes parameters by reference in the order they appear in the BASIC source code.

The BASIC source code to call an assembly language subroutine is much simpler in QuickBASIC than in interpreted BASIC, as you'll see when you examine the sample code on the following page.

```
DEFINT A-Z                          ' default all variables to integer type
DECLARE SUB MEDABS (A%)             ' declare the assembler subroutine

FOR X = -10 TO 10
 Y = X
 CALL MEDABS(Y)                     ' call the subroutine
 PRINT "ABS("; X; ")=";Y
 NEXT
END
```

The subroutine itself, however, is nearly identical to the version called from interpreted BASIC:

```
MEDABS_TEXT     SEGMENT byte public 'CODE'
                ASSUME  cs:MEDABS_TEXT

                PUBLIC  MEDABS
MEDABS          PROC    far             ; call with far CALL

                push    bp
                mov     bp,sp

                mov     bx,[bp+6]       ; BX = address of first parameter
                mov     ax,[bx]

                cwd
                xor     ax,dx
                sub     ax,dx

                mov     [bx],ax         ; leave result at parameter address

                pop     bp
                ret     2               ; far return, discard parameter value

MEDABS          ENDP

MEDABS_TEXT     ENDS
```

The only differences between this version of *MedAbs()* and the version used with interpreted BASIC are related to the way the subroutine is linked to the BASIC program. The compiled-BASIC version does not contain a BLOAD header because BLOAD isn't used to link the subroutine. Instead it contains a PUBLIC declaration for the name of the subroutine. When you use the linker to generate an executable program, the linker associates the PUBLIC name with the same name used in the BASIC program.

❏ NOTE: *QuickBASIC provides two different ways to link an assembly-language subroutine to BASIC programs. One is to use the BC compiler to compile your BASIC source code, and then to link the resulting object (OBJ) file with the assembled subroutine's object file. The other technique is to use LINK and LIB to create a Quick library so that the subroutine can be accessed within the QuickBASIC environment. The QuickBASIC manuals describe both techniques in detail.*

Data Representation

QuickBASIC's data representations resemble those used in interpreted BASIC. QuickBASIC supports interpreted BASIC's 2-byte integers and an additional 4-byte LONG data type that is represented by a variable name with a terminal ampersand (for example, *X&*). Floating-point values are the same size as in interpreted BASIC (4 bytes for single-precision; 8 bytes for double-precision), but the floating-point representation follows the 8087-compatible, IEEE standard instead of the unique representation used in interpreted BASIC.

Like interpreted BASIC, QuickBASIC dynamically allocates memory for strings, so strings are represented by a two-part string descriptor. QuickBASIC's string descriptor is 4 bytes in size compared to 3 bytes in interpreted BASIC. Because the string length is represented in 2 bytes instead of 1, the maximum length of a QuickBASIC string is 65,535 bytes.

Turbo Pascal

We'll conclude this chapter with a look at Borland's widely used Turbo Pascal compiler. Turbo Pascal's data formats and support for assembly-language subroutines are different from those found in traditional Pascal compilers like IBM's or Microsoft's. However, you can use the same principles of subroutine interface design in Turbo Pascal that you use in any other language.

❏ NOTE: *Our description of the subroutine interface applies to version 4.0 of Turbo Pascal. Versions 3.0 and earlier used a somewhat different interface that isn't compatible with the one we're about to cover.*

The Subroutine Interface

Turbo Pascal version 4.0 uses a large memory model, with multiple executable code segments and multiple data segments. However, Turbo Pascal compiles all the executable code in the body of a program into a single segment, so assembly-language subroutines that you declare within the main body of a program should use a near call-return sequence. In contrast, Turbo Pascal uses separate segments for subroutines declared in the INTERFACE section of a Turbo Pascal UNIT. (A *UNIT* in Turbo Pascal is a collection of predefined subroutines and data items.) Such subroutines must be accessed through a far call-return sequence; data is accessed using far addresses. When you write an assembly-language subroutine for Turbo Pascal, be sure you use the right call-return sequence.

The following example is a Turbo Pascal variation of our absolute-value function. Because it is designed to be called from the main body of a Pascal program, it uses a near call-return sequence.

```
CODE            SEGMENT byte public
                ASSUME  cs:CODE

                PUBLIC  AbsFunc
AbsFunc         PROC    near            ; call with near CALL

                push    bp
                mov     bp,sp

                mov     ax,[bp+4]       ; AX = value of parameter
                cwd
                xor     ax,dx
                sub     ax,dx           ; AX contains the result

                pop     bp
                ret     2               ; near return

AbsFunc         ENDP

CODE            ENDS
```

If you assemble this subroutine into the object file ABSFUNC.OBJ, you can link it into a Turbo Pascal program by using the $L compiler directive and declaring *AbsFunc( )* as an EXTERNAL function:

```
{$L absfunc}        { object filename }
FUNCTION AbsFunc(x: INTEGER): INTEGER; EXTERNAL;
```

Turbo Pascal uses a large memory model, so data pointers are always passed to subroutines as 32-bit addresses. You can see this by writing the same subroutine as a PROCEDURE instead of a FUNCTION and declaring x as an integer variable. The VAR keyword in the parameter list instructs the Turbo Pascal compiler to pass the parameter by reference, that is, to pass the parameter's address instead of its value:

```
{$L absproc}              { object filename }
PROCEDURE AbsProc (VAR x:INTEGER); EXTERNAL;
```

The subroutine differs from the previous one in that it must obtain the 32-bit address of x from the stack in order to obtain the actual value of x:

```
CODE            SEGMENT byte public
                ASSUME  cs:CODE

                PUBLIC  AbsProc
AbsProc         PROC    near            ; call with near CALL

                push    bp
                mov     bp,sp

                les     bx,[bp+4]       ; ES:BX = segmented addr of x
                mov     ax,es:[bx]      ; AX = value of x
                cwd
                xor     ax,dx
                sub     ax,dx

                mov     es:[bx],ax      ; leave result in x

                pop     bp
                ret     4               ; near return

AbsProc         ENDP

CODE            ENDS
```

This subroutine resembles *LargeAbs()*, our large-model example for Microsoft C. The important difference is that Turbo Pascal's subroutine-calling convention requires a near subroutine call because the subroutine was declared in the body of a Pascal program. Had we declared *AbsProc()* in the INTERFACE portion of a UNIT, the subroutine would have used a far call-return sequence.

Data Representation

Like the other languages discussed in this chapter, Turbo Pascal supports integer, floating-point, and string data types. Integers are stored in the familiar 2-byte format, but floating-point and string representations present some novelties.

Turbo Pascal version 4.0 supports five types of floating-point (real) numbers. The REAL type is a 6-byte, floating-point representation designed by Borland. The other four (SINGLE, DOUBLE, EXTENDED, and COMP) are representations used by the 8087 math coprocessor.

Turbo Pascal stores strings in a simple data structure: a 1-byte count that is followed by the string data itself. (See Figure 20-2.) The count byte is treated as an unsigned value, so the maximum length of a string is 255 (FFH) bytes.

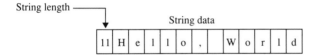

Figure 20-2. *String data representation in Turbo Pascal.*

Turbo represents other Pascal data types in equally reasonable ways. For example, Boolean values are represented in a single byte (01H = true, 00H = false). Sets are represented as bit strings in which the position of each bit corresponds to the ordinal value of one member of the set. (See Figure 20-3.) The low-order bit in each byte corresponds to an ordinal value that is evenly divisible by 8. The compiler stores only as many bytes as are needed to represent the set.

```
TYPE LETTERS = 'a' .. 'z'; {ordinal values 97 through 122}
VAR X :SET OF LETTERS;

X := ['a', 'b', 'c', 'y', 'z'];
```

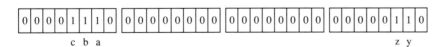

Figure 20-3. *Representation of a set in Turbo Pascal. The set X is represented as a 4-byte bit string in which each bit corresponds to one of the ordinal values 'a' through 'z' (decimal 97 through 122). The bits are aligned so that ordinal values evenly divisible by 8 are represented in bit 0 of each byte.*

A Parting Comment

In this chapter we examined five programming language translators. We covered the major design issues involved in building an executable program that calls subroutines. Figures 20-4, 20-5, and 20-6 summarize some characteristics of the language translators we discussed.

Language	Default Memory Model
Interpreted BASIC	Medium
QuickBASIC	Medium
Microsoft C	Small
Turbo Pascal	Large

Figure 20-4. *Default memory models for several popular programming languages.*

Language	Default Parameter-Passing Method	Parameter Order
Interpreted BASIC	Reference	Forward
QuickBASIC	Reference	Forward
Microsoft C	Value	Reverse
Turbo Pascal	(Varies)	Forward

Figure 20-5. *Parameter-passing conventions for several popular programming languages.*

Language	Registers Used by Language Translator
Interpreted BASIC	DS, ES, SS, BP
QuickBASIC	DS, SS, BP, SI, DI
Microsoft C	DS, SS, BP, SI, DI
Turbo Pascal	DS, SS, BP

Figure 20-6. *Register usage conventions followed by several popular programming languages. Preserve these registers if you change them in a subroutine.*

Even if you never plan to write an assembly-language program or link subroutines written in different languages into the same program, we hope you've found it interesting to see how these different language translators do their work.

Appendix A

Installable
Device Drivers

Two features introduced with DOS version 2.0 require special discussion: installable device drivers and the ANSI driver (ANSI.SYS). Although these features are related by their common introduction in DOS version 2.0 (and by the fact that the ANSI driver is itself an installable device driver), they are radically different topics from a programming perspective. We'll begin by looking at device drivers in general, give you some details about how DOS device drivers are implemented, and then review how a typical DOS device driver, ANSI.SYS, can be used in DOS applications.

Overview

DOS can work with most common computer devices, such as ordinary disk drives, serial communications lines, printers, and, of course, the keyboard and display screen. However, many other kinds of devices can be attached to PCs and PS/2s. Most of these devices require additional software support — *device drivers* — to connect to DOS and to DOS programs.

Since the release of version 2.0, DOS has been able to incorporate into its own operations any device driver that follows a standard set of integration rules. During start-up, a disk file named CONFIG.SYS tells DOS when there is a device driver to be loaded. The name and file location of each device driver are identified by the command line DEVICE = *filespec* in the CONFIG.SYS file. For each DEVICE = command line, DOS locates the program file, loads it into memory, and goes through the series of steps necessary to welcome the device driver into the DOS fold.

Typically, a device driver supports a new kind of device in an old way. For example, a device driver that supports a disk drive whose detailed control commands are new to DOS but whose overall features are similar to other kinds of disk drives will most likely follow the program format laid down by its more common predecessors. Likewise, a device driver that supports the addition of a mouse or joystick may treat them as keyboard-like devices.

On the other hand, device drivers can perform functions that have little or nothing to do with the addition of new hardware devices to the computer; witness the ANSI device driver, which we'll be discussing in the following section. The ANSI device driver doesn't *add* new hardware to the computer; instead, it *modifies* the operation of the computer's standard hardware (the keyboard and the display screen).

All the technical details of writing a device driver really belong in a book specializing in DOS systems programming, but we can give you the main points here.

How Device Drivers Work

There are two kinds of device drivers: those for *character devices,* which, like the keyboard, printer, and communications port, work with a serial stream of characters, and those for *block devices,* which, like a disk drive, read and write blocks of data identified by some form of block address. Character devices are identified by their own names (similar to the names LPT1 and COM1). Block devices are identified by a drive letter that DOS assigns (D:, E:, F:, and so on).

In a program, you generally treat character devices like files. A character device can be opened using its name and then read from or written to. On the other hand, your program sees block devices as if they were disk drives. This is the point of using installable device drivers — the usual DOS interrupt 21H function for files and disks let you access any device as long as the device driver conforms to DOS's format.

DOS maintains a chained list of device drivers in which each device driver contains the address of the next device driver in the list. The chain starts in the heart of the DOS kernel, beginning with the NUL device. When you use an interrupt 21H function to identify a character device, DOS searches the list of device driver names before it searches disk directories.

Every installable device driver consists of three main structural elements; a *device header*, a *strategy routine*, and an *interrupt routine.* The device header is a data structure that contains a device attribute word as well as the addresses of the strategy and interrupt routines. DOS communicates with a device driver through a data structure called a *request header.* DOS uses the request header to pass I/O function numbers and buffer addresses to the device driver. The device driver uses the same data structure to return status and error codes to DOS.

To initiate an I/O request, DOS builds a request header, calls the device driver's strategy routine to pass it the request header's address, and then calls the driver's interrupt routine. The interrupt routine examines the request header, initiates the data transfer to or from the hardware device, waits for the completion of the data transfer, and updates the request header with a status code before it returns to DOS.

> ❏ NOTE: *It may seem curious that DOS actually makes two separate calls to a device driver for each input/output request. This somewhat redundant design is actually similar to that used in device drivers in multitasking operating systems like UNIX (after which the DOS design is modeled) and OS/2.*

459

In a multitasking system, the two-part design makes good sense because it allows I/O operations to take place in parallel with other system functions. The strategy routine starts the I/O operation and then returns control to the operating system, which can perform other tasks without waiting for the hardware device to transfer data. When the data transfer is complete, the interrupt routine gains control and cleanly terminates the operation.

Writing a device driver is similar to writing the I/O service programs that are at the heart of DOS and at the heart of the computer's built-in ROM BIOS. It is among the most sophisticated and intricate programming that you can do.

The ANSI Driver

One example of an installable device driver that comes as an optional part of DOS is the *ANSI driver,* a program that enhances the handling of keyboard input and screen output. As with any installable device driver, the ANSI driver is active only when you load it into DOS through the CONFIG.SYS file. The following CONFIG.SYS command activates the ANSI driver:

```
DEVICE = ANSI.SYS
```

Although the ANSI driver is an optional part of the IBM versions of DOS, it is an integral part of the DOS used on some computers similar to (but not fully compatible with) the IBM PC family. In such computers, the ANSI driver isn't installable—it's built into DOS, like the CON and PRN drivers.

The ANSI driver monitors both the screen output and the keyboard input that pass through the standard DOS screen and keyboard services. (Keyboard or screen data that bypasses DOS is never seen or processed by the ANSI driver.)

In monitoring the screen output, the ANSI driver looks for special codes that identify commands for the driver. The driver takes note of and then removes these commands so that the special command codes do not appear on the display screen. Instead, these driver command codes are sent to the command processor.

Commands for the ANSI driver are identified by a special 2-byte code: The first byte is the "escape" character, ASCII 1BH (decimal 27), and the second is the left-bracket character [, ASCII 5BH (decimal 91). Following these identifying bytes are the command parameters and finally the command code itself. The command parameters are either numbers (in the form of ASCII numeric characters interpreted as decimal digits) or strings of ASCII characters enclosed in quotes, like this: "a string parameter." Multiple parameters are separated by semicolons. The command code itself, which completes the ANSI driver command, is always a single alphabetic character. Commands are case-sensitive; for example, lowercase *h* is one command, and uppercase *H* is an entirely different one.

To show what these commands look like, here are two examples, one simple and one complex (the caret stands for the escape character, 1BH):

```
^[1C
^[65;32;66;"Re-mapped B"p
```

The ANSI driver recognizes a large number of commands, but they all fall into two broad categories: *screen control commands* and *keyboard translation commands*. Let's look at screen control first.

ANSI Screen Control

Although the ROM BIOS services for the PC let you move the cursor anywhere on the screen and basically give you full-screen control, the standard DOS services do not. In fact, the DOS screen output services are completely oriented to "glass teletype" output — output that encompasses only what can be done with a printer. This, of course, ignores the richer potential of a display screen. This lack of full-screen output in DOS forces most programs to bypass the DOS services and use lower-level services, such as the ROM BIOS services.

The screen control commands of the ANSI driver remedy this situation by providing a set of full-screen commands that can be used to do nearly anything that the display screen is capable of doing. The commands include moving the cursor, clearing the screen, setting the display attributes (color, underscore, blinking, and so on), and changing the mode from text to graphics and vice versa. As an additional level of sophistication, some commands can save the current cursor location so that you can move the cursor to display information and then return it to its original position.

461

ANSI Keyboard Control

The other type of command accepted by the ANSI driver is a keyboard translation command. When one of these commands is given to the driver, the driver monitors keyboard input and replaces one key character with another single character or even a whole string of characters. This allows the ANSI driver to act as a crude but effective keyboard-enhancer program.

The two ANSI driver commands are very different in their purpose and use, but they are both passed to the driver in the same way — through a stream of screen output characters.

The Pros and Cons of the ANSI Driver

You can look at ANSI driver commands in two ways: from the perspective of the user, who can use the ANSI driver to perform a few beneficial tricks, and from the perspective of the programmer, who can use it as an aid to program development.

Many users often regard the ANSI driver as a poor man's keyboard enhancer. By using the keyboard translation commands, as we mentioned earlier, you can roughly simulate the keyboard ''macro'' features of commercial keyboard-enhancer programs.

You can also use the ANSI driver as a DOS command-prompt enhancer. Usually the keyboard commands are activated by placing them in a text file and sending them to the screen (and therefore to the ANSI driver) with the TYPE command. By embedding ANSI driver commands into the prompt string, however, you can move the cursor to the top of the screen, display the date and time in reverse video, and then return the cursor to its regular position, or you can even clear the screen and then paint a complete menu display. The possibilities are endless.

From a programmer's point of view, the ANSI driver has two main benefits to offer:

- It makes the most crucial BIOS-type services available to any programming language.

- It lets you write programs for any DOS computer (not just the PC family) that uses the ANSI driver.

Despite these apparent advantages, we generally believe that relying on ANSI driver commands in your programs is not a good idea. For one thing, it requires that the ANSI driver be installed in any computer that your programs are used on, which complicates the instructions that you have to prepare to accompany the programs. It is difficult enough trying to explain the setup and use of your programs to both novices and experts without adding extra layers of complexity, such as the explanation of how to install the ANSI driver.

More important, however, is the fact that, compared to other methods that are available, the ANSI driver is pathetically slow in generating full-screen output. For a direct comparison of the relative speed of the ANSI driver, the ROM BIOS services, and direct-to-memory screen output, play with the NU program in the Norton Utilities set. The NU program contains three screen drivers that use these three output methods. If you try them all, you'll quickly see how much slower the ANSI driver is. Unless little screen output will be displayed, the ANSI driver is too slow to be satisfactory.

Appendix B

Hexadecimal Arithmetic

Hexadecimal numbers crop up in computer work for the simple reason that everything a computer does is based on binary numbers, and hexadecimal notation is a convenient way to represent binary numbers.

Hexadecimal numbers are built on a base of 16, exactly as ordinary decimal numbers are built on a base of 10; the difference is that hex numbers are written with 16 symbols whereas decimal numbers are written with 10 symbols (0 through 9). (From here on, we'll use the terms "hexadecimal" and "hex" interchangeably.) In hex notation, the symbols 0 through 9 represent the values 0 through 9, and the symbols A through F represent the values 10 through 15. (See Figure B-1.) The hex digits A through F are usually written with capital letters, but you may also see them with the lowercase letters *a* through *f*; the meaning is the same.

Hex numbers are built out of hex digits the same way that decimal numbers are built. For example, when we write the decimal number 123, we mean the following:

    1 times   100   (10 times 10)
 + 2 times   10
 + 3 times   1

If we use the symbols 123 as a hex number, we mean the following:

    1 times   256   (16 times 16)
 + 2 times   16
 + 3 times   1

There does not seem to be a standard way to write hex numbers, and you may find them expressed differently in different places. BASIC uses the prefix &H to identify hex numbers, and this notation is sometimes used

Hex	Dec	Hex	Dec	Hex	Dec	Hex	Dec
0	Zero	4	Four	8	Eight	C	Twelve
1	One	5	Five	9	Nine	D	Thirteen
2	Two	6	Six	A	Ten	E	Fourteen
3	Three	7	Seven	B	Eleven	F	Fifteen

Figure B-1. *The decimal value of the 16 hex digits.*

elsewhere, as well. In C, hexadecimal numbers start with the characters 0x (zero followed by lowercase x). Occasionally, the prefix # or 16# is used, but more often (and throughout this book) a hex number is simply followed by an upper- or lowercase *H*. Another common way to express hex numbers, especially in reference information, is without any special notation at all. You are expected to understand from the context when a number is written in decimal notation and when it is written in hex. When you see a number in any technical reference information that seems to be a decimal number, check carefully; it may actually be in hex.

When you need to work with hex numbers, you can use interpreted BASIC as an aid (see page 445), or you can work with them by hand. Whichever method you choose, you may find the conversion and arithmetic tables located toward the end of this appendix helpful. But before we get to the tables, we'll first explain why hex numbers and binary numbers are so compatible. Then we'll describe one of the most common uses of hex numbers in PC and PS/2 programming: segmented addressing.

Bits and Hexadecimal

Hex numbers are primarily used as a shorthand for the binary numbers that computers work with. Every hex digit represents 4 bits of binary information. (See Figure B-2.) In the binary (base 2) numbering system, a 4-bit number can have 16 different combinations, so the only way to represent each of the 4-bit binary numbers with a single digit is to use a base-16 numbering system. (See Figure B-3.)

When you're using 2-byte words, remember the reverse, or "backwords," order in which they are stored in memory. See Chapter 2, page 24.

Hex	Bits	Hex	Bits	Hex	Bits	Hex	Bits
0	0000	4	0100	8	1000	C	1100
1	0001	5	0101	9	1001	D	1101
2	0010	6	0110	A	1010	E	1110
3	0011	7	0111	B	1011	F	1111

Figure B-2. *The bit patterns for each of the 16 hex digits.*

Bit	Word	Byte	Value Dec	Hex
0	 1	 1	1	01H
1	. . . . 1 .	. . . . . . 1 .	2	02H
2	. . . . 1 . .	. . . . . 1 . .	4	04H
3	. . . . 1 . . .	. . . . 1 . . .	8	08H
4	. . . . 1	. . . 1	16	10H
5	. . . . 1	. . 1	32	20H
6	. . . . 1	. 1	64	40H
7	. . . . . . 1	1	128	80H
8	. . . . . . 1		256	100H
9	. . . . . . 1		512	200H
10	. . . . . 1		1024	400H
11	. . . . 1		2048	800H
12	. . . 1		4096	1000H
13	. . 1		8192	2000H
14	. 1		16,384	4000H
15	1		32,768	8000H

Figure B-3. *The hexadecimal and decimal equivalents of each bit in a byte and each bit in a 2-byte word.*

Segmented Addresses and Hexadecimal Notation

One of the most common uses of hex numbers is for memory addressing. You may recall from Chapters 2 and 3 that a complete 8086 address is 20 bits, or 5 hex digits, wide. Since the 8086 microprocessor can work only with 16-bit numbers, addresses are broken into two 16-bit words, called the *segment* and the *relative offset*. The two parts are written together as 1234:ABCD. The segment is always written first, and both segment and offset are given in hexadecimal form.

The 8086 treats the segment of an address as if it were multiplied by 16, which is the same as if it had an extra hex 0 written after it. The two parts, added together, yield the actual 20-bit address that they represent. For example, the segmented address 1234:ABCD converts into a complete address like that shown on the following page.

```
  1 2 3 4 0     (note the zero added on the right)
+     A B C D
-----------------
  1 C F 0 D
```

If you need to calculate the actual address that a segmented address refers to, follow this formula. The addition tables on page 473 may also help.

On the 8086, many different segmented addresses correspond to the same location in memory. For example, the address 00400H (where the ROM BIOS keeps its status information) is equally well represented as 0000:0400H and 0040:0000H. (Of course, this does not hold true in protected mode on an 80286 or 80386, as we saw in Chapter 2.)

There is no one best way to break an actual 8086 address into its segmented format. One simple way is to take the first digit of the actual 20-bit address followed by three zeros as the segment-paragraph part, and the remaining four digits as the relative part. Following this rule, the address above, 1CF0D, would be separated out as 1000:CF0D. IBM's listing for the ROM BIOS in the *IBM PC Technical Reference Manual* follows this convention, so all relative addresses appearing there have the (unshown) segment of F000.

When you are working with real segmented addresses, the segment will represent the actual contents of one of the segment registers and could point to nearly anywhere in memory. The relative offsets typically vary with usage. Information in executable code and data segments generally starts at a low relative offset. For example, the first instruction of a COM program is always at offset 100H in its segment. In contrast, stack segments usually use high relative offsets because stacks grow toward lower addresses.

To see the sort of segmented addresses in use when a program is executed, run the DOS DEBUG program. When DEBUG begins, it will give you a command prompt of –. When you enter the single-letter command D, DEBUG will display part of memory; the addresses on the left are typical segmented addresses.

Decimal-Hexadecimal Conversion

The tables in Figure B-4 show the decimal equivalent of each hex digit in the first five digit positions, which covers the complete address-space arithmetic used in the 8086. As we'll demonstrate, you can use these tables to convert between hexadecimal and decimal numbers.

First Position				Second Position			
Hex	*Dec*	*Hex*	*Dec*	*Hex*	*Dec*	*Hex*	*Dec*
. . . . 0	0	 8	8	. . . 0 .	0	. . . 8 .	128
. . . . 1	1	 9	9	. . . 1 .	16	. . . 9 .	144
. . . . 2	2	. . . . A	10	. . . 2 .	32	. . . A .	160
. . . . 3	3	. . . . B	11	. . . 3 .	48	. . . B .	176
. . . . 4	4	 C	12	. . . 4 .	64	. . . C .	192
. . . . 5	5	. . . . D	13	. . . 5 .	80	. . . D .	208
. . . . 6	6	. . . . E	14	. . . 6 .	96	. . . E .	224
. . . . 7	7	. . . . F	15	. . . 7 .	112	. . . F .	240

Third Position				Fourth Position			
Hex	*Dec*	*Hex*	*Dec*	*Hex*	*Dec*	*Hex*	*Dec*
. . 0 . .	0	. . 8 . .	2048	. 0 . . .	0	. 8 . . .	32,768
. . 1 . .	256	. . 9 . .	2304	. 1 . . .	4096	. 9 . . .	36,864
. . 2 . .	512	. . A . .	2560	. 2 . . .	8192	. A . . .	40,960
. . 3 . .	768	. . B . .	2816	. 3 . . .	12,288	. B . . .	45,056
. . 4 . .	1024	. . C . .	3072	. 4 . . .	16,384	. C . . .	49,152
. . 5 . .	1280	. . D . .	3328	. 5 . . .	20,480	. D . . .	53,248
. . 6 . .	1536	. . E . .	3584	. 6 . . .	24,576	. E . . .	57,344
. . 7 . .	1792	. . F . .	3840	. 7 . . .	28,672	. F . . .	61,440

Fifth Position			
Hex	*Dec*	*Hex*	*Dec*
0	0	8	524,288
1	65,536	9	589,824
2	131,072	A	655,360
3	196,608	B	720,896
4	262,144	C	786,432
5	327,680	D	851,968
6	393,216	E	917,504
7	458,752	F	983,040

Figure B-4. *The decimal equivalent of each hex digit position.*

Here is how you use these tables to convert a hex number to a decimal number. We'll use number A1B2H as an example. Look up each hex digit in the table corresponding to its position and then add the decimal values:

2	in the first position is	2
B	in the second position is	176
1	in the third position is	256
A	in the fourth position is	40,960
	The total is	41,394

To use these tables to convert a decimal number to hex, the process is equally simple to perform, but slightly more complicated to describe. Once again, we'll work through an example. We'll use the decimal number 1492.

Work from the table for the fifth position to the table for the first position. In the fifth-position table, find the biggest hex digit with a value that isn't greater than 1492, write down the hex digit, subtract its decimal value from 1492, and continue to the next table with the new value (that is, the difference after subtracting). Go from table to table until the number remaining is 0. The process is shown in Figure B-5. The result is 005D4H, or 5D4H without the leading zeros.

Position	Largest Hex Digit	Decimal Value	Remaining Decimal Number
Starting			1492
5	0	0	1492
4	0	0	1492
3	5	1280	212
2	D	208	4
1	4	4	0
Result	005D4		

Figure B-5. *Converting the decimal number 1492 into a hexadecimal number.*

471

Using BASIC for Hex Arithmetic

One easy way to manipulate hex numbers is to let interpreted BASIC do the work. To do this, activate the BASIC interpreter and use the command mode (without line numbers) to enter any operations you want to perform.

To display the hexadecimal equivalent of a hex number, such as 1234H, you can simply do this:

```
PRINT &H1234
```

Be sure to prefix any hex number with &H so that BASIC knows it is a hex number. To get the best display of decimal numbers, particularly large numbers, use the PRINT USING format, like this:

```
PRINT USING "###,###,###"; &H1234
```

To display the hexadecimal equivalent of a decimal number, such as 1234, you can simply do this:

```
PRINT HEX$( 1234 )
```

The examples so far have used only decimal and hex constants. You can as easily have BASIC perform some arithmetic and show the result in decimal or hexadecimal. Here are two examples:

```
PRINT USING "###,###,###"; &H1000 - &H3A2 + 16 * 3
PRINT HEX$(17766 - 1492 + &H1000)
```

By using variables to hold calculated results, you can avoid having to retype an expression or a complicated number. Variables that hold hex numbers should always be written as double-precision variables (with a # at the end of the variable name) so that you get the maximum accuracy. For example:

```
X# = 1776 - 1492 + &H100
PRINT USING "###,###,###"; X#, 2 * X#, 3 * X#
```

Hex Addition

To add hex numbers, you work digit by digit, exactly as you do with decimal numbers. To make addition easier, use Figure B-6, which shows the sum of any two hex digits. To use this table, find the row for one hex digit and the column for the other. The hex number located at the intersection of the row and column is the sum of the two digits.

	0	1	2	3	4	5	6	7	8	9	A	B	C	D	E	F
0	0	1	2	3	4	5	6	7	8	9	A	B	C	D	E	F
1		2	3	4	5	6	7	8	9	A	B	C	D	E	F	10
2			4	5	6	7	8	9	A	B	C	D	E	F	10	11
3				6	7	8	9	A	B	C	D	E	F	10	11	12
4					8	9	A	B	C	D	E	F	10	11	12	13
5						A	B	C	D	E	F	10	11	12	13	14
6							C	D	E	F	10	11	12	13	14	15
7								E	F	10	11	12	13	14	15	16
8									10	11	12	13	14	15	16	17
9										12	13	14	15	16	17	18
A											14	15	16	17	18	19
B												16	17	18	19	1A
C													18	19	1A	1B
D														1A	1B	1C
E															1C	1D
F																1E

Figure B-6. *Addition of two hex numbers.*

Hex Multiplication

To multiply hex numbers, you work digit by digit, as you do with decimal numbers. To make multiplication easier, use Figure B-7, which shows the product of any two hex digits. To use the table, find the row for one hex digit and the column for the other. The hex number located at the intersection of the row and column is the product of the two digits.

	0	1	2	3	4	5	6	7	8	9	A	B	C	D	E	F
0	0	0	0	0	0	0	0	0	0	0	0	0	0	0	0	0
1		1	2	3	4	5	6	7	8	9	A	B	C	D	E	F
2			4	6	8	A	C	E	10	12	14	16	18	1A	1C	1E
3				9	C	F	12	15	18	1B	1E	21	24	27	2A	2D
4					10	14	18	1C	20	24	28	2C	30	34	38	3C
5						19	1E	23	28	2D	32	37	3C	41	46	4B
6							24	2A	30	36	3C	42	48	4E	54	5A
7								31	38	3F	46	4D	54	5B	62	69
8									40	48	50	58	60	68	70	78
9										51	5A	63	6C	75	7E	87
A											64	6E	78	82	8C	96
B												79	84	8F	9A	A5
C													90	9C	A8	B4
D														A9	B6	C3
E															C4	D2
F																E1

Figure B-7. *Multiplication of two hex numbers.*

Appendix C

About Characters

The IBM personal computer family uses 256 distinct characters. These characters have numeric byte codes with values ranging from 00H through FFH (0 through decimal 255). The characters are of two types:

- The first 128 characters, 00H through 7FH (decimal 0 through 127), are the *standard ASCII character set*. Most computers handle the standard characters in the same way (with the exception of the first 32 characters — see page 483).

- The last 128 characters, 80H through FFH (decimal 128 through 255), are special characters that make up the *extended ASCII character set*. Each computer manufacturer decides how to use these special characters.

All models of the IBM personal computers use the same extended ASCII character set. Computers that closely mimic the IBM personal computers use this set as well, but other computers often have their own set of special characters. Be aware of this when you convert programs from other computers or when you write PC programs that you plan to convert for use on other computers.

The Standard and Extended Character Sets

The following BASIC program displays all 256 characters along with their numeric codes in both decimal and hexadecimal notation. The characters are also listed in Figure C-1.

```
1000 ' display all the PC characters
1010 '
1020 MONOCHROME = 1
1030 IF MONOCHROME THEN WW = 80 : HH = &HB000
     ELSE WW = 40 : HH = &HB800
1040 GOSUB 2000                              ' initialize DS register
1050 FOR I = 0 TO 255                         ' for all character codes
1060   GOSUB 3000                             ' display the information
1070 NEXT I
1080 PRINT "Done."
1090 GOSUB 6000
1092 COLOR 0,0,0
1095 SYSTEM
1999 '
2000 ' initialize
2010 '
2020 DEF SEG = HH                             ' set up DS register for poke
2030 KEY OFF : CLS                            ' set up the screen
```

```
2040 WIDTH WW : COLOR 14,1,1
2050 FOR I = 1 TO 25 : PRINT : NEXT I
2060 PRINT " Demonstrating all characters"
2070 GOSUB 5000                              ' periodic subheading
2080 RETURN
2099 '
3000 ' display character information
3010 '
3020 PRINT USING " ###      ";I;
3030 IF I < 16 THEN PRINT "0";
3040 PRINT HEX$(I);"          ";
3050 POKE WW * 2 * 23 + 34, I                ' insert the character
3060 GOSUB 4000                              ' print any comments
3070 IF (I MOD 16) < 15 THEN RETURN          ' pause after each 16 characters
3080 GOSUB 6000
3090 IF I < 255 THEN GOSUB 5000
3100 RETURN
3997 '
3998 ' character comments
3999 '
4000 IF I =   0 THEN PRINT "shows blank";
4007 IF I =   7 THEN PRINT "beep (bell)";
4008 IF I =   8 THEN PRINT "backspace";
4009 IF I =   9 THEN PRINT "tab";
4010 IF I =  10 THEN PRINT "linefeed";
4012 IF I =  12 THEN PRINT "page eject";
4013 IF I =  13 THEN PRINT "carriage return";
4026 IF I =  26 THEN PRINT "end text file";
4032 IF I =  32 THEN PRINT "true blank space";
4255 IF I = 255 THEN PRINT "shows blank";
4997 PRINT                                   finish the line
4998 RETURN
4999 '
5000 ' periodic subheading
5010 '
5020 COLOR 15
5030 PRINT
5040 PRINT
5050 PRINT "Decimal - Hex - Char - Comments"
5060 PRINT
5070 COLOR 14
5080 RETURN
5999 '
6000 ' pause
6010 '
6020 IF INKEY$ <> "" THEN GOTO 6020
6030 PRINT
```

```
6040 COLOR 2
6050 PRINT "Press any key to continue..."
6060 COLOR 14
6070 IF INKEY$ = "" THEN GOTO 6070
6080 PRINT
6090 RETURN
```

Char	Number Dec	Hex	Control	Char	Number Dec	Hex	Control
	0	00H	NUL (Null)	#	35	23H	
☺	1	01H	SOH (Start of heading)	$	36	24H	
●	2	02H	STX (Start of text)	%	37	25H	
♥	3	03H	ETX (End of text)	&	38	26H	
♦	4	04H	EOT (End of transmission)	'	39	27H	
♣	5	05H	ENQ (Enquiry)	(	40	28H	
♠	6	06H	ACK (Acknowledge)	)	41	29H	
•	7	07H	BEL (Bell)	*	42	2AH	
◘	8	08H	BS (Backspace)	+	43	2BH	
○	9	09H	HT (Horizontal tab)	,	44	2CH	
◉	10	0AH	LF (Linefeed)	-	45	2DH	
♂	11	0BH	VT (Vertical tab)	.	46	2EH	
♀	12	0CH	FF (Formfeed)	/	47	2FH	
♪	13	0DH	CR (Carriage return)	0	48	30H	
♫	14	0EH	SO (Shift out)	1	49	31H	
☼	15	0FH	SI (Shift in)	2	50	32H	
►	16	10H	DLE (Data link escape)	3	51	33H	
◄	17	11H	DC1 (Device control 1)	4	52	34H	
↕	18	12H	DC2 (Device control 2)	5	53	35H	
‼	19	13H	DC3 (Device control 3)	6	54	36H	
¶	20	14H	DC4 (Device control 4)	7	55	37H	
§	21	15H	NAK (Negative acknowledge)	8	56	38H	
▬	22	16H	SYN (Synchronous idle)	9	57	39H	
↨	23	17H	ETB (End transmission block)	:	58	3AH	
↑	24	18H	CAN (Cancel)	;	59	3BH	
↓	25	19H	EM (End of medium)	<	60	3CH	
→	26	1AH	SUB (Substitute)	=	61	3DH	
←	27	1BH	ESC (Escape)	>	62	3EH	
∟	28	1CH	FS (File separator)	?	63	3FH	
↔	29	1DH	GS (Group separator)	@	64	40H	
▲	30	1EH	RS (Record separator)	A	65	41H	
▼	31	1FH	US (Unit separator)	B	66	42H	
<space>	32	20H		C	67	43H	
!	33	21H		D	68	44H	
"	34	22H		E	69	45H	
				F	70	46H	
				G	71	47H	
				H	72	48H	

Figure C-1. *The IBM PC and PS/2 family character set.* *(continued)*

Figure C-1. *continued*

Char	Dec	Hex	Char	Dec	Hex	Control	Char	Dec	Hex
I	73	49H	v	118	76H		ú	163	A3H
J	74	4AH	w	119	77H		ñ	164	A4H
K	75	4BH	x	120	78H		Ñ	165	A5H
L	76	4CH	y	121	79H		ª	166	A6H
M	77	4DH	z	122	7AH		º	167	A7H
N	78	4EH	{	123	7BH		¿	168	A8H
O	79	4FH	¦	124	7CH		⌐	169	A9H
P	80	50H	}	125	7DH		¬	170	AAH
Q	81	51H	~	126	7EH		½	171	ABH
R	82	52H	Δ	127	7FH	DEL	¼	172	ACH
S	83	53H	Ç	128	80H		¡	173	ADH
T	84	54H	ü	129	81H		«	174	AEH
U	85	55H	é	130	82H		»	175	AFH
V	86	56H	â	131	83H		░	176	B0H
W	87	57H	ä	132	84H		▒	177	B1H
X	88	58H	à	133	85H		▓	178	B2H
Y	89	59H	å	134	86H		│	179	B3H
Z	90	5AH	ç	135	87H		┤	180	B4H
[	91	5BH	ê	136	88H		╡	181	B5H
\	92	5CH	ë	137	89H		╢	182	B6H
]	93	5DH	è	138	8AH		╖	183	B7H
^	94	5EH	ï	139	8BH		╕	184	B8H
_	95	5FH	î	140	8CH		╣	185	B9H
`	96	60H	ì	141	8DH		║	186	BAH
a	97	61H	Ä	142	8EH		╗	187	BBH
b	98	62H	Å	143	8FH		╝	188	BCH
c	99	63H	É	144	90H		╜	189	BDH
d	100	64H	æ	145	91H		╛	190	BEH
e	101	65H	Æ	146	92H		┐	191	BFH
f	102	66H	ô	147	93H		└	192	C0H
g	103	67H	ö	148	94H		┴	193	C1H
h	104	68H	ò	149	95H		┬	194	C2H
i	105	69H	û	150	96H		├	195	C3H
j	106	6AH	ù	151	97H		─	196	C4H
k	107	6BH	ÿ	152	98H		┼	197	C5H
l	108	6CH	ö	153	99H		╞	198	C6H
m	109	6DH	Ü	154	9AH		╟	199	C7H
n	110	6EH	¢	155	9BH		╚	200	C8H
o	111	6FH	£	156	9CH		╔	201	C9H
p	112	70H	¥	157	9DH		╩	202	CAH
q	113	71H	₧	158	9EH		╦	203	CBH
r	114	72H	ƒ	159	9FH		╠	204	CCH
s	115	73H	á	160	A0H		═	205	CDH
t	116	74H	í	161	A1H		╬	206	CEH
u	117	75H	ó	162	A2H		╧	207	CFH

(continued)

Figure C-1. *continued*

Char	Number Dec	Hex	Char	Number Dec	Hex	Char	Number Dec	Hex
⊥	208	D0H	α	224	E0H	≡	240	F0H
⊤	209	D1H	β	225	E1H	±	241	F1H
π	210	D2H	Γ	226	E2H	≥	242	F2H
⊥	211	D3H	π	227	E3H	≤	243	F3H
⊢	212	D4H	Σ	228	E4H	⌠	244	F4H
F	213	D5H	σ	229	E5H	⌡	245	F5H
π	214	D6H	μ	230	E6H	÷	246	F6H
╫	215	D7H	τ	231	E7H	≈	247	F7H
╪	216	D8H	Φ	232	E8H	°	248	F8H
⌐	217	D9H	Θ	233	E9H	•	249	F9H
⌐	218	DAH	Ω	234	EAH	·	250	FAH
■	219	DBH	δ	235	EBH	√	251	FBH
▄	220	DCH	∞	236	ECH	η	252	FCH
▌	221	DDH	φ	237	EDH	²	253	FDH
▐	222	DEH	ε	238	EEH	■	254	FEH
▀	223	DFH	∩	239	EFH		255	FFH

The BASIC program is designed to adjust itself to a monochrome or color video mode based on the value shown in line 1020: 1 (as shown) indicates a monochrome mode; 0 indicates a color mode. The value in line 1020 causes the program to set two values:

- The location, in screen memory, where the POKE command inserts display information

- The screen width (40 or 80 columns)

The POKE statement in line 3050 causes the characters to appear. This extra step is necessary because a few characters cannot be displayed by the ordinary PRINT statement. See "The First 32 ASCII Characters," page 483, for an explanation.

Each of the 256 characters is visually unique, except for ASCII 00H and ASCII FFH (decimal 255), which appear the same as the blank-space character, CHR$(32).

The Character Format

All characters that appear on the display screen are composed of dots drawn within a grid called a *character box* or *character matrix.* (See Figure C-2.) The size of the character box depends on your video hardware as well as on the video mode you're using. For example, the Monochrome Display Adapter (MDA) uses a 9 × 14 character matrix; the text modes on the Color

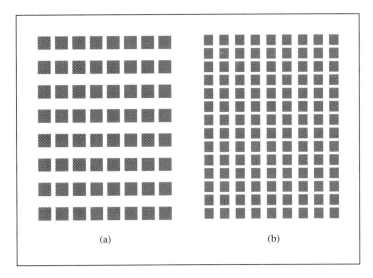

Figure C-2. *The dot-matrix pattern displayed by (a) the Color Graphics Adapter and (b) the Monochrome Display Adapter.*

Graphics Adapter (CGA) uses 8×8 characters; the default 80×25 text mode on the Enhanced Graphics Adapter (EGA) uses an 8×14 character matrix; and the default text modes on the Video Graphics Array (VGA) use 9×16 characters. Characters are created by filling, or lighting, the appropriate dots in the grid. The more dots in a grid, the sharper the characters appear.

Dot-matrix printers also draw characters with a grid of dots. However, each model of printer may have its own particular way of drawing characters that may not exactly match the screen characters dot for dot.

To see how characters appear, the three dot matrices in Figure C-3 illustrate a *Y*, a *y*, and a semicolon, using the 8×8 character box.

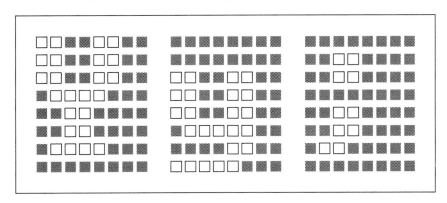

Figure C-3. *The dot pattern of three characters in an 8×8 character box.*

Several rules apply to the character drawings:

- For standard characters, the two right columns are unused, providing separation between characters. These two columns are used only by characters that are supposed to fill the entire character box, such as the solid block character, ASCII DBH (decimal 129).

- The top two rows are used for *ascenders* (the parts of characters that are above the ordinary character height). The ascender space is used for capital letters and for such lowercase letters as *b*, *d*, and *k*.

- The bottom row is used for *descenders* (the parts of characters that drop below the line), as in the lowercase letters *g* and *y*.

These general guidelines are occasionally compromised for overall effect. For example, the semicolon, our third example in Figure C-3, is shifted up one row from what you might expect so that it does not use the descender row.

The dots that form each character on the screen are placed there by a specialized component of the video subsystem called a *character generator*. The character generator's task is to convert ASCII codes into the corresponding pattern of dots that make up a displayed character. The character generator accomplishes this by using ASCII codes as an index into a memory-resident bit pattern table that represents the displayed character's dot patterns.

For example, Figure C-4 shows the table entry for an uppercase Y in an 8 × 8 character box. Note how the pattern of ones and zeros in the character definition corresponds to the pattern of dots displayed for the character.

| *Bit* | | | | | | | | *Value* |
7	6	5	4	3	2	1	0	*(hex)*
1	1	0	0	1	1	0	0	CCH
1	1	0	0	1	1	0	0	CCH
1	1	0	0	1	1	0	0	CCH
0	1	1	1	1	0	0	0	78H
0	0	1	1	0	0	0	0	30H
0	0	1	1	0	0	0	0	30H
0	1	1	1	1	0	0	0	78H
0	0	0	0	0	0	0	0	00H

Figure C-4. *The coding of the 8 character bytes for the Y character.*

In some video modes, you have no control over the bit patterns that define the displayed characters. The MDA's character definitions, for instance, are stored in special ROM chips that can be accessed only by the adapter's character-generator circuitry. In many video modes, however, the character definition table resides in RAM, allowing you to redefine the bit patterns used by the character generator and create your own fonts or character sets. (See Chapter 9 for more about RAM-based character definitions.)

The First 32 ASCII Characters

The first 32 ASCII characters, 00H through 1FH (decimal 0 through 31), have two important uses that just happen to conflict with each other. On one hand, these characters have standard ASCII meanings; they are used for both printer control (for example, ASCII 0CH (decimal 12) is the formfeed character) and communications control. On the other hand, IBM also uses them for some of the most interesting and useful display characters, such as the card-suit characters (hearts, diamonds, clubs, and spades) — ASCII 03H through 06H, and the arrow characters ($\uparrow$, $\downarrow$, $\rightarrow$, and $\leftarrow$) — ASCII 18H through 1CH (decimal 24 through 27).

When DOS transmits characters to the video screen or to a printer, it acts on the ASCII meaning of the characters instead of showing the character's picture. For example, the beep/bell character, ASCII 07H, has a dot for a picture. However, if you use DOS (or a programming language such as BASIC that relies on DOS for output), nothing happens on screen when you try to display this character: Instead, the speaker will beep. But if you put the character directly onto the screen by using the POKE command like this:

```
DEF SEG = &HB800 : POKE 0, 7
```

the character's picture will appear. You can always make characters appear on the screen by poking them into the screen buffer. However, it's much easier to use the PRINT statement to display characters. Store characters directly into the video buffer only if you can't display them with PRINT.

Most of these 32 characters can be written to the screen, but the display characters may vary, depending upon which language is used. Figure C-5 shows some of these differences. The characters not shown, ASCII 00H through 06H (decimal 0 through 6) and ASCII 0EH through 1BH (decimal 14 through 27), can always be written to the screen with predictable results.

| ASCII Character | | Result | |
Hex	Dec	In BASIC	In Most Other Languages
07H	7	Beeps	Beeps
08H	8	Character appears	Backspace action
09H	9	Tab action	Tab action
0AH	10	Linefeed and carriage-return action	Linefeed action
0BH	11	Cursor to top left	Character appears
0CH	12	Screen clears	Character appears
0DH	13	Carriage-return action	Carriage-return action
1CH	28	Cursor moves right	Character appears
1DH	29	Cursor moves left	Character appears
1EH	30	Cursor moves up	Character appears
1FH	31	Cursor moves down	Character appears

Figure C-5. *The results obtained when certain characters are written to the screen using different languages.*

The Box-Drawing Characters

Among the most useful of the special extended ASCII characters are the characters designed for drawing single- and double-lined boxes: characters B3H through DAH (decimal 179 through 218). Because they are difficult to combine properly, you may find the information in Figure C-6 helpful.

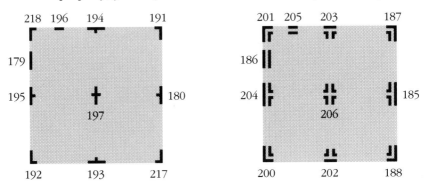

Figure C-6. *The box-drawing characters and their corresponding ASCII codes.*

(continued)

Figure C-6. *continued*

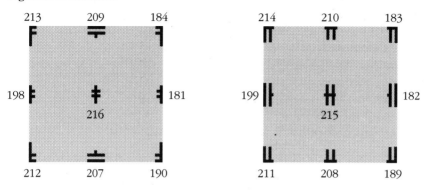

The Graph and Block Characters

In addition to the box-drawing characters, two series of characters are designed for graphs and block drawings. (See Figure C-7.) One series consists of four characters that fill the entire character box but are shaded in different densities (that is, some of the character's dots are on, or set to the foreground color, and the remaining dots are off, or set to the background color). The other series consists of four block characters that provide a solid color covering half the character box. The solid character, ASCII DBH (decimal 219), is also used with these half-characters.

ASCII 176		ASCII 220	
ASCII 177		ASCII 221	
ASCII 178		ASCII 222	
ASCII 219		ASCII 223	

Figure C-7. *The two sets of graph and block characters.*

Text File Formatting Conventions

Many programs work with files of text. As a result, most programmers have adopted text file formatting conventions that make it easier for text files to be used by different programs. The formats are defined by embedded characters that perform such functions as carriage returns, linefeeds, and backspaces.

When you write a program that reads text files, you can make it more flexible by having it recognize a variety of different text file formats. Conversely, when you design a program to write files with a simple text format, other programs can more easily share your program's output. In this section, we'll describe the ordinary text format recognized by most text-processing programs, and then go on to discuss some of the text formats used in word-processor files.

Ordinary Text File Formats

Ordinary text files are made up of only the standard ASCII characters and do not use the extended ASCII characters. In the ASCII coding scheme, the first 32 characters, ASCII 00H through 1FH (decimal 0 through 31), have special meanings: Some are used for formatting text and others are generally used for communications control. These control characters are rarely displayed or printed.

Only a handful of formatting characters are widely used in ordinary text files. They were originally developed as commands to tell a printer how to format a printed page and how to recognize the end of a file. Now their use extends to all output devices. We'll discuss each of the main formatting characters in turn.

ASCII 1AH (decimal 26) marks the true end of a text file. This character may come before the end of the file indicated by the file size in the directory entry. This is because some text-processing programs read and write files, not byte by byte, but in larger chunks — 128 bytes at a time. When they transfer data in this way, DOS sees only the end of the 128-byte block and does not recognize the actual end of the file delimited by the end-of-file character.

ASCII 0DH (decimal 13) and ASCII 0AH (decimal 10) normally divide a text file into lines by marking the end of each line with a carriage return (ASCII 0DH) and a linefeed (ASCII 0AH), usually in that order. Many text-processing programs have difficulty with lines of more than 255 characters, and some are limited to 80 character lines.

A carriage return can be used by itself. Unfortunately, such usage can be interpreted as either of two things: the end of a line with a linefeed that is implied and automatically provided by some printers; or a return to the beginning of the current print line, which causes the entire line to be overprinted. (The backspace character, ASCII 08H, is also sometimes used to make a printer overstrike a character.)

ASCII 09H, the *tab character,* is sometimes used to represent one or more spaces, up to the tab location. Unfortunately, as yet, there is no universal convention on tab settings, which makes the use of the tab character uncertain. However, one of the most common tab settings is every eight spaces.

ASCII 0CH (decimal 12), the *formfeed* or *page eject,* is another format character. This character tells a printer to skip to the top of the next page.

Other formatting characters, such as the vertical tab (ASCII 0BH, decimal 11), are available but are not widely used with personal computers.

You can avoid many difficulties by having programs create text files with simple formats. The simplest formats allow lines no longer than 255 characters and use only the carriage-return (ASCII 0DH), linefeed (ASCII 0AH), and end-of-file (ASCII 1AH, decimal 26) formatting characters. Many programming languages, including BASIC and Pascal, can automatically generate these formatting characters when creating text output.

Most compilers and assemblers expect to read source code in this ordinary, plain format. Rarely can a language translator work with the more complex formats created by some word processors.

Word-Processor Text Formats

Word-processing programs have special needs for formatting text files. The files that these programs create are rarely simple and typically have many exotic additions to the simplest ASCII format. Generally, each word processor has unique formatting rules; luckily, there are some common features.

Many of the special format codes used by word processors are created by using an extended ASCII code that is 128 higher than a normal ASCII code. This is equivalent to setting the high-order bit of an otherwise ordinary byte. For example, a "soft" carriage return, ASCII 8DH (decimal 141), is coded by adding 128 to an ordinary carriage return, ASCII 0DH (decimal 13). Soft carriage returns indicate a tentative end of line, which can be changed when a paragraph is reformatted. On the other hand, an ordinary carriage return, can mark the end of a paragraph that isn't changed by reformatting. This kind of coding in word-processing text can cause some programs to treat an entire paragraph as one single line.

"Soft" hyphens (ASCII ADH, decimal 173), whose ASCII value is 128 greater than ordinary hyphens (ASCII 2DH, decimal 45), are sometimes used to indicate where a word may be split into syllables at the end of a line.

Ordinary "hard" hyphens are treated as regular characters and cannot be used or removed by the word-processing program in the same way that soft hyphens can.

Even ordinary alphabetic text can have 128 added to its character code. Some programs do this to mark the last letter in a word. For example, a lowercase *a* is ASCII 61H (decimal 97); but when it appears at the end of a word, as in *America*, it may be stored as ASCII E1H (decimal 225), because 225 is the sum of 97 + 128.

Programs intended to work with a variety of text and word-processing data should be prepared, as much as possible, to cope with the variety of text formats that these examples suggest.

Appendix D

DOS Version 4

New Features in DOS Version 4

DOS version 4's full-screen interface shell gives it a very different look from the "glass teletype" interface familiar to users of previous DOS versions. Nevertheless, from a programmer's perspective, DOS version 4 is quite similar to its predecessor, version 3.3.

The most important changes in DOS version 4 are related to its ability to manage larger disk and memory resources. When the IBM PC and DOS were new, the lack of support for more than 1 megabyte (MB) of RAM or 32 MB of disk space was hardly a shortcoming. But by July 1988, when DOS version 4 appeared, both of these limits had become important to many DOS users. DOS version 4 avoids the limitations of previous versions by improving the way it manages memory and disk space.

DOS version 4 provides access to larger fixed-disk partitions by using 32-bit logical sector numbers instead of the 16-bit sector numbers used in previous versions. With 16-bit logical sector numbers, the maximum number of sectors in a fixed-disk partition is 65,536. Thus, with a default 512-byte sector size, the largest disk partition you can support is 32 MB. With DOS version 4's 32-bit logical sector numbers, the maximum number of logical sectors in a partition is not limited to 65,536. This means that DOS version 4 can manage fixed-disk partitions larger than 32 MB without increasing the default sector size. (See Chapter 5 for more about logical sectors.)

DOS version 4 supports expanded memory by incorporating the functionality of version 4.0 of the LIM (Lotus-Intel-Microsoft) Expanded Memory Specification, which consists of a set of function calls invoked through software interrupt 67H. (See Figure D-1.) Because DOS supports the LIM interface, you needn't install a separate device driver in order to use expanded memory in a PC or PS/2.

One immediate benefit of EMS support is that DOS itself can use expanded memory for its internal buffers. (The /E switch with BUFFERS= in the CONFIG.SYS file places DOS disk buffers in expanded memory; the /E switch on FASTOPEN places FASTOPEN's directory/file cache in expanded memory.) This lets your applications use more conventional memory in the first 640 KB of the 8086 address space.

These features of DOS version 4 make the DOS application-programming interface different from previous versions in several ways. The differences are evident in several interrupt 21H functions, in the services provided through interrupts 25H and 26H, and in the way DOS version 4 formats disks. The following sections describe these differences.

EMM Function	Function Hex	Dec	Description
1	40H	64	Get status.
2	41H	65	Get page frame address.
3	42H	66	Get unallocated page count.
4	43H	67	Allocate pages.
5	44H	68	Map/unmap handle page.
6	45H	69	Deallocate pages.
7	46H	70	Get EMM version.
8	47H	71	Save page map.
9	48H	72	Restore page map.
10			(Reserved.)
11			(Reserved.)
12	4BH	75	Get EMM handle count.
13	4CH	76	Get EMM handle pages.
14	4DH	77	Get all EMM handle pages.
15	4EH	78	Get/set page map.
16	4FH	79	Get/set partial page map.
17	50H	80	Map/unmap multiple handle pages.
18	51H	81	Reallocate pages.
19	52H	82	Get/set handle attributes.
20	53H	83	Get/set handle name.
21	54H	84	Get handle directory.
22	55H	85	Alter page map and jump.
23	56H	86	Alter page map and call.
24	57H	87	Move/exchange memory region.
25	58H	88	Get mappable physical address array.
26	59H	89	Get expanded memory hardware information.
27	5AH	90	Allocate raw pages.
28	5BH	91	Alternate page map register set.
29	5CH	92	Prepare expanded memory for warm boot.
30	5DH	93	Enable/disable operating system/ environment functions.

Figure D-1. *LIM Expanded Memory Support functions supported in DOS version 4 through interrupt 67H.*

Interrupt 21H Functions in DOS Version 4

DOS version 4 supports all (and enhances some) interrupt 21H functions available in DOS 3.3. In addition, it supports a new interrupt 21H function (function 6CH, Extended Open/Create). We'll summarize the new features here, but be sure to compare the functions supported in DOS version 4 to those offered in previous DOS versions. (See Chapters 15, 16, and 17.)

Function 33H (decimal 51): Get/Set System Value

In DOS versions prior to version 4, function 33H (decimal 51) can be used only to examine or update the DOS internal flag that controls Ctrl-C checking. (See Chapter 17.) DOS version 4 supports a third subfunction that returns the drive ID of the disk drive used to boot the system.

To determine the boot drive ID, call function 33H with AL = 5. DOS version 4 returns the drive ID in register DL. Drive ID values can be 1 (drive A) or 3 (drive C).

Function 44H (decimal 68): IOCTL — I/O Control for Devices

Subfunction 0CH has been enhanced for double-byte character support (DBCS). See the *DOS Version 4 Technical Reference Manual* for details.

Function 65H (decimal 101): Get Extended Country Information

In DOS version 4, interrupt 21H, function 65H (decimal 101) supports subfunction 07H, which returns the segmented address of a *DBCS vector*, a table of byte pairs that can be used to translate characters in non-ASCII character sets that represent each character with 2 bytes instead of one. Each byte pair indicates a range of values. The values in each range do not, themselves, represent individual characters; instead, each value identifies the lead byte of a 2-byte character code.

This support for double-byte characters is useful only in foreign-language DOS releases where the usual extended ASCII character set is inadequate. But if you want to experiment, here's how interrupt 21H, function 65H gives you access to the DBCS vector in DOS version 4.

Call this function with the register values shown in Figure D-2. Subfunction 07H updates the buffer at ES:DI with a subfunction ID byte (07H) followed by the segmented address of the byte-pair table. The table consists of a single word containing the number of entries in the table, followed by a sequence of byte-pairs. For example, in a DOS version 4 system installed with COUNTRY = 81 (Japan) in its CONFIG.SYS file, subfunction 07H returns a pointer to the following table:

06	00	81	9F	E0	FC	00	00

The first 2 bytes of the table indicate its length (6 bytes). The next two pairs of bytes indicate that each value in the ranges 81H–9FH and EDH–FCH represents the lead byte of a 2-byte character code. The table ends with a pair of zero bytes.

Call with	Returns
AH = 65H	*If error:*
AL = 07H	CF set
BX = code page number	AX = error code
(−1 = default)	
CX = buffer length (should be 05H)	*If no error:*
DX = country ID (−1 = default)	CF clear
ES:DI → empty buffer	ES:DI → extended country
	information

Figure D-2. *Registers used for interrupt 21H, function 65H, subfunction 07H.*

Function 6CH (decimal 108): Extended Open/Create

Function 6CH, introduced in DOS version 4, combines the functionality of several previously supported interrupt 21H functions. This function lets you specify several different actions at the time you open a file:

- You can open an existing file (as in functions 0FH and 3DH).

- You can create a file or truncate an existing file (as in functions 16H and 3CH).

- You can create a file that is guaranteed to be new (as in function 5BH).

- You can open a file for which every write operation is automatically committed to disk (as if you called function 68H after each write).

- You can disable interrupt 24H (critical-error) processing for the file.

When you call function 6CH, you select a combination of these actions by setting bits in registers BX (Figure D-3) and DX (Figure D-4). The other registers specify information required by DOS to open or create the file: CX contains the file-create attribute if you're creating a file; DS:SI contains a pointer to an ASCIIZ filename; and AL must contain 00H.

15	14	13	12	11	10	9	8	7	6	5	4	3	2	1	0	Value	Meaning
.	.	.	.	.	.	.	.	.	.	.	.	.	0	0	0	0	Access code: read only
.	.	.	.	.	.	.	.	.	.	.	.	.	0	0	1	1	Access code: write only
.	.	.	.	.	.	.	.	.	.	.	.	.	0	1	0	2	Access code: read/write
.	.	.	.	.	.	.	.	.	.	.	.	0	.	.	.		(Reserved)
.	.	.	.	.	.	.	.	.	0	0	0	.	.	.	.	0	Sharing mode: compatibility
.	.	.	.	.	.	.	.	.	0	0	1	.	.	.	.	1	Sharing mode: deny read/write
.	.	.	.	.	.	.	.	.	0	1	0	.	.	.	.	2	Sharing mode: deny write
.	.	.	.	.	.	.	.	.	0	1	1	.	.	.	.	3	Sharing mode: deny read
.	.	.	.	.	.	.	.	.	1	0	0	.	.	.	.	4	Sharing mode: deny none
.	.	.	.	.	.	.	.	0	.	.	.	.	.	.	.	0	Inherit: child inherits handles
.	.	.	.	.	.	.	.	1	.	.	.	.	.	.	.	1	Inherit: no inherited handles
.	.	.	0	0	0	0	0	.	.	.	.	.	.	.	.		(Reserved)
.	.	0	.	.	.	.	.	.	.	.	.	.	.	.	.	0	INT 24H: enabled
.	.	1	.	.	.	.	.	.	.	.	.	.	.	.	.	1	INT 24H: disabled
.	0	.	.	.	.	.	.	.	.	.	.	.	.	.	0	0	Auto-commit: disabled
.	1	.	.	.	.	.	.	.	.	.	.	.	.	.	1	1	Auto-commit: enabled
0	.	.	.	.	.	.	.	.	.	.	.	.	.	.	.		(Reserved)

Figure D-3. *Bit-field values in register BX for interrupt 21H, function 6CH.*

15	14	13	12	11	10	9	8	7	6	5	4	3	2	1	0	Value	Meaning
.	.	.	.	.	.	.	.	.	.	.	.	0	0	0	0	0	If file exists: fail
.	.	.	.	.	.	.	.	.	.	.	.	0	0	0	1	1	If file exists: open
.	.	.	.	.	.	.	.	.	.	.	.	0	0	1	0	2	If file exists: truncate and open
.	.	.	.	.	.	.	.	0	0	0	0	.	.	.	.	0	If file not found: fail
.	.	.	.	.	.	.	.	0	0	0	1	.	.	.	.	1	If file not found: create
0	0	0	0	0	0	0	0	.	.	.	.	.	.	.	.		(Reserved)

Figure D-4. *Bit-field values in register DX for interrupt 21H, function 6CH.*

If the create or open operation is successful, function 6CH returns with the carry flag clear, a file handle in AX, and a result code in CX. The possible result codes are 01H (existing file opened), 02H (new file created and opened), and 03H (existing file truncated and opened). If an error occurs, the function sets the carry flag and returns an error code in AX. Possible error codes depend on the type of operation you requested. They include 01H (invalid function), 02H (file not found), 03H (path not found), 04H (no handles available), 05H (access denied), and 50H (file already exists).

Interrupts 25H and 26H

In DOS version 4, the Absolute Disk Read and Write services — interrupts 25H and 26H (decimal 37 and 38) — have been augmented to process 32-bit logical sector numbers. You must use these services to access individual sectors in disk partitions that contain more than 65,536 sectors.

As in previous DOS versions, these interrupt services require you to use the CPU registers to pass a disk drive ID, a buffer address, a starting sector number, and a number of sectors. However, the registers are used differently in DOS version 4 (Figure D-5). To use a 32-bit sector number, you must execute interrupt 25H or 26H with CX = –1 and DS:BX containing the address of a *control packet*, a 10-byte data structure that contains the starting sector number, the number of sectors to read or write, and the buffer address (Figure D-6). If CX does not contain –1, DOS version 4 assumes that the other registers are used as in previous DOS versions to describe the read or write operation. (See Chapter 15 for details.)

Call with	Returns
AL = drive ID CX = –1 DS:BX → control packet	Previous contents of Flags register on top of stack *If error:* CF set AH = error code AL = error code *If no error:* CF clear

Figure D-5. *Registers used with interrupt 25H and 26H services in DOS version 4.*

Offset	Size (bytes)	Contents
00H	4	Logical sector number
04H	2	Number of sectors to read or write
06H	4	Segment:offset address of data buffer

Figure D-6. *The control packet used in DOS version 4 interrupt 25H and 26H services.*

The augmented DOS 4 versions of these services use the same codes to report errors as previous versions. If you do not use a 32-bit logical sector number when you access a disk partition that contains more than 65,536 sectors, these services return with AH = 02H (bad address mark) and AL = 07H (unknown media). This error occurs even if you try to access one of the first 65,536 logical sectors in the partition.

Before it can process an interrupt 25H or interrupt 26H request, DOS version 4 must know how the disk is formatted. For a fixed disk this isn't a problem, but for diskettes you can ensure that DOS knows the current diskette format by executing interrupt 21H, function 47H (Get Current Directory) before you call interrupt 25H or 26H.

The DOS Version 4 Disk Boot Sector

When it formats a disk, DOS records information about the disk in logical sector 0, the DOS boot sector. (See Chapter 5.) As in previous versions, DOS version 4 stores information about the size of the disk's sectors, clusters, FAT, and root directory in a table called the BIOS parameter block (BPB). But DOS version 4 records more information in the disk boot sector than do previous DOS versions.

The Extended BIOS Parameter Block

In DOS version 4, the BPB data structure contains an extra 4-byte field that can contain the number of logical sectors on the disk. (Compare Figure D-7 with Figure 5-9 on page 111.) As in previous DOS versions, DOS version 4 stores the number of logical sectors in the field at offset 13H and the number of hidden sectors in the field at offset 1CH. If, however, the sum of these two values is greater than 65,535, DOS stores a 0 in the field at offset 13H and uses the additional field at offset 20H to record the total number of logical sectors on the disk.

Offset in Boot Sector	Length (bytes)	Description
03H	8	System ID
0BH	2	Number of bytes per sector
0DH	1	Number of sectors per cluster
0EH	2	Number of sectors in reserved area
10H	1	Number of copies of FAT
11H	2	Number of root directory entries

Figure D-7. *The extended BIOS parameter block in the DOS version 4 sector.* *(continued)*

Figure D-7. *continued*

Offset in Boot Sector	Length (bytes)	Description
13H	2	Total number of sectors
15H	1	DOS media descriptor
16H	2	Number of sectors per FAT
18H	2	Number of sectors per track
1AH	2	Number of heads (sides)
1CH	4	Number of hidden sectors
20H	4	Total number of sectors (if field at offset 13H contains 0)

The Volume Serial Number

DOS version 4 also records a disk's volume label and volume serial number in a data structure that immediately follows the BPB in the boot sector. (See Figure D-8.) The volume label is the same 11-byte name that appears in a disk's volume-label entry in the root directory. You specify the volume label with the FORMAT or LABEL command, or with a call to interrupt 21H, function 16H. DOS itself computes the volume serial number.

When it formats a disk, DOS version 4 derives the disk's volume serial number from the current date and time. This means that volume serial numbers are almost always different among different disk volumes, so DOS version 4 can use the serial numbers to distinguish different disks with the same physical format. You can illustrate this in DOS version 4 by installing SHARE, opening a diskette file for input, and then changing diskettes. If you then try to read from the file, DOS version 4 generates an "invalid disk change" critical error. In a program, you can use your own critical-error handler to detect this error. It's easier, of course, to rely on the DOS version 4 default critical-error handler, which displays the volume label and serial number of the diskette that contains the open file.

Offset in Boot Sector	Length (bytes)	Description
24H	1	Physical drive number
25H	1	(Reserved)
26H	1	Signature byte (29H)
27H	4	Volume serial number
2BH	11	Volume label
36H	8	(Reserved)

Figure D-8. *Boot sector extensions in DOS version 4.*

A Sample Routine

The following sample routine reads the volume serial number from a DOS version 4 disk. The C program, which calls *Readabs()*, shows how you can access information in a DOS version 4 boot sector:

```
main( argc, argr )
int     argc;
char *  argv[];
        unsigned char   Buffer[512];
        unsigned long * LongPointer;
        int             DriveID = 02;           /* drive c */

        struct
        {
          unsigned long SectorNumber;           /* 4 bytes */
          unsigned int  Count;                  /* 2 bytes */
          void far *    BufferPointer;          /* 4 bytes */
        }
                ControlPacket;


        /* initialize control packet */
        ControlPacket.SectorNumber = 0;
        ControlPacket.Count = 1;
        ControlPacket.BufferPointer = (char far *)Buffer;

        /* read the DOS boot sector on the specified drive */
        if( argc == 2 )
          DriveID = (argv[1][0] | 0x20) - 'a';
        ReadAbs( DriveID, &ControlPacket );


        /* display the volume serial number if it's there */
        if( Buffer[0x26] == 0x29 )              /* check the signature */
        {
          LongPointer = (long *) (Buffer+0x27);
          printf( "\nThe volume serial number is %08lX", *LongPointer );
        }

        else
          printf( "\nNo volume serial number" );
}
```

The *Readabs()* routine illustrates how to use the DOS version 4 extended interrupt 25H function:

```
DGROUP          GROUP   _DATA
_TEXT           SEGMENT byte public 'CODE'
                ASSUME  cs:_TEXT,ds:DGROUP


                PUBLIC  _ReadAbs
_ReadAbs        PROC    near

                push    bp
                mov     bp,sp
                push    si
                push    di

; ensure that DOS knows the disk media format
; by executing interrupt 21H, function 47H
                mov     ah,47h
                mov     dl,[bp+4]
                inc     dx
                mov     si,offset DGROUP:Buffer
                int     21h

; use interrupt 25h to read the requested sector(s)
                mov     al,[bp+4]       ; AL = drive ID
                mov     bx,[bp+6]       ; DS:BX -> control packet
                mov     cx,-1
                int     25h             ; absolute disk read

                mov     ax,0            ; return AX = value of ...
                adc     ax,0            ; ... carry flag


                add     sp,2            ; discard flags pushed by DOS

                pop     di
                pop     si

                pop     bp
                ret

_ReadAbs        ENDP

_TEXT           ENDS
_DATA           SEGMENT word public 'DATA'
Buffer          DB      64 dup(?)
_DATA           ENDS
```

DOS Version 4 in Perspective

For the most part, DOS users — not DOS programmers — benefit most from DOS version 4. DOS version 4 support for expanded memory and larger fixed disks makes it easier for applications to take advantage of these resources. The full-screen command shell clearly resembles the command interface provided with OS/2 Presentation Manager and reflects the philosophy that the point-and-shoot graphics interface is what PC and PS/2 users want. But from a programmer's point of view, DOS version 4 support for these features presents few novelties.

DOS version 4 isn't revolutionary. It represents another step in the evolution of the predominant operating system for the IBM PCs and PS/2s.

Index

Numbers

501

Peter Norton

Peter Norton was reared in Seattle, Washington, and was educated at Reed College in Portland, Oregon. Before discovering microcomputers, he spent a dozen years working on mainframes and minicomputers for companies including Boeing and Jet Propulsion Laboratories. When the IBM PC made its debut, Norton was among the first to buy one. Now recognized as a principal authority on IBM personal computer technology, he is the president of Peter Norton Computing, Inc., a company that is a leader in developing and publishing PC utility software. Norton is also the author of the popular book *Inside the IBM PC,* now in its second edition from Brady Books.

Richard Wilton

Currently a fellow in the Medical Informatics program at the University of California, Los Angeles, Richard Wilton earned an M.D. from UCLA and completed his residency in pediatrics at the Childrens Hospital of Los Angeles. He has been programming computers since the late 1960s and has worked with IBM mainframes as well as with various microcomputers. Wilton has written about IBM PC and PS/2 programming for *BYTE, Computer Language,* and *The Seybold Outlook on Professional Computing.* He is the author of **PROGRAMMER'S GUIDE TO PC AND PS/2 VIDEO SYSTEMS,** published by Microsoft Press.

1952-28
22-04

DATE DUE